Mies in His Own Words
Complete Writings,
Speeches, and Interviews
1922–1969

Mies in His Own Words
Complete Writings, Speeches, and Interviews 1922–1969

Ludwig Mies van der Rohe
–
Edited by Vittorio Pizzigoni and
Michelangelo Sabatino

CONTENTS

8		Mies as Educator: Written and Spoken Words
14		Mies, a Kind of Modernity
28		Editorial Note With Archival Sources and Bibliography
32		Photo Essay

49		**Mies in His Own Words**
50	1	Two Glass Skyscrapers (1922)
51	2	Office Building (1923)
52	3	[Draft for a Newspaper Article] (1923)
52	4	Building (1923)
53	5	Solved Tasks: A Challenge for Our Building Industry (1923)
55	6	[Review of Paul Tropp, *Development and Organisation of Rent*] (1924)
55	7	The Industrialisation of Building Methods (1924)
57	8	[Lecture: What We Mean by Elementary Form-Giving] (1924)
61	9	Building Art and the Will of the Epoch! (1924)
62	10	[Lecture: The Nature of Building] (1926)
68	11	Letter to *Die Form* (1926)
68	12	An Interview With an Architect (1926)
70	13	For the New Year (1927)
72	14	On Form in Architecture (1927)
73	15	[Lecture: The Struggle for the Flat Roof] (1927)
74	16	[Foreword to the Catalogue for the *Die Wohnung* Exhibition] (1927)
74	17	[Foreword to *Bau und Wohnung*] (1927)
75	18	Concerning My Block (1927)
76	19	[Introduction to the Werkbund Exhibition in Stuttgart] (1927)
77	20	[On Flat and Pitched Roofs] (1927)
77	21	[Draft of a Letter] (c. 1927–28)
78	22	The Preconditions for Architectural Work (1928)
82	23	On the Topic of Exhibitions (1928)
83	24	We Stand at the Turning Point of Time: Building Art as the Expression of Spiritual Decisions (1928)
84	25	[The Adam Department Store] (1928)
85	26	[Stuttgart Bank Competition Report] (1928)
86	27	[On the Barcelona Pavilion] (1929)
86	28	Beautiful and Practical Buildings! Stop This Cold Functionality (1930)
87	29	[Art Criticism] (1930)
88	30	The New Time (1930)

89	31	Hall II at the Berlin Building Exposition (1931)
90	32	[Radio Address] (1931)
91	33	[Paul Klee Leaves the Bauhaus] (1931)
91	34	Expressways as an Artistic Problem (1932)
93	35	[On the Anniversary of the Werkbund] (1932)
94	36	[Bauhaus Berlin. Syllabus and Curriculum] (1932)
97	37	This is How the Future Berlin Bauhaus Will Look (1932)
98	38	[What Would Concrete, What Would Steel Be without Plate Glass?] (1933)
99	39	[Announcement of the Dissolution of the Bauhaus to Students] (1933)
99	40	[Letter on the End of the Bauhaus] (1933)
100	41	Competitions Proposal (1933)
101	42	Architects of Europe Today (1935)
103	43	The H. House in Magdeburg (1935)
104	44	[Inaugural Address as Director of Architecture at Armour Institute of Technology] (1938)
106	45	Architectural Education (c. 1938–39)
108	46	[AIT Curriculum] (c. 1939)
109	47	[The Stevens Chicago Note] (c. 1938–39)
109	48	[It is Performance That Matters] (c. 1938–45)
111	49	A Tribute to Frank Lloyd Wright (c. 1940)
112	50	[Vendôme Shop in Pittsburgh] (1941)
113	51	[A Museum for a Small City] (1943)
114	52	[Introduction to Ludwig Hilberseimer, *The New City: Principles of Planning*] (1944)
115	53	Only the Patient Counts: Some Radical Ideas on Hospital Design (1945)
118	54	[Library and Administration Building, IIT] (1946)
118	55	[Book by Philip Johnson] (1947)
119	56	[The IIT Campus] (1949)
120	57	Campus Design (1949)
123	58	What Should a Church Look Like? (1950)
124	59	Architecture and Technology (1950)
125	60	Broaden Vision, Architects Urged (1950)
125	61	The Training of Architects (1950)
126	62	People Who Live in Glass Apartments Throw Verbal Stones at Scoffers (1951)
127	63	Six Students Talk With Mies (1952)
130	64	[Mies' New Buildings] (1952)
132	65	[Commons Building, IIT] (1953)
133	66	A Chapel, IIT (1953)

CONTENTS

133	67	The End of the Bauhaus (1953)		164	85	[Conversation at the Architectural League in New York] (c. 1958–60)
136	68	On Walter Gropius (1953)		172	86	[Eulogy for Herbert Greenwald] (1959)
138	69	A Proposed National Theatre (1953)		173	87	[Story About the Barcelona Pavilion] (1959)
139	70	[Conversation Regarding the Future of Architecture, Part I] (1955)		174	88	[Conversation With Architecture Students in Chile] (1959)
143	71	[Dedication of Crown Hall] (1956)		181	89	[Acceptance Speech for the Cross of the Order of Merit] (1959)
143	72	Crown Hall, IIT (1956)		182	90	Speech on the Occasion of Receiving the Gold Medal of the Royal Institute of British Architects (1959)
144	73	Mies' Enormous Room (1956)		183	91	No Dogma (1959)
145	74	[Interview Given to the BBC] (1956)		187	92	An Address of Appreciation by HT Cadbury-Brown (1959)
151	75	At the Ground-breaking of Lafayette Park (1957)		194	93	Architect of the Clear and Reasonable (1959)
152	76	[Some Ideas Behind Mies' Work] (1957)		198	94	[On Value] (1959)
153	77	[Office] Organisation (1958)		198	95	Famed Architect Enjoys Thinking (1960)
153	78	Foreword to Rudolf Schwarz, *The Church Incarnate* (1958)		200	96	[On Civilisation] (1960)
154	79	Mies and the Glass Manufacturers (1958)		201	97	[Speech on the Occasion of Receiving the AIA Gold Medal] (1960)
155	80	Some Thoughts About Civilisation (1958)		202	98	[George Danforth Interviews Mies] (1960)
157	81	A Special Kind of Order (1958)		221	99	[Interview With Peter Blake] (1961)
160	82	Interview at Chicago Office: Eight Questions (1958)		236	100	[Speech on The Voice of America] (1962)
160	83	A Conversation With Mies van der Rohe (1958)		237	101	[Speech at Aachen Industrial School] (1962)
163	84	[Dedication of Cullinan Hall] (1958)		237	102	An Architect for His Time (1962)

242	103	[Eulogy for Rudolf Schwarz] (1963)		279	121	[Dirk Lohan Interview] (1969)
242	104	Acceptance Speech at the Presentation of the Gold Medal in Architecture (1963)		294	122	[Eulogy for Walter Gropius] (1969)
243	105	[Acceptance Speech for the Munich Cultural Award] (1963)				
244	106	Building Details (1963)				
245	107	[Conversation Regarding the Future of Architecture, Part II] (1964)		296	INDEX	
				302	ACKNOWLEDGEMENTS	
252	108	[Architecture Is Not a Martini Cocktail] (1964)				
255	109	Meet Mr Mies van der Rohe (1964)				
257	110	[Mies Speaks in Berlin] (1964)				
264	111	Against Arbitrary and Childish Play (1964)				
265	112	Modern Classicist (1965)				
268	113	[Peterhans' Seminar for Visual Training] (1965)				
269	114	[Eulogy for Le Corbusier] (1965)				
270	115	[My Professional Career] (1965)				
271	116	Mies van der Rohe, an Architect of Our Time (1965–66)				
272	117	Light 80 Candles on the Library (1966)				
273	118	The Life and Times of an Old Master (1968)				
275	119	I Really Always Wanted to Know About Truth (1968)				
276	120	The Will of the Epoch Shown in Construction (c. 1968)				

Mies as Educator:
Written and Spoken Words

Michelangelo Sabatino
IIT College of Architecture

During a consequential life that unfolded between Berlin and Chicago, Ludwig Mies van der Rohe (1886–1969) contributed to a profound rethinking of the foundations of modern architecture at a time of great upheaval in architectural practice and education. Intended as an accompaniment to analyses of his buildings, *Mies in His Own Words: Complete Writings, Speeches, and Interviews (1922–1969)* presents Mies' written and spoken words from a period of almost 50 years – from manifesto-like pronouncements on form creation as a young architect in Berlin in the 1920s to vivid recollections recounted to his grandson Dirk Lohan during the last three weeks of his life in the USA. We see Mies in a variety of settings and situations – reading voraciously while designing steel-and-glass skyscrapers in the 1920s; deftly managing the Bauhaus in its interactions with the Nazis during the 1930s; reacting to fellow architects including Peter Behrens, Walter Gropius, Le Corbusier, and Frank Lloyd Wright; and sitting in his pyjamas for three hours each morning 'Buddha-like' in his 'almost barren' apartment in Chicago as he did 'nothing but think'.

Although this collection of texts seems voluminous, Mies' written output is relatively modest compared to that of his contemporaries Le Corbusier and Frank Lloyd Wright. But, while Mies did not produce multiple tomes of architectural criticism or theory, he wrote carefully and with clarity in both German and English, eschewing the oftentimes hyperbolic tone of his more widely published peers. This collection of spoken and written words attests to the considerable energy Mies expended on foundational reading and writing about architecture and art in his native Germany prior to assuming leadership of the Department of Architecture at Chicago's Armour Institute of Technology (now Illinois Institute of Technology) in 1938. As he struggled to master the English language – even years after his arrival in Chicago, he retained a strong accent, clearly audible in recordings from the time – he gradually discovered the power of the spoken word, especially in educating his students. At the same time, he also understood the power of silence. It is no coincidence that numerous photos show him in conversation while surrounded by attentive students and colleagues gathered in SR Crown Hall, the architectural masterpiece he designed for the IIT campus. Despite his association with Crown Hall, the fact that it was realised in 1956, just two years prior to his retirement from IIT, meant that he spent relatively little time actually teaching in the building. These often crowded group photos, with Mies at the centre of a rapt audience, are in sharp contrast to the more well-known, often sombre, portraits of him staring sagely and silently into the distance. In almost all these two types of photos, Mies is seen holding his signature Montecristo No. 2

cigar in his right hand. According to his grandson, the architect Dirk Lohan (born 1938), Mies derived great pleasure from his cigars; but taking a puff also allowed him to gather his thoughts and formulate answers to questions before articulating a response in English. The delay associated with this diversion only added to his allure as a measured and thoughtful interlocutor who weighed his words carefully. (Figs. 1–3.)

The extraordinary consolidation of Mies' national and international reputation in the 1950s and 60s corresponds to the post-World-War-Two boom in affordable printed media that allowed architects to extend their reach and identity beyond professional and academic audiences. Mies was no exception. In a lengthy overview of his work and ideas published in an issue of the then popular and influential *LIFE* magazine (17 March 1957), Mies appears in photographs by Frank Scherschel and Hedrich Blessing. In the first of a sequence of four remarkably candid photographs, most likely taken by Hedrich Blessing, Mies is captured speaking with his eloquent hands in his office at IIT (Alumni Memorial Hall, room 215, where he was based for many years before the construction of Crown Hall) and amidst employees in his architectural office at 230 East Ohio Street. As part of a four-episode television programme titled 'Mies van der Rohe', broadcast in 1961 for the Heritage Program on WTTW, an affiliate of Chicago PBS, he was interviewed by his former student and collaborator, the architect and educator George Danforth (see pp. 202–221). In this television interview Mies went into great detail about his work and his architectural ideas. *BDA ehrt Mies van der Rohe in Berlin* (BDA Honours Mies van der Rohe in Berlin), a film produced in Germany in 1966 by the Bund Deutscher Architekten (Association of German Architects), features extensive interviews with Mies in German (see Figs. 4–11). And in 1964 *Look* and *LIFE* editor John Peter conducted a probing interview with Mies, during which the architect revealed the extent to which his time teaching in America had led him to think and communicate in a more concise manner in English:

> J.P.: Has working in America changed what you think or what you do?
>
> L.M.v.d.R.: I think you are always influenced by your environment. There's no doubt. I think that teaching helped me a lot. I was forced to be clear to the students. You know, students are funny people. They perforate you with questions. You look like a sieve. You have to make it really clear, and you cannot fool them. They want to know, and you

have to be clear. That forces me to think these things clear through so that I can answer them. I think teaching had this influence. It was in the direction I was going anyway.

John Peter, interview, 1964, *The Oral History of Modern Architecture*, New York, 1994, p. 164; see also p. 247 of this publication

The so-called 'Lohan Tapes', an extensive interview conducted with Mies in the summer of 1969, during the final days of his life, by his grandson Dirk Lohan, were published for the first time in 2021 with annotations by Fritz Neumeyer (see pp. 279–293 here). The insights about Mies' life and work contained in these candid interviews are of exceptional historical value. Finally, *Mies van der Rohe*, the 1986 film produced by Mies' daughter Georgia van der Rohe on the occasion of the centennial of his birth, features a number of excerpts in which Mies shares his thoughts, including excerpts from an interview Georgia did with him when the National Gallery in Berlin opened in 1968 (first released as Georgia van der Rohe and Sam Ventura, directors, *Beton, Stahl und Glas*; for an overview of Mies and film see Dietrich Neumann, 'Mies Media', *JSAH*, 66/1 [March 2007], pp. 131–135). Cumulatively, these examples demonstrate the extent to which Mies, particularly in the last decades of his life, relied upon the spoken word to disseminate his long-held beliefs to different generations of architects and students, as well as to a wider audience.

Since his brief but intense experience teaching at the Bauhaus in Germany, Mies had grown to appreciate his role as educator. He understood that alongside drawing and sketching, the written and the spoken word were key to the transmission of ideas. Over the years, scholarship has been produced that reinforces Mies' contributions to architectural pedagogy. Alfred Swenson and Pao-Chi Chang's *Architectural Education at IIT, 1938–1978* (1980) was followed by *Mies van der Rohe: Architect as Educator*, the catalogue for the exhibition held at IIT between 6 June and 12 July 1986. Edited by Rolf Achilles, Kevin Harrington, and Charlotte Myhrum, this catalogue was IIT's contribution to the Mies van der Rohe Centennial Project. In engaging in conversation with professionals as well as journalists and students. Mies grew to rely for teaching at IIT on a Socratic method of questions and answers in place of conventional podium lectures. Photos of him with his students almost invariably show him either sitting next to them, examining a model, observing a drawing, or sitting on a chair and speaking to them directly. His charisma and the endearing German accent with which he spoke only enhanced the appeal of his compelling vision of architecture and architectural education. What emerges fairly clearly during Mies' years in America is a preference for dialogue with his interlocutors (whether architects, journalists, or students), as opposed to expressing his thoughts in the form of controlled pieces of writing published in either article or book form. Even when he chose to write about various topics of interest – ranging from Frank Lloyd Wright to Rudolf Schwarz – he typically kept his writing brief. Although Mies tended to repeat himself in his written and spoken words, he would often introduce slight variations.

Although Mies did not attend university, he was an avid reader and was committed to self-education throughout his entire adult life. He looked to books to inform his vision of architecture and its relationship with contemporary culture, society, and architects. It is no coincidence that when Scherschel photographed Mies for the *LIFE* article, he was particularly intrigued by the architect's apartment at 200 E. Pearson (Fig. 12). In a couple of these informal photos Mies appears to be at ease as he holds a book in his left hand and a cigar in his right against the backdrop of his art, while perhaps listening to classical music in the background. Here, as with the photograph taken of Mies by Lohan shortly before he died, we see Mies engaged in the quiet and patient act of reading (Fig. 13). It is worth recalling Mies's frequent interactions with students and his discussions with them about the role that books played in his life (Figs. 14–15):

> I don't know if I told you about the time I had 3000 books in Germany. I spent a fortune to buy those books, and I spent a fortune to read them, to study them. I brought 300 books with me to America, and I can now send 270 books back, and I would lose nothing. But I would not have these 30 left if I had not read the 3000.
>
> **Six Students Talk With Mies, p. 128**

Mies understood that in order to really probe the depth of architecture's relationship with culture and society, architects must constantly seek out opportunities to put aside their professional tools and read the classic works of great thinkers of both the past and the present. It is no coincidence that Mies so frequently refers to epoch when discussing his architecture. Even as he appears keenly aware of the greater forces that shape his epoch he is stubbornly committed to setting his own agenda rather than superficially following fashionable trends. In 1958 he told Christian Norberg-Schulz that 'architecture begins when you carefully put two bricks together.' While some might understand this dictum in purely architectural terms, Mies most certainly understood that words, like bricks, need to be selected and positioned with great care. And that dedication to detail and dialogue is precisely what continues to make hearing and carefully reading Mies in his own words so enthralling.

Mies, a Kind of Modernity

Vittorio Pizzigoni
Università degli Studi di Genova

Ludwig Mies van der Rohe became a modern architect when he decided to fully embrace the new mass society and its means of communication. This is, in fact, what many other architects and artists of modernity were doing, but, unlike them, Mies skilfully blurred his public image by coexisting as both the radical Avant-garde architect and the master of a new Classical architecture.

At the end of the First World War Mies was already an established architect on the Berlin scene. In 1907 he built his first villa for the philosopher Alois Riehl, and it was during his visits to Riehl's house that he later met his future wife, Ada Bruhn. From 1908 to 1912, with some interruptions, he worked in the studio of Peter Behrens, the most important German architect of the time, and later worked independently for a bourgeois clientele. In 1919, at the end of the war, Walter Gropius organised a major exhibition in Berlin titled 'Ausstellung für unbekannte Architekten [Exhibition for Unknown Architects]' to showcase the new trends in the latest architecture. Mies wanted to be part of it and asked to display his unrealised project for the Kröller-Müller house-museum in Wassenaar, near The Hague but was excluded because, as he himself recalls, Gropius was 'looking for something quite different' (see p. 261). During this period Mies separated from his wife and three daughters and started living in his architecture studio at Am Karlsbad 24 in Berlin.

Between 1921 and 1924 Mies produced five projects: two variants of a steel and glass skyscraper, an office building in reinforced concrete, a house in reinforced concrete, and a brick house. Five programmatic projects that immediately earned him recognition as one of the masters of Modern Architecture and were intended not so much to be built as to be exhibited as manifestos in shows and exhibitions. In 1923, unlike in 1919, Mies' projects for a glass skyscraper and an office building were included in the exhibition *Internationale Architektur*, organised in Weimar by Gropius, who was now the director of the Bauhaus. At the same time, they were shown at Berlin City Hall, at the *Grosse Berliner Kunstaustellung* (Big Art Exhibition of Berlin), at the annual exhibitions of the Novembergruppe, one of which was curated by Mies himself (p. 207), and also in Paris at the exhibition *Les architects du groupe De Stijl* (The Architects of the De Stijl Group) in 1923. Simultaneously, they were published in Avant-garde magazines and newspapers, accompanied by incisive and aphoristic texts that reinforced their function as 'manifestos' for a new idea of architecture. These projects have an almost didactic quality: their names announce the materials of which they are made and seem themselves to adumbrate logical formal consequences, however radical or unexpected. They are drawn in charcoal, often used flat, with the intention that they impress and be clearly visible from a distance.

Mies' early writings serve the specific purpose of accompanying the publication of his projects, not only helping in their dissemination but also identifying them as Avant-garde. The texts are precise and detailed descriptions of what is drawn but are also preceded by brief and incisive polemical paragraphs that use the style of the Avant-garde manifesto to provoke debate and discussion. Some texts or remarks may seem almost deliberately provocative, calculated to cause annoyance and reaction. Examples are Mies' request that the name of the Werkbund magazine *Die Form* be changed (p. 70) and the statement 'we shall not build cathedrals' (pp. 57, 61), made in front of an audience that was requesting a new cathedral for modern architecture.

Mies' early writings present two concepts that helped him establish himself as an Avant-garde architect but were then reiterated throughout his career. The first is that architecture can only be the expression of its own time. Mies repeats this statement many times, modifying it slightly depending on the context: Building art is the will of the epoch expressed in space' (p. 51); 'Architecture depends on its time; it is the crystallisation of its inner structure' (p. 124); 'Architecture as a true symbol of our time' (p. 124); 'Architecture is the expression of an epoch translated into space' (p. 171); 'Architecture as the expression of the slow unfolding of an epoch' (p. 182). Mies recalled having read this concept somewhere (pp. 139, 152). From this point forwards he considered architecture to be the art that 'wrote the history of the epochs and gave them their names' (pp. 124, 221). Understanding and accepting this view of architecture led him to seek a shareable position, to avoid ephemeral fads and individualistic attitudes, and, in a sense, to balance the thrust of his Avant-garde positions from the beginning. This approach later led him to state that he didn't 'design' buildings: 'We "develop" a building' (p. 235).

The second concept present in his early writings concerns the centrality of construction over form: 'We know no forms, only problems of construction' (p. 52). While this position has the merit of grounding architectural discussion in specific aspects, it also seems to be a way to give value to his learning though practical experience, downplaying the fact that he had not had a formal education. This concept is initially formulated as the need to use 'new building materials' to create a new architecture: the architect does not have 'to invent materials but to use materials invented by others' (p. 174). The materials of the new mass society 'were often in glaring contrast to our traditional conception of architecture [...] I felt that it must be possible to harmonise the old and the new in our civilisation' (p. 270). Later, this concept was simplified as a preference for natural materials and the intention to understand the characteristics of 'natural or artificial' materials (p. 107) and to make the right use of them, or, even more schematically, as a call to make 'honest' use of them. The attention to the characteristics of building materials is also evident in his educational programmes: both the Bauhaus programme of 1930 and the programme for the School of Architecture at the Armour Institute of Technology in 1939 seem to echo, at least in part, the education that Mies himself received and the series of questions he had posed.

To emphasise the Avant-garde, manifesto-like nature of his projects from the early 1920s, Mies, who had been born with the name Maria Ludwig Michael, chose to sign them with a stage name: Ludwig Mies van der Rohe. As is well known, he added his mother's surname 'Rohe' to his father's, preceded by 'van der' to echo the German 'von' indicating aristocratic origin. Between 1921 and 1924 two Mieses coexisted: the Avantgardist Mies who was increasingly present in the national and European debate and the other Mies who continued to create Biedermeier-style projects for the Berlin bourgeoisie. Only around 1924 did Mies decide to fully dedicate himself to modern architecture. Perhaps to emphasise this decision, he again modified his name that year. By adding a diaeresis he changed the pronunciation from Mies (pronounced 'meece'), which in German is an adjective meaning 'miserable' or 'dud', to Miës (pronounced 'mee-yes'), which eliminates that bothersome assonance. Only when he moved to the United States, where the German assonance was no longer present, did he again start signing himself 'Mies van der Rohe' or, more simply, just 'Mies'. The detachment from his previous work as an architect was emphasised in 1925–1926 by his decision to destroy much of his archive, as recalled by his assistant Sergius Ruegenberg (Wolf Tegethoff, 'From Obscurity to Maturity', in *Mies van der Rohe: Critical Essays*, ed. F. Schulze, New York: MoMA, 1989, p. 33). Of all his previous works, many of which were destined to remain unknown, only Mies' project for the Kröller-Müller house-museum was to be included in monographs dedicated to him.

Writing was much more a central aspect of Mies' work than one might be led to believe. This was not just because he became 'Ludwig Mies van der Rohe' when he started writing, but rather because he regarded writing as one of the necessary tools for achieving a 'clear and reasonable' architecture (p. 145). Mies had only attended school until the age of 14. When arranging his draughting table as a young lad employed in a small architecture studio in Aachen, as he later recalled, he found two books: a pamphlet on the theory of Pierre-Simon Laplace and a magazine titled 'Die Zukunft [The Future]' (p. 245). From then on, he began to read. He spent part of his meagre salary on buying *Die Zukunft* every Monday morning, as well as on purchasing books, and devoted time to reading voraciously and haphazardly. When his first client, the philosopher Alois Riehl, visited his studio in Berlin and noticed Mies' library, he asked, 'For heaven's sake, who advised you on your library?' (p. 245), not imagining that Mies had chosen his books himself.

The importance of reading and writing as tools for reflecting on one's work is made clear in a 1960 interview that describes Mies' typical day in Chicago: he gets up around 9 a.m. and, after preparing breakfast, 'sits on a couch and thinks. For three hours or so he does nothing but think' (ibid.); occasionally, he reads something, sometimes writes a note, or smokes a cigar; 'otherwise, he does nothing but sit there, Buddha-like, and think' (p. 199). Despite the casual irony, Mies adds an important statement: 'A great deal of work is thinking. To draw is relatively easy' (ibid.). Theory and practice went hand in hand in Mies' work, or rather, as he explained himself: 'I thought about architecture, and then I tried architecture to prove it' (p. 223).

Through writing Mies defined various concepts that aided him in his work, sometimes formulating them himself, at other times drawing from past thinkers such as St Augustine or Thomas Aquinas, from writers like Charles Baudelaire (p. 129), Walt Whitman (p. 114), and Henry Milton (p. 145), or from philosophers like Giambattista Vico, Max Scheler (p. 149), and Alfred North Whitehead (p. 150). One of these concepts is the comparison between architecture and language. Mies states that he works 'on architecture as a language' (p. 142), meaning in a way that makes it possible to reuse what others have developed and where the replication of a solution only confirms its soundness and reasonableness. This is a classical approach, where the collective development of the discipline ultimately has greater value than individual inventions. Not surprisingly, when asked if he minded his architectural designs being copied, Mies replied that this was rather a sign that they were appreciated: 'that is the reason we are working, that we find something everybody can use'

(p. 140). In the end he was able to have a profound influence on the time in which he lived through a comparatively small number of buildings because this influence was 'based on its reasonableness' (p. 146).

Part of this inclination towards 'the Classical' was also the search for a 'common language' (p. 140) of modern architecture: a language useable for both prose and poetry and which enables the realisation of anything – be it a garage or a cathedral – using 'the same means, the same structural methods' (pp. 140, 152). If the very idea of a common language is viewed with suspicion in an era characterised by individualistic approaches and a fear of monotony, Mies responds by citing on different occasions the medieval city, so rich and varied despite the fact that 'the plans are the same' (p. 226), and the variety of seashells: 'There are about 10,000 species of seashells […] but only one spiral shell construction in all of them. The difference is in the rate of growth' (p. 126). Moreover, not all buildings should be alike. Indeed, Mies states that he does not want to build 'a church as a movie palace and […] a factory as a church' (p. 146) because each building has a different meaning and value within society and the city. Consistent with this, Mies strongly criticises the individualistic approach. He asserts on multiple occasions that 'if a man has to express himself, let him be a painter' (p. 275). When Wright's niece asks him 'what about self-expression in architecture?', he has her write her name on a piece of paper and adds, 'There […] so much for self-expression. Now let's design a good building' (p. 274). Mies vividly remembers the confused architecture of the late nineteenth century, when architects, despite being 'the strongest artistic talents' (p. 57) of their time, made their work irrelevant by taking an individualistic approach. He finds it surprising that, for example, John Ruskin could state that 'every decoration should be thrown out when it does not support the construction' (p. 197) and then proceed to operate in a completely different manner.

Another concept that sets Mies apart from the functionalist architecture of his time and aligns him with a Classical approach is his quest for flexibility in designed spaces and the idea that architecture is indifferent to its function. From the 1920s forwards, Mies extensively discussed this with his friend and studio companion Hugo Häring (p. 258): Häring was in favour of an architecture that perfectly adapted itself to its function, while Mies advocated for an architecture broad enough to accommodate both current and future functions. Later, Mies took up Louis Sullivan's aphorism 'form follows function' (p. 130), only to overturn it and propose an architecture capable of adapting to the rapid changes in our society's functions: 'if a building serves the programme of today and is flexible enough to serve tomorrow's programme too, it is really economical' (p. 121).

The Classical connotations of Mies' modern architecture became a tool of distinction and promotion while also making it possible to recover traditional compositional systems, such as symmetry, and reconnect with a tradition which Modernism had distanced. His fondness for Classical architecture emerges on many other occasions. For instance, in 1935, during an interview for the US magazine *Pencil Points*, he was asked about a print of an Ionic capital in his studio. After a long silence he responded, 'The old architects copy this sort of thing. We appreciate it' (p. 103). On another occasion he described the IIT chapel as 'monumental' (p. 133), a word until then banned from the vocabulary of modern architecture. Mies acquired the idea of monumentality from Peter Behrens and repeatedly defined it as the pursuit of a 'great form' (pp. 139, 152). Again, there is the fact that full-page photos of the Parthenon in Athens and the Temple of Hera II (formerly known as the Temple of Poseidon) in Paestum appeared in the book on his work written in 1956 by his close friend Ludwig Hilberseimer. On many occasions Mies stated, 'I learned the most from old buildings' (pp. 150, 182). He repeated this on 26 May 1959, when he received the gold medal from the Royal Institute of British Architects for his achievements in modern architecture. These works of the past are 'mostly very simple buildings' (p. 139), structures capable of belonging to all historical epochs and, in this sense, 'classical'. Mies cites, for example, Inuit tents and the Castle of Ghent (p. 54), Roman aqueducts and suspension bridges over the Hudson, but also Palazzo Pitti and the Basilica of Maxentius (p. 203). Alongside medieval Gothic architecture, which he often takes as an example, a passion for classical Greece is glimpsed, perhaps derived from his early studies of Friedrich Schinkel's work or the fact that Berlin was called 'Athens on the Spree' at the beginning of the twentieth century. In any case, on one of the few occasions when Mies allowed himself a vacation, in 1959, he travelled to Greece, where he stayed from 1 to 23 May. The Greek influence on his architecture is a characteristic that manifested itself especially in the large Greek temple he realised in Berlin at the end of his life, the Neue Nationalgalerie (New National Gallery).

From Hendrik Petrus Berlage, Mies learnt 'the use of brick and [...] the honesty of materials' (p. 139) and that 'architecture should be construction' (p. 223). Above all, however, Berlage's writings influenced him by revealing the new architecture of the United States and the work of

Frank Lloyd Wright. From that point forwards, Mies' interest in American architecture was to be constant, growing particularly strong in the 1920s as he studied the large industrial structures published by Werner Lindner. In 1926 he defended the approach taken by the Berlin exhibition *Neue Amerikanische Architektur* (New American Architecture), almost giving the impression that he was personally involved.

In 1938 Mies moved to Chicago, where he finally encountered the pragmatic American architecture that had long inspired him. Even though he ironically said, 'I really don't know the Chicago school […] I always take taxis to and from work' (p. 267), his close friend Ludwig Hilberseimer seemed to hold a different opinion when he explicitly wrote, 'It is surprising to see how faithfully [Mies'] work carries onward the Chicago school of architecture, originated by architects who aimed, as he does, at a structural architecture' (Ludwig Hilberseimer, *Mies van der Rohe*, Theobald, Chicago 1956, p. 21). Once in Chicago, Mies used his first major project, the IIT Campus, as a true laboratory to test an architecture suitable for the new American context.

Mies' thought is not as monolithic as it is often represented. In fact, it developed over the years. For example, in 1930, when he began teaching at the Bauhaus, he set his students the exercise of designing a low-rise housing scheme on the same land where Gropius had just completed a project consisting of tall houses, demonstrating the economic equivalence of the two types of settlement. Later, in the Lafayette Park housing complex in Detroit, he created a set composed of both tall and low houses and found tall houses to be much more economical. He then concluded, 'I would not be surprised if, in such town development schemes, we kill off the low house in the end' (p. 184). But, when asked whether people should live in tall or low houses, he responded with disarming pragmatism, 'People should live as they like to live' (p. 184). And even his interest in and understanding of 'the Classical' evolve and change over time.

Mies' own figure was partly a media construction that fed on anecdotes and myths that he himself constructed. For example, as a young man, he worked in a stucco firm, where he truly learned to draw full-size and on vertical walls, and one day, during the preparation of a Renaissance-style ceiling, the chief draughtsman fell ill. 'Mies stayed late one night and finished the drawing. There was a furore, of course, and when it was discovered who had done it, Mies was promoted from broom to draughting board' (p. 101). Through stucco Mies learned to draw every type of ornament, and, after doing it 'for three years' (p. 164), he didn't need to draw any more ornaments: 'That lasts for a lifetime' (p. 164). 'When I told my students about it, I often turned around, took a piece of charcoal, and made a drawing on the wall without even looking' (p. 260). Another example concerns his visit to a marble yard in Hamburg to choose the material for the central wall of the Barcelona Pavilion. Spotting a huge block of onyx, which was not available because it was already sold, Mies 'said, "Why don't you give me a hammer and I will show you how we did this at home." And then somebody brought a hammer, and they were very curious to see if I would knock off a corner from the block, but instead, I made a very hard stroke in the centre of the block and got a hand-size slice, very thin, which they polished so that I could see it' (p. 258). Another example is when a Nazi delegation visited the Bauhaus directed by Mies in Dessau; Paul Schultze-Naumburg, who led the delegation, criticised the students' work and argued for the need to build pitched roofs, but Mies responded, 'I know there are some difficulties. I once had to fix one of your [pitched roofs]!' (p. 233). It's hard not to accept the truth of this statement even if we could never have imagined that Mies' practical activities extended to repairing a roof made by Schultze-Naumburg.

Mies' undeniable charisma emerges particularly in stories of his relationships with clients. For example, in the case of the Riehl House, his first independent work, the clients wanted a young architect, but Sophia Riehl was concerned about his inexperience and asked him if it was not dangerous to rely on an architect who had never built a house before. Mies replied, 'Listen, if somebody would answer me that until I am 60, what would I do?' (p. 228). And he got the job. Another time, Eduard Fuchs showed Mies the design for a monument to Karl Liebknecht and Rosa Luxemburg. Mies replied: 'You must be nuts […] That is something for a banker! […] these people [died] in a bank or before a brick wall. Why don't you build a brick wall' (p. 230). Fuchs was disappointed because he had to decide which project to build, but the next morning he called Mies and asked him to build a brick wall. Mies let Fuchs insist for a while and then replied, 'I'll try' (p. 231). Even with the Tugendhat House, there were conflictual moments, especially at the end of construction when the owners refused to accept the furniture designed by Mies for their home, similar to what was to happen at the Farnsworth House. Mies still shipped the furniture to Brno and gave specific instructions for the delivery: ' "You keep the furniture and shortly before lunch call him out and say that you are at his house with furniture. He will be furious, but you must expect that." [Mr. Tugendhat] said, "Take it out," before he saw it. However, after lunch, he liked it' (p. 188). Mies' charisma also shines through in his dialogue with Samuel Bronfman for the commission to design the Seagram Building in New York. Bronfman says, 'I like bronze and marble,' perhaps envisioning a more traditional architecture, but Mies responds, 'That's good enough for me!' (p. 250). Mies explains the relationship between the architect and the client, stating that one should never 'talk to a client about architecture. Talk to him about his children [...] An architect of ability should be able to tell a client what he wants' (p. 185).

In other writings this shrewd approach of unsettling the interlocutor while maintaining a certain reasonableness is even clearer. Examples are the idea of using a series of trees alongside highways to replace road signs (p. 91), Mies' proposal to let architects participating in a specific architectural competition choose the jury for that competition (p. 100), and a certain inclination towards more limited urban growth (p. 116). Even ceremonial speeches became opportunities to construct a mythical narrative, such as reviving the ancient tradition of handing over the key of an inaugurated building to the client (pp. 143, 163) and Mies' acknowledgement of his debts to Wright, Gropius, and Herbert Greenwald, his most significant client.

Mies often pondered the characteristics of our time, recognising them in science, technology, industrialisation, and the economy. On the one hand, these are topics understandable to everyone and therefore capable of reaching a very broad audience. On the other hand, Mies distanced himself from more common interpretations, and, with a mix of pragmatism and irony, related these concepts to the field of architecture. For instance, when asked to judge a competition for small hospitals, he stated that all patients' rooms should face south or east: 'Architects have no business to be talking like bankers [...] putting patients on both sides of a corridor will be a little cheaper, yes, but the reasoning is wrong. Money isn't the point. Is there economy in war?' (p. 115). When questioned about why he used an expensive material like bronze in the Seagram Building, he replied, 'You [don't] have to pay for it' (p. 169). When discussing the decision to use plaster instead of bricks for the interior walls of the IIT campus buildings because it was cheaper, he identified this decision as 'a false economy' (p. 121). 'We don't even need to measure the cost in dollars,' he said (ibid.). For him economy was not so much about costs; it was rather 'an economy of means [...] It is the economy that has an influence on architecture' (p. 249).

In project descriptions Mies employed almost the opposite technique, used interchangeably in major projects like the Mannheim theatre (p. 161), as well as in smaller projects such as the Vendôme Shop built in a Pittsburgh department store for the Kaufmann family, who also commissioned Frank Lloyd Wright's nearby Fallingwater (p. 112). The descriptions are concise and prosaic, entirely focused on practical aspects such as the use of carpeting and sliding doors in the Concrete House or the size of spans in the IIT Commons Building. The justifications given for the project appear so obvious and consequential that it becomes almost impossible not to accept them as the best possible ones.

The impression that Mies built few buildings and wrote even less largely stems from his insistence on consistently showcasing only those projects and writings he deemed most exemplary. This reiteration, even using the same photographs, served to promote himself and his architecture. Each of his tall buildings thus became a particular case of the 860/880 Lake Shore Drive Buildings and each of his writings an elaboration on one of his aphorisms. It may be surprising that his most famous aphorisms, such as 'skin-and-bone buildings', 'less is more', 'God is in the details', and 'almost nothing', appear infrequently in this collection. These simplifications, at times excessively concise, do not aim to explain Mies' architecture and thought but rather to advertise him to the general public, to mass society. These phrases' promotional effectiveness is tremendous, as may be judged by the fact that in 1967 *The New York Times* asked him to use the expression 'less is more' in an underwear advertising campaign. Perhaps amused, he responded that he didn't care 'as long as the models wear beautiful underwear' (LoC, Box 4, A).

However self-evident, Mies' ability to use mass media as a tool to promote himself and his work never ceases to amaze. His entire career may be reinterpreted by focusing on how he wanted to present himself to the masses – the same masses that in 1927 did not seem to him 'quite as characterless as manufacturers of mass-produced packaging see them' (p. 73) (Beatriz Columina, *Manifesto Architecture: The Ghost of Mies*, Berlin: Sternberg, 2014; Juan José Lauherta, *Photography or Life. Popular Mies*, Barcelona: Tenov, 2015).

From a young age, Mies demonstrated an unusual skill in using the pioneering technique of photomontage. Already in 1910, in the competition for the Bismarck Monument, together with his brother Ewald, he presented highly realistic photomontages that combined drawing with photographic landscapes (Martino Stierli, *Montage and the Metropolis*, New Haven and London: Yale University Press, 2018). This tool, extensively used by the Avant-garde, was employed realistically by Mies, giving life to beautiful images of the glass and iron skyscraper on Friedrichstrasse and to the perspectival view of the Adam Department Store, with a level of detail so precise that one might even wonder whether the images of the Kröller-Müller house-museum are photographs or photomontages.

Writing was also part of this promotional strategy. If initially Mies' writings were dogmatic and polemical, placing themselves in the cultural debate of the time, from the 1930s onwards, their tone became more conversational and capable of reaching a broader audience. Alongside the written word, Mies also employed the spoken word, starting from 1931, in radio broadcasts. In the post-war period he increasingly expressed his ideas through interviews, a communication tool that was more accessible to the mass audience. Furthermore, if the sporadic interviews of the 1920s consisted of a few questions and lengthy answers, in the post-war period the way he talked became concise and almost colloquial – a trend that continued in the following years, eventually becoming his primary form of expression. The places where Mies' words were published also changed: from Avant-garde magazines in the 1920s and specialised press there was a slow shift towards widely circulated magazines and newspapers.

After the Second World War Mies' writing was marked by a profound linguistic shift: around 1945 he stopped writing in German and shifted to English. This change could even be said to have modified his ideas. In 1947 he translated his German writings for the volume edited by Philip Johnson (Philip Johnson, *Mies van der Rohe*, MoMA, New York, 1947). While the content remained the same, the presentation was significantly different: where the original text had sometimes been heavy and complex, the English version was light and fluid, purposely designed for a broader audience.

Mies' interest in and attention to new forms of communication led him to plan, in 1958, the script for a documentary about his work with the title 'A Special Kind of Order'. Initially, he planned 13 episodes and appointed Hans Richter, who in 1930 had directed the short film *Die neue Wohnung* (The New Habitation). The idea of making a film about a living architect and of '[communicating] "this story" through the media of television and motion pictures' (p.158) was entirely novel. After drafting several versions of the script, the work came to a halt. However, shortly afterwards, in July 1960, a documentary was produced by WTTW Television in Chicago: in the four episodes of the series Mies is in a television studio where, with the help of images printed on cardboard, he engages in a friendly dialogue with George Danforth, his former student and collaborator who had succeeded him as the director of the School of Architecture at IIT (Figs. 10–11). The idea of a more complex film, closer to the one planned in 1958, was finally realised in 1966 and produced by Bayerische Rundfunk Television. In it Mies' voice and explanations alternate with images of his buildings and footage of his work in the studio.

What is particularly surprising in Mies' writings is the persistent attention he dedicates to his own contemporaneity. This attention repeatedly led him to modify and clarify his positions, aiming to make them more closely aligned with reality, but without tracking it step for step. In his thoughts there was always a gap – the identification of a crisis point, a careful examination of a condition that cannot be accepted either for what it is or, above all, for what it appears to be. He acknowledged the pragmatic necessity of replacing an old building with a new one but believed that to achieve a good result, it is necessary to 'plan on a large scale large and complex projects' (p. 125). He never shied away from functional needs, but by analysing functions, he distorted the spatial consequences normally expected. While accepting economy as a guiding principle, he never devalued it into a mere and immediate saving.

This continuous reflection on reality, on assumptions that usually are taken for granted but never truly understood, remains perhaps one of the highest teachings of Ludwig Mies van der Rohe.

Editorial Note
With Archival Sources
and Bibliography

In this volume the reader will find a complete anthology of writings, speeches, and interviews by Ludwig Mies van der Rohe through which the development of the architect's thinking about architecture and architectural education may be understood. The writings produced while he lived in Germany were originally published in his native language, whereas those produced after he moved to America in 1938 were mostly in English. While many of these have been published in specialised and mainstream journals and magazines, as well as in books, a handful are presented here for the first time. Although we have included letters, we have avoided personal correspondence since we are primarily concerned with Mies as an architect and educator in the public realm. Even though strict authorial oversight is somewhat blurred when it comes to interviews / conversations that were subsequently transcribed and published without us knowing if final approval was given by Mies, we believe that only by accessing a variety of different types of textual sources in Mies's own words can we fully understand how his ideas formed over time. This is also true with regard to project descriptions that were likely the joint efforts of Mies and his staff. What might be lost in accuracy is hopefully made up for by access to a heterogeneous body of work. To be clear, this is not a critical academic edition. For example, sentences written and deleted by Mies are not reproduced, but sources are systematically provided for the individual documents in order to make it easier for those who wish to do so to consult the original source.

The three categories presented to our reader in the book's subtitle – writings, speeches, interviews – should be understood as somewhat general. For example, when we refer to 'writings,' we mean a broad variety of published and non-published texts ranging from brief statements to published letters and a handful of lengthier articles. We consider a 'conversation' to be a less structured variant of an interview. Also, our category 'speeches' includes both 'addresses' and 'lectures', which are somewhat similar in intent (but differ in terms of audiences). In short, the three groupings are intended to provide readers with general categories within which we include slightly different but related types.

At various times throughout the process of gathering and editing this anthology we experienced a series of challenges given the nearly five decades over which the writings, speeches, and interviews were produced. Added to this were issues concerning translation of texts from German to English. We were greatly helped in this endeavour by Fritz Neumeyer's pioneering *The Artless Word. Mies van der Rohe on the Building Art* (originally published in German in 1986 and first translated into English by Mark Jarzombek in 1991). Neumeyer's study significantly expands the number of Mies' texts first gathered in Philip Johnson's *Mies van der Rohe*, published in conjunction with the exhibition held at the Museum of Modern Art in 1947 (and subsequently re-issued in 1953 with an additional text). Although several other anthologies have included Mies' writings, Neumeyer's book and to a lesser degree Johnson's catalogue remain essential references, even if considerable differences exist in the translations. Worthy of mention is Moisés Puente (ed.), *Conversations with Mies van der Rohe* (New York, 2008), originally published as *Conversaciones con Mies van der Rohe* (Barcelona, 2006). Finally, Vittorio Pizzigoni's *Ludwig Mies van der Rohe, Gli scritti e le parole* (2010), published in Italian by Einaudi, served as a starting point for this publication.

As far as language goes, there are a number of inconsistencies throughout the text that we have tried to clarify. While we have endeavoured to be faithful to the original texts, we have taken some liberties regarding the correction of typos and clear grammatical errors in order to help with the flow of reading. For example, in certain instances where we have an unpublished typewritten text transcribed by others without any certainty that Mies oversaw the final version, we have tried to make the text more readable. For texts published before 1935, we almost always use translations by Mark Jarzombek (*The Artless Word*). Overall, we have worked to faithfully present Mies in his own words, even though there are several instances in which previous translators or transcribers have made choices that are hard to identify in retrospect.

Abbreviation

LMvdR: Ludwig Mies van der Rohe

Archives

– LoC: Library of Congress, Washington DC.
– AIC: Art Institute Chicago, Chicago IL.
– MoMA: Museum of Modern Art, New York NY.

Select Bibliography

– Blake 1970: Peter Blake, 'A Conversation With Mies van der Rohe', *Four Great Makers of Modern Architecture: Gropius, Le Corbusier, Mies, Wright* (New York, 1970).

– Blaser 1977: Werner Blaser, *Mies van der Rohe. Lehre und Schule* (Basel–Stuttgart, 1977), also published as Werner Blaser, *After Mies: Mies van der Rohe, Teaching and Principles* (New York, 1977).

– Hartman 2004: George E. Hartman, Jan Cigliano (eds.), *Pencil Points Reader: A Journal for the Drafting Room 1920–1943* (New York, 2004).

– Johnson 1947: Philip Johnson, *Mies van der Rohe* (New York, 1947; 2nd edition, 1953).

– Neumann 2020: Dietrich Neumann, David Caralt (eds.), *The Barcelona Pavilion by Mies van der Rohe. One Hundred Texts Since 1929* (Basel, 2020).

– Neumeyer (1986) 1991: Fritz Neumeyer, *The Artless Word: Mies Van Der Rohe on the Building Art* (MIT Press, 1991; first published as *Mies van der Rohe. Das kunstlose Wort: Gedanken zur Baukunst* [München, 1986]).

– Pizzigoni 2010: Vittorio Pizzigoni (ed.), *Ludwig Mies van der Rohe. Gli scritti e le parole* (Torino, 2010).

– Puente (2006) 2008: Moisés Puente (ed.), *Conversations With Mies van der Rohe* (New York, 2008; first published as *Conversaciones con Mies van der Rohe* (Barcelona, 2006)].

– Walter 2022: Axel Walter (translator), *Ludwig Mies van der Rohe. Gesammelte Schriften* (Leipzig, 2022)

– Wingler (1962) 1969: Hans M. Wingler, *Bauhaus, Weimer, Dessau, Berlin, Chicago* (Cambridge–London, 1969; first published as *Das Bauhaus: 1919–1933 Weimar, Dessau, Berlin* [Bramsche, 1962]).

– Zukowsky 1986: John Zukowsky, Ines Dresel, *Mies Reconsidered* (Chicago, 1986).

Photo Essay

Fig. 1
'Mies van der Rohe at Crown Hall',
photo by Dirk Lohan, 1965.

Fig. 3
Mies with students, photo by Frank Scherschel,
LIFE magazine, March 18, 1957.

Fig. 2
'Mies van der Rohe at Crown Hall, 1965,
Bust of Mies by Hugo Weber in Background',
photo by Dirk Lohan.

Fig. 5
Mies in his IIT office at Alumni Memorial Hall, photo by Hedrich Blessing, courtesy of Chicago History Museum [hb35283s].

Fig. 4
Mies in his IIT office at Alumni Memorial Hall, photo by Hedrich Blessing, courtesy of Chicago History Museum [hb35283u].

Fig. 6
Mies in his IIT office at Alumni Memorial Hall, photo by Hedrich Blessing, courtesy of Chicago History Museum [hb35283y].

Fig. 7
Mies in his IIT office at Alumni Memorial Hall, photo by Hedrich Blessing, courtesy of Chicago History Museum [hb35283z].

Fig. 8
Photo of Mies, Ludwig Karl Hilberseimer,
and Myron Goldsmith, Chicago, 1953,
Edward A. Duckett Collection, Ryerson and
Burnham Art and Architecture Archives, AIC,
Digital File #198602.Hilbs_Mies11.

Fig. 9
Photo of Mies, Ludwig Karl Hilberseimer, and Myron Goldsmith, Chicago, 1953, Edward A. Duckett Collection, Ryerson and Burnham Art and Architecture Archives, AIC, Digital File #198602.Hilbs_Mies7.

Fig. 10
Screenshot of Mies and George Danforth discussing Peter Behrens' Turbine Factory, Mies van der Rohe, WTTW, courtesy of American Archive of Public Broadcasting, 1961.

Fig. 11
Screenshot of Mies and George Danforth discussing Peter Behrens' Turbine Factory, Mies van der Rohe, WTTW, courtesy of American Archive of Public Broadcasting, 1961.

Fig. 12
Mies in his 200 E. Pearson St apartment, photo by Frank Scherschel, *LIFE* magazine, March 18, 1957.

Fig. 13
Mies in his 200 E. Pearson St apartment shortly before his death on 17 August 1969, photo by Dirk Lohan.

Fig. 14
Mies with students near Lugano
(left to right: Mies, Jack Rodgers,
Paul Naeff, Howard Dearstyne, and
with back to camera, E. Burzi),
photo by Fritz Schreiber, 1933,
courtesy of IIT.

Fig. 15
Mies with R Schneider, draughting
room at the Art Institute of Chicago,
photo by Thomas Burleigh, c. 1941,
courtesy of IIT.

Nota bene:
Square brackets appear throughout this publication. They signal editorial decisions made by the co-editors with the intention of clarifying or of filling in gaps. Titles of writings, speeches, and interviews by Mies placed in square brackets have been selected by the editors because there does not appear to be a definitive title assigned by Mies. Furthermore, with the exception of the preface and introduction by the co-editors, Roman text is used throughout only for Mies' own words, whereas italics are used for contributions by everyone else.

For all the texts published in *Mies in his Own Words*, we have endeavoured to identify, where possible, the source of the first publication while Mies was alive, as well as any subsequent publications during Mies' life. For unpublished work published after Mies' death we have identified the archival source and where it was first published. For unpublished work published for the first time in this anthology, we have identified the archival source.

Mies in His Own Words

1 Two Glass Skyscrapers

Published journal article (summer 1922).
Source: LMvdR, untitled, in Bruno Taut, Karl Peters (eds.), *Frühlicht. Eine folge für die verwirklichung des neuen baugedankens*, vol. 2, no. 4, 1922, pp. 122–124.
Translated from German by Mark Jarzombek.
Republished in Johnson 1947, p. 182; Neumeyer (1986) 1991, p. 240; Pizzigoni 2010, pp. 3–4; Walter 2022, pp. 11–12.

Only skyscrapers under construction reveal bold constructional thoughts, and then the impression of the high-reaching steel skeletons is overpowering. When the walls are raised, this impression is destroyed completely; the constructional thought, the necessary basis for artistic form-giving, is annihilated and frequently smothered by a meaningless and trivial jumble of forms. At very best, one remains impressed by the sheer magnitude, and yet these buildings could have been more than just manifestations of our technical skill. That would mean, however, having to give up the attempt to solve a new task using traditional forms and trying instead to give form to the new task based on the nature of this task.

The novel constructional principle of these buildings comes clearly into view when glass is used for the exterior walls, which are no longer load-bearing. The use of glass, however, necessitates new approaches.

In my design for the skyscraper at the Friedrichstrasse railway station in Berlin, intended for a triangular site, a prismatic form corresponding to the triangle appeared to offer the right solution for this building. I angled the respective façade fronts slightly toward one other to avoid the danger of the effect of lifelessness that often occurs if one employs large glass panels *[Glass Skyscraper, first version, angular]*. My experiments with a glass model showed me the way, and I soon realised that in employing glass, what mattered was not an effect of light and shadow but a rich interplay of light reflections. That is what I strove for in the other design published here *[Glass Skyscraper, second version, curved]*. At first glance the contour of the ground plan appears arbitrary, but in reality it is the result of many experiments on the glass model. The curves were determined by the need to illuminate the interior, the effect of the building mass in the urban context, and finally the play of the desired light reflection. Ground plan contours in which the curves were calculated from the point of view of light and shadow revealed themselves on the model, when glass was employed, as being totally unsuitable. The only fixed points in the ground plan are the shafts for the stairs and the elevators.

All other subdivisions of the ground plan are to be adapted to the respective needs and executed in glass.

2 Office Building

Published journal article (July 1923).
Source: LMvdR, 'Bürohaus', in G, no. 1, 1923, p. 3; LoC, Mies, Box 61, Articles about Mies.
Translated from German by Mark Jarzombek.
Republished in Johnson 1947, pp. 183–184; Neumeyer (1986) 1991, p. 241; Pizzigoni 2010, pp. 5–6; Walter 2022, pp. 13–14.

Any aesthetic speculation
any doctrine   } we reject.
and any formalism

Building art is the will of the epoch expressed in space.

Alive. Changing. New.

Not the yesterday, not the tomorrow, only the today is formable.

Only this building creates.

Creates form out of the nature of the task with the means of our time.

That is our work.

OFFICE BUILDING
The office building is a building of work, of organisation, of clarity, of economy.
Bright, wide workrooms, uncluttered, undivided, only articulated according to the organism of the firm. The greatest effect with the least expenditure of means.
The materials are concrete, iron, glass.
Ferroconcrete buildings are essentially skeleton structures.
Neither pasta nor tank turrets. A supporting beam structural system with a non-supporting wall. That means skin and bone structures.

The room depth was determined by the most practical distribution of the workstations; this is 16 metres. A double-shafted frame with a span of eight metres with four-metre-long lateral cantilever brackets on either side was determined to be the most economical construction principle. The distance between beams is five metres. This post-and-beam system supports the ceiling panel, which, angled vertically upward at the end of the cantilever arms, becomes exterior skin and serves as the back wall of the shelving, which has been moved to the exterior walls in order to keep the interior uncluttered. Above the two-metre-high shelving is a continuous band of fenestration reaching to the ceiling.

Berlin, May 1923

3 [Draft for a Newspaper Article]

Unpublished manuscript (2 August 1923).
Source: MoMA, Mies, Manuscripts, folder 3.
Manuscript as in *Deutsche Allgemeine Zeitung*, based on the preceding text, 'Office Building'.
Translated from German by Mark Jarzombek.
Republished in Neumeyer (1986) 1991, p. 241; Pizzigoni 2010, p. 7.

It is no coincidence that today important architectural questions are discussed in the newspapers. The art and technical journals that used to be focal points for artistic life have, due to their purely aesthetic orientation, failed to register the movement of modern building art away from the aesthetic to the organic, from the formal to the constructional. Modern building art has for a long time now refused to play a merely decorative role in our life. Creative building artists want to have nothing, nothing whatever, to do with the aesthetic traditions of past centuries. We leave this field without regret to the art historians. *[Such artists']* work shall serve life. Life alone shall be their teacher. They reject any tutelage by art specialists; building art is for them neither theory nor aesthetic speculation nor doctrine but the will of the epoch expressed in space. Alive, changing, new. The character of our time must be evident in our buildings. We want to shape the form of our buildings based on the nature of the task but using the means of our time. *[This article continues with word-for-word repetition of the text 'Office Building'.]*

4 Building

Published journal article (September 1923).
Source: LMvdR, 'Bauen', *G*, no. 2, September 1923, p. 1. LMvdR; 'Bauen', in Theo van Doesburg (ed.), *Bouwbedrijf*, vol. IV, no. 2, Jan. 1927, p. 74.
Translated from German by Mark Jarzombek.
Republished in Johnson 1984, pp. 183–184; Neumeyer (1986) 1991, p. 242; Pizzigoni 2010, pp. 8–10; Walter 2022, pp. 15–17.

We know no forms, only problems of construction.
Form is not the goal but the result of our work.
There is no form in and for itself.
The truly formal is conditional, fused with the task, yes, the most elementary expression of the solution of the task.
Form as goal is formalism; and that we reject. Nor do we strive for a style.
Even the will to style is formalism.
We have other concerns.
What concerns us in particular is to liberate building from aesthetic speculators and make it again the only thing it should be, namely

BUILDING
[The title 'Concrete Residential Building' appears only in the manuscript version.]
There have been repeated attempts to introduce ferroconcrete as a building material for construction of apartment buildings. Mostly, however, inept. The advantages of this material have not been exploited nor its disadvantages avoided. People think they have taken sufficient account of the material if they have rounded off the corners of a building and of the individual rooms. Round corners are totally irrelevant for concrete and are not even all that easy to execute. It will not do, of course, simply to translate a brick building into ferroconcrete. I see the main advantage of ferroconcrete in the possibility of considerable savings in materials. In order to realise this in an apartment building, one must concentrate the supports and

reinforcements in a few places in the building. The disadvantage of ferroconcrete, as I see it, lies in its limited performance as insulation and its poor sound absorption. This makes it necessary to provide additional insulation against exterior temperatures. The simplest way to remove the disadvantage of sound transfer seems to be to exclude everything that causes noise. Here I have in mind rubber floors, sliding windows and doors, and similar installations, but also spatial generosity in the ground plan. Ferroconcrete demands the most precise planning before its execution; here the architect still has everything to learn from the shipbuilding engineer. With brick construction it is possible, even if not particularly advisable, to let the heating and installation crews loose on the house as soon as the roof is up; they will in a short time transform the house into a ruin. With ferroconcrete such a procedure is impossible. Here only disciplined work will achieve the desired result.

The model illustrated above demonstrates an attempt to get closer to the problem of using ferroconcrete in a residential building. The main living section is supported by a beam system with four pillars. This construction system is encased in a thin concrete skin. The skin forms both walls and roof. The roof is slightly inclined from the exterior walls toward the centre. The incline of the two roof planes forms a groove that permits the simplest imaginable roof drainage. All gutterwork is thereby omitted. I have cut openings into the walls where I needed them for views or for illumination of the interior.

5 Solved Tasks: A Challenge for Our Building Industry

Published journal article (27 December 1923).
Source: LMvdR, 'Gelöste Aufgaben. Eine Forderung an unser Bauwesen', *Die Bauwelt*, vol. XIV, no. 52, 1923, p. 719.
Lecture given on 12 December 1923 at a public meeting of the Association of German Architects (Bund Deutscher Architekten) titled 'How can we Escape From the Housing Shortage? Building must be Resumed!' The lecture took place at the auditorium of the Berlin Arts and Crafts Museum, Prinz-Albrecht-Strasse 8, Berlin.
Republished in Neumeyer (1986) 1991, p. 243; Pizzigoni 2010, pp. 11–13; Walter 2022, pp. 18–21.

In the country it is natural practice to plough under a field overgrown with weeds without considering the few grains that have managed to survive. We, too, have no other choice if it is really our aim to take a new attitude toward building.

You are all familiar with the condition of our buildings, and yet I wish to remind you of Kurfürstendamm and Dahlem, so that you have before your eyes this total lunacy in stone.

I have attempted in vain to understand the meaning of these buildings. They are neither comfortable nor economical nor functional, and yet they were supposed to be homes for people of our time.

They do not think very highly of us, if they really think these boxes can fulfil our living requirements. There has been no attempt to comprehend and formulate in a basic way these totally different needs.

Our inner needs have been ignored; they believed they could get away with cleverly juggling historical allusions. These buildings are dishonest, stupid, and insulting.

What we ask for, by contrast, for buildings for our time is: absolute truthfulness and rejection of all formal cheating.

Furthermore, we demand:

that in planning apartment buildings, absolute priority be given to the organisation of the living arrangements;

rational economics be striven for; the employment of new technological means is a precondition that goes without saying.

Meeting these demands will give us an apartment building for our time.

Since the rental apartment house is just a multiplicity of individual apartments, in this case too the organism of the building is formed from the type and number of these apartments. This determines the form of the apartment block.

I can show you no illustrations of new buildings that correspond to these demands. Because even the latest attempts have failed to go beyond matters of form.

To help you look beyond the historical and aesthetic junk heaps of Europe to what is elementary and purposeful in housing construction, I have put together illustrations of buildings that lie outside the realm of Greco-Roman culture. I have done this deliberately because to me an axe stroke in Hildesheim is closer than a chisel stroke in Athens.

I will now show you dwellings clearly formed from purpose and material.

Fig. 1 (An Indian tent) This is the typical residence of a nomad. Light and transportable.

Fig. 2 (Leaf hut) This is the leaf hut of an Indian. Have you ever seen anything more perfect in terms of function and use of material? Is this not the best possible use of the shade of the jungle?

Fig. 3 (Eskimo [Inuit] house) Now I take you into night and ice. Moss and seal skins have here become building materials. Walrus ribs form the roof structure.

Fig. 4 (Igloo) We go even further north. The residence of a central Eskimo [Inuit]. Here there is only snow and ice. And yet man builds.

Fig. 5 (Summer tent of an Eskimo [Inuit]) This fellow even has a summer villa. The building material is skin and bones. From the stillness and loneliness of the north I now take you to warlike medieval Flanders.

Fig. 6 (Gravensteen, castle of the counts of Flanders in Ghent) Here the residence has become a fortress.

Fig. 7 (Farm) In the North German lowlands stands the house of the German farmer. His needs with respect to house, stable, and barn have likewise been met in this structure.

All the pictures I have shown correspond in every way to their inhabitants' needs.

For ourselves we demand nothing else.

Only means that are of our time.

Since there are no buildings that so completely meet the needs of modern man, I can only show you a structure from a related field that embodies a modern sensibility and meets the conditions that I too long for and strive for in our residential buildings.

Fig. 8 (SS Imperator, ship [ocean liner]) Here you see a floating apartment building formed from the needs and means of our time.

Now I must ask you again: have you ever seen anything more perfect in terms of fulfilment of purpose and fitness of materials?

We would be enviable if we had buildings on dry land that suited our needs so well. Only when we have a similarly fundamental feeling for the needs and means of our time shall we acquire a new approach to construction.

It is the purpose of my short speech to awaken an awareness of these matters.

6 [Review of Paul Tropp, *Development and Organisation of Rent*]

Published journal article (March 1924).
Source: LMvdR, 'Paul Tropp, Entwicklung und Aufbau der Miete', *Die Baugilde*, vol. VI, no. 5, 1924, p. 56.
Translated from German by Mark Jarzombek.
Republished in Neumeyer (1986) 1991, p. 251; Pizzigoni 2010, p. 14; Walter 2022, p. 28.

Under the title 'Entwicklung und Aufbau der Miete [*Development and Organisation of Rent*]', Paul Tropp presents the results of his in-depth investigation into the apartment economy with great detail and clarity. This is the first time that our apartment economy has been illuminated from the point of view of an expert. Tropp shows how it is and how it could be. He discusses existing apartment and tax economies, incomes and rents, capital costs, maintenance and repair costs, and ground rents and draws expert conclusions from his objective observations. This text has happily appeared at the very moment when enormous efforts are being made to restart the building economy and put it on a sound footing. As Tropp's book makes a valuable contribution to this effort, I would recommend it warmly to all interested circles.

7 The Industrialisation of Building Methods

Published journal article (April–June, 1924).
Source: LMvdR, 'Industrialisierung des Wohnungsbaues – eine Materialfrage', *Der Neubau*, VI, no. 7, April 1924, p. 77. Republished in a second version with the title 'Industrielles Bauen' in G, II (June 1924), no. 3, pp. 8–13. In this second version Mies adds an umlaut to his surname.
Translated from German by Mark Jarzombek and John Nicolson.
Republished in Johnson 1947, pp. 184–185; Neumeyer (1986) 1991, p. 248 (partially); Pizzigoni 2010, pp. 15–18; Walter 2022, pp. 25–27.

The article 'Industrialisation of Building methods' that appeared in issue 5 discusses the great complex of problems associated with new building, the social, economic, technical, and also artistic nature of which is still misunderstood today. *[These words appear only in the first version. They refer to an article by Walter Curt Behrendt, of which Mies reuses the title.]* Just a short time ago, the need to industrialise the building trade was denied by almost all participating circles. I consider it a step forward that this question can now be discussed seriously in a larger circle, even if only a few are really convinced. The industrialisation that is advancing in all areas would also have gripped the building trade without concern for outdated attitudes and convictions if very specific circumstances had not here barred the way. I see industrialisation of the building sector as the core problem for construction today. If we are successful in carrying out this industrialisation, then the social, economic, technical, and even artistic questions will solve themselves. The question how this industrialisation is to be achieved can perhaps best be answered if we point out what has prevented it so far. The belief that backward operational practices are the cause is wrong. They are not the cause but the result of a situation, and they do not conflict with the character of the old building economy. Attempts to modernise operational methods in the construction trade have been made repeatedly but have only succeeded in those areas that have been open to industrialisation. Furthermore, too much weight has undoubtedly been given to the assembly-based character of today's building. *[The words following 'Attempts to' were added in the second version.]* Everything concerning construction of the building frame structure and interior decoration has been executed using the same methods since time immemorial and is purely a matter of handcraft. This character cannot be changed by economic forces or work methods; and it is precisely this that guarantees the survival of the small firms. As new building practices have shown, materials and wages can, of course, be saved by using larger and other types of masonry, but that does not in any way alter construction's handcraft character; and it should still be noted that brickwork has undeniable advantages over the new building methods. What matters is not so much a rationalisation of existing work methods but a fundamental reorganisation of the building trade in general.

As long as we use essentially the same materials, the character of construction will not change, and this character, as I have already pointed out, determines, when it comes down to it, the form that the building firms take. The industrialisation of the building trade is a question of materials. That is why the demand for new building materials is the first prerequisite. Our technology must and will succeed in finding a building material that can be produced technologically and processed industrially and that is firm, weather-resistant, and acoustically and thermally insulating. It will have to be a lightweight material whose processing not only permits but actually requires industrialisation. Industrial production of all parts can only be properly rationalised in a factory process, and the work on the building site will then be exclusively a matter of assembly and can be compressed into an incredibly short time. This will bring with it a significant reduction in building costs. New architectural aspirations will also then have work to do. It is clear to me that this will bring with it the destruction of the building trade as we know it, but anyone who regrets that the house of the future will no longer be erected by artisans must keep in mind that the automobile too is no longer built by the wheelwright.

[The first version of this text stops here. The following words are included in the second version.]
WE CONSIDER NECESSARY A FUNDAMENTAL CHANGE IN OUR FORMS OF HABITATION!

Building contractors will have to decide whether they really want to build rationally or whether the aesthetic speculation (in whatever guise) that still prevails in Europe will determine what they produce.
The organisation of building enterprises, their structuring principle, will also ultimately determine how they develop. Large-scale works can only be achieved where firms are large-scale. Industrialisation of construction is by its very nature a matter of industrial enterprises.

In the next issues we shall publish and discuss projects by Sommerfeld that aim at rational and economical construction.

8 [Lecture: What We Mean by Elementary Form-Giving]

Unpublished lecture manuscript (19 June 1924).
Source: MoMA, Mies, Manuscripts, folder 4, untitled.
The initial part of this lecture is published in the article 'Building Art and the Will of the Epoch!'
Translated from German by Mark Jarzombek.
Republished in Neumeyer (1986) 1991, pp. 245–250; Pizzigoni 2010, pp. 19–24.

Ladies and gentlemen! Never before has construction been so much talked about as it is today, and never have we been further from understanding the nature of building. For this reason, the question of the nature of building art is today of decisive importance. For only when this has been clearly understood can the struggle for the principles of a new building art be conducted purposefully and effectively. Until then it must remain a chaos of confused forces. We shall have to realise that building art has always been the spatial expression of intellectual decisions, is tied to its time, and can only manifest itself in addressing vital tasks using contemporary means. It has never been otherwise.

For this reason it is a futile endeavour to use contents and forms from earlier periods today. Here even the strongest artistic talent will fail. We find again and again that even outstanding building masters are ineffective when their work does not serve the will of the epoch. For all their great talent, they ultimately remain dilettantes because when you do something wrong, the élan with which you do it is irrelevant. It is the essential that matters. You cannot walk forwards while looking backwards, and you cannot express the will of the epoch if you live in the past.

The structure of our age is fundamentally different from that of earlier epochs. That applies to both its spiritual and material aspects. These, however, determine our work of creation.

The striving of our epoch is directed toward the secular. The efforts of the mystics will remain just episodes. Although our understanding of life has become more profound, we shall not build cathedrals. Even the grand gesture of the romantics is meaningless for us, for we sense behind it the emptiness of the forms. Our epoch is undramatic; what we value is not the grand gesture but rationality and reality.

Our epoch's demands for practicality and functionality have to be met. If this is done with great sense, then the buildings of our time will demonstrate the greatness of which our time is capable, and only a fool can maintain that they are without greatness.

Questions of a public nature are of central interest. The individual is becoming less and less important; his fate no longer interests us. The decisive achievements in all fields are objective in nature, and their originators are for the most part unknown. It is here that the great anonymity of our time is revealed. Our works of engineering are typical examples. Gigantic dams, large industrial complexes, and important bridges arise with the greatest matter-of-factness, and yet we do not know who built them. These structures also show the technical means we shall have to use in the future.

The objection that these are only functional structures is irrelevant. A building's purpose is its own meaning. The buildings of all epochs have served purposes, and very real ones. These purposes have varied, however, in type and character. The purpose has always been decisive for a building. It gave it its sacred or profane form.

Our historical schooling has dulled the way we look at these things; that is why we are always confusing effect with cause. This accounts for the belief that buildings exist for the sake of architecture. Even the sacred language of temples and cathedrals is the result of a purpose. This is how it is, and not the other way around.

Each time, the purpose changes the language, and the same holds true for the means, materials, and technique.

People who lack a feeling for the essential always try to hold up the results of past ages as examples for our time and recommend the old work methods as the way to artistic success. Both are wrong; we can use neither. We need no examples. Those who propose working methods based on craftsmanship in our time prove that they have no idea of the interrelationships that give an age its coherence. Even handcrafts are only a work method and a form of economics, nothing more.

People tend to believe unquestioningly that handcrafts are better and attribute to them an innate ethical value. However, it is never a work method that has value but only the work itself.

I was born into an old family of stonemasons, so am very familiar with craftsmanship, and not merely as an aesthetic onlooker. My receptiveness to the beauty of craftsmanship does not prevent me from recognising that handcrafts as a form of economic production are done with. The few real craftsmen still alive in Germany are rarities whose work can only be acquired by very rich people. What really matters is something entirely different. Our needs have assumed such proportions that they can no longer be met using the methods of craftsmanship. This spells the end of the crafts: we cannot save them any more, but we can perfect the industrial methods to the point where we obtain results comparable to medieval craftsmanship. Whoever has the courage to maintain that we can still exist without industry must produce proof of that. The need for even a single machine abolishes craftsmanship as an economic form.

Let us keep in mind that all these theories about craftsmanship have been composed by aesthetes under the beam of an electric lamp. They embark upon their propaganda mission on paper that has been produced by machines, printed by machines, and bound by machines.

If people had devoted one percent of this effort to improving the book's bad binding, this would have been an opportunity to learn what immense capabilities are offered by industrial production methods. To waken these capabilities is our task. Since we stand only at the beginning of industrial development, we cannot measure its initial imperfections and weaknesses against a highly developed culture of craftsmanship.

That eternal preoccupation with the past is our downfall. It prevents us doing what needs to be done, that which alone can give rise to a viable building art. Old contents and forms, old means and work methods, have only historical value for us. Life confronts us daily with new challenges; they are more important than all the historical clutter. These challenges call for creative people, people whose gaze is directed forwards, who are sufficiently unafraid to tackle each task without prejudice from the bottom up, and who do not dwell excessively on the results. The result is a by-product. Each task presents us with new conditions and leads to new results. We are solving problems not of form but of construction, and the form is not the goal but the result of our work. That is the essence of our striving; and this viewpoint still divides us from many. Even from most master architects today. But it unites us with all our disciplines in modern life.

Just as we take the concept of building as not tied to old contents and forms, so it is also not bound to specific materials. The charm of ashlar and brickwork is very familiar to us. But that does not prevent us from today regarding glass and concrete and glass and metal as proper construction materials. In many cases, it is precisely these materials that best meet present-day purposes.

Steel serves today in skyscrapers as a structural skeleton, and reinforced concrete has often proven itself an excellent building material.

If a building is built using steel, what is the point of then suspending massive stone walls around it so as to give it the appearance of a tower? Even from the point of view of fire safety, this cannot be justified. It is similar nonsense to wrap a ferroconcrete structure in a sheath. In both cases more ideas instead of more materials would lead to the goal. *[The previous paragraph has been deleted in the manuscript.]*

The purposes of our tasks are for the most part very simple and clear. They only have to be recognised and formulated to lead of themselves to significant building solutions. Skyscrapers, office buildings, and commercial structures practically call forth clear, large-scale solutions, which can only be mutilated because people repeatedly try to adapt these buildings' purposes to outdated attitudes and forms.

The same applies to construction of residential buildings. Here too, certain ideas about houses and rooms lead to impossible results. Instead of simply developing a residential building based on its purpose, namely organising the activity of living, the building is treated as an object for showing to the world how far its owner has progressed in the realm of aesthetics. A residential building must only serve for living in. The construction site, the insolation, the spatial programme, and the construction materials are the most essential factors in designing a habitation. The building's organism should be formed on the basis of these conditions. The pictures so familiar to us with will then disappear, but in their place will arise residences that will be functional in all respects. The world did not become poorer when the stagecoach was replaced with the automobile.

Now I want to give you a few examples to explain what we mean by elementary form-giving.

(Fig. 1) This is the plan for the expansion of the city of Magdeburg designed by the much-reviled Bruno Taut. This plan contains nothing fantastic or arbitrary. It has been designed in response to the landscape, the traffic, and with respect for the people that have to live and work here. The plan has acquired its significant and distinctive form precisely because no form was striven for here.

(Fig. 2) This is a plan for a farm: a nursery under intensive management in the hands of a modern farmer who operates using scientific methods and with the help of the latest technical innovations. This method of operation determined the projected layout. The design is by the Berlin architect Hugo Häring.

I would have liked to show you other works of elementary design by other architects, but due to the scarcity of such works and the short time at my disposal, this is not possible. Excuse me, therefore, if I use my own work to demonstrate to you the influence exerted by the material and technology of the buildings.

(Fig. 3) The building site was triangular; I endeavoured to use it to the full. The depth of the lot forced me to split up the fronts to get light into the inner core. Since I consider it senseless to drape the building's steel structures with stonework, I gave the building a skin of glass. The objection has been raised that the glass wall does not take sufficient account of exterior temperatures. These fears are exaggerated. Buildings with large glass fronts already exist, and I know of no case in which the large glass planes are considered a defect. Furthermore, we now have Rudeglass, a material which possesses considerable insulating capacity due to its incorporation of a vacuum layer.

(Fig. 4) This is another design for a skyscraper. Here the objection has been raised that the building has not been properly formed but has got stuck at the schematic treatment stage. This reproach is typical. It stems from another way of thinking which still involves certain, albeit modern, architectonic concepts ... *[This sentence is incomplete in the manuscript.]* What is overlooked is that schematism is implied by the brief and is therefore expressed in the design.

(Fig. 5) This is the ground plan for the building just shown. Here too I attempted to approach the core of the building from the outside. This is where the deep recesses come from. Since my work with the problem of glass structures has taught me the dangers of too large areas of glass, I here chose polygonal curves for the ground plan to give a rich play of reflections.

(Fig. 6) This is the design for a reinforced-concrete office building. Ferroconcrete buildings are essentially skeleton structures. A tie-beam load-bearing structure with non-load-bearing walls. So, they are skin-and-bone buildings. The room depth was determined by the most practical distribution of the work stations and is 16 metres. A frame with two pillars with a span of eight metres and four-metre-long cantilever brackets on either side was found to be the most economical construction principle. The distance between the beams is five metres. This beam system supports the ceiling panel, which, angled upward at the perimeter, becomes exterior skin and serves as the back wall for the shelving, which has been moved to the exterior walls in order to keep the interior uncluttered. Above the two-metre-high shelving is a continuous band of fenestration stretching to the ceiling.

(Fig. 7) This picture illustrates an attempt to get closer to the problem of a residential building in ferroconcrete. The main living section is supported by a beam system with four pillars. This structural system is encased in a thin concrete skin. The skin forms both walls and roof. The roof is slightly inclined from the exterior walls towards the centre. The incline of the two roof planes forms a groove that permits the simplest imaginable roof drainage. All gutterwork is thereby omitted. I cut openings in the walls where I needed them for views or to provide illumination.

(Fig. 8) This house, for execution in brick, shows you, by contrast with the previous illustration, the influence of materials on the design of the forms. In the ground plan of this house I abandoned the usual concept of enclosed rooms and aimed at a series of spatial effects rather than a row of separate rooms. The wall loses its enclosing character and serves only to articulate the building organism.

I see the real value of the works I have shown you not so much in the quality of what has been achieved as in the particular approach taken to form-giving. Nothing illuminates more clearly the situation in which we find ourselves than the fact that Ford's book triggered such a strong reaction here in Germany. What Ford wants is simple and illuminating. His factories show mechanisation in dizzying perfection.

We agree with the direction Ford has taken but reject the level on which he moves. Mechanisation can never be the goal; it must remain the means. The means towards a spiritual purpose.

We want to stand with both feet firmly on the ground – but with our head in the clouds.

9 Building Art and the Will of the Epoch!

Published journal article (autumn 1924).
Source: LMvdR, 'Baukunst und Zeitwille!', *Der Querschnitt*, vol. IV, no. 4, 1924, pp. 31–36.
Translated from German by Mark Jarzombek.
Republished in Johnson 1947, pp. 186–187; Neumeyer (1986) 1991, pp. 245–247; Pizzigoni 2010, pp. 25–27; Walter 2022, pp. 22–24.

It is not architectural achievements that make buildings from earlier times appear so significant to us but the fact that the ancient temples, the Roman basilicas, and the cathedrals of the Middle Ages were not the work of individual personalities but the creations of entire epochs. Faced with such buildings, who asks for names, and what would the accidental personality of their builders mean? These buildings are by their very nature totally impersonal. They are pure representatives of the will of an epoch. That is their significance. Only thus could they become symbols of their time.

Building art is always the will of the epoch expressed in space, and nothing else. Only when this simple truth is clearly recognised can the struggle for the principles of a new building art be conducted purposefully and effectively. Until then it must remain a chaos of confused forces. This is why the question of the nature of building art is of decisive importance. What has to be grasped is that all building art is bound up with its epoch and can only manifest itself in addressing vital tasks with the means of its own time. It has never been otherwise.

For this reason it is a futile endeavour to use contents and forms from earlier periods of construction today. Here even the strongest artistic talent must fail. We find again and again that outstanding master architects fail because their work does not serve the will of the epoch. For all their talent, they ultimately remain dilettantes since if what you are doing is wrong, the élan with which you do it is irrelevant. It is the essential that matters. You cannot walk forwards while looking backwards, and you cannot be an instrument of the will of the epoch if you live in the past. It is an old fallacy committed by remote observers to make the epoch responsible for such tragic cases.

The striving of our epoch is directed toward the secular. The efforts of the mystics will remain just episodes. Although our understanding of life has become more profound, we shall not build cathedrals. Even the grand gesture of the romantics is meaningless for us for we sense behind it the emptiness of the forms. Our age is undramatic; what we value is not the grand gesture but rationality and reality.

Our epoch's demands for practicality and functionality have to be met. If this is done with great sense, then the buildings of our time will demonstrate the greatness of which our time is capable, and only a fool can maintain that they are without greatness.

Questions of a public nature are of central interest. The individual is becoming less and less important; his fate no longer interests us. The decisive achievements in all fields are objective in nature, and their originators are for the most part unknown. It is here that the great anonymity of our time is revealed. Our works of engineering are typical examples. Gigantic dams, large industrial complexes, and important bridges arise with supreme matter-of-factness, and yet we do not know who built them. These structures also show the technical means we shall have to use in the future.

If we compare the ponderous weight of Roman aqueducts with the spider-thin power system of a modern crane or bulky vaulted structural systems with the sleek lightness of new ferroconcrete structures, we get an inkling of how very different the form and expression of our structures are from those of earlier times. Industrial production methods too leave their mark. The objection that these are only functional structures is meaningless.

If we cast aside every temptation to look at things romantically, we will recognise incredibly bold engineering feats in the masonry structures of antiquity, the brick and concrete constructions of the Romans, and the cathedrals of medieval times too, and we can be certain that the first Gothic buildings were perceived, in their Romanesque setting, as alien bodies.

Only when, through fulfilling their purpose, they become instruments of the will of the epoch will our utilitarian structures become building art.

10 [Lecture: The Nature of Building]

Unpublished lecture manuscript (circa April 1926).
Source: MoMA, Mies, Manuscripts, folder 4, untitled.
First version of the manuscript is dated 17 March 1926.
Translated from German by Mark Jarzombek.
Republished in Neumeyer (1986) 1991, pp. 252–256; Pizzigoni 2010, pp. 28–38; Walter 2022, pp. 29–41.

Ladies and gentlemen! Never has building been so much talked about as it is today, and never we been further from understanding the nature of building. For this reason the question of the nature of building art is today of decisive importance. For only when this has been clearly understood, can the struggle for the principles of a new building art be conducted purposefully and effectively. Until then it must remain a chaos of confused forces. We shall have to realise that building art has always been the spatial expression of spiritual decisions, is bound up with its time, and can only manifest itself in addressing vital tasks using contemporary means. It has never been otherwise.

For this reason it is a futile endeavour to use contents and forms from earlier periods today. Here even the strongest artistic talent will fail. We find again and again that even outstanding building masters fail when their work does not serve the will of the epoch. For all their talent, they ultimately remain dilettantes because when you do something wrong, the élan with which you do it is irrelevant. It is the essential that matters. You cannot walk forwards while looking backwards, and you cannot express the will of the epoch if you live in the past. It can be fascinating to trace the spiritual impulses of a period in art and illuminate its formal problems. The spiritual forces of a period can also be effective here. Building art is not the implementation of specific formal problems, however much these may be contained in it.

The structure of our period is fundamentally different from that of earlier epochs. This applies to both its spiritual and material aspects. These, however, determine our work of creation. With or against our will. It is astonishing how little this simple fact is understood. We affirm modern life in thousands of ways. We use all the technical innovations. We are enthusiastic about new inventions, and we never hesitate for a moment to apply the boldest innovation if there are economic advantages to be derived from it. But we refuse to draw consequences for building art from these changes in living conditions. The reasons for this are manifold. We have specific preconceptions about what building art is, and we believe that what has existed until the present time is of eternal value. This should not astonish us, for it is also the mistake perpetuated in our schools.

What is astonishing, however, is the total lack of historical understanding connected with this love for historical things. People misconstrue the real interdependence of things, with regard to both the new and the old. Everything that has existed until now has been closely connected with life, out of which it arose, and a change of things always presupposes a change of life. Plato too perceived changes of forms in state and society and identified their cause in changes in the soul of the people who constitute state and society, while the soul in turn is influenced in myriad ways by the form of the life that surrounds it.

Each culture arises out of the landscape and its economic conditions. Only in this connection can we understand what is meant by 'culture'. Only someone who understands the full significance of the need for irrigation of the lower Nile Valley and its influence on societal structure can fully comprehend the nature of Egyptian culture. Ignorance of the economic basis and social structure of the Hellenes led to a complete misunderstanding of antiquity. Nordic culture, too, is just as much the result of very specific economic conditions without which it would either have failed to develop or would have developed differently. Transformations within cultures, too, depend on transformations of their economic structures. These too can succumb to political influences, just as they can impact on these influences in their turn. They change the living requirements of the people concerned, and this leads to a change in how this people expresses itself in forms. It is wrong, of course, to assume that an economic change in a society is automatically followed by a change in ideology. The change of the ideological superstructure takes place often very much later and infinitely much more slowly than the changes in the societal basis. The shell of the outer form of things, the crystallisation of a life process, persists even then and exerts an influence long after its kernel has been hollowed out. People continue to employ the forms even when they no longer comprehend their meaning; they continue to degrade their value and to alienate them even further from their original purpose. What once was the supreme expression of vital forces gradually deteriorates into the banality of senseless use unless power and grandeur can be summoned to impart new expression to the changed life content.

We ourselves are witnesses to such a tragedy. The sins committed in this respect today exceed what is imaginable. If an individual is unable to see effective interconnections and consequently makes mistakes, this is regrettable. But if new things are prevented by officials, it is our duty to fight this obstruction with everything we have since it has its roots in an indifference towards spiritual things and a complete misunderstanding of the past. Those who assume the right to intervene with regulatory action in the lives of individuals and the community are obliged to acquire adequate knowledge of things and their interconnections. Only superior abilities and real mastery give one the right to rule.

Neither sentimentality nor brute force are suitable preconditions for that. The force of life will one day push aside this farce and create its own form all the quicker. Nothing is more stupid than to assume that our will is sufficient to change the situation in which we live in this or that direction. Neither peoples nor individuals can attain their aims on their own. Only what lies in the direction of our life's goals can be fulfilled.

Before I address the modern movement and its principles, I want to give you a few examples to make clear what, by contrast with the various theories, building has always been about and to what conditions it has always been subject. This will make it much easier for us to understand the new. As we consider the development of building, we are confronted with two large areas of this discipline. One area concerns building for life in a general sense; the other is closely connected with very specific spiritual atmospheres that we perceive as clearly defined cultures.

Buildings of the first type are completely intertwined with the ground on which they stand; they and they alone are truly down-to-earth. They are formed from primal materials in the landscape. No one invented them, but they have grown in the truest sense of the word from the needs of their inhabitants and reflect the rhythm and character of the landscape in which they are embedded. These features are typical for all farmhouses regardless of where on earth they are located. Differences in their layouts are the consequence of different racial characteristics. But in everything, with their living quarters, stables, and barns, they correspond to the lifestyle habits of their inhabitants. The illustrations I shall now show you will make clearer than all words just how far human building forms express the character of their purpose.

(Fig. 1) I leave open the question of whether the single farm settlement that we find in the area west of the Weser on the Lower Rhine up to the coast of Holland and Flanders is the primitive form of the Germanic settlement or whether here it is Saar-Frankish influences that prevail.

(Fig. 2) These structures are erected in no particular order and without preference for orientation on open fields, surrounded by ramparts and ditches, near a spring or wooded area, in the middle of land assigned to farming, and far from any road.

(Fig. 3) The farmer lives as a free man on free land, dependent on no one, creating what he needs for his own life and that of his family. Only field paths connect the individual farms with one another.

(Fig. 4) The splitting up of families and the consequent contraction of operational resources may have led to the formation of dispersed settlements – to compensate for the reduced defence capabilities and to provide help in times of need. Even now, however, each builds in the old spirit of independence wherever he wants and where the land offers him sufficient possibility of making a living.

(Fig. 5) Neither do Germanic cluster villages follow a fixed plan; their formations follow the landscape with a natural matter-of-factness. Although denser, the houses stand about entirely without order.

(Fig. 6) There is no need for traffic of any type. Like individual farmsteads in previous times, the individual villages too are now self-sufficient. Only field paths connect the villages with one other.

(Fig. 7) These village formations come from the Germanic-Slavic border area and are built with improved defence in mind. The spaces between the individual farmsteads can easily be blocked in case of attack.

(Fig. 8) This settlement type is regarded as the original Germanic village. Here the distinctive old field divisions are still visible.

(Fig. 9) This village formation is undoubtedly of colonial origin. The village green is the centre of village life – the place where wagons are kept and judgements are pronounced, the feast and meeting place. The green now has a distinct influence on how the village is formed. The buildings orient themselves in respect to the green in a free, natural order. Little by little, handcrafts and trades emerge. Both continually gain in importance. Agricultural work gradually decreases. Traffic grows. The street gains in importance and eventually forms the backbone of the village settlement. Whereas once, when Romanesque churches were built, entire villages became depopulated as people sought to escape decades of forced labour in the praise of God and in the service of the church, now many seek protection against attacks in the shadow of fortified churches and castles. In exchange for promised protection, they have to participate in defence and perform services of other kinds. Although farmers too seek to settle near such protective locations, the latter are mainly inhabited by craftsmen and tradesmen.

(Fig. 10) Given the continual population growth, it is an obvious thing to do and in the communal interest to secure with walls the areas lying outside the castle or church area too.

(Fig. 11) Gradually, towns and cities are formed in which crafts and trades can develop undisturbed. The seclusion and limited size of these early urban formations forces their inhabitants to live very closely together, but it also forces them for the sake of securing their livelihoods to regulate production and consumption. This is entrusted to the individual trades. And this is how the guilds come into being. Life behind protective city walls combined with these economic ties must clearly have brought with it an incredible sense of community. This in turn intensifies religious feeling. A highly developed crafts system and the heyday of the German cities coincide with the unrestricted secular power of the church in Europe; both find their expression in the medieval township with its dominating cathedral.

(Fig. 12) Churches too undergo a change of form. Initially, they stood in open countryside and were for a long time heavily fortified; they too only gradually, under the protection of the fortified town, acquired full freedom of form. For a long time the guilds were able to control production and consumption. Increasingly, however, they have to ward off the forces of accumulating merchant capital. After losing more and more ground, they finally succumb in this struggle, leaving the way open for trade to develop to its full extent. This brings true prosperity and with it the growing power of the cities. The cities found schools and universities, often in competition with the church. With the invention of book printing, the crafts come into close contact with the highest spiritual aspirations; the cause of the Reformation is thereby much advanced. The cities acquire all kinds of rights and their own administration and defence system. The ornate guildhalls and town halls are the expression of a proud consciousness of power. At this point secularisation increasingly takes hold, launching the great bourgeoisification of German life.

(Fig. 13) The invention of gunpowder reduces the value of city walls. There is a transition to using fortified strongholds to protect the land.

(Fig. 14) Political development leads to the formation of principalities. This change, too, is more clearly seen in the development of the German cities.

(Fig. 15) Now it is the seats of the princes that have the decisive influence on the development of architecture. Here courtly life is clearly expressed. Furthermore, the new royal-residence cities clearly illustrate the stratification of political life.

(Fig. 16) The once so proud citizens have become vassals. Their habitations line the access routes to the castle and have the appearance of liveried servants. It is a specific achievement of Protestantism to put science in the service of technology and economics. This is a time of scientific experiments. This, coupled with an emphasis on reason that has been in ascendancy since the Middle Ages and with the onset of capitalism, which finds nourishment in the existing nations, leads to the development of industrial work methods. Traffic, which was previously tied to roads and waterways, expands immensely following the invention of the steam engine. Industry and trade now know no boundaries. The tempo of life accelerates in manifold ways. The population expands rapidly. Customs barriers fall, allowing the country's interior economy to develop freely. The technification of life progresses further. The unified German empire achieves world power status. International traffic and international trade shape life from now on. Metropolises of vast size develop. The speed of development leaves no time for reflection.

(Fig. 17) Endless sequences of street upon street are built. Industry experiences unprecedented expansion.

New technology with unimagined possibilities comes into being. Bold structural systems that have never been seen before are invented.

(Fig. 18) Traffic grows to immense size and intervenes with brutal violence in the organism of our cities.

(Fig. 19) Gigantic industrial complexes – yes, entire industrial cities – come into being.

(Fig. 20) The machine has long since been master of production. This is more or less the situation before the war. Even though the speed of this development slows with the outbreak of war, its direction is unchanged. On the contrary, the situation intensifies. If there were formerly a thousand reasons for managing with loose reins, now there are just as many reasons for making the sharpest calculations. The degree to which life for everyone before the war was tied to the economy only becomes fully clear to us when the war is over. Now there is only the economy. It dominates everything, politics and life. Ladies and gentlemen, I had no intention, of course, of giving you an extensive survey of economic or architectural development; I wanted only to show how closely all construction is bound up with living and how transformations in life are reflected in transformations of our building forms.

The situation in which we find ourselves today is, however, in no way comparable with that of earlier epochs. It is totally new and will find ways of expressing this in likewise new building forms. I have already pointed out that economic changes in a society are by no means instantly and automatically followed by changes in ideology but take a much longer time to unfold. It should therefore not surprise us that despite fundamental changes in the structure of our existence, the exterior form of our life has not yet been able to create a new expression for itself. This transformation will take place only very gradually, little by little. Specific necessities of life will articulate themselves increasingly and push out the old, long-obsolete forms of living.

(Fig. 21) It is well known that certain technical requirements lead to new forms of great expressiveness. But this must not be confused with expression of a spiritual kind. It is beauty of a technical kind. They are technical forms that stem from a technical, not a spiritual will. The degree to which a new technology influences the construction of a building can be seen in this picture.

(Fig. 22) That it makes no sense to drape this building with heavy masses of stone and give it the appearance of a tower is quite obvious.

(Fig. 23) These forms, too, are only possible thanks to a new technology.

(Fig. 24) How a new type of technical thinking can lead to new structural systems is shown by this wooden hall.

(Fig. 25) Ferroconcrete facilitates wide-span and cantilevered constructions.

(Fig. 26) The use of this type of beam system leads to a totally new form of structure and therefore to a new exterior appearance. That the uninhibited force of life cannot be held back by administrative regulations is shown by this picture.

(Fig. 27) Here the influence of building code restrictions is noticeable in the stepped setbacks. New forms have never been the result of regulations. But in our administered world this mistake too is understandable. In reality, however, only creative forces can truly create form.

If modern master architects are now embarking one after another upon the attempt to give new expression to our changed life, this is in no way a matter of arbitrariness or whimsy. Le Corbusier has addressed the problem of form in the metropolis.

(Fig. 28) His opinion is that the city of the future cannot do without skyscrapers. He sees the latter as an appropriate means for managing increasing traffic congestion. He arranges the skyscrapers in groups, puts an airport in their middle, and connects them with underground railways. Since he leaves the ground floors open, the traffic can easily flow through these buildings.

(Fig. 29) Residential buildings, too, exceed their previous height and enclose gardens and parks.

(Fig. 30) Continuing the work of Haussmann, Le Corbusier has proposed rebuilding the outdated medieval quarters of Paris.

(Fig. 31) Here too he has proposed using skyscrapers.

(Fig. 32) Le Corbusier's plans can only be properly understood from the Parisian point of view.

(Fig. 33) Due to its historical development, Paris is a city of representation.

German city building takes other paths. Academic theory is still struggling to understand the problems of medieval city planning. The charm of these cities is unforgettable. But life keeps going onwards and makes brutal demands without regard for individuals' arbitrary longings. Traffic poses problems. The senseless positioning of working and living quarters in relation to one another is leading, particularly in large cities, to unbearable increases in the cost of living. Entire residential quarters in industrial areas have to be torn down to create space and freedom of movement for industry. Further difficulties arise from the current division into administrative districts. Each district is administered without regard for the whole. That this lack of planning will in the short or long run inhibit and even kill off economic and industrial development seems gradually to be sinking in. Economic insights are gaining influence in city planning. The value of the location theory in urban planning has begun to be recognised. Industry must be positioned where it finds the most advantageous living conditions. That these difficulties are particularly evident in the industrial districts of Rhineland-Westphalia, the most developed economic centre, and that here the call for their elimination is loudest, is understandable. The creation of the Ruhr Settlement Association has united 325 urban administrations under a single urban-planning concept, creating the opportunity to establish a unified economic plan, independent of individual administrative districts, for an entire economic region. This economic plan is simply a planned distribution of work and residential areas and of railroad, agricultural, and recreational zones. The transport system is determined only on the basis of this allocation. This means that these traffic arrangements do not determine but follow the development of the plan, or, to put it another way, traffic planning is a consequence of economic development. Thus the lording of economic power over us is beginning to exercise its determinative influence at the most important locations in the planning of cities. Only thorough development of such thoughts can provide the conditions necessary to give our cities an organic form. Only when there is a basis of this kind can the industrial, residential, commercial, and administrative centres develop freely and in a way that suits their own nature. Only thus can the changed structure of our life find a suitable expression.

And only here can the spiritual capabilities of our time become effective. Building art is not the realisation of specific problems of form, no matter how much it may contain these problems. But it is always, I repeat, the spatial execution of spiritual decisions.

11 Letter to *Die Form*

Letter published in journal (May 1926).
Source: LMvdR, 'Briefe an die Form', *Die Form*, vol. I, no. 7, 1926, p. 179.
Translated from German by Mark Jarzombek.
Republished in Neumeyer (1986) 1991, p. 251; Pizzigoni 2010, p. 39; Walter 2022, pp. 42–43.

Volume 5 of *Die Form* contained an article on 'American Building Art' by Lewis Mumford, with an editorial claiming that the published article was more enlightening on the state of American architecture than the exhibition *Neue Amerikanische Architektur*, held not long before at the Academy of Arts.

Reading Mumford's article, I found the exhibition to be a particularly apt illustration of Mumford's beliefs. That speaks for the exhibition. The objection has been expressed in the Berlin press that the exhibition was not organised in accordance with a specific plan, but that only outstanding achievements of American architecture were presented. I consider it an advantage that the exhibition did not adhere to a specific and narrow programme but allowed the visitor to form his own judgment as to American building art.

However interesting it may be to learn how you yourself or how Mendelsohn, Paulsen, or Rading appraise America, it appeared to me necessary and desirable that each arrive at his own picture of the present state of the American art of building; this, as I see it, constituted the value of the Berlin exhibition.

12 An Interview With an Architect

Published article (December 1926).
Source: Heinrich Ritter, 'Ein Architektengespräch', *Stein Holz Eisen. Wochenschrift für moderne Bauwirtschaft und Baugestaltung*, vol. XL, no. 52, December 1926, pp. 668–669.
Translated from German by John Nicolson.
Republished in Walter 2022, pp. 44–47.

On the occasion of the Werkbund exhibition of 1927 three leading architects met in Stuttgart: a Frenchman, a Dutchman, and a German. In each of their countries these are the minds attuned to the most fundamental matters and therefore the most characteristic representatives of modern architecture.

Le Corbusier from Paris: someone who has worked and is very much accustomed to working – as is immediately apparent. Dogmatic without necessarily being a systematist. Gifted with all the puritan rigour of his homeland. He comes from the upper Rhone area, where the expelled Albigensians settled hundreds of years ago. The great rationalists Rabelais and Rousseau are his fellow-countrymen – a not unimportant fact. Le Corbusier built his first house when he was 17. It was then he realised that our houses are merely a compromise between medieval construction methods and modern furnishings and that their interior structures do not meet the requirements of the present day. He spent years travelling so as to gain a clear view of the elements of the art of building. His observations and conclusions were reflected in the journal which he founded and edited – L'esprit nouveau. *His book* Vers une Architecture, *which caused a stir and which we reviewed in detail in our issue no. 30 of 22 July, is an extract from this journal. Mart Stam from Rotterdam, one of the younger generation, rejects 'architecture' from the outset. For him there are only technical challenges – and no challenges relating to form or spatial design. Like Le Corbusier, he is a sharp-eyed observer. But he sees other things and with other eyes. As far as he is concerned, no art of building exists, so from the outset he excludes from his activities a large complex of concerns which provided the theme for Le Corbusier's book* Vers une Architecture.

Finally, Mies van der Rohe from Berlin is not the best known but certainly one of the most mature and full-blooded of the German 'moderns'. He is all inner gravity and stability. His broad shoulders have something about them that brushes aside all objections. He goes his way unswervingly, straight ahead, without beating about the bush. In his thinking and what he does Mies is astoundingly simple and straightforward. That is his stature.

Upon his arrival Le Corbusier said of the main railway station: 'It's an exceptional station, with very good proportions, and reminiscent of Italy, of Florentine cities. But the division into window-panes is bad. It brings in a pettiness of scale. Large, continuous window panes would be more beautiful. Because where the windows have not been inserted, on the left wing, the building looks better. The window is a hole; nothing can be done about it. Why try closing it with a wooden frame?' *Regarding the fighting between young and old, fights which have come to a head especially at the Werkbund exhibition, he said,* 'Why form value judgements out of differences of opinion that are purely about matters of principle? With these battles it's like with a horserace: the biggest enemies are not the first and last horses, but the first and second...'

'This is my second time in Stuttgart,' *said Le Corbusier.* 'I was here on a visit 20 years ago. I was looking for the court architect – what was his name? – to show him my things. I found what I wanted. He was the first to show me what is meant by architecture, and he paraded before my eyes all the beauties of the Fischer school. Later I went to Berlin. But I did not feel comfortable there. A lot of work gets done in Berlin. The German is a worker, but he does not have the art to conceal how hard he works. For him all thinking is difficult and effortful. In Paris too a lot of work is done, but the visitor doesn't notice. Life in Paris is more playful.'

Le Corbusier is Roman, hence his limitations. He is not entirely fair to Germans. When you get to know him, you realise he rejects the Gothic because buttresses are not beautiful.

It has been said that architecture is a suit that has to fit. 'No,' *objects Le Corbusier.* 'Architecture is more than a suit. The value of architecture does not depend on cloth and a person's stature. Sure, both are elements of it – technology and the spatial programme. But what is essential to architecture is the expression which can be achieved through it, the design. Architecture is a crystallisation.'

'What des crystallisation mean?' *asks Stam.* 'What does architecture mean? We create spaces – brightly illuminated, sufficiently insulated, provided with the necessary equipment. What happens in them, how they are subdivided, that is something no architect can determine or establish. Living and, together with it, the habitation are subject to constant change. What is crucial today for the architect is technical matters: how can I properly ventilate, illuminate, heat, furnish, and manage my house?'

Mies van der Rohe objects: Those are not questions for the architect. Those are things which concern the engineer. Discovering a new construction method, a window lock, or a roof structure – that doesn't make you an architect. It's a mark of the time that these questions are taken so seriously. Building art is not itself affected by them at all. It is something spiritual; it is part of a spiritual culture which we have entered today. Far from all sentimentalities and questions of art and aesthetics, far from all sentimental technical questions, because these too have essentially taken on sentimentality. That we must today establish the material bases is a necessary evil. In terms of the house, they are questions of construction, questions of the spatial programme: establishment of the residential function! *Le Corbusier points to how difficult* this task is. How do we establish residential functions? How do we create a good floor plan? In a situation where people today do not know themselves how they live or how they wish to live.

Bystanders found it interesting to note how in the end, in spite of the differences in opinion, in spite of these architects' different nationalities and distinctive characters, in their achievements they have arrived at similar or identical results. An encouraging sign that a new architecture has arrived which is not a fashion but a style – if you will – that will never be abandoned.

13   For the New Year

Letter published in journal (January 1927), together with reply from Walter Riezler.
Source: LMvdR, 'Zum neuen Jahrgang', *Die Form*, vol. II, no. 1, 1927, p. 1.
Translated from German by Mark Jarzombek and John Nicolson.
Republished in Neumeyer (1986) 1991, p. 257; Pizzigoni 2010, p. 40; Walter 2022, pp. 48–50.

Dear Dr *[Walter]* Riezler,
May I make a suggestion to you at the moment when you are taking on the editorship of the journal of the Deutscher Werkbund *[German Workers' Federation]*? Give the journal another title. A neutral title pointing to the workers' federation.
You may ask, what do I have against the present title? Do you not think that the title 'Die Form' makes too great a claim? A claim that obliges? That would not in itself constitute a danger; but does it not oblige in the wrong direction?
Are we not directing the reader's attention away from the essential? Is form really an aim? Is it not rather the result of the form-giving process? Is it not the process that is essential? Will a small change in preconditions not lead to another result? Another form?
That is why I would prefer to march without a flag. Think about my suggestion.
Yours, Mies van der Rohe

Dear Mr Mies van der Rohe,
Your wish is not entirely easy to fulfil: you don't change the name of a journal when the name is already established, and we would probably incur the wrath of the publisher if we approached him with such a request. The name 'Die Form [The Form]' has already become a kind of slogan, especially in connection with the 'books of Die Form', and at least possesses some weight. Admittedly, if this slogan points in a wrong direction, as you say in your letter, a different name should still be sought. But I am not

entirely convinced of this and believe that the two of us, as so often happens, merely mean something a little different when we talk of 'form'.

You think it suspicious when the outcome of the design process – which is nothing other than form – is taken to be more important than this process itself. I must confess I cannot see any strong contradiction here. What I understand by 'form' cannot be separated from the design process, and I do not think it possible to make the design process visible other than in form: the form of a tree is one with the process of its growth, which is a vitally organic process, just as the form of a machine is one with the powers that are organised within it. This cannot be said more beautifully than in the words of Goethe: 'For what is inside is outside.' And it is, of course, the same for art because artistic form is not what is added to the inner life, to the 'content' of a work of art, but is this life, this 'content' itself. You are absolutely right: even the slightest shift in the conditions of the design process leads to a change of form as a consequence. But that just proves the inextricable connection between the two factors. I know very well that you mean something different when you use the word 'form'. You are thinking of the abuse which has for a long time been – and still is being – committed less with the word than with the form itself. It is regrettably true that the age of precious form does not yet entirely belong to the past, that there is still such a thing as the external application of forms which have not grown in the place where they are used but have been transplanted there from somewhere else, like a lifeless specimen. If you are fighting against this concept of form, you find me, as I hardly need to tell you, firmly on your side. But I think we shall conduct the fight with better weapons if we set against this false concept of form the true concept – if we clearly and energetically ban 'formalism' from the realm of true 'forms'. It is of the greatest importance that we should attempt to identify the empty, external formalism which tries to insinuate itself here and there, also in the case of works in the new style of construction, a style which in its simplicity seems to contain nothing of the empty elements of form which make the architecture of past decades intolerable for us.

To this extent this would be merely a dispute of words, but I believe it can be proved that we cannot do without the word 'form'. There is – and this is true specifically of the time in which we live – also a design process which has remained stuck halfway, which means that it has not led to living form. Examples of this are at least as common as examples of empty formalism. And the danger that lies therein, that people are satisfied with this condition of embryonal design, so to speak, seems to me exceptionally great in an age that is under the spell of rationalisation and typification. Now we in the Werkbund in particular are here on the one hand to fight against empty formalism – but on the other hand to use all our powers to ensure that all those who have been entrusted with design work in our time should not rest until every thing, be it the most inconspicuous or the most important, is 'thoroughly formed' down to the last detail. In this I see the real purpose of our journal, and for this reason I believe it is right for it to bear the name 'Die Form'.

With cordial greetings,
Your Walter Riezler

14 On Form in Architecture

Letter published in journal (February 1927), together with reply from Walter Riezler.
Source: LMvdR, 'Über die Form in der Architektur', *Die Form*, vol. II, no. 2, 1927, p. 59. MoMA, Mies, Manuscripts, Folder 6.
Translated from German by Mark Jarzombek and John Nicolson.
Republished in Johnson 1947, pp. 187–188; Neumeyer (1986) 1991, p. 257; Pizzigoni 2010, pp. 41–42; Walter 2022, pp. 51–52.

Dear Dr *[Walter]* Riezler,
I am not arguing against form, only against form as a goal.
And I do so on the basis of multiple experiences and the insights they have given me.
Form as a goal always results in formalism. For this aspiration does not aim at something internal but at an external.
Only a vital inside, however, has a vital outside. Only intensity of life has intensity of form.
Every 'how' is supported by a 'what'.
The un-formed is not worse than the over-formed.
The former is nothing; the other is illusion. Effective form presupposes effective life. But not one that has been nor one that has been thought.
Therein lies the criterion.
We value not the result but the beginning of the form-giving process.
It is this that reveals whether the form has been taken from life or for its own sake.
This is why the form-giving process appears to me so important.
Life is what matters. In its complete fullness, in its spiritual and specific ties.
Is it not one of the most important tasks of the Werkbund to illuminate the spiritual and concrete situation in which we find ourselves, make it visible, order its currents, and thereby direct them?
Should one not leave all else to the creative forces?

[The following sentence appears only in the rough draft of the letter.]
Only a properly initiated and executed process of form-giving leads to the result. You value results; we value the point of departure. As certainly as a form-giving process is only recognisable by its result, so one that has been initiated properly will lead to a result. Is that not the most important, perhaps the only task? That is why I think it is more important to illuminate, make visible, and direct the currents of the spiritual situation in which we stand than to evaluate it.

Dear Mr Mies van der Rohe,
It's only now that I fully understand you and see that you are absolutely right – but that we mean almost exactly the same thing. I too believe that that just as the unformed is nothing, so the unformed is illusion and that real form only exists where there is real life. Unfortunately, we cannot name our journal 'Real Form' – otherwise we would probably be absolutely in agreement. But I also hope it will be possible to promote 'real forms' in Die Form *– and to keep not just the unformed, but also the overformed out of it or at least to accept them only with criticism.*
Cordial greetings,
Your Riezler

15 [Lecture: The Struggle for the Flat Roof]

Published newspaper statement (19 March 1927).
Source: 'Die Entwicklung der heutigen Kunst', *Das Berliner Tageblatt*, morning edition, p. 1 (thanks to Tom Lamberty and Merve Verlag for alerting us to the existence of this text); manuscript version in MoMA, Mies, Manuscripts, Folder 4, untitled.
Translated from German by Mark Jarzombek.
Republished in Neumeyer (1986) 1991, p. 262; Pizzigoni 2010, pp. 43–44; Walter 2022, pp. 53–54.

Even the building-art movement has its 'flag dispute'. It is the struggle for the flat roof. Here too the opponents are accused of being reactionary; the advocates, of being under alien influences. This battle is conducted with a seriousness as if it concerned the survival of building art. It is, however, only a fight over externalities, even though it is conducted by people with resounding names. It has nothing to do with the fight over the basis for a new art of building.

This struggle takes place on an altogether different plane and is only a part of the greater struggle over new forms of living – and not, as the academicians believe, the whimsy of a small clique. It is an attempt to confront changed conditions for living and working, new technology, and new materials. A changed world needs its own form. Not formal trends but mastery of real ties is the focus of these strivings.

For us, neither the lack of spirituality on the part of the intellectuals nor the historicising games of a tired society are significant. The need of financial and economical leaders to have workplaces that imitate the life forms of medieval merchant princes cannot deceive us with regard to the fact that it is their work in particular that has the greatest influence on how our lives are being changed. Nor are we surprised that theatres and movie houses are still decked with props from the period of La Pompadour and people today still prefer bad imitations of pleasure palaces for their residences. Everywhere there is the same striving to legitimise oneself. This behaviour is typical of the initial phases of great social upheavals. But one should not justify this jostling or, if you like, this 'drunken crowding' by claiming it serves the needs of the masses.

The masses do not appear to us quite as characterless as manufacturers of mass-produced packaging see them. It is the masses that demonstrate clear, strong impulses for living, as well as a great urge towards practicality and an undistorted affirmation of life. The forces residing in them will become effective and make themselves heard.

[Only in the manuscript] Because building art is only vital when it is supported by life in all its fullness, the leaders of the modern movement make an effort to identify the spiritual and material forces of our time, address them, and draw, without prejudice, the necessary conclusions. For only where building art leans on the material forces of a period can it be the spatial implementation of that period's spiritual decisions. That, however, is its actual purpose, and it has never been otherwise.

16 [Foreword to the Catalogue for the *Die Wohnung* Exhibition]

Published foreword (July 1927).
Source: LMvdR, untitled, in *Die Wohnung* (Stuttgart: 1927), p. 1.
The exhibition of the Deutscher Werkbund in Stuttgart titled 'Die Wohnung [The Habitation]' ran from 23 July to 9 October 1927. The construction of Weissenhofsiedlung was part of this exhibition.
Translated from German by Mark Jarzombek.
Republished in Johnson 1947, p. 188; Neumeyer (1986) 1991, p. 258; Pizzigoni 2010, p. 45; Walter 2022, pp. 55.

The problems associated with the new housing are rooted in the changed material, social, and spiritual structure of our time; only from this vantage point can these problems be understood.

The degree of structural change determines the character and extent of the problem. These are not subject to any arbitrary forces. They cannot be solved with slogans, nor can they be argued away with slogans.

The problem of rationalisation and typification is only part of the problem. Rationalisation and typification are only the means; they must never be the goal. The problem of the new housing is basically a spiritual problem, and the struggle for new housing is only an element in the larger struggle for new forms of living.

17 [Foreword to *Bau und Wohnung*]

Published foreword (circa July 1927).
Source: LMvdR, 'Vorwort', in Deutscher Werkbund (ed.), *Bau und Wohnung* (Stuttgart: 1927), p. 77.
Translated from German by Mark Jarzombek.
Republished in Neumeyer (1986) 1991, p. 259; Pizzigoni 2010, p. 46; Walter 2022, p. 56.

It is not entirely useless to expressly emphasise today that the problem of new housing is a problem of building art in spite of its technical and economic aspects. It is a complex problem and therefore can only be solved by creative forces rather than by calculation or organisation. Based on this belief, I thought it necessary, in spite of current slogans such as 'rationalisation' and 'typification', to extricate the tasks posed in Stuttgart from the atmosphere of one-sidedness and doctrinairism. I have made an effort to illuminate the problem comprehensively and have therefore invited the most distinctive representatives of the modern movement to take up positions regarding the housing problem.

To allow each as much freedom as possible to develop his ideas, I have avoided laying down guidelines or programmatic constraints. In establishing my development plan I thought it important to avoid everything schematic and exclude everything that could prevent people working freely.

18 Concerning My Block

Published journal article (July 1927).
Source: LMvdR, 'Vorwort [Foreword]', in Deutscher Werkbund (ed.), *Bau und Wohnung* (Stuttgart, 1927), pp. 76–77, 84–85.
Translated from German by Mark Jarzombek and John Nicolson.
Republished in Johnson 1947, p. 189; Neumeyer (1986) 1991, p. 259 (partially); Pizzigoni 2010, pp. 47–48; Walter 2022, p. 57.

Economic reasons today necessitate rationalisation and typification in the construction and production of apartment buildings. The increasing differentiation of our housing needs, however, demands on the other hand the greatest freedom of usage. In the future it will become necessary to do justice to both aspects. For this purpose, the skeleton structure is the most suitable system of construction. It makes rational production possible and yet permits total freedom of layout in the interior. If you limit yourself to designing the kitchen and bathroom as fixed spaces due to their installation, and if you then use moveable walls to divide the rest of the living space, I am sure that all legitimate residential requirements can thus be accommodated.

The structural system is an iron skeleton whose compartments have half-brick-deep walls and are covered with four-centimetre peat boards on the exterior walls to counter fluctuations in temperature; on top is a basis for the plaster. The staircase walls and the partition walls between the individual apartments are protected with two-centimetre peat boards providing acoustic insulation.
For the solid ceilings the following design was specified: brick-and-iron ceilings constructed using the Kleine system, topped by a two-centimetre layer of sand with gypsum screed as a basis for a covering of linoleum. Tectonic plates were prescribed as a basis for the plaster; these are attached to wooden bars clamped to the iron beams. The terraces are fitted with a Biehn seal. The roof consists of a solid ceiling covered with a double layer of Ruberoid. The entire block is served by a central hot-water and hot-water-preparation system. All pipes are detached from the walls; the wiring for the lighting is under the plaster. The building's outside surfaces are plastered with cement mortar. The windows are Rekord windows designed in such a way that the sashes can be placed on top of one another when open.

19 [Introduction to the Werkbund Exhibition in Stuttgart]

Published journal article (September 1927).
Source: LMvdR, untitled, *Die Form*, vol. II, no. 9, 1927, p. 257.
This text introduces a section of the magazine dedicated to *Die Wohnung*, an exhibition by the Deutscher Werkbund, and in particular to the Weissenhofsiedlung.
Translated from German by Mark Jarzombek.
Republished in Neumeyer (1986) 1991, p. 261; Pizzigoni 2010, pp. 49–50; Walter 2022, pp. 59–60.

In summer 1925, on the occasion of the meeting of the Deutscher Werkbund in Bremen, the request made by the Württemberg Work Collective of the Deutscher Werkbund to deal with the housing problem at an exhibition in Stuttgart was accepted, and I was entrusted with the implementation of this task.

On 29 July 1926 Stuttgart City Council accepted this proposal, and our building plans were approved. In mid-November 1926 the Verein Werkbund-Ausstellung 'Die Wohnung' *[Association for the Werkbund Exhibition on Housing]* was founded and by 1 March 1927 ground was broken for the excavations at Weissenhof.

Taking on this assignment, I knew that we had to realise it in contradiction of commonly held expectations since the complex character of the problem was clear to all who had occupied themselves seriously with the housing problem. The battle cry 'rationalisation and typification' and the call to cut costs in the housing industry represent only parts of the problem for, although important, they have significance only when seen in the right proportions. Next to them, or rather above them, stands the spatial problem of creation of a new habitation. This can only be solved by creativity rather than by calculation or organisation. I have therefore not issued guidelines but limited myself to soliciting the cooperation of those whose work leads me to expect interesting contributions to the housing question. The exhibition was conceived from the beginning as experimental and thus has value quite independently of the results achieved.

Each participating architect has investigated the new materials available in the marketplace in terms of applicability, and each has selected a construction according to his responsibility. The state of building technology has set limits to our efforts.

The organisational problem cannot be solved without the cooperation of the building trades. This was completely impossible in Stuttgart as we had no authority over the placing of contracts. This also meant that we were unable to exercise control over the quality of the execution. We were properly independent only with regard to spatial problems, which means questions in respect to the actual art of building.

20 [On Flat and Pitched Roofs]

Published newspaper statement (October 1927).
Source: 'Erklärung der Architektenvereinigung "Der Ring" zum Streit um Flachdach und Steildach', *Das neue Frankfurt. Monatschrift für die Fragen der Grossstadt-Gestaltung (Sondernummer: Das flache Dach)*, vol. I, no. 7, Oct.–Dec. 1927, p. 162.
Translated from German by John Nicolson.
Republished in Walter 2022, pp. 61–62.

On the practicality of the flat roof the decision has long been taken because for decades the flat roof has been used in industrial and agricultural buildings and in rental buildings in major cites – which is to say, where practicality and economic advantages tip the scales. It is therefore only natural that where these factors have gained in significance, there is today a general propensity for flat roofs.

Where aesthetic aspects determine the shape of the roof, there is no settled overall preference for a specific shape of roof. Whether a pitched or a flat roof is preferable in a particular case is always dependent on the design challenges of the time, as it is on those of the individual building.

[Signed by] Otto Bartning, Walter Curt Behrendt, Peter Behrens, Richard Döcker, Walter Gropius, Hugo Häring, Otto Haesler, Ludwig Hilbersheimer, Arthur Korn, Carl Krayl, Hans Luckhardt, Wassily Luckhardt, Ernst May, Erich Mendelsohn, Adolf Meyer, Ludwig Mies van der Rohe, Bernhard Pankok, Hans Poelzig, Adolf Rading, Hans Scharoun, Walter Schilbach, Karl Schneider, Hans Soeder, Bruno Taut, Max Taut, Heinrich Tessenow, Martin Wagner.

21 [Draft of a Letter]

Manuscript letter (circa 1927–1928).
Source: MoMA, Mies, Manuscripts, Folder 2, untitled.
This was probably intended to be a public letter in response to 'Schräges oder flaches Dach? [Sloping or Flat Roof?]', an article by Werner Hegemann in *Wasmuths Monatshefte für Baukunst*, vol. XI, no. 5, May 1927, pp. 120–127.
Translated from German by Mark Jarzombek.
Republished in Neumeyer (1986) 1991, p. 263; Pizzigoni 2010, pp. 51–52.

At that time the modern art of building did not yet exist. Berlage was a solitary giant and, having returned from America, had just drawn attention to Frank L Wright. Berlage, but not the modern Dutch achievement, has influenced me. My relationship with Holland is older than is thought.

The gentlemen do not know that I am one of the few German architects who has not been in Holland since 1913 and therefore can have no part in achievements in building art. I write this to you because I see in you not just a well-equipped mocker. The delight in mockery causes mistakes. First of all, it is fun, and secondly, it is healthy.

Should you have overlooked in your preference for Classicism that the flat roof, aside from all roof fashions, is nevertheless a prerequisite of the free ground plan?

The situation is such that a hot battle has erupted over the flat roof. This is exactly like round or fat butterballs: calculating natures work off their excess energies by rationalising. Overtime work.

The actual movement, far away from this battlefield, is struggling for new insights; it operates like science. Only so that the new results will gain ascendancy one day and the battle will be decided. This battle within building art will not only be conducted in the professional circle and decided there but is part of a larger dispute in all areas.

If only today's generation would assume real and positive attitudes toward today's life and its tasks and not follow a false tradition: real tasks as instruments of intellectual development.

Today's society feels obligated to hold onto an antiquated, ridiculous tradition, and we understand, of course, that the individual does not want to fall outside this norm.

We are furthermore aware that *[illegible]* the remark about the masses is inadequate, for who seriously wants to believe that they are really as lacking in character as the mass-production clothiers maintain? We feel particularly in them the strongest impulses for living and a strong urge toward functionality.

Is it not precisely a criterion what a person feels toward the masses? Is it not the duty of each generation to assume a positive attitude toward life rather than remain caught up in dusty thinking? Was that not once the most lively expression of the times?

Is it not a shame the extent to which large challenges are passed up? Is it really economically justifiable to hand over real tasks to mass-production clothiers and allow oneself to be satisfied with solutions that are already antiquated before they are completed? We are aware that the time has great potential but that it cannot be made visible as long as clothiers' attitudes and field marshals' conceits are in control. Has one forgotten that building art was always the spatial process of spiritual decisions?

[Added on a separate page] Why do you believe the Dutch have had this influence over me? I do not really place so much value on that building art.

22 The Preconditions for Architectural Work

Unpublished lecture manuscript (February 1928).
Source: LMvdR, 'Die Voraussetzungen baukünstlerischen Schaffens', LoC, Mies, Box 61, Addresses.
Lecture given at Staatliche Kunstbibliothek in Berlin in February 1928, repeated at the Arbeitsgemeinschaft für Frauenbestrebung (Work Association for the Women's Movement) in Stettin on 5 March and at the Frankfurter Gesellschaft für Handel, Industrie und Wissenschaft (Frankfurt Society for Trade, Industry, and Science) in Frankfurt am Main on 7 March.
Translated from German by Mark Jarzombek and John Nicolson.
Republished in Neumeyer (1986) 1991, p. 299 (partially); Pizzigoni 2010, pp. 53–61; Walter 2022, pp. 63–73.

Ladies and gentlemen! For me building art is not a subject for clever speculation. I do not expect anything from theories and specific systems. And especially from an aesthetic attitude that merely touches the surface. Building art can only be unlocked from a spiritual centre and can only be understood as a living process.

Building art is man's spatial dialogue with his environment. It demonstrates how he asserts himself therein and how he masters it. For this reason building art is not merely a technical problem nor a problem of organisation or economy.

Building art is in reality always the spatial execution of spiritual decisions. It is bound to its time and manifests itself only when addressing vital tasks with the means of its time. A knowledge of the time, its tasks, and its means is the necessary precondition for working in building art.

It is not a lack of talent but a lack of clarity in regard to these relationships that seems to me the cause of the confusing and inadequate products of today's building art. Since these products may not be instantly recallable by everybody with full precision, and since words have lost their unambiguous meaning, I shall clarify the present situation by means of a series of illustrations and conduct my investigation on this basis. It goes without saying that I will only show works that deserve to be taken seriously. The choice of pictures does not constitute a value judgment but only serves to clearly characterise the situation. Nor will I take a position in regard to these pictures since I am convinced that the chaotic character of our building art will be clear all by itself.

(Fig. 1) This is today's building art. We all have reason to infer corresponding causes from this result.

Chaos is always a sign of anarchy. Anarchy is always a movement without order. Movement without central direction. Chaos occurred before – when the order of antiquity degenerated into late antiquity. But out of this chaos came a new order, the order of the Middle Ages. On the basis of the Platonic theory of ideas, Augustine formulated the basic ideas of medieval belief. In the medieval idea of order lived, even if in a totally new dimension, that spirit of proportion exemplified and proven by Plato. The noblest legacy of antiquity.

The idea of order controlled the spiritual life of the Middle Ages and realised itself in its society, most of all in its social ideas. Society was, on account of the feudal system, immensely static. The classes were not only an economic but, above all, a daily and spiritual fact. Honour and duty, law and solidarity in all social things were inseparable. The order of rank corresponded to the objectively correct order of spiritual life values and economic values. This natural arrangement of classes was the basis for the health of the society of that time. The life of medieval man was determined through and through by a totally secured understanding of the meaning of life.

(Fig. 2) Strasbourg. Everything points to a spiritual aim. Insight stands before deed. Belief and knowledge have not yet gone separate ways. This idea of order is the point of departure for the change we want to demonstrate.

The deterioration of the medieval form of life was preceded by a deterioration of its spiritual structure. The process of disintegration began with the attempt by Duns Scotus to stake out a separate territory and law for knowledge. In stepping beyond the concept of almightiness William of Occam destroyed the idea of order, leaving behind only empty nomina. The victory of nominalism signals the victory of spirit turned toward reality long before it ever expressed itself in reality itself. This spirit was anti-medieval. With it the Renaissance began. While it reached back to the antique origins of the Middle Ages, it dealt with them more freely and spontaneously and already harboured the tendency to decay. Whereas man in the Middle Ages had been committed, internally and externally, to the community, now there occurred the great detachment of the individual, who conceived himself entitled to advance his talents and develop his powers.

This development became the basis for spiritual freedom, for the will to think autonomously and search independently. The result was a contrast between integration and separation. This contrast, which was to give a new form to the social situation in Europe, brought with it those problems that still lie before us today. This lack of integration was the cause of excessive exaggeration of the personality, an irrepressible will to power, and of unrestrained impulsiveness. More and more, spiritual life tended toward the will. The actions of the autonomous individual became ever more important. People studied nature. Control of nature became the yearning of the period. Its immense potential was recognised. The English statesman and philosopher Francis Bacon spoke out against pure science, against science for the sake of science, recognising its practical potential and demanding that it serve life. He put knowledge in the service of culture and introduced method and experimental science. We stood at the beginning of something new.

The same century brought the fateful alliance between iron and coal. Science entered into the service of technology and the economy, acquired a certain degree of understanding of the forces of nature, and invaded nature's domain. Steam, electricity, and chemical energy became detached from their natural contexts. Their rational laws were understood and their effectiveness unleashed.

Man developed a corresponding attitude in which will and capability undertook rational work. Carried along by this will, the powers of nature, heretofore isolated, came into play. Will freely set its aims, placed them in the service of use, and wrested performance from conquered nature. Nothing seemed impossible anymore. Thus began the reign of technology. Everything succumbed to its impact. Technology detached man from his restrictions, made him freer, and became his great helper, breaking down the isolation of geographical locations and bridging enormous distances. The world shrank more and more, became surveyable, and was investigated down to its remotest recesses. The characteristics of peoples become clear. Their social and economic structures were revealed. The result was world consciousness and a conscious awareness of mankind. Man, too, moved into the circle of consciousness. Physiological and psychological understanding became universal and determined the conduct of life. Technology offered a thousand means of increasing awareness. Nothing occurred anymore that was not observed. We surveyed ourselves and the world in which we stood. Consciousness was our very attitude.

(Fig. 3) Berlin Stadium. Simultaneously and interconnected with this development, there took place a huge increase in population. Masses formed, posing totally new problems of an economic and social nature.

(Fig. 4) Krupp. Technology was the means for these problems' solution.

(Fig. 5) Leipzig. Traffic developed.

(Fig. 6) New York. Traffic served the economy. The economy became the great distributor, interfering in all domains, forcing man into its service.

(Fig. 7) A New York street. The economy began to rule. Everything was pressed into the service of use. Profitability became law. Technology determined economic attitudes, transformed material into power and quantity into quality. There was a conscious effort to make the most effective use of power.

Ladies and gentlemen! It seemed to me necessary to trace the course of development, even if in large jumps, for this alone leads to a comprehension of the condition of our time. We have laid bare the structure of our period and have established that our givens are consciousness, economy, technology, and the fact of the masses. The effect of this structural change can be demonstrated by the following examples:

(Fig. 8) Aqueduct. Earlier ages were compelled to work with natural materials, and the tie to these materials set limits on what could be achieved. Arched structures made from stone permit only a limited span width.

(Fig. 9) The Hudson Bridge. With the help of new materials and new self-supporting structures our age is able to span great widths.

(Fig. 10) In previous ages dams were enormous walls. Reinforced concrete can now be used to make thin partition walls.

The influence of materials and construction methods is also clear in dome construction. Despite an increase in span width, a substantial reduction in quantities of materials may be noted. The weight of the dome of St Peter's in Rome is about 10,000 tonnes, while its width is 40 metres. *[This reveals a discussion with L. Hilberseimer, at this time working on his book* Hallenbauten *(Leipzig, 1931).]*

(Fig. 11) Breslau. The dome of the Jahrhunderthalle in Breslau seen in this picture is in the region of 6300 tonnes with a span of 65 metres. The weight of the single dome at the new Large Market Hall in Leipzig with the same span width is only 2100 tonnes.

(Fig. 12) Jena. At the Planetarium in Jena the dome consists of nothing more than a thin concrete skin injected into a cobweb-thin web of iron bars.

(Fig. 13) Mies. The effort to replace quantity with quality leads to the formation of a skeleton system.

(Fig. 14) Corbusier. Thin, non-load-bearing struts are clamped between load-bearing supports.

(Fig. 15) Acoustic Paris. Scientific effort for the understanding of the laws of acoustics is applied and begins to influence the planning of large halls. This picture shows a concert hall in Paris for 3000 people [*Salle Pleyel (Paris 1927), later published in L. Hilberseimer,* Hallenbauten *(Leipzig, 1931)*].

(Fig. 16) Hannes Meyer. And this picture shows the design of the Palace of the League of Nations and a cross-section through the large auditorium.

(Fig. 17) Lamp, lamp rays. This picture shows another effect of scientific work: the demonstration of light rays based on the Poulsen lamp [*a design by Poul Henningsen for Louis Poulsen*].

(Fig. 18) Lamp. This is the result of this purely technical-scientific work. This lamp is not the result of a design but of construction.

These are amazing achievements; all are results of will, of rigorous discipline. Technology follows its own laws and is not man-related. Economy becomes self-serving and calls forth new needs. Autonomous tendencies in all these forces assert themselves. Their meaning seems to be the attainment of a specific phase of development. But they assume a threatening predominance. Unchecked, they thunder along. Man is swept along as if in a whirlwind. Each individual attempts to brace himself against these forces singly. We stand at a turning point in time. The degree and the intensity of this experience are determined by the attitude of the individual. This explains the chaotic appearance of these phenomena, the multiplicity of currents.

You can now understand why the result in building art is necessarily so confusing, as I have demonstrated. But even in this chaos various types of structure are clearly discernible. You saw that one group subscribes to the belief that even in our changed world the means and methods of past epochs can be applied to solve the tasks of our time. Their work is determined by the fear that invaluable treasures could be lost. And also by the belief that it is impossible, in the hard and clear atmosphere of technology and consciousness, for artistic and spiritual values to unfold. We are not entitled to hold their achievements in low respect, even if we believe that the world to which they incline and in which they are rooted is inevitably sinking. We are obliged to appreciate their efforts, for they transmit values and insights that we must not lose sight of. They still believe in the vitality of the old order.

A few stand in the middle, still committed to the old yet alert to the new. For the remaining group, the old habitual order has lost its meaning and vitality. It cannot be suffered anymore. This group affirms the new world and fights with its means. It is feeling its way toward new possibilities of form-giving. It experiments, is unrestricted in its work, and no longer stands under the protection of conventions.

At the beginning of my lecture I pointed out that building art is always bound to its own time and can manifest itself only in vital tasks and through the means of its own period. I have attempted to trace the changes of our time and make visible the forces at work in it. Our time is not an external course on which we run. It has been given to us as a task that we must master. We see its immense power and its will. The determination with which it stands ready to fight.

We have to affirm [*our time*] even if its forces still appear menacing to us. We have to master the unleashed forces and build them into a new order, an order that permits free play for the unfolding of life. Yes, but an order that is also related to mankind.

But this cannot happen based on the technological problems themselves, but only on living men. No matter how immense knowledge may be, how huge the economic apparatus, or how powerful technology, all this is only raw material, compared to life.

We do not need less technology but more. We see in technology the possibility of freeing ourselves, the opportunity to help the masses. We do not need less science but a science that is more spiritual; not less economic energy but energy that is more mature. All this will only become possible when man asserts himself in objective nature and relates it to himself.

It must be possible to heighten consciousness and yet keep it separate from the purely intellectual. It must be possible to let go of illusions, to see our existence sharply defined, and yet gain a new infinity, an infinity that springs from the spirit. It must be possible to solve the task of controlling nature and yet simultaneously create a new freedom. It must be possible to see elitism disappear and admit the fact of the masses, the fact that each of the many has a right to life and to goods. Mass must not be a cliché for us. It must be articulated from within itself, for only thus can the forces residing in it be made serviceable for all.

The way leads from the extensive to the intensive. But all this can only happen if we regain our belief in the creative powers, if we trust the power of life.

23 On the Topic of Exhibitions

Published journal article (April 1928).
Source: LMvdR, 'Zum Thema: Austellungen', *Die Form*, vol. III, no. 4, 1928, p. 121.
It is not clear if this article refers to a specific exhibition. It might be a reference to the Barcelona Exhibition of the following year, as suggested by Mies in a later discussion (see 'Six Students Talk with Mies'). Translated from German by Mark Jarzombek.
Republished in Johnson 1947, pp. 189–190; Neumeyer (1986) 1991, p. 304; Pizzigoni 2010, pp. 62–63; Walter 2022, pp. 75–76.

Exhibitions are instruments of economic and cultural work. They must be handled with care.

An exhibition depends both as to type and effect on the basic problem it poses. The history of the great exhibitions has shown that only those exhibitions were successful that dealt with current problems and that employed means corresponding to their goals.

The period of impressive exhibitions that make a profit is past. What is decisive for us is the productive achievement of an exhibition; an exhibition's value can only be demonstrated by its cultural impact.

Economic, technological, and cultural preconditions have changed fundamentally. Technology and the economy face totally new problems. It is of crucial importance that these be correctly recognised and that meaningful solutions be found; not only for the economy and technology but for our entire social and cultural life.

If the German economy, and beyond it the European, wants to maintain its position, it must recognise its specific task and act on it. Its way forward is from quantity to quality, from the extensive to the intensive. On this itinerary, the economy and technology encounter important forces in spiritual and cultural life. We stand in the middle of a transformation, a transformation that will change the world.

To point to this transformation and further it will be the task of upcoming exhibitions. Only if they succeed in illuminating this transformation suddenly and forcefully will they achieve a productive effect. Only if the central problem of our time – the intensification of life – becomes these exhibitions' content will they find meaning and justification.

They must be demonstrations of leading forces and bring about a revolution in our thinking.

24 We Stand at the Turning Point of Time: Building Art as the Expression of Spiritual Decisions

Published magazine article (June 1928).
Source: LMvdR, 'Wir stehen in der Wende der Zeit. Baukunst als Ausdruck geistiger Entscheidungen', *Innendekoration*, vol. XXXIX, no. 6, 1928, p. 262.
Translated from German by Mark Jarzombek.
Republished in Neumeyer (1986) 1991, p. 304; Pizzigoni 2010, p. 64; Walter 2022, p. 74.

Building art is not the object of clever speculation; it is in reality only understandable as a life process – it is an expression of man's ability to assert himself and master his surroundings. A knowledge of the time, its tasks and means, is a necessary prerequisite for the work of a building artist; building art is always spatial expression of spiritual decisions.

Traffic is increasing. The world is shrinking more and more, is coming more and more into view down to its remotest recesses. The results are world consciousness and consciousness of mankind.

The economy is beginning to rule; everything is in its service. Profitability is becoming law. Technology brings with it economical attitudes, transforms material into power and quantity into quality. Technology presupposes knowledge of natural laws and works with their forces. Power is most effective when it is used deliberately. We stand at the turning point of time.

25 [The Adam Department Store]

Unpublished letter describing a project (2 July 1928).
Source: MoMA, Mies, Later German Projects, Folder 1, untitled. This project was subsequently published in C. Gravenkamp, 'Mies van der Rohe: Glashaus in Berlin', *Das Kunstblatt*, vol. XIV, no. 3, 1930, pp. 111–113. Translated from German by Mark Jarzombek.
Republished in Neumeyer (1986) 1991, p. 305; Pizzigoni 2010, pp. 65–66.

Yesterday my project was delivered to your office at Leipziger Strasse n. 121. I take the liberty to present briefly the thoughts that determined the project. The variability you want is best served by an undivided expanse on the individual floor levels; for this reason I have placed the supports in the exterior walls. Your request that the building be divisible both horizontally and vertically to accommodate the workshops you need makes three staircases necessary. I have arranged the secondary staircase for the workshops so that it is accessible from Friedrichstrasse as well as from Leipziger Strasse. Right and left of it are the two freight elevators so that each can be used from either part of the building. In the stairwells the toilets for the employees are accessible from the landings. Each of the two main staircases is easily reached from Friedrichstrasse and Leipziger Strasse respectively. These stairwells contain the elevators for visitors to the building and the elevators for internal use. Next to the stairwells are the toilets for managers and customers.

You have indicated in your requirements that in general a building with vertical articulation would conform to your tastes. May I say in all frankness that in my opinion a building has nothing to do with taste but must be the logical result of all requirements that result from its purpose. Only if these are established can one speak of the intrinsic forming of a building. You need layered floor levels with clear, uncluttered spaces. Furthermore, you need a great deal of light. You need publicity and more publicity.

We stand at the beginning of new developments. Your building must not appear obsolete in two or three years; it must last for years to come, an important and never-failing instrument in your hands. All this requires not only from the architect but also from the client a good dose of boldness. I therefore suggest to you making the skin of your building of glass and stainless steel, with the bottom floor of transparent glass and the others of opaque glass. Walls of opaque glass give the rooms a wonderfully mild but bright and even illumination. In the evening this is a powerful body of light, and you will have no difficulty in affixing advertising. You can do as you like, regardless of whether you write on it 'For Summer Vacation', 'For Winter Sports', or 'Four Bargain Days'. Advertising so brightly lit on an evenly illuminated background will have a fairy-tale effect.

Additionally, for the back walls of the display windows I would recommend coloured plate glass – in mouse-grey. Your building should exhibit the character of your business and fit in with sailboats and automobiles or, to put it another way, with the modern time and with people that embody it.

Respectfully, Ludwig Mies van der Rohe

26 [Stuttgart Bank Competition Report]

Competition statement (circa November 1928).
Source: document saved from destruction by Martin Werwigk, architect of the Württembergische Landesbank, located by Ines Dresel.
Translated from German by Ariane Nowak and Robert V Sharp.
Republished in Zukowsky 1986, p. 171.

The author is of the opinion that the banking house should be clearly separated from the business building. This conception is the basis for the whole project. The competition rules state that the bank should stand in the less valuable part of the site, and the author has therefore chosen the part at Hindenburgplatz and Lautenschlagerstrasse for business use, with the bank having but one entrance on Lautenschlagerstrasse. The actual bank building extends parallel to Lautenschlagerstrasse towards the courtyard. It contains all the space desired and is sufficient for its purposes.

The location of the bank buildings seems to the author no less critical, so he intends to cover the whole structure, including the bank, with plate-quality glass with a matt finish. This will prevent a view of an unpleasant environment and give all rooms in the complex excellent diffused light. Only the shops on the ground floor will have transparent glass windows. The bank as well as the business building will be of skeleton construction. There will be no limitation on how the inner sections may be divided; this will guarantee that the divisions of the rooms can be changed for later uses.

The rules further say that the building must be suitable for the installation of advertisements. The author thinks that advertising will develop to an extent that might now seem unrealistic but be common within the next five years. He believes that advertising will become a factor more and more relevant in the economy and that it will soon be the reason for changes in the arrangement of buildings' façades. The author bases his arrangement of the building's exterior on this idea. He tries, as the model clearly shows, to keep the entire front empty for advertisements. Thus he also tries to use the illumination of the interior for the effectiveness of the advertising. The building would glow at night. Any kind of advertisement could then be installed on these glowing glass walls.

Everything else will be clear from the plans, photographs, and model.

The following has to be said with regard to urban development: for artistic reasons the railway station's strong grouped forecourt needs opposite it a building of quiet appearance made from a seemingly monumental material that does not really compete with the view of the railway station. The author chose glass and non-rusting steel as the materials so as to create an impression of the building's lightness and to create a nice contrast with the fine construction of the railway station.

27 [On the Barcelona Pavilion]

Published interview (2 June 1929).
Source: LMvdR, 'El arquitecto Van der Roch [sic] creador del Pabellón de Alemania [Architect Van der Rohe, Creator of the German Pavilion]', *Diario Oficial de la Exposición Internacional Barcelona 1929*, no. 12, p. 25.
Translated from Spanish by Dietrich Neumann.
Republished in Neumann 2020, pp. 50–51.

Life has changed in the last few years. Today we live differently, and what satisfied us yesterday leaves us indifferent today. We have other needs, and it is logical for architecture to change as the way we live also changes.

Life today demands simplicity and brevity. The complications of the past no longer have reasons to exist. It is therefore natural that our buildings, our furniture, and the interiors of our homes respond to this new way of life, which is becoming more and more apparent with every day.

The danger of this new kind of architecture is the possible elimination of artistic taste. Modern architecture, so thoroughly accepted in Germany, tends to combine art and simplicity. There can and should be art in the new architecture. Using true and simple lines and smooth planes, one can solve the problem of architecture without compromising its aesthetic. For this we have to employ rich materials. Marble in different colours, bronze, and glass are obligatory elements of the modern style.

When I constructed the German pavilion at the international exhibition in Barcelona, I was given complete freedom. Only thus can an architect carry out his work.

The furniture complements the architecture, in my opinion. I have designed a new type of furniture made from materials not previously used. The results are very comfortable and resonate with the building.

28 Beautiful and Practical Buildings! Stop This Cold Functionality

Published newspaper article (26 January 1930).
Source: LMvdR, 'Schön und praktisch bauen! Schluß mit der Kalten Zweckmäßigkeit", *Duisburger General Anzeiger*, vol. XLIX, 1930, p. 2.
Translated from German by Mark Jarzombek.
Republished in Neumeyer (1986) 1991, p. 307; Pizzigoni 2010, pp. 67–68; Walter 2022, pp. 77–79.

There is not the slightest doubt that in today's architecture the artistic is being short-changed. I believe that sometime in the future we will have to come to a decision whether architecture should be merely practical or also beautiful. How this decision will turn out cannot be predicted with any degree of certainty.

What appears totally evident to me is that with our changed requirements and with the new means made available by technology we will arrive at a new type of beauty. That we will ever again befriend 'beauty per se', however, I find unlikely. But how does a medieval sentence put it so nicely? 'Beauty is the radiance of truth!' Yes, in the final analysis, beauty is coupled to truth; it does not float around in the air but is attached to things and irrevocably connected to the forms of the real world. Real truth will therefore only be attained by those who work with a mind open to reality.

The architecture of old was not as function-proclaiming as ours. But in spite of its 'beauty' it was tied to the conditions and to the forms of existence and appearance of its time and was in that sense reality-bound.

It is fundamentally wrong to assume that the problem of modern architecture has been recognised as soon as one admits the need for a rational solution. This belief, today taken as self-evident, is only a precondition. If one wants to produce beautiful objects or beautiful houses, one must first of all be able to produce them in the most economical – that is, the most practical – way. This verity, as banal as it is, is today often heralded as the ultimate goal, whereas in reality it is not an artistic nor a building aim but simply a necessary precondition, a basis.

It is a natural, human characteristic not just to consider the purposeful but also to search out and love beauty. Due to the powerful advance of technology, this self-evident awareness seems to be somewhat repressed. It often appears as if our time would content itself with technical perfection. But this will not remain so. Our time has enormously many means for form-giving at its disposal. It just has not yet learned to master them – perhaps because mastery of the means, the technical difficulties alone, in itself requires so much energy that nothing is left over to apply these means also in a form-giving way.

What we consider today as impractical, what we would therefore no longer build today, is simple forms that have lost their meaning. But what we call practical today does not stand in opposition to what was always and at all times practical – namely meaningful. Only what has become meaningless should and must be thrown overboard; we must not in blind reversal reject the concept of the beautiful for our times.

And what finally is beauty? Certainly nothing that can be calculated or measured. It is always something imponderable, something that lies in between things. Beauty in architecture, just as necessary and just as desirable as in former times, can only be attained if in building we have more than the immediate purpose in mind.

29 [Art Criticism]

Published journal article (June 1930).
Source: LMvdR, untitled, *Das Kunstblatt*, vol. XIV, no. 6, 1930, p. 178.
MoMA, Mies, manuscript, Folder 4, with the preparatory version of the lecture.
Publication of a lecture on art criticism given at the congress of Verband der Kunstkritiker (the Union of Art Critics) in April 1930.
Translated from German by Mark Jarzombek.
Republished in Johnson 1947, p. 191; Neumeyer (1986) 1991, p. 308; Pizzigoni 2010, p. 69; Walter 2022, pp. 80–81.

Do not fear that I will add to the long chain of reproaches and attacks. Are misjudgements not a matter of course?

Is criticism then so easy? Is real criticism not just as rare as real art? I would like therefore to direct your attention to the basic preconditions of any criticism because I believe that without adequate clarity on this issue real criticism cannot be engaged in and demands will be made of criticism that it is unable to fulfil.

Criticism is the testing of an achievement in regard to its meaning and value. In order to test an achievement, it is necessary to assume an attitude toward the object to be tested – to get a handle on it. This is not so easy. Works of art have a life of their own. They are not accessible to all. For them to speak, one must approach them in the way they demand. This constitutes the obligation of the critic.

Another obligation of criticism concerns the gradation of values. Here criticism finds its measuring scale. Real criticism is ultimately in service to value.

30 The New Time

Published journal article (1 August 1930).
Source: LMvdR, 'Die neue Zeit', *Die Form*, vol. V, no. 15, 1930, p. 406.
MoMA, Mies, manuscript, Folder 4, with the text of the lecture.
The subtitle of the first publication reads: 'Concluding words of Mies van der Rohe's speech at the Vienna Days of the German Werkbund, Vienna 22–26 June 1930'.
Translated from German by Mark Jarzombek.
Republished in Johnson 1947, p. 190; Neumeyer (1986) 1991, p. 309; Pizzigoni 2010, pp. 70–71; Walter 2022, pp. 82–83.

The new time is a fact; it exists whether we say 'yes' or 'no' to it.

But it is neither better nor worse than any other time. It is a pure given and in itself undifferentiated. That is why I shall not pause long to describe the new time and point to its relationships and lay bare its support structure.

Similarly, we do not want to overestimate mechanisation, typification, and standardisation.

Even the changed economic and social conditions we shall accept as facts.

All these things go their fateful, value-blind way.

What is decisive is only how we assert ourselves toward these givens.

It is here that the spiritual problems begin.

What matters is not the 'what' but only the 'how'. That we produce goods and the means by which we produce them say nothing spiritually.

Whether we build high or flat, with steel or with glass says nothing as to the value of this way of building.

Whether one aims for centralisation or decentralisation in urban planning is a practical question, not one of values.

But it is exactly this question of values that is decisive. We must set new values and indicate ultimate goals in order to gain new criteria.

For the meaning and justification of each epoch, even the new one, lie only in providing conditions under which the spirit can exist.

[The following part of Mies' conference speech was not published.]

Ladies and gentlemen!

I would like to begin with a practical question, namely with the question as to the organisational structure of the exhibition. This question appears to me to be of particular importance in regard to an international exhibition, for only the right choice of organisational basis permits us to perform our work.

So far it has been the practice at international exhibitions to set the theme in terms of nationalities. This means that specific conditions of individual countries have been emphasised. This principle has led to constant repetition and to confusion; it has, however, enabled easier and more relaxed execution due to the fact that financing has been available on a national basis and due to decentralisation of responsibility. A different solution would be to go a step further. One could strive for a transnational approach to intellectual issues, but with economic contributions being made along national lines. This would, however, lead to fragmentation of the exhibition, for it implies that one part of it would be ordered in accordance with an ideal and the other with an economic point of view. This approach also appears to me unsuitable for Cologne as it deprives us of the necessary orientation for the industrial sector.

What is called for is a transnational treatment of all problems, economic problems included; this requires preparation and execution by international committees. Only thus can the emphasis on the theme be guaranteed and transnational economic aims be approached. All this, of course, leads to a much more complex organisation for it calls for an expansion of responsibility and demands common financing. It will not be easy to achieve this aim. But here we put all our confidence in Professor Jackh, who will create the basis for this new type of exhibition.

As to the three groups that I am supposed to elaborate on, I cannot yet submit practical suggestions. That lies in the nature of the matter. Real tasks can only be taken into consideration when it has been established at what time the exhibition will take place – for each situation is unique and calls for a special point of view. I will, however, briefly give my views on the problems raised:

The new time is a fact; it exists whether we say 'yes' or 'no' to it. *[...] [The remainder of the manuscript is identical with the text printed above.]*

31 Hall II at the Berlin Building Exposition

Published journal article (15 July 1931).
Source: LMvdR, 'Die Halle II auf der Bauausstellung', *Die Form*, vol. VI, no. 7, 1931, pp. 241–9.
Description of the building programme arranged by Mies for the Berlin Building Exhibition in 1931.
Translated from German by Mark Jarzombek.
Republished in Neumeyer (1986) 1991, p. 310; Pizzigoni 2010, p. 72; Walter 2022, p. 84.

The dwelling of our time does not yet exist. But changed living conditions demand its realisation.

The precondition for this realisation is clear definition of actual dwelling needs. This will be the main purpose of the exhibition.

A further task will be to demonstrate the means required for satisfaction of these dwelling needs.

Only thus can we combat the present discrepancy between real dwelling needs and wrong dwelling expectations, between genuine demand and inadequate supply. To overcome this is a burning economic necessity and a precondition for cultural reconstruction.

32 [Radio Address]

Radio speech (17 August 1931).
Source: MoMA, Mies, Manuscripts, Folder 4.
Translated from German by Mark Jarzombek.
Republished in Neumeyer (1986) 1991, p. 311; Pizzigoni 2010, pp. 73–74; Walter 2022, pp. 85–86.

It might appear strange to discuss artistic building in times of economic depression. And yet I want to use the few minutes that are available to speak of this.

The call for economical methods and functionality in new building is not the result of the economic distress in which the world finds itself today. It is much older than the worldwide economic crisis and has quite different causes. Yet this economic depression encourages to a very great degree an orientation on economical and functional building. Insofar as economics and functionalism constitute preconditions for the new building, the present situation will exercise a considerable influence on building's development.

There is, however, a danger connected with this development. It could contribute to further spreading the misconception prevalent in many circles that the new building is merely a question of function and economy and thus cause serious damage to the development of building art. Because this belief is wrong. No matter how much function and economics are preconditions for new building, the ultimate problems are of an artistic nature. No matter how much function and economics determine our building, they say very little as to its artistic value.

They do not prevent it, however. The artistic appears in step with the structure of purpose and function, or rather, it realises itself in that structure. But not in the sense of adding to it; rather, in the sense of giving form to it. The artistic expresses itself in the proportions of things, often even in the proportions between things. Essentially it is something immaterial, something spiritual. And thus independent of the material conditions of a period. It is a wealth that even a materially poor period need not renounce, indeed must not renounce. We do not want to add to the material loss a cultural one. The need for simplicity need not be equivalent to cultural deprivation as long as we attempt to lock in as much beauty as possible.

33 [Paul Klee Leaves the Bauhaus]

Published note (December 1931).
Source: *bauhaus, zeitschrift für gestaltung*, IV, n. 3, dec. 1931, p. II.
Translated from German by John Nicolson.
This document is in lower case, as was typical of the Bauhaus.
Republished in Walter 2022, p. 87.

in paul klee the bauhaus is losing an outstanding pedagogue and – which is most irreplaceable – a great personality, and we are all losing in him a real friend.

34 Expressways as an Artistic Problem

Published magazine article (October 1932).
Source: LMvdR, 'Autobahnen als baukünstlerisches Problem',
Die Autobahn, no. 10, 1932, p. 1; also in *Pariser Zeitung*, 7, no. 44, 1932, p. 1.
(Published in Frankfurt am Main, *Die Autobahn* was the organ of HAFRABA [Haupt-Ausschuss für den Reichs-Autobahn-Bau].)
Translated from German by Mark Jarzombek.
Republished in Neumeyer (1986) 1991, p. 313; Pizzigoni 2010, p. 75–77; Walter 2022, pp. 88–90.

Is there even such a thing as an artistic problem in expressways? Such a question is not without meaning in regard to a configuration that is so overwhelmingly economic and technical in nature.

And yet this question must be affirmed if we keep in mind that expressways, as the most important traffic routes of the future, will not only cut through landscapes with their stations, intersections, overpasses, and valley spans but will also, in those areas where they lie embedded in the landscape, unlock new landscapes as we drive through them. Here too – even if in a more passive vein, more as consequence – questions of form-giving arise. These formal questions are of a particular type but nevertheless essential.

That economic and technical reasons determine the routeing of expressways is self-evident. But beyond that, much can be done to protect the peculiarity and the particular character of a landscape. Yes, one could even hold that the laying out of traffic routes, beyond the obligation to protect farming interests, can even, under certain circumstances, entail the obligation to heighten the landscape.

Certainly, such questions can only be dealt with very circumspectly and only in cooperation with district and village administrations. Our time can no longer afford the recklessness of the previous century that erected technical structures without regard to the farm economy.

Mr Becker, the regional planning officer, has made suggestions on plantings along expressways [Hafraba Circular, no. 7, 1930]. These suggestions arise apparently out of a desire to fit the traffic routes organically into the landscape. This striving goes so far as to extend even to the traffic signals. It appears to me doubtful, however, that the proposed means are suitable in each specific case for achieving the goal.

For example, the obelisk-like treatment of the border plantings seems to me rather to lead to an emphasising of the road within the landscape, instead of a fitting in. From the point of view of the expressway, this arrangement of border plantings cuts through the landscape image where it should fuse with it. And in a fast-driven car this cutting apart is heightened, becoming a disagreeable chopping up of the landscape. Also, I do not believe that the suggested signalling of curves and overpasses by means of individual trees or groups of trees can be accomplished because it would presuppose that all terrain adjoining the route would have to be kept free of trees. Here other means must be searched for.

When we talked above of preserving the landscape, in which, by the way, village views should also be included, it was taken for granted that the usual highway advertising should under no circumstances be permitted. Commercial interests, however, may not be willing to renounce advertising rights in regard to the traffic network of the future and possibly cannot even do without them. This would mean that a way would have to be found that permits legitimate economic interests to find opportunity without, however, allowing a rampant spread of advertising to take place. I could conceive that groups of advertisements could be clustered to indicate danger zones, or that the installations of advertisements be restricted to the circumference of cities and furthermore that all advertising be subject to a central control. This agency should, however, not operate with fixed rules but take into account ongoing change and fluctuating conditions; otherwise, a pedantic rigidity and bureaucracy will set in, destructive to advertising and destroying what may specifically be artistic and valuable in it. This would involve more an attitude than regulations, more an artistic sense than restrictive measures. All in all, more form-giving than administration.

35 [On the Anniversary of the Werkbund]

Manuscript of speech (October 1932).
Source: MoMA, Mies, Manuscripts, Folder 5, D.1, untitled.
Lecture to the anniversary meeting of the Deutscher Werkbund in October 1932 in Berlin, unpublished hand- and type-written draft.
Translated from German by Mark Jarzombek.
Republished in Neumeyer (1986) 1991, pp. 311–312; Pizzigoni 2010, p. 78.

One speaks much these days of a new Germany. Who would doubt the need to rearrange the German space? The new arrangement also applies to our work, and it is our hope that genuine arrangements will be found with a reality content sufficiently large for authentic life to be able to unfold in them. But life that – vitally secured – will allow space for the unfolding of the spirit. Then, so we hope, the German soil will again assume human features.

Even in the days of our need we remain firmly convinced that the value of our existence lies only and exclusively in offering the spirit in the most comprehensive sense the possibility for realisation.

Ladies and gentlemen,

You have been introduced to the work of the Werkbund up to now. There also have been hopes expressed as to the future of the Werkbund's work. I will explain in a few short words how we visualise such work.

One speaks now of a new Germany. We too are profoundly convinced that it is necessary to recognise the German space. It is our hope that genuine arrangements may evolve.

Form-giving work for all that serves spiritual progress and the benefit of mankind; in young Germans an attitude of work ethics to keep awake bold utopian thought.

I do not consider it right to foreground questions that deal with reform of economic life. It is obvious that one will not have to take a position on this. These questions are especially controversial [but] may not have the weight that one attributes to them. It is a clear tendency of our time to want to set limits to economics and subject it to stricter controls. The concept of the apartment is totally unclear. In fact the apartment must be defined from the point of view of man. The question of the basic forms of houses, whether small house, large house – surely there are intermediate forms.

Also, we shall concern ourselves with the metropolis as we do not believe that it can of itself bring forth the right form. It appears necessary to issue rules.

We too want to investigate the potential residing in the German space and its landscapes. We want to expand the question of formal form-giving in products of craftsmanship and industry to a critique of the production of goods, for here not only the 'how' but also the 'what' becomes crucial.

Furthermore, we are interested in the question of school policy insofar as it relates to questions of work, form, and art.

The second way.

One must know that the world is formed and that this form matters.

We want to confine ourselves to work in those fields in which we are recognised as specialists. This work must be conducted in a thorough manner with underlying problems solved by the best experts.

We shall investigate the entire field of settlement housing. Villages and metropolises.

Given this basic orientation, individual fields will be worked on by diverse work groups. We shall deal with the question of settlement, the question of education, the question of products – not unilaterally but from all points of view.

First criticism, then clarification, then reconstruction. The Werkbund suffers like everything else under the confusion and insecurity of the present situation; all feel this turbulence and unrest and suffer from it. One gropes in the dark, one fears to speak up, one wants to see things ripened and matured. One must not allow oneself to be seduced into doing nothing, out of fear of doing the wrong thing or of acting immaturely and like a dilettante.

Especially now, one must remain loyal to oneself, remain constant and firm. Insist on what one has rightly recognised as essential.

We refuse to approach things and questions only from the outside – which can bring about only organisation, only formal, quick solutions. Our concern is with a deepening of the work process that should bring us to the unquestionable kernel of the problems. The Werkbund cannot, must not, go with the times. The Werkbund can only concern itself with the contents of things, always the 'how'.

36 [Bauhaus Berlin. Syllabus and Curriculum]

Published curriculum (October 1932).
Source: Bauhaus Archive, Berlin.
While the author is not explicitly named, we assume, given the context, that Mies, as director of the school, was involved.
The entire document is written in lower case, as was typical of the Bauhaus.
Translated from German by Wolfgang Jabs and Basil Gilbert.
Republished in Wingler (1962) 1969, pp. 182–184.

<u>bauhaus berlin</u>

the bauhaus, founded in weimar as a state school of higher learning and continued at dessau as a school of design, is an independent teaching and research institute.

direction: ludwig mies van der rohe.

<u>the curriculum</u>

of the bauhaus is divided into three stages of instruction and covers seven semesters.

in the <u>first stage</u> students who differ with respect to previous education and talent are brought to a common standard.

at the time of acceptance into the <u>second stage</u> the students decide upon their specialised area of study: 1. architecture and interior design; 2. commercial art; 3. photography; 4. weaving; 5. fine art.

in this stage students are given a practical, technical, and scientific background for their work in the various special fields. theoretical instruction is supplemented by practical experimental work in order to develop a sense for design and quality in manual and technical work.

based on technical knowledge and professional capabilities, in the <u>third stage</u> a start is made on independent design work.

in addition to specialised education, lectures and guest courses are designed to confront the student in depth with the problems of our time.

teaching staff

l. mies van der rohe   j. albers   f. engemann
l. hilberseimer   w. kandinsky   w. peterhans
lilly reich   a. rudelt   h. scheper

requirements for admission

enrolments take place in april and october. any student whose talent and previous education are deemed sufficient and who is more than 18 years of age may be admitted to the bauhaus as a full-time student. no particular kind of previous education (matriculation or similar) is required. if possible, the students should have had previous practical experience. in cases where a student has had greater previous professional training, he may, as an exception, be admitted to one of the advanced semesters, providing he makes up indispensable courses in lower semesters. the director's office decides upon the applications of admission. admission is complete when the student has received written confirmation of the decision and when he has paid all fees required.

students who do not enrol for the prescribed course of studies may be admitted as guest auditors, space permitting.

enrolment

application for admission should be made on the application form which is provided. the following is to be included in the application: 1. curriculum vitae (previous education, nationality, personal situation); 2. means of support; 3. police certificate of good conduct; 4. health certificate; 5. photograph; 6. certificates of previous manual or theoretical training; 7. original drawings or projects requiring craftsmanship. foreigners are to submit german translations, certified by their consulates, of these documents.

expenses

the following fees will be charged:
for germans, germans residing outside germany, and german-austrians

1. a non-recurring admission fee of rm. 20.
2. tuition fees: a. for full-time students, summer semester rm. 100, winter semester rm. 200; b. guest auditors, 10 rm. for each hour per week per semester.
3. premium for accident insurance, rm. 5 per semester. foreigners pay twice the admission and tuition fees.

fees due per semester are to be paid to the secretariat at the beginning of each semester. student identification cards are handed out only after the fees have been paid, and only then is the student entitled to take classes.

semester fees are non-refundable.

talented students having no financial support may be exempted from paying tuition fees in part or altogether only within the limits of the available means.

studies

semesters begin and finish punctually. the summer semester runs from april to july, the winter semester from october to april. summer vacations are, if possible, to be spent obtaining practical experience (working on actual construction, etc.). summer courses will be held during vacation as required.

daily hours: 9:00 a.m. to 1:00 p.m., 2:00 p.m. to 5:00 p.m., saturday – independent work. classes are compulsory. students are required to attend classes regularly. enrolment in a chosen course makes regular attendance mandatory for the duration of the course. exemption from specific classes or admission to other courses is possible only with written permission of the director. exemptions can be granted only where there is proof of adequate proficiency in the material of the course.

leave of absence has to be applied for in writing, with reasons given.

work is judged at the end of each semester; the result of this determines continuation of studies and admission to the next higher semester.

upon leaving, each student may apply for a certificate stating the duration and nature of his work at the bauhaus.

the bauhaus diploma can be earned only after completing the required course of studies and is dependent upon satisfactory completion of an independently carried out project for the diploma.

certificates, diplomas, etc. are only issued when all obligations to the bauhaus have been fulfilled.

the director's office of the bauhaus must be informed in writing when a student intends to leave before completion of his course of studies. the director reserves the right to suspend students from the bauhaus. students whose behaviour disturbs work will be expelled.

students are to give the secretariat their home address. changes of address are to be reported immediately.

each student is held liable for any damage caused as a result of negligent or wilful action. the bauhaus is entitled to the copyright on all work carried out at the bauhaus. when such is economically exploited by the institute, special financial arrangements may be made. moreover, the bauhaus reserves the right to keep student work at its disposal for a period of up to one year after the student has completed his studies. consequently, the publication, exhibition, and sale of such work is only possible with the permission of the director. publications which, by addition of the names 'bauhaus' or 'bauhaus berlin' to the name of the author or which, by the way they are worded, create the impression of being statements by the institute, require the approval of the director. the use of the name 'bauhaus' or 'bauhaus berlin' by students on their projects and on private or business letters is not permitted.

the curriculum is subject to change.

the work of the institute is covered by house rules.

accident insurance all students are insured against accidents within the building and on the way to and from the institute. for further information apply to the secretariat of the bauhaus.

1st stage = 1st semester practical instruction – for the purpose of developing a sense for materials and space | mathematics (geometry and algebra) | descriptive geometry | representational drawing | lettering | science of materials | colour theory | workshop practice | special field | theoretical subjects are supplemented by experimental work

2nd stage = 2nd and 3rd semesters
architecture and interior design structural and decorative work in connection with construction | strength of materials | static, steel, and reinforced concrete | structures | heating and ventilation | installation and lighting | cost estimating | design of furniture | perspective | colour theory
commercial art practical experimentation: topography, printing, and reproduction processes | cost estimation of printed matter | life drawing and drawing of figures | instruction in photographic techniques
photography practical and theoretical fundamentals of photography | experimentation and discussion based on actual tests with copy techniques | reproduction of grey values and colours | lighting and reproduction of material
weaving study of materials, binding techniques | introduction to the different techniques of weaving | exercises in combinations of material and colour
fine art seminar-type practical and theoretical exercises | independent work | group discussions of independent work
general instruction colour theory | descriptive geometry representational drawing | lettering | life drawing and drawing of figures | practical experimentation

3rd stage = 4th–7th semesters
architecture, interior design, and city planning small residential building and housing projects | dwelling and office building construction, hotels, schools, etc. | strength of materials | steel-skeleton structures and structures for auditoriums, gymnasiums, hangers, etc. | interior design | furnishing of apartments, individual homes, hotels, etc. | single pieces of furniture | combination of materials

commercial art instruction in the theory of advertising | independent and experimental work in the field of advertising | printed advertising matter | exhibition stands, etc. | statistical and diagrammatic presentation
photography transition from purely technical experimentation to independent work with reference to the requirements of advertising and reporting
weaving continuation of the practical exercises at looms | manufacture of textiles to independent designs or to given projects, using different materials and techniques and with respect to the requirements of contemporary interior design

37 This is How the Future Berlin Bauhaus Will Look

Published statement (15 October 1932).
Source: Bauhaus Archive, Berlin: *Volksblatt für Anhalt*, Dessau, 15 October 1932.
While the author is not explicitly named, we assume, given the context, that Mies, as director of the school, was involved.
Translated from German by Wolfgang Jabs and Basil Gilbert.
Republished in Wingler (1962) 1969, p. 182.

The Bauhaus has been set up in Berlin right on time. Its director, Mies van der Rohe, actually intends that winter semester classes at the Bauhaus in Berlin-Steglitz will open on 18 October.
Of course, it is out of the question for the institute to be taken over by the state of Prussia under Papen and Bracht; and the city of Berlin does not have the financial means to rebuild the Bauhaus. In such a situation the strength of the creative idea proves successful: the Bauhaus is going to support itself. The 80,000-mark subsidy from the city of Dessau is no more, but this will be compensated for by prospects for new commissions and new opportunities in the much larger city of Berlin. A helping factor under these circumstances is the royalties the Bauhaus has acquired and the contracts of employment of its teachers, a number of whom will continue for several years to receive their salaries from Dessau because of the city's contractual obligations, meaning that they can teach in Berlin without pay. The most difficult problem, that of finding a site for the school, has already been solved: the buildings of the former Berlin Telephone Company in the district of Steglitz have been leased. Although not a replacement for the institute's buildings in Dessau, they nevertheless yield 12 studios when subdivided by partitions, etc. For the beginning, these are enough.
The National Socialists have caused Dessau a lot of trouble: the city has lost the cultural and economic

advantages given it by the Bauhaus. On the other hand, Berlin, and particularly Steglitz, is gaining an invaluable source of energy in the institute's teaching and practice.

38 [What Would Concrete, What Would Steel Be Without Plate Glass?]

Unpublished manuscript (13 March 1933).
Source: LoC, Mies, Box 2, V, untitled.
On March 13 Mies sent this text to the Verein Deutscher Spiegelglas Fabriken (Association of German Plate-Glass Factories) in Cologne.
Translated from German by Mark Jarzombek.
Republished in Neumeyer (1986) 1991, p. 314; Pizzigoni 2010, pp. 79–80; Walter 2022, p. 93.

What would concrete, what would steel be without plate glass?

The space-toppling power of both would be undermined, yes, even cancelled, would remain empty promise.

A glass skin, glass walls alone permit the skeleton structure its unambiguous structural appearance and secure its architectonic possibilities. Not only in large functional structures. Although in the latter, on the basis of function and necessity, a development is underway that needs no more justification but whose full unfolding will not occur in this field but in the realm of residential buildings.

Here, in greater freedom and without immediate obligation to narrow functionality, the artistic value of these technical means may be proven.

[Concrete and steel] are genuine building elements from which a new, richer building art can arise.

They permit a measure of freedom in spatial composition that we shall never relinquish. Only now can we articulate space, open it up, and connect it to the landscape.

Now it is again apparent what walls and openings are and what floors and ceilings are.

Simplicity of construction, clarity of tectonic means, and purity of material shall show the radiance of original beauty.

39 [Announcement of the Dissolution of the Bauhaus to Students]

Speech (10 August 1933).
Source: Bauhaus Archive, Berlin.
Published in Hans M. Wingler, *Das Bauhaus: 1919–1933, Weimar, Dessau, Berlin*, Bramsche 1962.
Translated from German by Wolfgang Jabs and Basil Gilbert.
Republished in Wingler (1962) 1969, p. 189; Pizzigoni 2010, pp. 83–84; Walter 2022, p. 91.

To the students of the Bauhaus.
At its last meeting the faculty resolved to dissolve the Bauhaus. The reason for this decision was the institute's difficult economic situation.
The Office of the State Secret Police, the Prussian Ministry for Science, Art, and Education, and the school administration have been informed of this decision.
This announcement has crossed with a notification from the Office of the State Secret Police in which we are informed that 'in agreement with the Prussian Ministry for Science, Art, and Education, the reopening of the Bauhaus is made dependent upon the removal of certain objections.'
We would have agreed to these conditions, but the economic situation does not allow the institute to continue.
Faculty members are, of course, available to students for advice at any time. Grade records for all students will be issued by the secretariat.
From now on please address all letters to Professor Mies van der Rohe, Berlin W 35, Am Karlsbad 24.
Mies van der Rohe

40 [Letter on the End of the Bauhaus]

Typewritten letter (24 August 1933).
Source: Stiftung Bauhaus Dessau, I 43377.
Translated from German by John Nicolson.
The document is in lower case, as was typical of the Bauhaus.
Republished in Walter 2022, p. 92.

closure of the bauhaus
at the local community meeting of 22.8.1932 it was decided to close the bauhaus on 30.9.1932.
i shall try to continue the house in another place; whether i shall succeed it is not possible to say at the moment. on the success of my efforts i shall send further information to students by the middle of september.
also, the work scheduled for the end of the holidays in the workshops (from 5 september forwards) can no longer take place due to the dissolution of the bauhaus, which is now already underway.

41 Competitions Proposal

Unpublished article (circa 1933).
Source: LoC, Mies, Box 22, W, 'Wettbewerbsvorschlag'.
Translated from German by John Nicolson.
Republished in Pizzigoni 2010, pp. 81–82.

The results of the most recent large competitions show the impossibility of awarding prizes and of – relatedly, in many cases – realising new thinking in building art.

This situation has its foundations in the competition system but above all in the choice of jurors and in the preliminary review process.

In many cases the competition programmes have conditions that go beyond what is objectively necessary and, usually unintentionally, bind the competition entrants to a programme which proves a fundamental mistake when the competition brief is tackled in detail.

The choice of jurors is almost always decisive for the outcome of the competition.

Until now this choice has been made, with or without advice, by the body organising the competition, and this has given each competition a specific flavour of its own.

This practice may have produced results in the past when renowned architects were appointed jurors.

It is my conviction that this practice is no longer sufficient and in no way ensures an objective verdict.

At turning points in development new thoughts in building art emerge that are not necessarily understood by every renowned architect yet which perhaps contain the germ of a new building art. It is precisely the youngest among us who are the bearers of new ideas, and I demand that they be given space in which to freely realise their powers – in the interest of the development of building art and likewise in the interest of our young building artists, who often live and create true to their convictions under the most difficult conditions.

That is why I am in favour of those who are to work on the competition briefs being given an influence on the choice of jurors.

I put forward the following proposal for discussion: Exhibitions being held should, as previously, be supervised by a competition committee formed by the Association of German Architects and the Association of German Architects and Engineers.

The choice of specialist jurors should be made by the competition entrants themselves, with each entrant proposing such and such a number of jurors.

The jurors who collect the most votes shall be deemed chosen and are to name a substitute in the event of being incapacitated.

The competition committee is to appoint in advance a preliminary examiner who is to make the results of his examination known to the selected jurors.

The jurors, however, are to determine whether a competition design entry is to be excluded as a result of a violation of the competition rules.

This seems to me to be necessary in order to prevent the exclusion of competition entries that perhaps violate one or another of the conditions but are significant from the point of view of building art.

42 Architects of Europe Today

Published interview (September 1935).
Source: George Nelson, 'Architects of Europe Today. 7–Van der Rohe, Germany', *Pencil Points*, vol. XVI, no. 9, 1935, pp. 453–460.
Republished in Hartman 2004, pp. 420–427; Pizzigoni 2010, pp. 87–91.

On the top floor of a rather dowdy old house in Berlin there lives a man who, in spite of having built little, spoken less, and written not at all, has somehow come to be considered one of the greatest architects of his time. Such is the power of personality and an idea.
[...] When I mentioned the attacks on Le Corbusier for his frequently excessive use of glass, [Mies] brushed the matter aside with the comment, The glass façade is not modern architecture.
[...] On the subject of Frank Lloyd Wright he was more willing to talk and, like most of Wright's European admirers, found it hard to understand why he had had so little influence in his own country. Wright, *said Mies*, was the greatest artist in setting buildings in a given landscape who had ever lived. *So much for the prophet without honour in his own land! As the conversation progressed to matters of mutual interest, Mies gradually unbent, and we both had a much better time. I left enormously impressed by the keenness and extraordinary personal force of the man.*
Mies van der Rohe was born in Aachen, in 1886. His father, a stonemason, had hopes that the boy would continue in the business, but there was a certain quality in his son that he mistook for stupidity. He apprenticed him to an architect, thinking that in this way he might acquire a certain amount of business acumen – curious idea! A story which Mies himself tells of this time indicates with what unconscious accuracy his father had selected his profession for him. It happened that during the preparation of an important drawing of an elaborate ceiling in the Renaissance manner the head designer fell ill and there was nobody in the office who could be trusted to finish it. Precisely like the child wonders who appear in the stories of the Italian Renaissance, Mies stayed late one night and finished the drawing. There was a furore, of course, and when it was discovered who had done it, Mies was promoted from broom to draughting board. Shortly after this rise in life he went to Berlin, worked with Bruno Paul for a time as a furniture designer, and then went into the office of Peter Behrens. Behrens was the greatest single influence in modern German architecture, and in his effect on his assistants he was very like that of the late Bertram Goodhue. Here Mies finished his architectural education and was entrusted with work of importance. After about three years of this, however, the association came to a sudden and violent end. Behrens entered a competition, and Mies, of course, worked on it. Apparently unsatisfied with Behrens' solution, he did one of his own outside the office, winning first prize with it [Bismarck Memorial Competition, 1910. Mies' design was one of 26 mentioned out of 379 submissions]. The scene which followed, as Behrens swore with mighty Teutonic oaths that Mies had copied his scheme, may well be imagined. Mies, no weakling himself, did a bit of bellowing on his own but, finally wearying of the argument, announced that he was resigning and going to Switzerland to ski. The resignation was quite unnecessary, but ski he did – for five months. When he returned, he opened an office of his own. Behrens never forgave him.
It was not until several years after the war that he was heard from. In 1921 and the years immediately following he published a brilliant series of studies: the Glass Skyscraper, which proved nothing; a cantilevered office building consisting of alternate horizontal bands of window and spandrel, a scheme used by [Erich] Mendelsohn with great effect on Columbus Haus in Berlin; and several country house projects. None of these, it will be noted, were ever

built; but they were published far and wide, and by means of the printing press Mies entered upon the road to fame.

[...] Mies designed the first metal chairs in Germany [MR10, 1927]. Others were working on them, and that he did any at all was accidental. He designed a silk exhibition room in Berlin with Lilly Reich, his collaborator on most interiors, and when the room was finished, he suddenly remembered that there were no chairs. Unwilling to put common chairs in this rich setting, Mies went back to the office and in one evening designed the chair that has since been copied all over the world. Four days later, when the exhibition opened, the chairs were there. They were a great success, and a manufacturer made arrangements with Mies to produce them. He made a slight variation in them, however, and Mies in a rage cancelled the contract and bought up all the chairs that had been made. Anything that went out under his name, he stormed, had to be perfect.

[...] On the strength of the Barcelona Pavilion Mies was made director of the important Berlin Building Exposition. Here he had sufficient power to select as architects the younger men in the Werkbund and thereby incurred the enmity of most of the more established architects. A movement arose to remove him from office at the next election, and at the meeting Mies had perhaps 20 people in the large audience who were for him. Before a vote was taken, he got up and made one of the longest speeches of his career – 15 minutes – and when he had finished, he was re-elected with one dissenting vote – his own [see 'The New Time']. Shortly after this [in November 1932], he retired, however, which was rather fortunate because six months later, the Nazis came in, and that ended the Deutscher Werkbund.

Another phase of his career is linked with the Bauhaus. [Walter] Gropius built it and was succeeded as director by Hannes Meyer, a functionalist and a communist to boot. More interested in communism than architecture, apparently, Meyer changed the character of the school radically. It must have been a rather hectic place, with a wild group of students agitating for one thing and another, and turning out a large crop of illegitimate babies, much to the horror of the staid citizens of Dessau. So bad did things become that Gropius was invited back, but he was busy and suggested Mies, who accepted. Mies was completely indifferent to communism, or any political system for that matter, and his students objected to him violently, calling him a reactionary. He stayed a year, however, doing some interesting work. Gropius had just finished a study of a tract of land in Berlin, proving that the solution of the housing problem was to put everybody in 12-storey houses, set a considerable distance apart. Mies, never much taken in by this sort of thing, put his students to work on the same tract of land, and proved that the same number of people could be settled for the same amount of money in small two-storey houses. This little experiment showed exactly what Mies wanted it to show, that there are several ways of doing almost anything. Most of his students were too busy talking to get the idea.

At the present time, oddly enough, Mies is on the upgrade. Hitler and his aides have condemned modern architecture repeatedly, evincing a preference for a kind of bombproof Nuremberg style, but Mies, who has never shown much love for pitched roofs, has been made head of the architects in the German Academy. And only a short while ago, his competition drawing for a new Reichsbank won first prize, although his design will not be built [Mies' design was one of six equal winners]. Whatever it is that accounts for his enviable position, it is to be hoped that he will get some jobs out of it. With [Erich] Mendelsohn, the Tauts [Bruno and Max], and Gropius out of the country, there surely ought to be a commission or two for those who remain, and it would be interesting to see what Mies would do on an important building.

[...] His reaction to a remark about the Beaux Arts was brief and to the point. It's dead, *he said.*

As I got up to leave, I noticed a beautiful engraving of an Ionic capital, prominent in the modern room, and asked what it was doing there. Mies looked at it seriously for a moment before replying. The old architects, he said finally, *copy this sort of thing. We appreciate it.*

43 The H. House in Magdeburg

Published journal article (1935).
Source: LMvdR, 'Haus H., Magdeburg', *Die Schildgenossen*, vol. XIV, no. 6, 1935, pp. 514–515.
Translated from German by Mark Jarzombek.
Republished in Neumeyer (1986) 1991, p. 314; Pizzigoni 2010, pp. 85–86; Walter 2022, p. 94.

This house was to be built on an island on the Elbe in Magdeburg, under old beautiful trees with a far-reaching view over the Elbe. It was an unusually beautiful place for building. Only the exposure presented problems. The beautiful view was to the east; to the south the view was dull, almost disturbing. This defect would have had to be corrected by the building plan.

For that reason I enlarged the living quarters with a garden courtyard surrounded by a wall and so locked out this view while allowing full sunshine. In the direction of the river, the house is entirely open and melts into the landscape.

Thereby I not only entered into the situation but achieved a beautiful alternation of quiet seclusion and open spaces.

This articulation also corresponds to the dwelling needs of the client, who, although living alone in the house, wanted to cultivate a relaxed social life and hospitality. This too is reflected in the interior layout, where we find a combination of the requisite privacy and the freedom of open room forms.

44 [Inaugural Address as Director of Architecture at Armour Institute of Technology]

Published speech (20 November 1938).
Source: LMvdR, 'Mies van der Rohe's Address, Delivered at a Banquet Held in his Honour', *Armour Engineer and Alumnus*, vol. IV, no. 2, 1938, pp. 19, 24. Drafts in: AIC, Hilberseimer, 070383, Box 13, Folder 3; LoC, Mies, Box 61, Addresses.
Speech delivered at Palmer House in Chicago.
Translated from German by Mark Jarzombek.
Republished in Johnson 1947, pp. 191–195; Neumeyer (1986) 1991, p. 321; Pizzigoni 2010, pp. 92–96; Walter 2022, pp. 95–99.

All education must be directed, first of all, towards the practical side of life. But if one may speak of real education, then it must go further and extend to the personal sphere and lead to a moulding of the human being.

The first aim should be to qualify the person to maintain himself in everyday life. This means equipping him with the necessary knowledge and ability for this purpose. The second aim is directed towards a formation of the personality. This should qualify him to make the right use of this knowledge and ability.

Genuine education is aimed not only at specific ends but also at an appreciation of values. Our aims are bound up with the special structure of our epoch. Values, on the contrary, are anchored in the spiritual destination of mankind. The ends towards which we strive determine the character of our civilisation, while the values we set determine our cultural level.

Although aspirations and values are of different origins, they are actually closely associated. For our standards of value are related to our aspirations, and our aspirations obtain their meaning from these values.

Both these concepts are necessary to establish full human existence. The former assures the person his vital existence, but it is only the latter that makes his spiritual existence possible.

Just as these propositions have a validity for all human conduct, even for the slightest differentiation of value, so are they that much more binding in the realm of architecture. Its simplest forms are rooted entirely in the useful, but architecture extends over all the degrees of value into the highest sphere of spiritual existence, into the sphere of the significant: the realm of pure art.

Any architectural education must take account of this circumstance if it is to achieve its goal. It must take account of this organic relationship. It can, in reality, be nothing other than an active unfolding of all these relationships and interrelationships. It should make plain, step by step, what is possible, what is necessary, and what is significant.

If education has any sense whatever, then, it must form character and develop insight. It must lead us out of the irresponsibility of opinion into the responsibility of insight, judgment, and understanding; it must lead us out of the realm of chance and arbitrariness into the clear light of intellectual order.

Therefore we guide our students along the disciplinary road from material through function to form.

We are determined to lead them into the wholesome world of primal buildings, where every axe stroke meant something and where every chisel cut was a veritable statement. Where does the structural fabric of a building appear with greater clarity than in the wooden buildings of our forefathers? Where else is there an equal unity of material, construction, and form? Here lies concealed the wisdom of the entire race. What a sense for material, and what a power of expression these buildings proclaim. What warmth they radiate, and how beautiful they are.

In stone buildings we find the same. What natural feeling is expressed by them! What clear understanding of material, what sureness in its use, what a feeling for that which can and should be done in stone! Where else do we find such richness of structure? Where do we find healthier strength and greater natural beauty than here? With what self-evident clarity does a beamed ceiling rest on these old stone walls, and with what feeling has a door been cut in them.

Where else should young architects grow up than in the fresh air of this wholesome world, and where else should they learn to work simply and prudently than with these unknown masters?

Brick is another schoolmaster. How clever is this small, handy unit, useful as it is for every purpose. What logic its bonding shows; what liveliness its jointing! What richness the simplest wall surface possesses, yet what discipline this material imposes!

Thus each material possesses its special qualities, which one must know in order to be able to work with them.

This is also true of steel and concrete. We expect absolutely nothing from the materials in themselves but only through our right use of them.

Then too, the new materials do not ensure superiority. Any material is only worth that which we make out of it.

Just as we are determined to know materials, so we are determined to know the nature of the purposes for which we build. We shall analyse them clearly. We are determined to know what their content is; wherein a dwelling is really different from another kind of building. We want to know what it can be, what it must be, and what it should not be. Therefore we must get at their essentials. Thus we shall examine every function which appears and determine its character and make its character the basis for our conception and our form.

Just as we procure a knowledge of materials – just as we acquaint ourselves with the nature of the uses for which we build – so we also learn to comprehend the spiritual and intellectual environment in which we find ourselves. This is a prerequisite for proper conduct in the cultural sphere. Here too we must know what exists, for we remain dependent upon our epoch.

Therefore we must learn to recognise the sustaining and compelling forces of our times. We must make an analysis of their structure; that is of the material, functional, and intellectual forces of today. We must clarify wherein our epoch is similar to former epochs and wherein it differs from them.

Here the problem of technology will come within the student's compass. We shall try to propound genuine questions: questions about the value and meaning of technology. We shall demonstrate that it not only offers us power and magnitude but that it also embraces dangers, that it contains good and evil, and that here mankind must decide aright.

Yet every decision leads to a definite clarification of principles and values. Therefore we shall elucidate the possible principles of order and clarify their bases.

We shall mark the mechanical principle of order as an overemphasis of the materialistic and functional tendency. This does not satisfy our feeling that 'the means' is a menial function, nor does it satisfy our interest in dignity and worth.

The idealistic principle of order, on the other hand, can, with its overemphasis of the ideal and the formal, satisfy neither our interest in truth and simplicity nor the practical side of our intellect.

We shall make the organic principle of order clear as a scale by which to establish the significance and proportion of the parts and their relation to the whole. We shall adopt this last principle as the basis of our work.

The long road from material through function to form has only one goal: to create order out of the unholy confusion of today. We want, however, an order which gives everything its proper place. We want to give to everything that which is its due, in accordance with its nature.

We are determined to do this in such a perfect way that the world of our creation will begin to flower from within. We want nothing more – nor can we do more. Nothing will express the aim and meaning of our work better than the profound words of Thomas Aquinas: 'Beauty is the radiance of the Truth.'

45 Architectural Education

Lecture manuscript (circa 1938–1939).
Source: LMvdR, 'Architectural Education at Armour Institute',
'Architectural Education, 1938–1949', LoC, Mies, Box 62, writings by
Mies General; AIC, Mies, 1984.2, Box 2, Folder 19; MOMA, Mies, IIT,
Folder 142.
Read at the 72nd conference of AIA, 24 May 1940; reused in identical
form in an IIT booklet of 1947.
Republished in Blaser 1977, pp. 52–53; Neumeyer (1986) 1991, p. 336
(partially); Pizzigoni 2010, pp. 97–100.

The curriculum of the Architectural Department of Armour Institute of Technology is designed not only to equip the student with the knowledge and ability required for the professional practice of architecture but also to give him a cultural education to enable him to make the right use of this knowledge and ability.

Architecture in its simplest forms is concerned primarily with the useful. But it extends from the almost purely practical until in its highest forms it attains its fullest significance as pure art. This relationship leads to a curriculum which makes clear, step by step, what is possible in construction, what is necessary for use, and what is significant as art.

This is accomplished in the curriculum by so interrelating the different fields of instruction that the student is always conscious of and is always working in the whole sphere of architecture in its fullest sense of designing a structure for a purpose, ordering it so that it attains significance as art, and working out the conception so that it may be realised in the executed building.

The curriculum leads therefore from the study of the means with which one builds into the sphere of architecture as an art. This is the synthesis of the entire curriculum: the fundamentals of the art of architecture, the artistic principles, the means, and their expression in the executed building. The student applies the principles in free creative architectural design and works his designs through in collaboration with the construction and construction staff of the department. Actually, these fields of instruction are initially kept separate and developed as far as possible independently, with the limitation that they complement each other at every stage; as the curriculum advances, they result in an architecture which appeals both to the heart and to the mind.

Such a method of instruction must be carried out by a unified faculty. With these ideas in mind let me briefly describe the curriculum.

The student studies the materials and construction of simple wood, stone, and brick buildings and then the structural possibilities of steel and concrete. This work is studied in such a way that the significant relationship between the materials, the construction, and the architectural expression is made apparent.

The knowledge of materials and construction leads to a study of function. The functions of the principal kinds of buildings are studied on the basis of an exact analysis. This analysis establishes wherein each architectural problem is distinguished from every other; wherein the real essence of each problem lies. After the essentials of each problem have been clearly established, buildings are designed whose conception and expression are based on these essentials.

The study of function is carried beyond individual buildings into groups of buildings and then into communities in the field of city planning in order to demonstrate the interdependence of all building in relation to the city as an organic whole.

Throughout the curriculum the student is given training to develop a feeling for the expression of and relationship between form, proportion, structure, and materials.

In conjunction with the curriculum there is a clarification of the cultural situation today so that the student may learn to recognise the sustaining and compelling forces of his times and to comprehend the intellectual and spiritual environment in which he lives. The material, intellectual, and cultural aspects of our era are explored to see wherein they are similar to those of former epochs and wherein they differ from them. The buildings of the past are studied so that the student will acquire from their significance and greatness a sense for genuine architectural values and because their dependence upon a specific historical situation must awaken in him an understanding for the necessity of his own architectural achievement.

[The version below is slightly different from the one given above.]
The architecture department aims, by means of its building programme, to teach the required knowledges and skills to architectural students. Through its pedagogical methods, however, it aims at forming the students so that they can apply the acquired knowledges and skills in the proper way. The theory therefore aims at function, while the pedagogical training aims at values. For it is the meaning of education to train and teach accountability. It must add the binding force of insight to the casualness of opinion and must lead from the realm of the accidental and arbitrary to the lucid laws of a spiritual order. Building art in its simplest forms is still rooted in purpose, but it reaches through the whole scale of value into the highest realms of spiritual being, into the sphere of pure art. All teaching of building must be based on this understanding. Step by step, it must make intelligible what is possible, necessary, and meaningful. This is why the individual fields of instruction have to be interconnected so that they result on each level in an organic order and the student always works with the entire field of building and all that relates to it in full view.

Aside from scientific instructions, the students must first of all learn how to draw in order to master this skill and to train eye and hand. Practice should instil in them a sense for proportions, structure, form, and material and make their relationship and expressive possibilities clear. Then, students should become acquainted with materials and the construction of simple wood, stone, and tile buildings; after that, with the constructive uses of iron and ferroconcrete. Simultaneously, they should be made acquainted with the meaningful interrelationships of these building elements and their immediate formal characteristics. Each material, whether natural or artificial, possesses specific characteristics that one must know if one wants to work with it. New materials and new constructions too are not necessarily indicative of superiority. What matters is the right application. Each material is only worth what we make of it. Subsequent to an understanding of materials and constructions comes purpose. This must be clearly analysed and its contents understood. It must be demonstrated in which respect one building task differs from another, what constitutes its intrinsic nature. An introduction to the problems of urban planning should teach its principles and the relationship of all buildings to each other and to the entire urban organism.

And finally, as a synthesis of the entire programme, follows an introduction to the artistic principles of building, to the nature of the artistic, the manner and application of its means, and its applicability in building. Together with this course of study, the spiritual nature of the epoch on which we depend should also be illuminated. We should investigate to what extent our epoch conforms with earlier ones and in which material and spiritual aspects it differs. For this reason the buildings of the past are to be studied and a vivid demonstration of them given. Not only to gain an architectural appreciation of their magnificence and significance but also to demonstrate that they are bound to an unrepeatable historical situation and thus present a challenge to us to bring forth our own creative achievements.

[Handwritten note]
We shall always pursue the same method.
Only then shall we investigate the structure of the aesthetic and cultural spheres, in order to obtain their full clarity.
We believe that only such a way will lead the students to surety from the necessary *[things to]* the suitable to the beautiful.

46 [AIT Curriculum]

Published school programme (circa 1939).
This programme is designed in a sort of pattern published the first time in upper case and the second time in lower case. The similarities with the curriculum developed less than a decade earlier for the Bauhaus are interesting (see 'Bauhaus Berlin. Syllabus and Curriculum').
Republished in Kevin P. Harrington, Rolf Achilles, Charlotte Myhrum (eds.), *Mies Van Der Rohe: Architect as Educator* (Chicago, 1986), p. 57.

PROGRAMME FOR ARCHITECTURAL EDUCATION

General Theory: Mathematics and Natural Science, The Nature of Man, The Nature of Human Society, Analysis of Technics, Analysis of Culture, Culture as Obligatory Task.

Professional Training: Architectural Drawing, Freehand Drawing and Life Drawing, Structural Design, Mechanical Equipment and Design, Specifications, Estimating, Financing, Law, Supervision, Office Practice.

(First Stage) MEANS: Wood, Stone, Brick, Steel, Concrete (filling, surfacing, enveloping and other materials).

Material Where and how obtained, How worked, Physical properties, Structural properties, Aesthetic qualities.

Construction Different methods of construction (wood, stone, brick, steel, concrete), Application of these materials in various types of construction.

Form Creation of Elementary Building Forms.
Based on, and including detailing of, types of construction in: Wood, Stone, Brick, Steel, Concrete. Various combinations of the above materials.

(Second Stage) PURPOSES: Dwellings, Commercial Buildings, Industrial Buildings, Public Buildings. Single-family dwelling, Multi-family dwelling, Apartment house, Hotel, Club, Resort, Dormitory, Institution, etc.
Store, Office, Display space, Bank, Restaurant, Warehouse, etc.
Light manufacturing, Heavy industry, Assembly plant, etc.
School, Library, Church, Auditorium, Theatre, Museum, Hospital, Transportation Building, Government Building, etc.
Analysis of various functions of buildings. Interior furnishing. Materials, Construction, Purpose, Arrangement.

Their ordering into groups and unified communities
According to the social requirements of: Dwelling, Work, Public administration, Recreation, Culture.
According to the technical requirements of: Topography, Kind of building development, Hygiene and sanitation, Transportation.

Reorganisation of Existing Cities

Regional Planning

(Third Stage) PLANNING AND CREATING

Dependence upon the Epoch. The Material Structure. The Functional Structure. The Spiritual Structure. An analysis of the supporting and compelling forces of the times.

Possible Principles of Order. The Mechanical as overemphasis of the material and functional. The Idealistic as overemphasis of the ideal. The Organic as the determining factor for the essential significance and proper proportioning of the purposes and functions of the various parts and their relation to the whole.

The Elements of Architectural Form: Wall and Opening, Surface and Depth, Space and Solid, Material and Colour, Light and Shadow, Lightness and Massiveness.

The Structure of Architectural Form: The dependence of architectonic structure upon distinct forms of organisation and working methods.

The Obligation to Realise the Potentialities of Organic Architecture.

Architecture, planning, and sculpture as a creative unity.

47 [The Stevens Chicago Note]

Manuscript for a speech (circa 1938–1940).
Source: AIC, Mies Collection, 1984.2.
Speech possibly given at the Stevens Hotel in Chicago.
Translated from German by Jan Frohburg.

At the Armour Institute we do not have the intention to shine with abstractions. In fact we consider abstractions hostile to the necessary and healthy. But this is the aim we pursue.
Our students must learn to build from the foundation up.
Therefore they first have to study materials. Their properties and possibilities regarding construction and design.
Then they will be introduced to the purposes of building. Based on exact analyses, the conditions of the individual building types will be explored.
Those results will serve as the basis for designs.
We do not follow any formal principle but the necessities of life.
The same holds true for city planning. Here too clarification of the basis through analysis serves as point of departure for designs.
At the last stage we shall examine the possible principles of order in the cultural and spiritual realm.
We believe that with such an organisation of the curriculum the students will surely find [a way] from the necessary via the appropriate to the beautiful.

48 [It is Performance That Matters]

Lecture manuscript (circa 1938–1945).
Source: LoC, Mies, Box 61, Miscellaneous.
Translated from German by Mark Jarzombek.
Republished in Neumeyer (1986) 1991, p. 325; Pizzigoni 2010, pp. 104–107; Walter 2022, pp. 355–361.

Ladies and gentlemen! The attempt to revitalise building art from the direction of form has failed. A century's worth of effort has been wasted and leads into the void. That heroic revolution of extremely talented men at the turn of the century had the time span of a fashion. The invention of forms is obviously not the task of building art. Building art is more and different. Its excellent name already makes it clear that building is its natural content and art its completion.
Building, where it has become great, has almost always been indebted to construction, and construction has almost always been the conveyor of its spatial form. Romantic and Gothic demonstrate this in brilliant clarity. In both cases structure expresses meaning, expresses it down to the last remnant of spiritual value. But if that is so, then it must follow that the revitalisation of building art can only come from construction and not by means of arbitrarily assembled motifs. But construction, that loyal safekeeper of the spirit of an epoch, had rejected all that was arbitrary and created an objective basis for new developments. And so it has happened here too. The few authentic structures of our period exhibit construction as a component of building. Building and meaning are one. The manner of building is decisive and of testimonial significance.
Construction not only determines form but is form itself. Where authentic construction encounters authentic contents, authentic works result – works that are genuine and intrinsic. And necessary. Necessary in themselves and as members of a genuine order. One can only order what is already ordered in itself. Order

is more than organisation. Organisation is the determination of function.

Order, however, imparts meaning. If we were to give to each thing what intrinsically belongs to it, then all things would easily fall into their proper place; only there they could really be what they are and there they would fully realise themselves. The chaos in which we live would give way to order, and the world would again become meaningful and beautiful.

But that means to let go of the self-will and do the necessary. To articulate and realise the timely and not prevent what wants to and must become.

In other words: to serve rather than rule. Only those who know how hard it is to do even simple things properly can respect the immensity of this task. This means to persevere humbly, renounce effects, and do what is necessary and right with loyalty.

Only yesterday one spoke of the eternal forms of art; today one speaks of its dynamic change. Neither is right. Building art is beholden neither to the day nor to eternity but to the epoch. Only a historical movement offers it space in which to live and allows it to fulfil itself. Building art is the expression of what historically transpires. Authentic expression of an inner movement.

Fulfilment and expression of something immanent. This may also be the reason why the nineteenth century failed. Unsuspected and deep beneath all the confused attempts of that time ran the quiet current of change, fed by the forces of a world that was intrinsically already different, and a jungle of new forms broke out. Forms that were unusual and of wild power. The world of technical forms – *[forms that were]* large and forceful.

Genuine forms of a genuine world. Everything else that occurred looked, next to this, pale and marginal. Technology promises both power and grandeur, a dangerous promise for man, who has been created for neither one nor the other. Those who are truly responsible feel depressed and respond to this promise by searching for the dignity and value of technology.

Is the world as it presents itself bearable for man? Further, is it worthy of man or too lowly? Does it offer room for the highest form of human dignity? Can it be shaped so as to be worthwhile to live in?

And finally: is the world noble enough to respond to man's duty to erect a high and magnanimous order? These are questions of immense weight. One can quickly affirm them and quickly negate them, and one has done that.

To the careful, however, beyond all prejudices and misjudgements, technology appears as a world which is what it is, specific and narrow, dependent on the panorama of its own time, just like any other building art, and precluding a host of possibilities.

There is no reason to overestimate this form. But it is, like all other authentic forms, both deep and high. Called to the one, attempting the other. A real world. If that is true, then technology too must change into building art to complete itself. It would be a building art that inherits the Gothic legacy. It is our greatest hope.

But none of this comes by itself. History does not come about by itself. History must be performed. And historical measurements are shorter than many realise. Only 30 life spans separate us from the Acropolis. And the breathing span of the Middle Ages was too short for it to complete its cathedrals.

Furthermore, the technological age is not as young as it may appear. *[Alfred North]* Whitehead moved the hour of its birth to the seventeenth century. That may be. The ultimate reasons for what occurs today may be found in the discussions of lonely monks behind quiet, Romanesque monastery walls.

With infinite slowness arises the great form whose birth is the meaning of the epoch. Not everything that happens takes place in full view. The decisive battles of the spirit are waged on invisible battlefields.

The visible is only the final step of a historical form. Its fulfilment. Its true fulfilment. Then it breaks off. And a new world arises.

What I have said is the ground on which I stand; that which I believe and the justification of my deeds. Convictions are necessary, but in the realm of one's work they have only limited significance. In the final analysis it is performance that matters.

49 A Tribute to Frank Lloyd Wright

Published journal article (circa 1940).
Source: LMvdR, 'A Tribute to Frank Lloyd Wright', *The College Art Journal*, vol. VI, no. 1, 1946, pp. 41–42. Republished in *Emporium*, vol. LIV, no. 107, 1948, p. 119; *Arts and Architecture*, vol. LXVII, no. 10, 1950, p. 30; and many other publications. Working Drafts in LoC, Mies, Box 40, MoMA1; Box 61, Articles about Mies B; Box 62, Writings Mies General.
Initially written for the never-published catalogue for the Frank Lloyd Wright exhibition at MoMA in 1940.
Republished in Johnson 1947, p. 195–196; Neumeyer (1986) 1991, p. 321; Pizzigoni 2010, pp. 101–103; Walter 2022, pp. 100–102.

About the beginning of this century, the great European revival of architecture instigated by William Morris grew over-refined and began gradually to lose its force. Distinct signs of exhaustion became manifest. The attempt to revive architecture from the standpoint of form was apparently doomed. Even the greatest efforts of artists could not overcome the patent lack of any useable convention. Then, however, these efforts were limited to the subjective. But the authentic approach to architecture must always be objective. Accordingly, the only valid solutions at that time were in cases such as industrial building, where objective limitations made subjective license impossible. Peter Behrens' significant creations for the electrical industry *[AEG]* are a vivid illustration. But in all other problems of architectural creation the architect ventured into the dangerous realm of the historical; to some of these men the revival of Classical forms seemed reasonable, and in the field of monumental architecture even imperative. Of course, this was not true of all early-twentieth-century architects. *[Henry]* Van de Velde and *[Hendrik Petrus]* Berlage, especially, remained steadfastly loyal to their own ideals. Once a way of thinking had been accepted as essential, Van de Velde's intellectual integrity and Berlage's sincerity and almost religious faith in his ideal allowed no compromise. For these reasons the former won our highest respect, the latter our special veneration and love.

Nevertheless, we young architects found ourselves in painful inner conflict. We were ready to pledge ourselves to an idea. But the potential vitality of the architectural ideal of this period had, by that time, been lost. This, then, was the situation in 1910.

At this moment, so critical for us, there came to Berlin the exhibition of the work of Frank Lloyd Wright. This comprehensive display and the extensive publication of his works enabled us really to become acquainted with the achievement of this architect *[F.L. Wright, Ausgeführte Bauten und Entwürfe (Berlin, 1910); F.L. Wright, Chicago: VIII Sonderheft der Architektur des XX Jahrhunderts (Berlin: 1911); both are in Mies' library at the University of Illinois in Chicago]*. The encounter was destined to prove of great significance to the development of architecture in Europe.

The work of this great master revealed an architectural world of unexpected force and clarity of language and also a disconcerting richness of form. Here finally was a master-builder drawing upon the veritable fountainhead of architecture who with true originality lifted his architectural creations into the light. Here, again at last, genuine organic architecture flowered.

The more deeply we studied Wright's creations, the greater became our admiration for his incomparable talent, for the boldness of his conceptions, and for his independence in thought and action. The dynamic impulse emanating from this work invigorated a whole generation. His influence was strongly felt even when it was not actually visible.

After this first encounter, we followed the development of this rare man with eager hearts. We watched with astonishment the exuberant unfolding of the gifts of one who had been endowed by nature with the most splendid talents. In his undiminishing power he resembles a giant tree in a wide landscape, which, year after year, ever attains a more noble crown.

50 [Vendôme Shop in Pittsburgh]

Project report (circa April 1941).
Source: LoC, Mies, Box 36, Kaufmann Edgar.
Translated from German by John Nicolson.

The Small Vendôme has become a difficult problem. I have tried many different solutions but have always come back to the one shown in the model and drawings. This solution seems to me the best for the required purpose and is, I think, elegant and attractive. From the model you will see that I tried to structure the available space by inserting screens and display cases in such a way that the entire thing looks elegant and impressive when seen from both outside and in.

The inserted screens have a dual function. They are intended to intercept the view from afar and at the same time provide a beautiful background for the pieces exhibited.

Additionally, they provide opportunity for a double-sided display.

My idea is to make the curved screens from glass pipes or glass rods. One in a champagne colour, the other of clear glass with a slightly green shine to it; the third wall, I think, should be silver-coloured. In front of these *[polished]* screens I would place low pedestals, perhaps of *[polished]* travertine, and on the glass tubes perhaps shelves could be placed adjustably; the attached drawings will give you an approximate impression of the effect of these screens.

I think the display cases should be glass and metal. The storage case should be of ebony with glass drawers.

It will be necessary to install a new ceiling to conceal the pipes and to contain pinhole lighting. This ceiling can be made from large plywood boards and painted white. This would make it possible to access the sprinkler system at any moment.

Now I have to apologise that all this has taken so long. I hope, however, that you will now also like my proposal.

51 [A Museum for a Small City]

Published journal article (1943).
Source: LMvdR, 'Museum', *Architectural Forum*, vol. LXXVIII, no. 5, 1943, pp. 84–85.
Republished in Johnson 1947, p. 197; Neumeyer (1986) 1991, p. 322; Pizzigoni 2010, pp. 108–109; Walter 2022, pp. 103–105.

The museum for the small city should not emulate its metropolitan counterparts. The value of such a museum depends upon the quality of its works of art and the manner in which they are exhibited.

The first problem is to establish the museum as a centre for the enjoyment, not the interment of art. In this project the barrier between the art work and the living community is erased by a garden approach for the display of sculpture. Interior sculptures enjoy an equal spatial freedom because the open plan permits them to be seen against the surrounding hills. The architectural space thus achieved becomes a defining rather than a confining space. A work such as Picasso's *Guernica* has been difficult to place in the usual museum gallery. Here it can be shown to greatest advantage and become an element in space against a changing background.

The building, conceived as one large area, allows every flexibility of use. The structural type permitting this is the steel frame. This construction permits the erection of a building with only three basic elements: a floor slab, columns, and a roof plate. The floor and paved terraces would be of stone.

Under the same roof, but separated from the exhibit space, would be the administrative offices. These would have their own toilet and storage facilities in a basement under the office area.

Small pictures would be exhibited on free-standing walls. The entire building space would be available for larger groups, encouraging a more representative use of the museum than is customary today, and creating a noble background for the civic and cultural life of the whole community.

Two openings in the roof plate (3 and 7) admit light into an inner court (7) and into an open passage (3) through one end of the building. The outer walls (4) and those of the inner court are of glass. On the exterior, free-standing walls of stone would define outer courts (1) and terraces (10). Offices (2) and wardrobes would be free standing. A shallow recessed area (5) is provided, around the edge of which small groups could sit for informal discussions. The auditorium (8) is defined by free-standing walls providing facilities for lectures, concerts, and intimate formal discussions. The form of these walls and the shell hung above the stage would be dictated by the acoustics. The floor of the auditorium is recessed in steps of seat height, using each step as a continuous bench. Number (6) is the print department. Above it is a space for special exhibits. Number (9) is a pool. *[Numbers refer to the plan originally published together with this text.]*

52 [Introduction to Ludwig Hilberseimer, *The New City: Principles of Planning*]

Published introduction (1944).
Source: LMvdR, 'Introduction', in L. Hilberseimer, *The New City. Principles of Planning* (Chicago: Paul Theobald, 1944), p. XV.
The introduction is preceded on p. XIII by Walt Whitman's poem 'Where the Great City Stands'.
Republished in Neumeyer 1991, p. 323; Pizzigoni 2010, pp. 111–112; Walter 2022, pp. 106–107.

'Reason is the first principle of all human work.' Consciously or unconsciously, L Hilberseimer follows this principle and makes it the basis of his work in the complicated field of city planning. He examines the city with unwavering objectivity, investigates each part of it, and determines for each part its rightful place in the whole. Thus he brings all the elements of the city into clear, logical order. He avoids imposing upon them arbitrary ideas of any character whatsoever.

He knows that cities must serve life, that their validity is to be measured in terms of life, and that they must be planned for living in. He understands that the forms of cities are the expression of existing modes of living, that they are inextricably bound up with these, and that they, with these, are subject to change. He realises that the material and spiritual conditions of the problem are given, that he can exercise no influence on these factors in themselves, that they are rooted in the past and will be determined by objective tendencies for the future.

He also knows that the existence of many and diverse factors presupposes the existence of some order which gives meaning to these and which acts as a medium in which they can grow and unfold. City planning means for the author, therefore, the ordering of things in themselves and in their relationships with each other. One should not confuse the principles with their application. City planning is, in essence, a work of order; and order means – according to St Augustine – 'the disposition of equal and unequal things, attributing to each its place.'

53 Only the Patient Counts: Some Radical Ideas on Hospital Design

Published interview (1945).
Source: Mildred E. Withcombe, 'Only the Patient Counts: Some Radical Ideas on Hospital Design by Mies van der Rohe', *The Modern Hospital*, vol. 64, no. 3, 1945, pp. 65–67.
Republished in Pizzigoni 2010, pp. 113–118; Walter 2022, pp. 108–115.

The patient is our master. We in our modern medical workshops function only as highly skilled, often consecrated servants. On that relationship our credo is constructed.

A world-famous architect is inclined to question whether we are entirely sincere in our ideal of the patient-centred hospital. Is the hospital building of today built for the patient primarily? Or are the patient's best interests frequently subordinated to limitations on cost, muddled planning, faulty selection of site and orientation – even to an imaginary pedometer attached to the ankle of a pretty nurse?

When the jury for awards in 'The Modern Hospital' competitions for small hospital and health centre designs met last December, the quietest man on the jury was that 'pure artist in architecture', Mies van der Rohe, one of the most advanced architects of the modern school.

[...] Mr Van der Rohe is polytheistic, architecturally speaking. His gods are Order, Light, and Space. He regards False Economy, Restrictions, and Compromise as hound-like evil deities ever snapping at the architect's heels.

To confront the evil forces first, let's hear his objections to economy per se.

Architects have no business to be talking like bankers. Economics is not their main concern. Their job is to design a good building on the understanding that only as much of it will be constructed at the time as is consistent with a perfect plan. Anything less than perfection is unacceptable.

Nature is a proper guide for Man. Nature produces all that is necessary to suit her purposes. To Nature nothing is too cheap, nothing too expensive. Nor does she stoop to compromise with optimum principles of design; she does not turn out three-legged horses to limp through life.

Our German-American has lived up to Nature's tenets, which is probably the reason why he has built relatively little, although he has designed much and freely.

You hospital folk say, 'We can't build every patient's room to face south. It is not economical.' I say that to put patients both sides of a corridor will be a little cheaper, yes, but the reasoning is wrong. Money isn't the point.

Is there economy in war? No one argues strongly against paying the cost of war, and yet this disorder of the body politic is necessary only because somebody made mistakes 50 years ago.

Patients' rooms should have southern exposures – all of them. East exposures are not quite so bad, but west exposures – 'never'. The late afternoon sun beats boldly in at the windows, yet much of the day's sunshine is lost. We must situate rooms where they ought to be. It doesn't make sense to place them elsewhere. Some say that the patient is in the hospital for a few days only, so that the exposure of his room is not of vast importance. It may be only a few days, but consider his weakened condition; consider the physical and emotional healing powers of light.

Hospitals belong in the best and most healthful sections of the city. They belong in parks, where the air is purest, away from the smoke screens that smog our cities.

One man will contend that there are mechanical ways of eliminating smoke. True, but there are not mechanical ways of avoiding the noise of railways and elevated lines and heavy vehicular traffic or of removing industrial gases and carbon monoxide from the atmosphere. Hospital planning must be of a piece with city planning. There is no logic in locating a new hospital in the spot where the old one stood. The chances are great that it does not belong there.

Our cities are monstrosities. Small cities have expanded into metropolises and through such unruly growth have managed chiefly to centralise their difficulties. We erect new and taller buildings in the core of our cities and thereby pile up new and taller troubles. Then, so that armies of workers and shoppers can converge upon this congested centre, we bore subways, and they serve enormously to augment our troubles. So chaos is compounded.

Cities have a normal size beyond which they should not be permitted to expand, just as our bodies have a normal size; normal growth is optimum growth. Suppose man shot upward to the height of 15 feet; he would certainly have need of another skeleton.

Paris, London, Berlin, New York, Chicago – there they had freedom to build, and in exercising that freedom their troubles multiplied with their populations.

'What is the optimum size of a city?' Mr Van der Rohe was asked; the interviewer could see that to him hospital planning and city planning are indivisible.

According to some theories, it is 50,000; to others, 500,000. I personally believe we cannot fix the limits. We have to find the one solution appropriate for any situation.

Then this modern planner went on to develop decentralisation – not the decentralisation now taking place in cities, where people move out to the suburbs for sunlight and pure air, for new and comfortable housing, only to find that in 30 or 40 years the suburbs have begotten little slums of their own, but rather a planned and ordered decentralisation.

People talk and argue and gesticulate in defence of this chaos of our cities, of the cramped and unhygienic location of many of our present-day hospitals. Why don't they use a little of this energy to buy Order?

You are not really living in a house or an apartment on Moving Day, with the entire load of household effects dumped into a single room, Mr Van der Rohe pointed out. You plainly, if not silently, suffer there until furniture and equipment are put into their rightful places. The home has its various elements, and the furnishings must be assigned to the elements in which they are to function appropriately.

So it is with cities and with hospital sites within cities; they must be located by plan; nothing must be accidental. The various elements of community life must be composed in the plan, and then all new buildings may rise unashamedly in the right places. In the matter of 40 or 50 years a new city will emerge. In this process there is not even economic waste because without ordered planning almost every building within that length of time will be renewed of modern necessity. Under Order our cities will grow into places where people can work and live healthfully and happily and where they can be treated for disease in environments in which Nature as healer so satisfactorily supplements modern science.

As the general hospital gathers under its motherly wings new fledglings – buildings or wards for convalescents, for long-term patients, for early psychotics – the park site becomes clearly essential. With such extension of services it becomes impossible to disassociate hospitals from parks since recreation, as well as sunlight and pure air, becomes a necessary part of therapy. Those who oppose the inclusion of these groups in the general hospital of the future often do so because they fail to picture the buildings in an ample park environment.

All the talk thus far has concerned city hospitals. How about rural hospitals? How about regional reorganisation?

Mr Van der Rohe is not counting heavily on a postwar airplane service that will swoop up patients from their homes and deposit them politely at a city medical centre. The drama of flight is for emergency service only – to bring the extreme case to the specialist and to specialised equipment or to carry the specialist to the bedside of the remote patient who cannot be moved. To Mr Van der Rohe new discoveries serve to provide us with the possibility of greater differentiation, and it is ridiculous to utilise every medium and every material that we possess. The character of transport should not be out of step with actual needs.

The normal measurement of distance from the farthest patient to a primary unit of hospitalisation is the ability to make the trip for examination or treatment back and forth comfortably in a single day – by motor car, by train, or by boat. This should determine the location of the community hospital or the outpost health station.

For every hospital except large city hospitals, this modern designer disapproves of multi-storey structures. In fact, he does not favour them even in big cities. His park-hospital, in which the number of steps expended daily by nurses is not the chief criterion of the plan, would be of the pavilion or the unit type.

As to the hospital structure, once it is related to a park site with patients' rooms facing south and including a part of the outdoor world, Mr Van der Rohe thinks any clear simple statement of function will provide a pleasing exterior.

In the skeletal building we have found the perfect construction. We need not wait for slow-moving experimentation on promised postwar materials; we can build aesthetically satisfying structures with our present materials. We possess today all the materials that are necessary if we will but make use of them in the right manner.

If the architect sets out to design a building that will be 'different', it will be wrong. To be functional is the first condition of beauty. Reason is the prime principle in architecture, as in medicine. Once having developed and arranged the building's functional elements, then it becomes a question of proportions only. To make the building right for the patient is all that is needed to make it harmonious.

In the end we find that Mr Van der Rohe would like the patient to be at home in the hospital, a desire all hospital administrators share. But homes, as Mr Van der Rohe designs them, are open, not closed. They are wholesomely illuminated by natural sunlight. The rooms seem to extend into the garden plot, and the serenity of the garden seems to step softly into the rooms.

A hospital, if designed in his idiom, would be a place of Order, Light, Space. How is this different from the physician's own prescription for his patients? There would seem to be complete compatibility.

Special mention was given by the contest jury to this small hospital designed by Edward J. Toole of Hingham, Mass. All patients' rooms are located on the south side of the building and give upon a terrace, thus embodying Mr Van der Rohe's concept that in hospitals, as in homes, the rooms should seem to extend into the garden plot, while the serenity of the garden steps softly into the rooms.

Special mention was also given to the design submitted by John C Harkness and Charles D Wiley of Washington DC The plot plan and rendering show that patients' areas are concentrated on the south, and the service facilities, many of which are combined in an inside area necessitating complete air conditioning, are on the north side.

54 [Library and Administration Building, IIT]

Published journal article (1946).
Source: 'Architecture "Speaking for itself". Library and Administration Building IIT', *Architectural Record*, vol. 100, no. 6, December 1946, pp. 85–90.
This is one of several project descriptions for Mies' American buildings that appear to have received direct input from Mies and his office.

When not another single line may be removed, when no part can be more simplified in form or more generalised in use, when nothing can be more accurately placed, Mies van der Rohe is prepared to release a design that may have occupied years of study. It is, as an English writer has declared, 'that sensitivity of line and that precision, purity, and sensitivity of design in general' which 'has placed its author among the handful of contemporary leaders in architecture, in spite of the small amount of work he has executed.'

55 [Book by Philip Johnson]

Published collection of writings (1947).
Source: Philip Johnson, *Mies van der Rohe*, MoMA, New York 1947, pp. 182–197; LoC, Mies, Box 61, Articles About Mies.
The texts included in the collection are the following: 'Two Glass Skyscrapers'; 'Office Building' (as 'The Office Building'); excerpts from 'Office Building' and 'Building' (as 'Aphorisms on Architecture and Form'); 'The Industrialisation of Building Methods'; 'Building Art and the Will of the Epoch' (as 'Architecture and the Times'); 'On Form in Architecture' (as 'A Letter on Form in Architecture'); 'Foreword to Catalogue for the "Die Wohnung" Exhibition' (Policy of the Stuttgart Exposition); 'Concerning my Block' (as 'The Design of Apartment Houses'); 'On the Theme: Exhibitions' (as 'Expositions'); 'The New Time' (as 'The New Era'); 'Art Criticism'; 'Inaugural Address as Director of Architecture at Armour Institute of Technology'; 'A Tribute to Frank Lloyd Wright' (as 'Frank Lloyd Wright'); 'A Museum for a Small City'; 'Architecture and Technology' (in the 1953 reprint). Here we publish the first text, 'Two Glass Skyscrapers', in order to show the freer translation Mies approved for his own texts.

Skyscrapers reveal their bold structural pattern during construction. Only then does the gigantic steel web seem impressive. When the outer walls are put in place, the structural system which is the basis of all artistic design is hidden by a chaos of meaningless and trivial forms. When finished, these buildings are impressive only because of their size; yet they could surely be more than mere examples of our technical ability. Instead of trying to solve the new problems with old forms, we should develop the new forms from the very nature of the new problems.

We can see the new structural principles most clearly when we use glass in place of the outer walls, which is feasible today since in a skeleton building these outer walls do not actually carry weight. The use of glass imposes new solutions.

In my project for a skyscraper at the Friedrichstrasse Station in Berlin I used a prismatic form which seemed to me to fit best the triangular site of the building. I placed the glass walls at slight angles to each other to avoid the monotony of over-large glass surfaces.

I discovered by working with actual glass models that the important thing is the play of reflections and not the effect of light and shadow as in ordinary buildings.

The results of these experiments can be seen in the second scheme published here. At first glance the curved outline of the plan seems arbitrary. These curves, however, were determined by three factors: sufficient illumination of the interior, the massing of the building viewed from the street, and, lastly, the play of reflections. I proved in the glass model that calculations of light and shadow do not help in designing an all-glass building.

The only fixed points of the plan are the stair and elevator shafts. All the other elements of the plan fit the needs of the building and are designed to be carried out in glass.

56 [The IIT Campus]

Note written on a typewriter (9 March 1949).
Source: LoC, Mies, Box 62. Partially used in Peter Carter, 'Mies van der Rohe. An Appreciation on the Occasion, this Month, of his 75th Birthday', *Architectural Design*, March 1961, p. 105; Montreal Museum, Manuscript Division, Ludwig Mies van der Rohe Papers, Box 30 (thanks to Tom Lamberty and Merve Verlag for sharing the typescript). Republished in Walter 2022, pp. 155–157.

Beginning:
No abstract talk – Architecture in action (Hauld)
Imagination – Courage – Simplicity – Spring 1939 – Commission – Survey
Centralisation or Decentralisation
Decentralisation – different needs – money – architectural possibilities
Campus a space problem
Survey analysis
Classroom – Drafting rooms – laboratories – lecturerooms – shops – 24 by 24 or more – Switzerland and Sweden
Not across the campus – model for design – garuatis [sic] for order – woodblocks – numerous possibilities – first scheme
Dearborn Street
Larger areas more freedom – Dearborn Street – Changing needs – more buildings – Armour Research Foundation – athletic field
Decision on new plan
Metals Research Building – type of construction – Steel Brick and Glass Factory – Not much talk about architecture – First Metallurgy Building – Huge hall with laboratories – change in the programme – many clessrooms – lectureroom – laboratory hall – 2-storey building
Decision of building type – importance of this decision – would decide the character of the Campus – efficiency of work, first principle – Efficiency depends on flexibility – So it was clear that we would use the

Skeleton construction – Skeleton depends on 2 materials – Steel and concrete – Superiority of Skeleton – Economic Reason – Generally accepted – Never clearly expressed.

Only a clear expression of the structure could give us an architectural solution which would last. We had to be sure of that.

We anticipated a building period of ten years. And we could think that the first buildings would be outmoded before the last was finished. We wanted an honest expression of what is going on inside. An expression of the sincere work of a great scientific and technological institution. There was no doubt that this could be done. The Administration and Student Union building confronted us with another problem. Since I wanted these two buildings in the centre of the campus to have a more monumental character – an expression of the dignity of a great institution. Could that be done with the same means? That was a real question. I designed this building three years ago. *[...]* This building is at the moment in the centre of discussions in architectural circles all over the world. That shows its importance. I said before that when we started, we anticipated a building period of ten years.

These ten years are gone by now. It may take us ten more years to finish the campus. But I am not afraid of that. It will not be outmoded. For two reasons: it is radical and conservative at once. It is radical in accepting the driving and sustaining forces of our time – Science and Technology. It has a scientific character, but it is not science. It uses technological means, but it is not Technology. It is conservative as it is not only concerned with a purpose but also with a meaning, as it is not only concerned with a function but also with an expression. It is conservative as it is based on the eternal laws of architecture: Order, Space, and Proportion.

57 Campus Design

Published interview (April 1949).
Source: Mildred E. Whitcombe, 'Campus Design: an Interview with Mies van der Rohe', *College Business*, vol. VI, no. 4, April 1949, pp. 12–15. Republished in Pizzigoni 2010, pp. 119–122.

In ten years you may not recognise your own campus from its 1949 photographs. [...] When President [Henry] Heald of the Illinois Institute of Technology commissioned the director of his architecture department, Ludwig Mies van der Rohe, to design the new campus, Mr Van der Rohe, one of the several great German-American architects, and his staff made a survey of the needs of each department. The results showed that most of them had the same general requirements: classrooms, laboratories, draughting rooms, shops, lecture rooms.

The professor of architecture next determined the optimum size of classroom and laboratory, arriving at a module of 24 feet. He then drew a 24-by-24-foot net across the campus plot, and in this net he designed clusters of single buildings.

Whether to erect one enormous structure (or perhaps two very large buildings) or to decentralise was a problem given initial study. The decision to decentralise was based on three points: each smaller building could be more accurately tailored to its special needs; to acquire successive sums of $600,000 or $800,000 for smaller buildings would be simpler and quicker than to accumulate several millions for a college Pentagon Building; and the aesthetic possibilities would be greater owing to a nice use of courts, walks, and landscaping features.

Even had the centralised plan been adopted, the skyscraper treatment was taboo. Mr Van der Rohe considers the skyscraper an inappropriate expression of the educational enterprise.

On a campus not strictly metropolitan but located in a rolling, tree-shaded park, suburb, or the countryside, Mr Van der Rohe would have evolved a less symmetrical plan, taking his cue from the natural contours.

In the Illinois Tech plan the architectural personality of the buildings is derived from the nature of the curriculum. Emphasis on science and technology seems to call for directness and sincerity of expression. With two larger structures, the administration building and the union, another characteristic is achieved, that of dignity.

The 24-foot-square classroom is the basic unit of the enlarged Illinois Tech campus. The laboratory is one and one-and-a-half or two 24-foot modules in length and one, two, or four modules in width. Shops may be two or three bays wide and as long as needed. Office space consists of the basic classroom unit divided by two.

This inherent flexibility means much to an institution with a prewar enrolment of 2500 and a present enrolment of 7000. If necessary, it can expand farther; with equal ease it can be converted as space requirements change and as technology swings forward with giant strides.

One principal characteristic of modern architecture is the skeleton system. Nearly all our larger buildings are skeleton buildings. Windows and walls merely fill in the space between the steel framing members. Use of the steel form allows great expanses of glass; brick walls need be only curtain walls.

Mies van der Rohe's buildings at Illinois Tech and elsewhere differ from many others in the modern system in that the skeleton is exposed. As in all true Modern buildings, the essential elements are expressed; nothing is formalistic; all is honest and forthright. Ornament and all else that fails to make sense are eliminated.

'You maintain that modern architecture costs less. How is that?' Mr Van der Rohe was asked.

The module system, being repetitive, reduces construction costs. The simplicity of a modern building is another saving factor; all decorative solutions are usually more expensive.

The exposed skeleton and the non-load-bearing walls are economies. At Illinois Tech we use large expanses of glass, but it is not double or triple glass. We feel that this extra expense is unnecessary. We bring the steel mullions inside and outside in one piece – that brings down cost.

Our buildings are strictly fireproof, and this is reflected in the insurance rates.

More important, our buildings fit the educational programme. The greatest efficiency in education is the greatest economy. We don't even need to measure the cost in dollars. If a building serves the programme of today and is flexible enough to serve tomorrow's programme too, it is really economical.

As to maintenance, spartan simplicity in planning and wise selection and frank use of materials make for ease and economy, *Mr Van der Rohe asserts.*

For example, we had planned to use brick for the interior walls, but we switched to plaster because it was cheaper. That was a false economy. A student drapes his lanky figure against the wall like this – *Mr Van der Rohe puts his hands behind him, rests his head, back, and palms against the plaster, and plants the sole of one brown shoe just above the baseboard.* – In the end it would have been cheaper to use a brick wall that would wash.

'Do you favour radiant heating for college buildings?' the former Bauhaus director was asked.

Certainly not for laboratories, *he came back instantly.* There it is a dangerous practice. You never know at what moment the laboratory director may demand a hole in a floor or ceiling to accommodate something promising in new equipment. With radiant heating coils in floor or ceiling, his hands and your hands are tied.

Why do so many universities that have schools or departments of architecture step outside the walls for a campus designer, Mr Van der Rohe?

Some of it is rejection of the new, provided the school is attempting to interpret our own times. The trustees personally may resent the new architecture, just as the first Gothic buildings must have been viewed as intruders in the Romanesque surroundings. Too, the trustees know they will have to defend their choice of Modern against attack from powerful segments of the alumni, although it has actually come to pass here and there within the last year that approval of traditional campus designs requires stronger defence by boards and building committees.

A more logical basis for opposition is that some architectural schools or departments do not maintain an architectural office. They are not set up as practising professionals. All our schools need better staff men.

Suppose an architect is commissioned to design one building on a traditional campus. Should he make it wholly modern, or should it be transitional in an effort to tie it in with the older style or styles?

If the architect is not well schooled in the new idiom, he may turn out not a truly modern design but a 'modernistic' design, *the master planner explained*. In that case almost anyone will immediately feel the contrast between the old and new. 'Modernistic' is a kind of formalism – what is normally called 'style.' You can't build a campus in the manner of the fashion. The first building will be outmoded before the last is finished.

However, if the new building on the old campus is modern in the true and accepted sense, it will fit in with older buildings. In the design it becomes chiefly a matter of scale. If the scale is correct in relation to adjacent structures, the result will be a harmony.

These days, the better schools are turning out many fine fledglings in modern architecture, and to give them practical experience there exists a limited but growing number of architectural firms capable of sound modern design and construction. To these firms or to pioneer consultants more and more colleges will turn for an apt expression of their educational ideas and ideals through campus architecture.

There is an unconscious compatibility between modern architecture and the goal of education, Mr Van der Rohe concludes. A college can't teach its students experience – they must get that on the job. A college exists to teach the fundamental principles only.

If students are surrounded by a building or by a group of buildings expressed in terms of simple elements and the first principles of design, this environmental influence should be reflected in the students' search for first principles and should result in the triumph of reason over rote.

58 What Should a Church Look Like?

Radio interview (1–2 April 1950).
Source: LoC, Box 57, University of Chicago; LoC, Box 61, Miscellaneous. Mies joined the round table on the subject 'What Should a Church Look Like?', followed by a recording session at the Mitchell Tower Studios, Radio Office, University of Chicago on 1 April with an additional recording session on 2 April. The round table organised by George E. Probst of the University of Chicago was moderated by Mr Christ-Janer.
The recording was not found on file. Here we publish a transcription of Mies' preparatory notes.

1) What should a Church look like? About the Appearance.
2) What should a Church be? About the Essence.
The inner structure. Its True Expression. With the Means of our time.
3) Collection of Churches of the last 20 years.
Desperate confusion. Confusion not only as architectural expression. A confusion in general thinking and acting.
4) Let us go back to the question about the Essence. That is certainly not a question the architect can answer.
Let me ask our theologians what they think about that. After we know more about the essence or the inner structure, we could ask how to build this structure. Only then are we confronted with an architectural problem.
Two talks with two bishops. The one ping pong. The other fear of fashion.
Subjective and objective.

The question of truth. The significance of facts. The construction as the truest guardian of the spirit of a time.
Real material. Real construction. Its expression. Spirituality. Sublimation. Radiance of Truth. Hierarchy. United nation and a small church.
Monumentality. A question of dignity, of not heaviness.

Order. Is the disposition of equal and unequal things attributing to each its place.
Veritas est adequatio intellectus et rei / Truth is the concordance of the intellect *[and]* the thing. Truth is the significance of the facts.

A human attitude is a symbolical attitude.
Impressive – effective.
Symbolism or symbol. Real symbol as expression of intrinsic qualities. Symbolism is allegory.

59 Architecture and Technology

Speech and published magazine article (17 April 1950).
Source: LMvdR, 'Architectur und Technik', *Der Aufbau*, vol. X, no. 2, February–March 1952, p. 41.
Address at the Blackstone Hotel on the occasion of the celebration of the addition of the Institute of Design to Illinois Institute of Technology. On this occasion, after Mies had spoken, Serge Chermayeff and Walter Gropius also gave speeches.
Republished in Johnson 1953, pp. 203–204; Neumeyer (1986) 1991, p. 324; Pizzigoni 2010, pp. 123–124; Walter 2022, pp. 116–117.

Technology is rooted in the past.
It dominates the present and tends into the future.
It is a real historical movement – one of the great movements which shape and represent their epoch.
It can be compared only with the classical discovery of man as a person, the Roman will to power, and the religious movement of the Middle Ages.
Technology is far more than a method; it is a world in itself.
As a method, it is superior in almost every respect.
But only where it is left to itself, as in gigantic structures of engineering, does it reveal its true nature.
There it is evident that it is not only a useful means – that it is something, something in itself, something that has a meaning and a powerful form, so powerful in fact that it is not easy to name it.
Is that still technology, or is it architecture?
And that may be the reason why some people are convinced that architecture will be outmoded and replaced by technology.
Such a conviction is not based on clear thinking. The opposite happens.
Wherever technology reaches its real fulfilment, it transcends into architecture.
It is true that architecture depends on facts, but its real field of activity is in the realm of significance.
I hope you will understand that architecture has nothing to do with the invention of forms. It is not a playground for children, young or old. Architecture is the real battleground of the spirit.
Architecture wrote the history of the epochs and gave them their names.
Architecture depends on its time.
It is the crystallisation of its inner structure, the slow unfolding of its form.
That is the reason why technology and architecture are so closely related.
Our real hope is that they grow together, that someday the one will be the expression of the other.
Only then will we have an architecture worthy of its name:
Architecture as a true symbol of our time.

60 Broaden Vision, Architects Urged

Published newspaper interview (21 April 1950).
Source: James Benet, 'Broaden Vision, Architects Urged', *San Francisco Chronicle*, vol. 170, no. 99, 21 April 1950.
Republished in Pizzigoni 2010, pp. 125–126; Walter 2022, p. 118–119.

Architects must broaden their vision beyond single buildings to their whole communities and the immense modern problems of humanity, they were told yesterday.
J Robert Oppenheimer, director of the Institute of Advanced Studies at Princeton, [… during] a session of the American Institute of Architects convention [in San Francisco, said]: 'It is part of the architect's job to give expression and meaning to human aspiration and human life, to recognise and create order and above all a kind of public order, an order which will not be limited to one community but extend to all who have converse with their buildings, their structures and their cities.'
The same point was made at a press conference in a vigorously matter-of-fact way by the second speaker, Ludwig Mies van der Rohe, who will receive the AIA's highest award, its gold medal, at a dinner here tonight.
People want to live in the country – I always wanted to live in the country myself – but we have to live in the city, he said. And the city is so ugly. There is no reason why it can't be really fine and good. We are only at the beginning of the new architecture. But we can't just let things grow up in the old way; we must plan on a large scale, large and complex projects. *[…]*
It is the immense and fast-rising cost of downtown land which makes such large buildings and large projects necessary, Mies said, *and he gave instances of cites in his own experience that doubled in million-dollar values within three years.*

61 The Training of Architects

Published note transmitted by telegram (June 1950).
Source: Nikolaus Pevsner, 'The Training of Architects: Interim Survey', *The Architectural Review*, vol. 107, no. 642, June 1950, p. 371.

[…] Visualisation of space must be supported by structural knowledge. Design without sufficient structural knowledge will result in dilettantism. For this reason we make construction a prerequisite to architectural planning. *[…]*

62 People Who Live in Glass Apartments Throw Verbal Stones at Scoffers

Published newspaper interview (28 September 1951).
Source: Grace Miller, 'People Who Live in Glass Apartments Throw Verbal Stones at Scoffers', *The Christian Science Monitor*, Boston, vol. 43, no. 258, 28 September 1951, p. 7.
Republished in Pizzigoni 2010, pp. 127–129; Walter 2022, p. 120.

Mies van der Rohe's glass apartments on Chicago's Lake Shore Drive are winning hearty 'ayes' from their first tenants. [...] Mr Van der Rohe wanted, for instance, to give city apartment dwellers the feeling of living close to the out of doors, as people in suburbs do who have floor-to-ceiling picture windows in their houses. The lake-front location seemed ideal for glass apartments.
Plate-glass walls are practical, Mies van der Rohe claims. Contrary to what the uninitiated think, it is the steel skeleton of a building that gives it stability, not the brick walls. The outer walls, he says, *do not actually carry weight.*
In this view the real structure of any building is its framework. He tried to preserve the beauty of its lines, and not clutter or cover them with unnecessary overlays of brick or other opaque materials. When some learned architectural contemporaries warn that the doctrine of structural integrity can be carried to extremes – that too great severity sacrifices formal beauty and the gay and pleasant of past architectural patterns – Mr Van der Rohe laughs. He appreciates the challenge.
I don't know, *he says, with a delighted grin,* whether we will ever add 'flowers' to glass-and-steel buildings. Decoration is another element.
Our time is governed by science and technology. If technology is a guiding influence today, architecture will have a technological character, not a decorative one. We should ask for a clear structure, and not care how it looks.

Should there be much repetition of this type of building, the effect need not be boring, *he claims.*
There are about 10,000 species of seashells, *he says*, but only one spiral shell construction in all of them. The difference is in the rate of growth. When the shells grow fast, they become flat. When they grow slowly, they become round.
Gothic architecture has lasted through the years and is still good, Mr Van der Rohe thinks, because it had a structural approach. Every line was designed, he explains, to carry the eye upward – to give a feeling of verticality and lightness. Baroque architecture, on the other hand, he claims, was not a beginning but an end. Its aim is to be decorative.
In the glass apartments the steel mullions ordinarily set behind windows run outside, to form vertical accents. There are 3000 windows. The mullions serve somewhat, too, as wind braces.
Some architects have questioned what lake-front weather may do to the buildings because there are no louvers (or windshield wipers) over the windows. The answer is that water sometimes climbs up a window if it rains hard enough or there is a strong wind. Louvers, then, would do no good, it is argued. Instead, windows in the glass apartments have double weather stripping. For winter heating there are convector coils beneath the windows and radiant heat coils in the ceilings. Each apartment controls its own heat individually. Neutral window shades are supplied to all tenants, so there is a unified appearance to the outside of the buildings. Inside, families can decorate as they choose. Modern, traditional, or provincial furnishings go equally well with the simple architectural pattern of the apartments, interior decorators find.
Each apartment has a steel kitchen. On the ground floor there is to be a grocery and a mail room. There are complete electric laundries and frozen-food lockers. An underground garage has stalls for 116 cars. Any overflow, it is hoped, can be taken care of on adjoining vacant land. [...]

63 Six Students Talk With Mies

Published interview (spring 1952).
Source: 'Six Students Talk With Mies', *Student Publications of the School of Design (North Carolina State College)*, vol. II, no. 3, spring 1952, pp. 21–28.
Republished in Pizzigoni 2010, pp. 130–136; Walter 2022, pp. 121–133.

In what way, specifically, do you train your young architects to understand technology. Do you encourage them going out into industry?
We try to train and educate them at the same time. To train them to do something and to educate them to understand what they are doing and what they should do.
Do you think you can take students in a college and they can be trained to became architects, or is it a process that is peculiar to each individual?
They can be trained to a certain degree. I think everybody can be trained to a certain degree, but he has to grow at the same time.
In other words, the training part consists of the use of his tools, but, beyond that, he must train himself and grow?
Certainly.
I know that same students feel that architectural schools in general are really teaching a craft rather than a profession. They are not teaching architecture any longer in the sense of the master builders of the past. I think we both agree that this is very important.
Certainly. You know, it is very difficult to train and educate somebody to be a master builder. I think that in the medieval times they had to start as an apprentice and then they learned something and then they worked more and more and became a master, and so on; there was a great tradition. The trouble nowadays is that there is no tradition whatsoever.
We haven't accepted a tradition, but actually this is our heritage. Don't you feel we should continue from that basis rather than cast it aside and start a new one? I don't believe we can start a new one.

No, certainly not. But to understand it is another thing. Some people, when they see a cathedral, think it is a grand idea. A caprice. But that is not so. It is the logical consequence of what the Romanesque master builder formed when he tried to build a solid roof on the cathedrals.
Do you feel the single greatest characteristic of our society is our technology?
Yes. Some people think our problem is the human situation today, but that is a general problem. That is not an architectural problem. That is a sociological problem.
In what way specifically, should the architect be acquainted with technology, and do you feel he should be actively engaged in determining its future nature?
You know, technology is neutral. It can go for good or evil. It can be used for good or evil, and architecture should use it for the good, not let it go.
Nor resort to older handicraft methods?
Yes.
Do you feel, as we are often forced to feel as young architects, that architecture is part of a parasite on society, and the way bankers, financiers, and real estate men move around, we are just called in as bystanders who are going to take whatever they give us and do something with it. I know you are not in that position, but you no doubt can understand how we feel.
You know, there are, in the whole structure of civilisation, some facts which are given which cannot be changed. Facts which come from the past. Some have done something, and it has influence. We can lead and guide these factors of reality, but we cannot change them.
You mean we cannot change the character of reality, but we can change its direction?
Yes, but our effect is quite limited because these facts take their ultimate way.
What you mean is that you may for a time force a deviation, but eventually they will fall back into their former line of force.
Yes. That is a mistake many people make. They believe they can change reality, but that is not the case.

To get back to the question of technology. As an example, let us consider the Gothic period, which had a very logical development and was the solution of a functional problem. Do you think the attempts of the Gothic architects to achieve verticality and use stone in pure compression were entirely due to the idea of solving a vaulting problem, or do you feel that the religious fervour of the period was also instrumental?
It may have had an influence on finding a way of doing things. All these factors of reality and ideology are interplaying, but in fact the reality is all-important. For instance, the Romanesque architects could have said that the wooden roof was good enough, but technology, for instance, in our time, depends on the masses and the masses depend on technology. We could not live otherwise. And technology is what we see. Our whole way of seeing and thinking is determined by it. For instance, we like a very simple glass. We take preference to the simple form, the technological form.
Yes, but as you were talking of St Thomas Aquinas and logic in your seminar, a thought kept running through my mind about the distinction between logic and emotion. Logic is not only an analytic state of mind.
Yes, but you can prove something logical by reason. You cannot prove feelings. Everyone has emotions, and this is the hell of our time. Everyone says they have a right to their opinion, but they really only have the right to express their opinion.
However, in attempting to prove something by reason don't you feel that you are guided along a certain path by intuition? Logically, one might not be able to determine an ultimate result by any of its effects. Intuitively, however, you feel one or another direction is proper. Once you have determined your course, you may begin applying reason.
Why, certainly, I often experience that my thoughts have to be controlled by the work I have done. Sometimes, out of the work I have done I have a certain direction. I am convinced of the importance of technology, but that was a long process. I could not read it in a book, and it wasn't dessert served on a lunch plate. Little by little, one thought is put to another. One is doubtful of a thousand things in this process, but by experience and logic you may build upon these thoughts until you achieve a real conviction, and in the end you have such a strong conviction that no one or anything in the world could change it. That is the way it has to be. I don't know if I told you about the time I had 3000 books in Germany. I spent a fortune to buy those books, and I spent a fortune to read them, to study them. I brought 300 books with me to America, and I can now send 270 books back and I would lose nothing. But I would not have these 30 left if I had not read the 3000.
In the real analysis those book rejections were as valuable as the ones you kept because they provided you with a very valuable negative knowledge.
Most certainly. It is exactly what research means. Research does not mean to get only positive results but rather to get at the facts. I don't know if someone told me or I heard it on the radio concerning this story of Edison. His assistant was deploring the failure of 800 experiments on filaments for electric lamps and the resulting waste of time. Edison said, 'What! Waste of time? We have proved that 800 things do not work.'
That is saying in essence that any success is a compilation of failures.
Yes, that may be said.
I'm glad you brought up this question of people having the right to their opinion because that is one of the misconceptions of a democracy.
Yes, but we must organise our considerations in a more concrete manner. In a democracy we have the right to express our opinion, but as human beings, we have the duty to formulate a clear opinion. Not just some assumption out of the clear blue sky.
Yes, but the general masses conclude that since everyone has the right to his own opinion, every man's opinion is as good as the next man's. It really is an encouraging thing to find two people who have a great

deal of faith in technology and in man's ability to control his thoughts, his actions, and his environment, for instance, as Mr [Buckminster] Fuller and yourself, and arrive at completely different solutions to their problems while completely within the framework of technology.

Why, certainly. The whole world is similar. There are fir trees and pine trees growing in the same environment.

For example, there are millions of solutions to the same problem.

I would say there are a variety. Somewhat they are limited. Let us take the closed plan and the open plan. In designing a house you could use the open plan and develop one, two, three, maybe ten solutions. With a closed plan you would find that you can produce one, two, three, maybe ten solutions. You know, people think with the open plan we can do everything – but that is not the fact. It is merely another conception of space. The problem of space will limit your solutions. Chaos is not space. Often I have observed my students, who act as though you can take the free-standing wall out of your pocket and throw it anywhere. That is not the solution to space. That would not be space.

The problem of accuracy always presents itself when you think of Mies van der Rohe. One gets the idea that there is an exact place for each element in a building and it must be exact. However, there is a certain magnitude of accuracy. How close does it have to be? In talking to a number of your students, they have discussed how they work for days upon the preciseness of a composition. I wonder if that preoccupation with accuracy is the fundamental thing, or whether it is superfluous to the real concept.

If you have the conception, why should it not be executed with the greatest accuracy?

I am only trying to get it straight whether you may not have the conception without the extreme accuracy.

You could, but it would not be an accurate expression of your conception. Accuracy is not the conception, but you must have the clearest expression to get at the essences. Take a sentence. When I have a thought and try to express it, I work on it and I work on it and I work on it. May I repeat a few sentences from what I read at the close of my seminars?

'Architecture depends upon its time; it is the crystallisation of its inner structure.' I worked on these sentences for weeks. It is not just saying things. It is thinking them. Let me give you another example.

'Form must be the form of the mind, the manner not of saying things but of thinking them.' John [*sic*] Cocteau said that. I have something else. 'Construction, the framework, so to speak, is the surest guarantee of the mysterious life of the works of the mind.' 'Everything that is beautiful and noble is the result of reason and calculation.' Now tell me who said that? [Charles] Baudelaire, the French poet. Even he thinks construction is important. Only the architect does not think so.

Whenever one thinks of exhibition buildings, one thinks of the Barcelona Pavilion. What social implications do you feel exhibitions have?

Philip Johnson's book on me contains my thoughts concerning the nature of exhibitions, and I still believe in them, so if you read his book, it would answer this question *[see Philip Johnson,* Mies van der Rohe *(New York: the Museum of Modern Art), 1953]*. I will tell you a story of the Barcelona Pavilion, however, which might interest you. One evening as I was working late on that building, I made a sketch of a free-standing wall, and I got a shock. I knew that it was a new principle.

I'm glad you mentioned that because I'm sure you are aware that the general conception exists that your architecture comes from the intellect and therefore is very cold and calculating. However, we are aware, and this statement is a confirmation, that this idea is incorrect.

I am not a sentimentalist. The so-called humanists say that. They should define what is human. Let me ask a question. Do they have a patent on humanity? I'm living too. I have talked to people like that and asked them why they think they are the only ones who are human. But one thing is sure. I am not a sentimentalist.

When you say you got a shock, it is obvious that such an experience is extremely emotional, and this immediately puts the lie to these rather uninformed statements.

Certainly. The shock is emotional, but the projection into reality is by the intellect.

I was very interested in your statement that you were not doing furniture anymore because you could not find anyone to make models. Real craftsmen.

Yes. In Europe you find many small shops to do this type of work. In our country the large factories are interested in terms of 100,000 chairs. They are not interested in getting chairs but in making them. I have used many modern chairs, and I become tired after 10 or 15 minutes. When I made a chair, I sat in it for hours. I did not answer the phone or anything because I wanted to discover when I would get tired. A simple ordinary old-fashioned chair such as the one you are sitting upon *[a high-back maple chair with some seat]* is more comfortable than most modern chairs. You do not become tired because you can move a little. In the modern chairs you cannot move. The angle prevents movement.

You have to leave now, but before you go, let me express my deepest gratitude for your consent to this interview, and be assured that you leave us with a great amount of respect. We sincerely hope you will return soon.

64 [Mies' New Buildings]

Published excerpts of interview (November 1952).
Source: 'Mies van der Rohe', *Architectural Forum*, vol. 97, no. 5, November 1952, pp. 93–111; Walter 2022, pp. 134–137.

[…] His biggest interest is in what he calls 'the structure'. But we are not decorating, he says. This is structure. We put up what has to be built, and then we accept it. This acceptance, however, is not pure complaisance to structural engineering. […]

He is an admirer of Louis Sullivan, his historical predecessor in straight steel building in Chicago, but he does not observe the ringing dictum 'form follows function'. We do the opposite. We reverse this, and make a practical and satisfying shape, and then fit the functions into it. Today this is the only practical way to build because the functions of most buildings are continually changing, but economically the buildings cannot change.

[…] In a world which each month sees more Mies-like structures built here are some real Mies buildings by the man who has said I hope you will understand that architecture has nothing to do with the inventions of forms. It is not a playground for children, young or old. Architecture is the real battleground of the spirit. *Mies should know; he has been there.*

860 Lake Shore Drive is a pair of 26-storey, steel-and-glass cooperative apartments that stand by Lake Michigan on one of the choicest sites, both naturally and socially, in Chicago. […] This stirring pair of apartment towers was built for a very sober price. Pace Associates, who were collaborators in the design and construction with Holsman, Holsman, Klekamp & Taylor and Mies – Without them, *he says*, it would never have been built *– reported the construction cost per square foot as $10.38. They point out that this is 5 to 10% below the cost of most conventional apartment houses in Chicago. […]*

The repetitive vertical use of steel sections across the exterior walls of the apartment towers has raised the eyebrows of some architects, who say they are surprised at Mies because this is not entirely 'functional' (the steel sections occur not only at window divisions but also on the columns of the building frame). These have been called pilasters, usually by people who do not like pilasters. But there could not be an explanation for them more functionally honest than Mies'. He says: Now, first, I am going to tell you the real reason, and then I am going to tell you a good reason by itself.

It was very important to preserve and extend the rhythm which the mullions set up on the rest of the building. We looked at it on the model without the steel section attached to the corner column, and it did not look right. Now, the other reason is that this steel section was needed to stiffen the plate which covers the corner column so this plate would not ripple, and also we needed it for strength when the sections were hoisted into place. Now, of course, that's a very 'good' reason, *he laughs*, but the other reason is the real reason.

[...] The same basic structure used in 860 Lake Shore Drive was also projected for a small four-storey office building to be erected in the Midwest; it emphasises Mies' feeling that the proportions of structural members are not dictated only by the height of the structure. He accepts the strength of steel as a useful generality and lets his sense of proportion set the exact sizes – checked by engineers, of course. Mies wanted to build this of stainless steel, which he prefers to black-painted steel. He would still maintain the depth of surface with outstanding mullions, however. [...] Illinois Institute of Technology [...] now partially complete [...] is constructed on the same grid module, with bays of 12 or 24 feet. [...] Orderliness is the real reason, *he shrugs, and then smiles.* But of course, if you ever have to fill in a space, it's good to have it in this way. With the standard column spacings you don't have to reach for your buttonhole. It is there.

[...] He says about the design of the buildings of the campus, It was the biggest decision I ever had to make. It was more than ten years ago that we started, and by now it was all supposed to be finished – but of course, it will be another 12 years yet. And you know, if you build one building, you can go away and leave it. But 25 years is a long time these days – and I know our way of building has to reach across this time and not become out of style. And we do not have a lot of money. The gifts do not come $10 million at a time, and perhaps this is good because if a man gives $10 million, maybe he wants to say what the building looks like. But if you give only $10,000 or $20,000 towards a building that is going to cost $200,000, you are perhaps willing to let someone else say what it should look like. *[...]*

65 [Commons Building, IIT]

Typewritten project report (circa 1953).
Source: MoMA, Mies, IIT, folder 113.
While the author is not named, we assume, given the context, that it was Mies.
Republished in Pizzigoni 2010, pp. 145–146.

This building is designed to serve the students and faculty residents of the dormitory and apartment buildings at the Illinois Institute of Technology, Technology Center, Chicago, Illinois.

The 96-by-168-foot building provides 32,000 square feet of floor area, divided between basement with nine-foot ceiling and main floor with 16-foot ceiling. Foundations and basement are of reinforced concrete, with superstructure of structural steel frame, forming 32-by-24-foot bays.

The exterior walls have seven feet of buff face brick, then a two-foot band of moveable sash, on top of which is seven feet of quarter-inch polished plate glass set in steel frames. On two sides of the building are 72-foot-long sections completely of glass to the height of 16 feet so that of the entire exterior two-thirds is glass.

Roof is pre-cast concrete panels covered with two inches of rigid insulation, then four-ply roofing finish with tar and gravel. There is mechanical ventilation in cafeteria and basement, natural ventilation in the stores. Heat is provided by forced-flow convectors around perimeter of building, with centre section using hot air from mechanical vent above kitchen core. There are no permanent structural partitions in the building, all interior dividers being removeable for re-arranging space units to meet future variations in campus requirements. Dividing walls are of unpolished plate glass to seven feet, with polished plate glass above. Stores are separated by seven-foot-high walls of fine-finished, lightweight concrete block.

On the grade floor, in addition to the cafeteria-style dining room accommodating 160, are stores for books, drugs, valet, post office, currency exchange, barber shop, self-service market, and medical suite. The basement has lounge services, storage space, and provision for a bowling alley.

66 A Chapel, IIT

Published journal article (January 1953).
Source: LMvdR, 'A Chapel. Illinois Institute of Technology', *Arts and Architecture*, vol. LXX, no. 1, January 1953, pp. 18–19.
Republished in Neumeyer 1991, p. 328; Pizzigoni 2010, pp. 143–144; Walter 2022, pp. 138–139.

I chose an intensive rather than an extensive form to express my conception, simply and honestly, of what a sacred building should be. By that I mean a church or chapel should identify itself rather than rely upon the spiritual associations of a traditional fashion in architecture, such as the Gothic. But the same motives of respect and nobility are present in both instances. [...]

I know there are those who may take exception to the chapel, but it was designed for the students and staff at the school. They will understand it.

Architecture should be concerned with the epoch, not the day. The chapel will not grow old ... It is of noble character, constructed of good materials, and has beautiful proportions ... it is done as things should be done today, taking advantage of our technological means. The men who did the Gothic churches achieved the best they could with their means.

Too often, we think of architecture in terms of the spectacular. There is nothing spectacular about this chapel; it was not meant to be spectacular. It was meant to be simple; and, in fact, it is simple. But in its simplicity it is not primitive but noble, and in its smallness it is great – in fact, monumental. I would not have built the chapel differently if I had had a million dollars to do it.

67 The End of the Bauhaus

Published magazine interview (spring 1953).
Source: 'The End of the Bauhaus', *North Carolina State University School of Design*, vol. 3, no. 3, spring 1953; also LoC, Mies, Box 62, Interview With Mies, 'transcribed as it was told to six students of the School of Design'.
See 'Interview with Peter Blake' (text 99. p. 221) for comparison.
Republished in Pizzigoni 2010, pp. 137–142; Walter 2022, pp. 140–146.

I became director of the Bauhaus only because *[Walter]* Gropius came one morning with the mayor of Dessau *[Fritz Hesse]* and told me, 'The school will break to pieces if you don't take it.' He said that if I took it over, it would go ahead. And later, in 1932, the Nazis came. Nobody's position was strong enough for that. In 1933 I closed the Bauhaus. Maybe that is interesting to you.

You know the rise of the Nazi movement was not so sudden. It began at Dessau. That was the first state that became by election Nazi. After the Nazis came to power, the mayor told me they wanted to see what the Bauhaus was doing and so on. They wanted an exhibition for criticism, and he said, 'I know you would like a vacation for two weeks. I am delighted to give you a vacation,' and I said, 'No. I'd like to stay here. I'd like to see these people.' And I did.

Then they came. It was a long talk. There was one man; his name was *[Paul]* Schultze-Naumburg, and he wrote early on, you know, about 1900, works on cultural tendencies in general *[a series of books titled 'Deutsche Kulturarbeiten' (German ideas about culture)]*, about old buildings and about the factories ruining the country – sentimental, aesthetic, typical of the misunderstanding of his day. He wanted to change. He wanted to save wonderful towns. You cannot save wonderful towns; you can only save wonderful towns by building new ones. That's all you can do. He was a man in the Nazi movement, very old with a gold medal *[a gold party badge, which only the early members of the party had]*. There were only about 90 that had these gold medals. He was one of these men. And he came, and we gave an exhibition at the Bauhaus. I tried everything, to keep that in order. And we made a wonderful exhibition, and I had a heck of a time, you know, with *[Wassily]* Kandinsky. Kandinsky had his constructions of old pictures, these geometric analyses. I said, 'Do we have to show these?' And he had a fit. So I said, 'Keep it.' And we put it on the table that was in the centre of a huge room. Everything was around, and this analysis was on the table. When these people came, we had a talk, and then I showed them what we were doing. I moved them, you know, around the walls. They never saw the table.

It was then I knew it was absolutely hopeless. It was a political movement. It had nothing to do with reality and nothing to do with art. I had nothing to lose, nothing to win, you know. I didn't want to win. But now we talk about what really happened in the end. The city of Dessau decided to close the Bauhaus. They stopped us, and they said, 'You have to go.' The mayor, who loved the Bauhaus and wanted to help us, said, 'Take all the machinery, all the weaving looms, and just leave.'

So I rented a factory in Berlin. I did that on my own. It cost me 27,000 marks for three years. It cost 9000 marks a year. That was a lot of money in Germany, nothing in America. So I rented this factory that was terrible, black. We started to work – all of us – every student. Many Americans who were with us will remember that we cleaned it all up and painted everything white. This was a solid, simple factory painted clean – wonderful, you know. And just on the outside, on the street, there was a broken-down wooden fence, closed. You couldn't see the building. And I can assure you there were a lot of people who when they came there and saw this fence, went home. But the good ones, they came through and stayed. They didn't care about the fence. We had a wonderful group of students.

One morning, I had to come from Berlin in the streetcar and walk a little, and I had to pass over the bridge from which you could see our building; I nearly died. It was so wrong. Our wonderful building was surrounded by Gestapo–black uniforms, with bayonets. It was really surrounded. I ran to be there. And a sentry said, 'Stop here.' I said, 'What? This is my factory. I rented it. I have a right to see it.'

'You are the owner? Come in. Come in.' He knew I never would come out if they didn't want me to. Then I went and talked to the officer. I said, 'I am the director of this school,' and he said, 'Oh, come in,' and we talked some more, and he said, 'You know there was an affair against the mayor of Dessau, and we are just investigating the documents of the founding of the Bauhaus.' I said, 'Come in.' I called all the people and said, 'Open everything for inspection, open everything.' I was certain there was nothing there that could be misinterpreted.

The investigation took hours. In the end the Gestapo became so tired and hungry that they called their headquarters and said, 'What should we do? Should we work here forever? We are hungry,' and so on. And they were told, 'Lock it and forget it.'

Then I called up Alfred Rosenberg *[author of* Der Mythus des XX. Jahrhunderts, *the bible of Nazi philosophy]*. He was the party philosopher of the Nazi culture, and he was the head of the movement. It was called 'Bund Deutsche Kultur' *[Kampfbund für deutsche Kultur – 'Militant League for German Culture']*. I called him up and said, 'I want to talk with you.' He said, 'I am very busy.'

'I understand that, but even so, at any time you tell me I will be there.'

'Could you be here at eleven o'clock tonight?'

'Certainly.'

My friends *[Ludwig]* Hilberseimer and Lilly Reich and some other people said, 'You will not be so stupid as to go there at 11 o'clock?' They were afraid, you know, that they would just kill me or do something. 'I am not afraid. I have nothing. I'd like to talk with this man.'

So I went that night and we really talked, you know, for an hour. And my friends Hilberseimer and Lilly Reich were sitting across the street in a café window so they could see when I came out, if I were alone, or under guards, or what.

I told Rosenberg the Gestapo had closed the Bauhaus and I wanted to have it open again. I said, 'You know, the Bauhaus has certain ideas, and I think that it is important. It has nothing to do with politics or anything. It has something to do with technology.' And then for the first time he told me about himself. He said, 'I am a trained architect from the Baltic states, from Riga.' He had a diploma as an architect from Riga. I said, 'Then we certainly will understand each other.' And he said, 'Never! What do you expect me to do? You know the Bauhaus is supported by forces that are fighting our forces. It is one army against another, only in the spiritual field.' And I said, 'No, I really don't think it is like that.' And he said, 'Why didn't you change the name, for heaven's sake, when you moved the Bauhaus from Dessau to Berlin?' I said, 'Don't you think the Bauhaus is a wonderful name? You cannot find a better one.' He said, 'I don't like what the Bauhaus is doing. I know you can suspend, you can cantilever something, but my feeling demands a support.' I said, 'Even if it is cantilevered?' And he said, 'Yes.' He wanted to know, 'What is it you want to do at the Bauhaus?' I said, 'Listen, you are sitting here in an important position. And look at your writing table, this shabby writing table. Do you like it? I would throw it out of the window. That is what we want to do. We want to have good objects that we don't have to throw out of the window.' And he said, 'I will see what I can do for you.' I said, 'Don't wait too long.'

Then from there on I went every second day for three months to the headquarters of the Gestapo. I had the feeling that I had the right. That was my school. It was a private school. I had signed the contract. It was 27,000 marks – a lot of money.

And when they closed it, I said, 'I will not give up that thing.' And it took me three months, exactly three months, to get to the head of the Gestapo. He must have had a back door somewhere, you know. And he had a bench in the waiting room not wider than four inches, to make you tired so that you would go home again. But one day I got him. He was young, very young, about your age, and he said, 'Come in. What do you want?' I said, 'I would like to talk to you about the Bauhaus. What is going on? You have closed the Bauhaus. It is my private property, and I want to know for what reason. We didn't steal anything. We didn't make a revolution. I'd like to know how that can be.'

'Oh,' he said, 'I know you perfectly, and I am very interested in the movement, the Bauhaus movement, and so on, but we don't know what is with Kandinsky.' I said, 'I make all the guarantees about Kandinsky.' He said, 'You have to, but be careful. We don't know anything about him, but if you want to have him, it is OK with us. But if something happens, we pick you up.' He was very clear about that. I said, 'That is all right. Do that.' And then he said, 'I will talk with Göring, because I am really interested in this school.' And I really believe he was. He was a young man, about your age.

That was before Hitler made a clear statement. Hitler made this statement in 1935 at the opening of the Haus Der Deutschen Kunst, the House of German Art, in his speech about the cultural policy of the Nazi movement. Before, everybody had an idea. Goebbels had an idea; Göring had an idea. You know, nothing was clear. After Hitler's speech the Bauhaus was out. But the head of the Gestapo told me he would talk with Göring about it, and I told him, 'Do it soon.' We were just living on the money we still got from Dessau. Nothing else came to us.

Finally, I got a letter saying we could open the Bauhaus again. When I got this letter, I called Lilly Reich. I said, 'I got a letter. We can open the school again. Order champagne.' She said, 'What for? We don't have money.' I said, 'Order champagne.' I called the faculty together: *[Josef]* Albers, Kandinsky, they were still around us, you know, and some other people, Hilberseimer, *[Walter]* Peterhans, and I said, 'Here is the letter from the Gestapo that we can open the Bauhaus again.' They said, 'That is wonderful.' I said, 'Now, I went there for three months every second day just to get this letter. I was anxious to get this letter. I wanted to have the permission to go ahead. And now I make a proposition, and I hope you will agree with me. I will write them a letter back: "Thank you very much for the permission to open the school again, but the faculty has decided to close it!".'

I had worked on it for this moment. It was the reason I ordered champagne. Everybody accepted it, was delighted. Then we stopped.

That is the real end of the Bauhaus. Nobody else knows it, you know. We know it. Albers knows it. He was there. But the talk about it is absolute nonsense. They don't know. I know.

68 On Walter Gropius

Published speech (18 May 1953).
Source: LMvdR, 'On Walter Gropius', in S. Giedion, *Walter Gropius, Work and Teamwork* (New York: Reinhold Publishing Corporation, 1954), pp. 17–18; LoC, Mies, Box 61, Miscellaneous.
Republished in Neumeyer (1986) 1991, p. 328; Pizzigoni 2010, pp. 149–151; Walter 2022, pp. 150–152.

During a large Chicago luncheon in honour of Gropius on his 70th birthday, 18 May 1953, the ever-silent Mies van der Rohe unexpectedly rose to his feet and said:

I don't know if Gropius remembers that 43 years ago today *[in 1910]*, we, the office of Peter Behrens, the great German architect, had a birthday party for him. This party was in the back room of a very cheap restaurant in a suburb of Berlin. I remember this party very well. We had a very good time. I have never seen Gropius so happy. I think Gropius had the best time in his life. Then he had no idea he would carry this awful burden of fame.

Gropius, a few years older than most of us, left the office of Peter Behrens and started on his own. He built a factory constructed of steel, glass, and brick *[Fagus Factory, Alfeld an der Leine, 1910]*. You can see that it is still going on. But this building was so excellent that he became, with one stroke, one of the leading architects in Europe.

A few years later, he built, for the exhibition in Cologne, a complex of several buildings, office buildings, and machinery halls *[office and factory buildings at the Werkbund Exhibition, Cologne, 1914]*. This building was still more radical than his first one, though he proved there that the first one was not an accident.

After that, the First World War stopped all work for four long years. After the war, Gropius took over the Academy of Weimar. It was headed before the war by *[Henry]* Van de Velde, the great Belgian architect. Now, it is always very difficult to succeed a great man, but Gropius did. He took over this academy and changed it from top to bottom and called it the Bauhaus.

The Bauhaus was not an institution with a clear programme – it was an idea, and Gropius formulated this idea with great precision. He said, 'Art and technology – the new unity.' He wanted to have painting, sculpture, theatre, and even ballet on the one hand and, on the other, weaving, photography, furniture – everything from the coffee cup to city planning.

For art he asked the Russian [Wassily] Kandinsky, the German [Paul] Klee, and the American [Lyonel] Feininger to work with him – at that time, very radical artists. Today everyone knows them as some of the great masters of our time.

In 1923 Gropius wanted to show some of his work and to demonstrate his idea: the Bauhaus. There was a Bauhaus week in Weimar, and during this time people from all over Europe came to look at his work and pay him tribute for what he did.

I said before, it was an idea. The fact that it was an idea, I think, is the cause of this enormous influence the Bauhaus had on every progressive school around the globe. You cannot do that with organisation; you cannot do that with propaganda. Only an idea spreads so far.

By 1926, when Gropius moved the Bauhaus to Dessau and built his own school buildings there, Gropius was interested in industrialisation. He saw the necessity of standardisation and of prefabrication. I am glad that I had once the possibility in Stuttgart to give Gropius a hand so that he could demonstrate his ideas on industrialisation and standardisation and on prefabrication [House 16–17 (now demolished), Weissenhofsiedlung, 1927]. He built two houses there, which were the most interesting houses in the exhibition.

But later on, Gropius became interested in the social importance of housing – that was when he left the Bauhaus. He was the most important member of the board of the Federal Housing Research Institute in Germany. He built large housing developments in several parts of Germany. He was one of the most important members, with Corbusier, of the International Congress of Modern Architecture [CIAM] with its chapters in nearly every country.

When the Nazis came, Gropius went to England, worked there with friends together for a few years, and then he was called to Harvard. I think most of you know his work from here on. He trained and educated a great number of students. A lot of them are in leading positions today in our large architectural offices, from the east to the west. I do not have to tell you that Gropius is one of the great architects of our time, as well as the greatest educator in our field; you know that too. But what I want to say, and what you may not know, is that he was always a gallant fighter in the never-ending battle for new ideas.

69 A Proposed National Theatre

Published project report (October 1953).
Source: 'A Proposed National Theatre for the City of Mannheim', *Arts and Architecture*, vol. LXX, no. 10, October 1953, pp. 17–19.
While the author is not named, we assume, given the context, that it was Mies. Republished in Pizzigoni 2010, pp. 147–148; Walter 2022, pp. 147–149.

The building is proposed to house the National Theatre, which will seat 1300 people, and a smaller, intimate theatre, which will seat 500 people. The large theatre will be used for all important artistic spectacles, such as opera, operettas, ballet, and pageants. The smaller theatre will be used for plays, lectures, chamber music, and movies.

An analysis of the building programme indicated a need for two types of space. The stages and workshops required large column-free areas, while relatively small rooms provided adequately for the dressing rooms, administrative and business offices, costume workshops, etc. This led to the use of a two-storey structure with an upper storey 12 metres in height and a lower storey four metres high. This clear separation of the functions and their spatial expression on separate planes have the advantage of great flexibility, a basic requirement for the modern theatre and its economic and efficient management.

The proposed building uses the site which the city has [assigned] for it. On the lower floor between these two theatres, and partly embracing them, are the rooms for the orchestra, the theatre and business administration, the dressing rooms with adjoining costume storage, the rehearsal rooms, a large lounge for the artistic personnel, the cafeteria, the kitchen, the delivery area with adjoining freight elevator, and garage. These rooms are organised in accordance with their functions and are connected with each other in a simple manner by two main corridors. At the end of the corridors two staircases lead up to the stages.

On the upper floor, immediately adjoining the staircases, are the dressing rooms and lounge for the soloists. Both stages are directly connected with the scenery workshops. The paint shops are placed in the centre of the building, with the workshops and the storerooms adjoining. A simple system of corridors connects all these rooms.

I came to the conclusion that the best way to enclose this complicated spatial organism was to cover it with a huge column-free hall of steel and coloured glass or, to express it differently, to place this whole theatre organism inside such a hall. The lower storey and the core of the upper storey comprising the stages, workshops, and storage rooms are separated from the hall construction by means of a light, fireproof material. The width of the hall exceeds the width of the lower storey by eight metres, forming loggias four metres wide. These adjoin the parking lots. A small basement for heating, ventilation, and electric plant extends under the full width of the building but is only 16 metres wide.

We have not concerned ourselves with many of the details of the theatre's operation and production, as this can only be solved by consultation with the theatre personnel. What we tried to accomplish was to create a well-organised and ample spatial arrangement suitable for any artistic intention on the stage and behind it. During the early stages of this work we planned to extend the main floor over the entire area enclosed by the hall and to enclose the auditoriums, thereby separating them from the foyers. A further step led us to open the auditoriums and, finally, for the large theatre, to combine both the upper and lower storeys into an imposing and festive hall.

70 [Conversation Regarding the Future of Architecture, Part I]

Published interview (1955).
Source: John Peter, 'Conversation with Mies', in J. Peter, *The Oral History of Modern Architecture: Interviews with the Greatest Architects of the Twentieth Century* (New York: Harry N. Abrams, 1994), pp. 154–173. Mies was interviewed in his suite at the Waldorf Towers, New York. Published with excerpts of the audio recording together with 'Conversation Regarding the Future of Architecture, Part II' (see p. 245). Republished in Puente (2006) 2008, pp. 49–87; Pizzigoni 2010, pp. 152–160; Casabella, no. 800, 2011, pp. 120–123; Walter 2022, pp. 364–388.

Were there great works or great masters who influenced your own thinking about architecture?
Yes, there is no question. I think if somebody takes his work seriously, and even if he is relatively young, he will be influenced by other people. You just cannot help that, you know. It is a fact.
First of all, I was influenced by old buildings. I looked at them; people built them. I don't know the names, and I don't know what it was, you know … mostly very simple buildings. When I was really young, you know, not even 20 years old, I was impressed by the strength of these old buildings because they didn't even belong to any epoch. But they were there for 1000 years and still there, you know, and still impressive, and nothing could change it. And all the styles, the great styles, passed, but they were still there. They didn't lose anything. They were ignored through certain architectural epochs, but they were still there and still as good as they were on the first day they were built.
Then I worked with Peter Behrens. He had a great sense of the great form. That was his main interest; and that I certainly understood and learned from him.
By 'great form' what do you mean?
Oh, let us say like the Palazzo Pitti *[in Florence]*. It is something, the monumental form. Let me put it this way: I was lucky enough, you know, when I came to the Netherlands and I was confronted with *[Hendrik Petrus]* Berlage's work. There it was the construction. What made the strongest impression on me was the use of brick and so on, the honesty of materials and so on. I never forget this lesson I got there just by looking at his buildings. I had only a few talks with Berlage, but not about that. We never talked about architecture together.
Do you think he knew that you sensed what he was doing?
No, I don't think so. I cannot see any reason why he should have because we didn't talk about it. I was really a young boy then. But I really learned this idea from him. I must have been open to this particular view because of the old buildings I had seen.
And I learned a lot from Frank Lloyd Wright. I would say that. I think more as a liberation, you know. I felt much freer by seeing what he did. You know, the way he puts a building in the landscape and the free way he uses spaces and so on.
Then those were the influences in your approach to architecture?
But my architectural philosophy came out of reading philosophical books. I cannot tell you at the moment where I read it, but I know I read it somewhere, that architecture belongs to the epoch and not even to the time, to a real epoch. Since I understood that, I would not be for fashion in architecture. I would look for more profound principles. And since I know by reading and studying books that we are under the influence of science and technology, I would ask myself, 'What can that be? What result comes from this fact? Can we change it, or can we not change it?' And the answer to this question, you know, gave me the direction which I followed, not what I liked. I throw often things out I like very much. They are dear to my heart, but when I have a better conviction, a better idea, a clearer idea, then I follow the clearer idea. And after a while, you know, I find the Washington Bridge most beautiful, the best building in New York. Maybe at the beginning I wouldn't. That grew. But first, I had to conquer the idea, and later I appreciated it as beauty.

So you sought what was characteristic of the epoch.
What is the essence of the epoch. And that is the only thing we really can express and that is worth expressing.

There is another thing that just comes to my mind. Thomas Aquinas, he says, 'Reason is the first principle of all human work.' Now when you have grasped that once, you know, then you act accordingly. So I would throw everything out that is not reasonable.

I don't want to be interesting. I want to be good.

You know, you find often in books – books that may have nothing to do with architecture – very important things. Erwin Schrödinger, you know, the physicist, he talks here about general principles, and he said the creative vigour of a general principle depends precisely on its generality *[E. Schrödinger, Nature and the Greeks (Cambridge, UK, 1951)].* That is exactly what I think about when I talk about structure in architecture. It is not a special solution. It is the general idea.

Sometimes people say, 'How do you feel if somebody copies you?' and so on. I say that is not a problem to me. I think that is the reason we are working, that we find something everybody can use. We hope only that he uses it right.

In other words, copies are an affirmation that you have found a general solution.
Yes, that is what I call the common language too. That is what I'm working on. I am not working on architecture, I am working on architecture as a language, and I think you have to have a grammar in order to have a language. It has to be a living language, but still you come in the end to the grammar. It is a discipline. And then you can use it, you know, for normal purposes and you speak in prose. And if you are good at that, you speak a wonderful prose, and if you are really good, you can be a poet. But it is the same language; that is the characteristic. A poet doesn't produce a different language for each problem. That's not necessary; he uses the same language, he uses even the same words. In music it is always the same and the same instruments, most of the time. I think that is the same in architecture.

You know, if you have to construct something, you can make a garage out of it or you can make a cathedral out of it. We use the same means, the same structural methods for all these things. It has nothing to do with the level you are working on. What I am driving at is to develop a common language, not particularly individual ideas. I think that is the biggest point in our whole time. We have no real common language. To build that, if it is possible, if we can do that, then we can build what we like and everything is all right. I see no reason why that should not be the case. I am quite convinced that will be the task for the future.

I think there will be certain influences, climatic influences, but that will only colour what is done. I think a much greater influence is the influence of science and technology that is worldwide and that will take all these old cultures away, and everybody will do the same. Just this light colouration.

In other words, you feel we are in a period where there can be an architectural vocabulary?
Oh, certainly, there's no question about that. I think that this is a human desire to do something reasonable. I see no difference if there is something reasonable in California, in the Mediterranean, or in Norway. They should do it with reason. If they worked with reason and did not have fancy ideas, particularly architectural ideas, everything would be much better.

You would say that people recognise a reasonable and honest approach?
Certainly. Let us take an example – the mechanic in a garage today. He is very much interested in all the technological means we have. He takes all that for granted. You have no personal ideas about these things. When he sticks to that, then he is on the common plane.

Do you mind working with engineers?
No, just the opposite, I love it if I get a good one. There are things that cannot be done without engineers. You

cannot know everything. I think architects should understand more about engineering and engineers should know a little more about architecture.

Will new materials greatly change the style of our times?

No, I don't think so, because what I tried to do in architecture is to develop a clear structure. We are just confronted with the material. How to use it in the right way is what you have to find out. It has nothing to do with the shape. What I do, what you call 'my kind' of architecture, we should just call it a structural approach. We don't think about the form when we start. We think about the right way to use the materials. Then we accept the result.

Grand ideas, you know, we keep them high in the air when we are working. We don't want them to come down. Often we are ourselves surprised what comes out of it. I collect the facts. As many facts as I can get. I study these facts, and then I act accordingly.

Maybe one of the problems of Wright's style is that it is not a vocabulary in that sense.

It is not that. It is much too individualistic to be that. We know he's a genius. There is no question about that. But I think he cannot have real followers. In order to do things as he does, you need a lot of fantasy and, if you have fantasy, you will do it differently. I am quite sure it is an individualistic approach, and I don't go this way. I go a different way. I am trying to go an objective way.

Have there been architects in the past who have developed a style that lasted as a vocabulary?

[Andrea] Palladio, certainly. You know, it lasted. It is still among us in certain cases. Even though his forms have changed, his spirit is still there in many cases.

Do you think there is a desire on the part of people for natural materials that are in a sense rich? For instance, I've always felt disappointed that the Resor House was never built.

Yes, I was sorry, too. I think it is a very good building.

Do you think these rich materials tend to give a humanity to it?

It is not necessary, but it can be rich. But it is not necessary. It could very well be simple. It would not change that.

You mean the Resor House wouldn't have had to be built with teak?

No, it was not necessary at all. It could have been in any other kind of wood and still be a good building. It would be not as fine as teak.

In fact, I think that the Barcelona Pavilion, if I had built it in brick, would have been as good a building. I am quite sure it would have been not as successful as marble, but that has nothing to do with the idea.

What do you think of the use of colour in architecture?

On our IIT campus I painted the steel black. At the Farnsworth House I painted it white because it was in the green. It was in the open. I could use any colour.

And you've even been known to chrome it, as you did in the Barcelona Pavilion.

Oh, certainly, yes. I would do that. I love natural materials or metallic things, you know. I have very seldom used coloured walls, for instance. I would really like to give it to Picasso or to Klee. In fact, I ordered from Klee a large picture, two pictures, one side white and the other black. I said: 'I don't care what you paint on it.'

So if it were a problem of colour, you would give it to a master.

Oh, certainly, yes. I would do that.

[Break]

You once told me how the Barcelona Pavilion evolved around a slab of marble that you found.

[...] I had the idea about the building and I had to look around. We had very little time. It was deep in the winter. You cannot move marble from the quarry in the winter because it is still wet inside and it would freeze to pieces. You have to find a piece of material which is dry. We had to go and look around in huge depots. There I found an onyx block. This marble block had a certain size, so I had only the possibility of taking twice the height of the block. Then making the pavilion twice the height of the onyx block. That was the module.

Would you be interested in doing another exhibition type of building?
You know, I've been through a lot of different possible types of building. There are only a few left. I would like to do this convention hall. This is an enormous building, 720 feet by 720 feet. I would like to see it myself. I know the drawings. I know the idea behind it. But, in fact, there is a certain size that is a reality. Take the pyramids in Egypt, and make them only 15 feet high. *[That would be]* nothing. There is just this enormous size that makes all the difference.

Do you feel in the Seagram Building on Park Avenue that the size of the sheer wall going up will have a lot to do with its impact?
Yes, I am quite sure. Because of its simplicity again it will be much stronger. Some other buildings are much higher and richer in the grouping and so on. I think, at least that is what I hope, that the Seagram Building will be a good building.

I must say that when I came first to this country, I lived at the University Club *[in New York]*. I saw the main tower of the Rockefeller Center every morning from my breakfast table and it made a great impression on me. That slab, yes. It has nothing to do with style. There you see that it is a mass. That is not an individual thing – thousands of windows, you know. Good or bad, that doesn't mean anything. That is like an army of soldiers or like a meadow. You don't see details anymore when you see the mass. I think that is the quality of this tower.

[Break]

Do you think that new ways of living will change things?
No, I think in principle it will be the same. It can be richer as it develops. You know, it is very difficult just to make something clear. Then express it in a beautiful way. They are two different things. But first, it has to be clear. I cannot help it if somebody wants to have 40-storey apartments and the apartments have to be all the same. I can only try to express it in such a way that it really comes out and that in the end it is beautiful.

Are you optimistic about the future of architecture?
Certainly, I am. I am absolutely optimistic. I think you should not plan too much and not construct too much these things.

So do you envision a time later when a person working from your architectural style may evolve a richer …
I would not even use this word 'style' for that. I would say if he used the same principle, the same approach. Then he, certainly, if he is talented, he can make it richer. That depends, but it would in principle not be different.

There is obviously visible now a reaction to my approach in architecture. There is no question, but I think it is just a reaction. I don't believe it is a new approach. It is a reaction against something that is there. The reaction is a kind of fashion.

71 [Dedication of Crown Hall]

Typescript of a dedication speech (30 April 1956).
Source: The Mies van der Rohe Society, Chicago.
Republished in Walter 2022, pp. 158–159.

Dr Rettaliata,
As the architect of the building, I have been asked to present to you the key of the building as it is often done at a dedication.
Working here for so long, I could not help thinking that you, as the President of this Institute must have a master key for all the buildings of the campus. So to give you a second key would be a nice but somewhat empty gesture.
In the days of old it was different.
People took a ceremony like this quite seriously. It was not so much a formality as a symbolic act. I thought I should take up this old and wise tradition. For this reason I ordered a golden key of the building.
Let the brightness of the gold be a symbol of our high appreciation for your great personal efforts to make this building a reality. But gold is not only bright. It has other more hidden qualities. I am thinking of its purity and its durability. Properties which very well could symbolise the character of the work which we hope will be performed in this building.
Let this building be the home of ideas and adventures. Real ideas. Ideas based on reason. Ideas about facts. Then the building will be of great service to our students and in the end a real contribution to our civilisation.
We know that will not be easy. Noble things are never easy. Experience teaches us that they are as difficult as they are rare.

72 Crown Hall, IIT

Project report and dedication speech, typewritten and in manuscript form (shortly after 30 April 1956).
Source: LoC, Mies, Box 33, IIT Department of Architecture, 'Crown Hall. Illinois Institute of Technology'; LoC, Mies, Box 40, Montreal Museum.
Republished in Pizzigoni 2010, pp. 161–162; Walter 2022, pp. 153–154.

Crown Hall houses the Department of Architecture and City and Regional Planning and the Institute of Design.
The one-storey welded steel structure, which has a full basement, is 120 feet by 220 feet with a ceiling height of 28 feet on the main floor. Suspending the roof plate from four steel girders spaced 60 feet apart and spanning the 120-foot dimensions provided a column-free main floor interior hall. The floor level of the hall is six feet above the ground to permit natural light and ventilation into the basement work areas. The enclosing walls of the building are of plate glass with the lower sections of obscure glass. The floor is terrazzo with the exterior stairs and terraces of the north and south entrances being travertine.
The main hall is mechanically ventilated and contains two large draughting areas on either side of a central core area defined by low, free-standing oak panels which form areas for administrative offices, a library, and an exhibition hall which can be used for assembly purposes.
In the basement are located the studios and workshops of the Institute of Design, as well as a student lounge and service and mechanical facilities. *[In the basement are various rooms whose functions require complete enclosure; i.e. studios, workshops, storage rooms, lecture rooms, as well as toilet and mechanical facilities.]*
The landscaping of almost all of the campus consists of honey locust trees and hawthorn cockspur bushes and was done under the direction of Alfred Caldwell. The building, named in honour of SR Crown,

co-founder and first president of the Material Service Corporation, was dedicated on 30 April 1956.

[The additional paragraphs below are found in another document contained in the same LoC folder pertaining to Crown Hall.]
Since the roof is suspended from six-foot-deep exterior steel girders carried on columns at the building's periphery, the large room is completely free of structural elements and great freedom is therefore permitted in its sub-division.

The room is subdivided by six-foot-high freestanding wood-panelled walls into two student work areas, a large central exhibition lounge, and an administrative space.

A single large room for 300 students is the physical expression of both the contiguity and the anti-ivory-tower aspects of the curriculum. The students, not isolated from the years above or below, clearly see their position at a particular time as a point within a consistent progress.

73 Mies' Enormous Room

Published article (August 1956).
Source: 'Mies' Enormous Room', *Architectural Forum*, vol. CV, no. 8, Aug. 1956, pp. 105–106.
Republished in Walter 2022, pp. 160–162.

Crown Hall, on the campus at Illinois Institute of Technology, is the summation of a century of steel and glass buildings.
The main floor of Crown Hall is one room, 220 [feet] long, 120 wide, 19 1/2 high, walled with panels of obscure and clear glass framed in steel. Within this immense room there is not one structural column, and even the partitions are more inference than actuality – low, fencelike planes which define exhibition space and offices in the centre and two large student draughting rooms at the ends. At any point in the big room you can see the top part of all four sides of it. Out front is a wide steel-framed porch with steps for sitting between classes, and downstairs are classrooms and shops with high windows.
The structural clarity of IIT's newest building is unlikely ever to be surpassed in steel.
I think this is the clearest structure we have done, the best to express our philosophy, *says architect Ludwig Mies van der Rohe, and it is difficult to see how the next century can contradict this builder, or how he himself can.*
This is the first building Mies has completed with his long-sketched plan of suspending the roof from plate girders, getting the girders up out of the building, as an exterior skeleton. It is also his widest span structure, and because it qualifies under the local code as a single-storey building, the steel framework did not have to be fattened with concrete fireproofing. The steel stands there in the reality of its slim strength.
Beyond this, architecturally, Crown Hall is also the most universal of Mies' buildings. This great room

would with facility house a factory, a sound stage, a newspaper plant, an insurance company – almost anything. It is a room under an oversheltering structure, a free space to be shaped to its use. And it is very cheap space: $13.71 per sq. ft., 780 per cu. ft., a total of $746,850. It needs further expenditure, for summer air conditioning; but this had been anticipated – ductwork and diffusers are in.

So far, the building may seem adroit. But behind the facts in all great buildings are the feelings in them; and in this building Mies again shows his ability to build a remarkable architectural atmosphere. His enormous, beautifully proportioned room is a very serene place to be. In some intricate way the space is balanced against the assertion of the construction to result in a large calm place for working. It is a good place in which to be alone in a crowd.

Another demonstration by this building: the powerful Mies idiom, under perfect control, does not depend on elegant execution or perfect material. His idiom can indeed reach a point of frailty, or emptiness, if it is too delicately or perfectly rendered. Crown Hall is welded neatly, nothing more, and derives a part of its great vigour from this kind of simplicity. Like the best poets, Mies uses a simple language.

What is our philosophy? It is honesty. Years ago, when I was designing the German Pavilion for the fair in Barcelona, my client was an official in the German government at that time, and I wanted him to understand what I wanted to do in this simple building, so I explained.

'Honesty?' he said, 'Yes I know, my grandmother told me always to be honest. Yes, I know all about that!' So I told him: 'Yes, and that's the way you should build.'

74 [Interview Given to the BBC]

Broadcast interview (6 October 1956).
Source: British Library, London, audio recording.
Mies was interviewed by Graeme Shankland. The interview was broadcast on the BBC's Third Programme.
In the following articles use is made of a mix of quotations from this text and the text 'No Dogma': Conrads, U., 'Mies van der Rohe. Ich mache niemals ein Bild [Mies van der Rohe. I Never Take a Picture]' in *Die Bauwelt*, vol. LIII, no. 32, 1962, pp. 884–885; Conrads, U., 'Mies van der Rohe, Baumeister einer strukturellen Architektur [Mies van der Rohe, Builder of a Structural Architecture]', *Jahrbuch Preussischer Kulturbesitz*, vol. VI, no. 6, 1968, pp. 57–74.
Republished in Pizzigoni 2010, p. 208.

[When Mies van der Rohe came to Britain this year,] he was preceded by his reputation as a kind of architectural Delphic oracle, unapproachable, taciturn, and cryptic. I found him to be none of these things. He had measured the value of his achievement and equipped the sharp sense of humour [with] discrimination without false pride. He is in love with logic, but also in love with his own building expression of it, and he is a master craftsman who religiously senses skills and handles material and structure. Mies [...] is one who brings quality to the inevitable. Like Milton, he is a poet of the 'clear and reasonable.' [...] As an illustration of one kind of architectural order, he takes the example of one of his buildings, the architects' building [SR Crown Hall, IIT, Chicago, 1956] on the campus of the Illinois Institute of Technology. This consists of one vast hall supported on a basement and free of internal columns and fixed partitions, its roof hung from four deep and exquisitely detailed, bare, black steel girders which stand up clear of the roof, outside the building. It is sheathed from floor to ceiling in glass. The whole campus – the buildings and the spaces between them – is planned on a grid, and I put it to him that this was an example of his search for a kind of order as a guiding and directing force.

You have to realise there are different stages of order. The real order is the one of which St Augustine spoke about the disposition of equal and unequal things according to their nature. That is real order. You know, if you compare the architects' building with the other campus buildings, you can see that. When I put a grid over the whole campus, that was more a mechanical help. After that we did not have to speculate where we put our columns. We put our columns on the crossing points of the grid, all the way through. In the architects' building I went away from the grid. You know, I took just the grid in a larger measure, but the elements are not in the grid anymore. The grid was 24 feet in the normal buildings, and here the columns are 60 feet apart. And I think the architects' building is the most complete and the most refined building, and the simplest.

And this more fundamental idea of St Augustine's which you referred to ... How have you sought to ...? How has this helped your work?

I would not build a church as a movie palace, and I would not build a factory as a church. So we make a clear distinction about what the values of these buildings are. There is not only a hierarchy of values; there is a hierarchy of works too.

But at the same time, in that gramophone record which you made a few years ago I heard you say that you should be looking for the same. You said that there should be the same kind of language for a garage as for a cathedral. [See 'Conversations Regarding the Future of Architecture, Part I']. Now how do you distinguish between these?

We use the same principles because ... Like the Gothic used the same principles for a cathedral as for a barn. And that is what I meant by that. But the expression is quite different.

In the same recording you said that we should search for a grammar in order to speak prose well. Occasionally there will be poets, but the important task for architects was to search for this grammar.

Yes.

Now it seemed to me you were saying something to all architects who are alive.

Certainly. I am not ... I don't want to express myself. I am looking for a grammar that can be understood by and used by everybody. That it has a personal character, that is unavoidable. But that is not a tendency. The tendency is the highest objectivity.

Your own work has had a big influence all over the world, in Europe and in America. How do you see the effect on the work of other architects?

I think the influence of my work has ... is based on its reasonableness. Everybody can use it without being a copyist because it is quite objective. And I think if I find something objective, I will use it. It doesn't matter who did it or ...

So to that extent you could be said to have suggested a grammar.

Yes, but that became clear to us much later, to me at least. It was not a tendency, but later on, I found that everybody could use it to his greatest advantage. And it is not a subjective affair. If it were subjective, nobody *[would have to]* use it, but I think if there's something objective, everybody is compelled to use it.

To analyse this thing a little more closely, it seems to me that it is a process of refinement and rejection. You've said, 'When I have a clearer idea, I follow it.' You've also said that you throw out everything that is not reasonable.

Yes.

That is a correct description, is it?

Certainly, yes. Often I have to throw out things I like, then I ... strike them out.

You think this process of rejection and refinement makes your work more objective, is that the point?

Yes. Certainly, yes, that is.

Mies not only discards what he discovers to be illogical or confused but severely limits the types of building structure he explores, isolating those he considers most important, like the multi-storey glass tower and the single-storey glass hall and subjecting them to an uncompromising aesthetic discipline in the search for the clearest possible architectural expression. To use his own words, We intentionally restrict ourselves to those structures which are possible at the moment and try to work them out in all the details. In this way we want to create a basis for further development. *He can do this because for him architecture is structure and, as such, not something to be played about with. Neither is it a question of just selecting a convenient or economic structure and leaving it to the structural engineers to work it out. He approaches architecture in the same spirit as the successive designers of the Gothic cathedrals who worked for 300 years to perfect one type of structure. I asked him how he worked with his structural engineers. As I expected, he said that mostly he had to tell them what to do.*

There are some structural engineers you wouldn't have to tell. In fact they go their way alone. But the others, they know how to figure out things, but they don't know the meaning of their work. So we have to say what structure is. They know nothing about structure. They know everything about construction.

To take the example now of your houses, it seems to me, it must seem to many people, I think, that there are not many different ways in which one could live in one of your houses. The way they are planned ...

Would you like a cigar?

Thank you very much. I'd like one very much ... Even the way the furniture is arranged is something that flows directly from the plan of the buildings, and the open planning principles, of course, do impose a certain way of living in a house. Could you tell us a bit about how you came to this idea of the open plan? Does it, for instance, have any relation to the ideas of Mondrian and the aesthetic ideas that were prevalent ...?

No. I think that was a mistake that the Museum of Modern Art made. They interpreted it this way, but that has nothing to do with it. I never make a painting when I want to build a house. But our plans, we like to draw our plans carefully. That is why they were taken as a kind of painting.

But nonetheless the open planning idea which you, Frank Lloyd Wright, and many architects since have adopted is an aesthetic idea.

Certainly, yes.

There have been criticisms by people who live in this country of open-plan houses, that they don't find them very convenient. They're draughty and they have no privacy, and that kind of thing ...

Yes. I would not like to live in a cubic house, with a lot of small rooms. I would rather live on a bench in Hyde Park.

[They laugh.]

What kind of house, if you were designing one for yourself now, what kind of house would you design for yourself?

I would build a very simple but very large house, so that I can do inside whatever I like.

You would like to change things around occasionally?

I would do that.

Like the Japanese do in their houses.

Yes, something like that.

There have been criticisms of modern architects that they are seeking to impose a way of life, a way of living, particularly in houses, particularly through open planning, on people. You reject that idea ...

Yes, we don't do that. You know, we use the principle of flexibility. For instance, in one of our tall buildings, on Lake Shore Drive, we have 400 apartments in the building, and I cannot remember that two apartments were similar. We cannot help fixing the bathrooms and the kitchens in one place, but otherwise it is quite flexible. You can take the walls out or put more walls in.

So you regard open planning in this context as a liberating thing?

Oh, certainly. And the flexibility is in my opinion about a necessity, for instance in office buildings. What Sullivan said, 'form follows function,' I think, has changed in our time very much. Function is very short-lived today, and our constructions last much longer, so it only makes sense to plan very flexibly.

The most perfect small house Mies has built is Farnsworth House. This is a classic example of the open plan: a single space glazed on all four sides, free of partitions, and with only a service core with bathrooms, a kitchen, and mechanical equipment rising to the ceiling in the centre. Was this not an aesthetic idea imposed on a reluctant client? I told Mies that the Italian critic Bruno Zevi said this was not a house at all but a museum.

No, that is not a fact. It was a house for a single person. That made the problem more simple. Later, I made a house in glass with five bedrooms and five bathrooms, and even a room for the help [row houses, Bensenville IL, 1954]. That is really a difficult problem. From my point of view, the open plan, when it is possible, makes you work really much harder. Well, Farnsworth House is, I think, not really understood. I have seen it. I was in the house morning to evening. I didn't know how colourful nature really is. But you have to take care to use neutral colours on the inside because you have the colours outside. This absolutely changed ... and I must say it's beautiful.

You had raw silk curtains, I think, in the same house ...

Yes, and a very neutral primavera wood, and the house's entire floor was Roman travertine – kitchen, bathrooms, altogether, and the terrace too.

And that was why, I think, you painted the columns white, as you told us ...

Yes, that was in the countryside, you know, against the green. I think, white ... It does not always have to be black. But I like black too. Black particularly for cities. Even in our tall glass buildings, where you are in an apartment and you have these huge glass walls. You see the sky and even the city changing every hour. I think that is really new in our concept.

Here not only does Mies reject the suggestion that the open plan could be a tyranny, but he claims for it not just the practical advantages of flexibility but a more important spiritual one of setting the scene for a really new and profound relationship between man and nature in town and in country. I then took up with him the question of prefabrication. In a modern industrial society based on factory production every serious architect has to make up his own mind on what terms he approaches this question. In his own work Mies has always used the individual products of modern industry but never designed completely prefabricated buildings. Why was this?

I don't think it is an advantage to build [entirely] prefabricated houses. I think the value of prefabrication is the value of getting elements which we can use freely. As we have. We have doors; we have bathtubs. Now, in our steel buildings, we have about 3000 windows, in only two shapes. I think that is the best way of prefabrication. To prefabricate a house, you must standardise the house from top to bottom. It's just too complicated a process. I think it is much better to deliver elements which we can use in a free way. Otherwise, it could be terribly boring. And I don't think it will happen.

And at the same time there has been in Europe, as you know, on a very wide scale now, and in Germany and in Russia, this use of this 'Groß-Plattenbau', I think they call it, system of large-plate building or the use of systems of construction involving an entire wall being put in position by crane and so forth ... but that doesn't seem to have interested you. You think this is a limiting factor on an architect, this kind of thing?

Yes, and I think it is not right. I think when I can build a skeleton where I have very thin columns, they are much stronger than these heavy walls. I'd rather use a skeleton and put glass in it, a light material again. It's wonderful; glass is the best material, you know. I have had the possibility to drink wine out of glasses that were 2000 years old. They were in the ground, and nothing had happened; they only decoloured a little, but they were otherwise perfect. And it's the same with bronze. That is why I like the Seagram Building. Nothing will happen to the walls; only it will colour. Things are also coloured; they turn black, maybe a little green.

This moving tribute to glass and bronze reminded me that Mies came to building first as a craftsman, an apprentice in his father's stonecutting shop in Aachen. He has not forgotten his first-hand impact with materials but transcended it in an ability to extract the last drop of character from every material he uses. The Seagram Building, New York's latest skyscraper, in its luxurious purity and calm authority, makes all earlier ones seem clumsy or at best pretty. It also represents the culmination of 40 years of intense study of glass towers, of ideas that first took preliminary shape in Europe but which, rejected in Nazi Germany, would be realised only in America. I asked him what other projects and ideas he still hoped to realise. You are listening to a man of 73.

You see, I'm not interested in building a lot. When we have a good idea, we want to build it. I am not a businessman, [I'm] an architect. But there is not much I would like to build – for instance, a convention hall [convention hall, Chicago, 1954] I designed for Chicago and some other things. Maybe a house for myself. [Laughs.]

You've had news today of a new job .... which you're going to do ...

Well, that is a federal court building in Chicago with many courtrooms. It's quite a complicated building. We have even to put a prison on the top of it. I am curious what comes out of it ... [They laugh.]

Apart from that, which is an actual commission, what buildings would you still now particularly like to do that you haven't done so far?

I would like to build one of these huge halls we designed. I don't know if you remember this design for the convention hall in Chicago. It was 720 by 720 feet without any support inside. And the Bacardi Building for Cuba, that is 65 metres by 65 metres without any support inside. But it's an office building, and this man came to me when he saw the designs for the architects' building. He wanted just one large room for his whole office.

He didn't regard the open plan as an obstacle ...
The opposite!

Finally, we turn to the question nearest to my own heart as an architect-planner – to the city. First, to the only project in town planning as a coordinating exercise he has ever realised, the Weissenhof Siedlung in Stuttgart in 1927. Here he conceived a three-dimensional master plan to guide a collective demonstration of what contemporary architecture can do to produce an environment for a whole community, and he invited 16 leading modern architects to design individual buildings. Did he regret not having had an opportunity to do this kind of thing in America?

I will tell you it was an ordeal to do it in Stuttgart, and I can imagine it would be more difficult in America.

Much more so, I think ...

And I don't see the necessity to repeat things like that. In Stuttgart that was a certain hour in history, that we could show, at once, that all these forces were at work but never visible really. That was the reason we wanted to build this Weissenhof Siedlung, to show it at once clearly, that there is a new way of building houses and apartment buildings.

We were talking over lunch about the city, the future of the metropolis.

Yes.

Many people, as you know, are throwing up their hands in despair today, saying it has no future. What's your view on that?

I think we are just at the beginning of changing the cities, but not in a romantic way. I am quite sure that the economic situation will have a great influence on the way our cities will be. I don't believe that we – I mean architects – we can just plan a city out of the blue sky. There are economic forces; they are so strong, we cannot change them. We can give guidance, that is about all. There is this problem of the idea in relation to the objective facts, and that was quite unknown and unclear until Max Scheler, a philosopher from Cologne, wrote his book on the forms of knowledge in society [Max Scheler, Die Wissensformen und die Gesellschaft *(Leipzig: Der Neue Geist Verlag, 1926)*]. He really clarified this problem.

That was in fact a very interesting year, 1926. In this year Schwarz, Rudolf Schwarz, wrote his book on technology *[Rudolf Schwarz,* Wegweisung der Technik, *Potsdam: Müller & Kiepenheuer Verlag, 1928); Schwarz may have started to work on this book in 1926].* There again, for the first time, this problem was really clarified. And in the same year, '26, Whitehead started his talks which he later published under the title 'Science and the Modern World' *[Alfred North Whitehead,* Science and the Modern World *(Cambridge: Cambridge University Press, 1926)].* A strange year ... *[See 'No Dogma'.]*

When Mies' own career began, he and his contemporaries had to break away from Art Nouveau. They found, at hand in Berlin, the Neoclassical buildings of Schinkel, built some 80 years earlier.

The Art Nouveau or Jugendstil people, you know, they *[exhausted]* this movement. Around 1910. And Schinkel was really the greatest representative in Berlin. His Altes Museum in Berlin ... a beautiful building. You could learn everything in architecture from it, you know. Well, I tried to do that.

You found in Schinkel's work certain key, leading ideas or an approach which you have found useful since?

Yes. In the Altes Museum he separated the windows very clearly, he separated the elements, the columns, and the walls and the ceiling, and I think that is still visible ... *[laughs]*

Yes.

... in my later buildings.

Finally, we spoke of a moral idea – that a building ought to express its structure. This central idea of the Modern Movement is expressed in Mies' buildings more than in those of any other architect, but it derives from men like Ruskin and Viollet-le-Duc, who practised something very different. Mies points to this paradox.

That Ruskin had quite romantic ideas about that. When he talks about it, it's like Viollet-le-Duc. He said, you know, every decoration should be thrown out when it doesn't support the construction ... and look what he did himself. It's very strange, you know, that somebody can have a clear idea and then work in a different way because he is a son of his time.

But you are the son of yours, in the sense that you have based your work on this scientific and objective and rational approach, helped by the philosophers you've been mentioning.

Yes. But I learned the most from old buildings.

Because they were scientific and rational too?

No, but they were 'clear and reasonable', and that is what we do too.

75 At the Ground-breaking of Lafayette Park

Handwritten manuscript of speech (circa 1957).
Source: LoC, Mies, Box 61, Miscellaneous, 'Lafayette Park'.
Republished in Pizzigoni 2010, pp. 163–164; Walter 2022, pp. 166–168.

Mayor *[Albert]* Cobo, what I am going to say will be short, but my task is a very pleasant one. I want to thank you for all the support and cooperation we received during this work, from you and all the departments of your government.

You, as mayor, have been the patron of this project. This fact reminded me of the patrons of older times, whose interest and support did so much for the development of their cities. In those days it was the custom to strike coins in commemoration of occasions like this. It was a noble custom.

Since I have not the power to coin money and still like the custom, I decided to give you an ancient coin. I have chosen a coin of Alexander the Great – not because he was a warrior, but because he founded and rebuilt many cities in Egypt and the near East. Among them Alexandria, situated on the delta of the River Nile. A harbour city and a great centre of commerce. A city with a mixed population, and as far as we know, the first city with a public park. I give you this coin as an expression of our appreciation and as a reminder to you of this ceremony.

(1) Never has city planning been so much talked about as today. But never have we been further from its real understanding.

(2) Most of the discussion has been about its technical aspects. Some see the problem simply as a traffic problem. Others think everything could be solved by clearing the slums. Still others think city planning is exclusively an architectural task. But only a few see the city as an entity subject to a principle of order without which it cannot exist.

(3) We have lost the sense for the integrated whole. We no longer seek the essence of things. We no longer understand the relationship between the individual and the community. We no longer believe in the necessity for an objective order.

(4) If we did, as we should, we would understand the nature of the elements involved in city planning and act accordingly.

(5) The medieval towns, for example, were based upon such an understanding. Their structure and beauty reflected it.

I know of no better definition of order than that of St Augustine: 'Order is the disposition of equal and unequal things, attributing to each its place.'

76 [Some Ideas Behind Mies' Work]

Published journal article (February–March 1957).
Source: LMvdR 'Source of Inspiration', in *Print*, vol. 11 (1), February–March 1957, p. 39.
This text contains quotes from different sources.
Republished in Walter 2022, pp. 163–165.

I think if somebody takes his work seriously and even if he is relatively young, you know, he will be influenced by other people. You just cannot help that, you know, it is a fact. I was influenced by old buildings. I looked at them. People built them, and I don't know their names and I don't know what it was, you know: mostly very simple buildings. When I was really young, you know, not even 20 years old, I was impressed by the strength of these old buildings, you know, because they didn't even belong to any epoch, you know. But they *[had been]* there for 1000 years and *[were]* still there and still impressive and nothing could change it, you know. And all the styles, the great styles, passed but they were still there – didn't lose anything. They were ignored through certain architectural epochs, but they were still there and still as good as they were the first day they were built.

Well, I worked with Peter Behrens. He had a great sense – a great form – that was his main interest and that I certainly understood and learned from him.

I was lucky enough, you know, when I came to the Netherlands and was confronted with Berlage's works – the construction was what made the strongest impression on me, you know, the use of brick, the honesty of materials, and so on. I never forget this lesson I got there, you know, just by looking at his buildings – after only a few talks with Berlage, but not about that, we never talked about architecture together.

And I learned a lot from Frank Lloyd Wright – I would say, more as a liberation. You know, I felt much freer by seeing what he did. You know, the way how he puts a building in a landscape, you know, and the free way how he uses space and so on.

I am working on architecture as a language, and I think you have to have a grammar in order to have language. You can use it, you know, for normal purposes. And you speak in prose and if you are good at that, you speak in wonderful prose and if you are really good, you can be a poet. The same language! Yes, that is the characteristic. And I think it is the same in architecture. You know, if you have to construct something, you can make a garage out of it or you can make a cathedral out of it. It is the same means, the same structural methods we use for all these things.

I cannot tell you at the moment where I read it that architecture belongs to the epoch and not even to the time, to the real epoch. What is the essence of the epoch? And that is the only thing that we really can express, what is worth to express, you know.

Until I understood that, I would not be for fashion in architecture. I would look for more profound principles. And since I know by reading and studying books that we are under the influence of science and technology, I would ask myself, you know, what can that be, you know, what result comes from this fight. Can we change it, or can we not change it? And the answer of the question, you know, gives me the direction which I followed, not what I like, you know. I throw out often things I liked very much, they are dear to my heart, but when I have a better conviction, a better idea, a clearer idea, better, then I follow the clearer idea. And after a while, you know, I find the Washington Bridge most beautiful, the best building in New York. Maybe at the beginning I wouldn't, you know, that grew. But first I had to conquer the idea, and later I appreciated it as a beauty.

Thomas Aquinas says, 'Reason is the first principle of all human work.' Now when you have grasped that once, you know, then *[you act]* accordingly. So I would throw out everything that is not reasonable. I don't want to be interesting, I want to be good.

77 [Office] Organisation

Typewritten manuscript (circa 1958).
Source: LoC, Mies, Box 62, Writings by Mies General, 'Organisation'.
At the end of 1958 Mies moved his office to 230 East Ohio Street, Chicago.
Republished in Pizzigoni 2010, pp. 210; Walter 2022, pp. 361.

My idea on the organisation of an architectural office has always been to have as much freedom and flexibility as possible. The freedom to choose and work on various types of buildings of significance demands an organisation which can expand or contract but without losing its effectiveness in the performance of a task, whether the task involves a large group of buildings or a small individual building. I have been able to have this flexibility, and thus freedom of choice, by maintaining a relatively small staff of 20. There are seven registered architects in the office, all well versed in the various duties necessary in the practice of their profession. When the office load is light, we carry out the work within our staff. When there is a great deal of work, we shall either expand to meet the current situation or employ an associate, but with the staff acting as a control group.

This method of organisation has proved an efficient tool in the performance of my architectural services.

78 Foreword to Rudolf Schwarz, *The Church Incarnate*

Published foreword (1958).
Source: LMvdR, 'Foreword', in Rudolf Schwarz, *The Church Incarnate. The Sacred Function of Christian Architecture* (Chicago, 1958), p. VII.
Republished in Neumeyer (1986) 1991, p. 330; Pizzigoni 2010, p. 167; Walter 2022, p. 175.

This book was written in Germany's darkest hour, but it throws light for the first time on the question of church building and illuminates the whole problem of architecture itself.

Rudolf Schwarz, the great German church builder, is one of the most profound thinkers of our time. His book, in spite of its clarity, is not easy reading – but he who will take the trouble to study it carefully will gain real insight into the problems discussed. I have read it over and over again, and I know its power of clarification. I believe it should be read not only by those concerned with church building but by anyone sincerely interested in architecture. Yet it is not only a great book on architecture; indeed, it is one of the truly great books – one of those which have the power to transform our thinking.

I have always felt it should be translated into English. Now, thanks to Cynthia Harris, it can be studied by anyone in the English-speaking world.

79 Mies and the Glass Manufacturers

Typewritten transcription of a conversation (15 January 1958).
Source: LoC, Mies, Box 62, Miscellaneous, 'Mies and the Glass Manufacturers'.
Republished in Pizzigoni 2010, pp. 165–166.

Mies told of his difficulty in getting the glass people to make the brown-tinted glass for the Seagram Building – there was none on the market. At three o'clock one night in New York City he got the idea of investigating who makes the coloured glass for Seagram's bottles and would have called up Miss Phyllis Lambert then and there had it not been so late, though, he said, she was probably still up dancing. So he called her in the morning. She arranged for a meeting with Libbey-Owens-Ford officials, and a whole group of them flew in for the meeting – they had a rough flight in stormy weather. He met with them at the University Club. They began talking about how much they had done for the architects. Mies said, What have you done for us? We've been working for you since 1922 *(referring to his glass skyscraper project).* Then a vice-president asked Mies if he would guarantee them a certain volume of sales if they made the brown glass for him. Mies pointed at the chairman of the board and said, If I were him, I'd fire you for that question!
Mies had previously said, when they told him they had sent various representatives to see him, Yes, first you sent me a salesman. I didn't want to buy anything. I threw him out. Then you sent me an advertising man. What business did I have with him?
Mies told them he could get coloured glass from Europe, and they didn't like this. He said that when he built the Barcelona Pavilion, he had had a choice of seven or eight coloured glasses, but only two of them had been any good, the bottle green and mouse grey. He had used these in the building.

Mies didn't say from whom he eventually got the brown-tinted glass. Evidently, it was not from Libbey-Owens-Ford.

80 Some Thoughts About Civilisation

Audio-recorded speech (25 January 1958).
Source: IIT, Galvin Library, University Archives and Special Collections, no. 1998.159, audio recording.
Speech at Graduation Saturday night at Illinois Institute of Technology.
Republished in Walter 2022, pp. 169–174.

Dr Rettaliata *[John T. Rettaliata, IIT president]*, members of the faculty, and ladies and gentlemen, when I first heard this list Dr Rettaliata made known to you, I wondered – I was asked to speak here, and before I knew what I would say, I had to give a title because the programme had to be printed *[audience laughter]*. So I thought maybe I would talk on civilisation, but after a while I thought that was a very ambiguous title that could mean a lot *[of different things]*. It could mean the whole history of civilisation, or it could mean Greek civilisation, or it could mean medieval civilisation. But that was not what I wanted to talk about. I think many of these things you could find much better in books than I could tell you. So I reduced the title, even though I didn't know yet what I would say, to 'some thoughts', and *[now]* I have enough room to find something. But, I thought, what about civilisation may be of value to you? Now, what is civilisation? I think it is a state of special culture marked by advances in all the world of men. That sounds like a description out of the dictionary; I know that. But to talk about civilisation on the whole would take a long, long time. I would not give a course on Civilisation in a semester, so you can imagine that I cannot talk much here about that. I thought through my life *[to see]* if I could find something that would be valuable enough to tell you. By doing that, I remembered my first job as a draughtsman. There was no light in the room, no artificial light. We were sent home when it would get dark, and only in the case of an emergency did they give us candles. A little later, we got oil lamps and still a little later, there came a plumber, who fixed some pipes and we got the first gas lamps. They were improved again, the stoppings, until there came somebody who called himself an electrician. He put wires around the place and gave us some bulbs. So that was, in my opinion, an advantage against this other kind of light because it was flexible. At least, we could have it where we needed it. But I cannot say that this improvement of light helped our work. When that was improved, it was done by a single draughtsman, by his efforts *[Mies himself]*. I think these improvements of the lights may have helped to make that a little easier, but it didn't become better. My definition about civilisation was not a real, full one. There's no question that we have advanced in science, and I have seen it at least for more than 50 years and have seen that it has advanced rapidly. And my impression is that we have not to worry about this advancement of science and of technology, but rather the opposite. I have got the impression that these things have got so strong in themselves that they go on forever and that the main problem would be to be able to guide these things a little. And that is again the question of civilisation: the question whether we can educate ourselves enough to become able to regulate things that otherwise would go out of hand. So I think it is important that we educate ourselves. It is important that wisdom advances too, not only science. I see it as a necessity that we need a lot of scientists, and I have really nothing against it. But I believe on the other hand that we would need a few good philosophers. But I want to go on a little about my own life. When I took a new job, I was then 17 years old *[in Aachen]* and a place was assigned to me to work at, and I looked in a drawer and there was a magazine that was called 'The Future' and there was a print of the Kant Laplace Theorie. Since my education had stopped at 14 and I worked as an apprentice for a year and we didn't have books in our offices, that was a great surprise to me, and I became interested in reading it. First, the magazine was interesting to me because it had a lot of different articles and it was a weekly magazine, so I could go on reading. And it may have been that I didn't understand the Kant Laplace Théorie. By reading this magazine I became interested in it, and I started to borrow this magazine. At this time I earned the salary of 50 marks that I gave to my father. He, in turn, gave me one mark every week. Every Monday morning, I bought this magazine that cost half a mark. With the other half I bought cigars. But these two things were of great importance to me. They started, really, my education. I read these articles, started to buy books [...]. And certainly, my little library must have been as confused as our time, maybe a little more because I bought these things at random.

The first books had more the character of a technical nature. They were not books about technology. They were not books about architecture. I must say, I have read very few books in my own field, but they had a technical nature. And much later, I became more and more interested in problems of a general nature if you will, of a philosophical nature. I wanted to understand the world I was living in. Certainly, I learned through work and at this time the architectural situation was not clear, absolutely confused, like maybe everything else was. And it was a great trouble to find out, when we got a job, what to do with it. Nobody knew. We had to count our buttonholes, and this brought me to think about that, about what kind of architecture is possible and what is not. On my way to work I met or I saw every day a very old house I liked particularly, I didn't know then why. But I liked it more and more. And then I asked myself, what is the quality of this house, what is it? It was not that it belonged to a certain style; it was plain, but to me a very fine house. By looking at it carefully I found that the brickwork was done very well, that the stone frames of the windows were done very well, and that the timberwork was done very well. It had no particularly elegant proportions, but it had very good proportions. And the purpose of the house seemed equally good and reasonable.

Everything was in harmony with the other parts, and I think that gave this house the beauty I saw. And that is what I think is civilisation. When I got my first house, just to come back to my little library, I had to build a house for a philosopher *[Riehl House, Potsdam, 1907]*. And he came one day to my studio to discuss some of these problems. Then he saw my books, and he was surprised about my little library. He said, 'Who helped direct you to build up this library?' I said, 'First, I don't think it is a library; it is just a heap of books.' And I had chosen these books myself. But he was, I think, interested in the confusion which lay reflected in all these books, in all these fields. Later, in his house, I read a sentence from William the Silent: 'You do not need hope in order to start; indeed, you do not need success in order to persevere.' That was a sentence I have never forgotten. When I came to America, my assistant proposed that I should have a radio in order to get used to English pronunciation. So I ordered this radio, and when I turned it on, somebody with a very deep voice was talking, and he brought William the Silent again into the picture. This sentence I knew so well and have loved so well all my life. The next speaker was [...]. He talked about international relations, and he closed his talk by saying, 'Let us be nice to each other; it costs so little and it means so much.' I was glad to hear the first sentence of William the Silent here again in Chicago, but what [...] said I didn't know. But I must say that he was very right and that it is a typical American attitude, to be nice to other people. I felt that was really an American virtue. I have seen in other countries that people are polite, but they are not always friendly. Now I bought books and I was reading all my time when I had free time. I was never a Sunday painter. You could say I was a weekly reader or something like that. I loved to read and to study, and I bought more and more books, and the character of the books I bought changed little by little. At first I didn't realise what it was until I felt that I was after not knowledge but understanding.

When I left Germany, I had about, let's say, 3000 books, and I lived in a hotel here when I came to Chicago. But when I rented an apartment, I thought I should get some of these books, so I made a list of about 300 books, and now I must say I could send 270 back. But there are very important books I would not like to miss, and they are the books that are mostly concerned with civilisation and culture. Now you could say, 'What promotes advances in civilisation?' I think it is the effort of men and women in all fields, and it, it is you. You have to build up this civilisation. You have to build up the world you want to live in, and nobody else can do it for you. I have one more thing to say: don't worry about success. I always tell my students success is just the by-product of good, simple, and honest work. And this simple and honest work, I think, is the essence of civilisation.

81 A Special Kind of Order

Proposal and tentative script for a film (12 February 1958).
Source: LoC, Box 9, IIT, Mies Film; LoC, Box 62, interview with Mies. There are surviving traces of episodes nos. 1, 2, 3, 7, and 8 and a draft of the screenplay for episode 6. The introduction and screenplay for episode 6 are transcribed below. 'A Special Kind of Order' was the title for the planned film.

Mies van der Rohe. A Special Kind of Order, presented by IIT under the supervision of John B. Buckstaff and Donald P. Anderson, with Howard B. Dearstyne, Reginald F. Malcolmson, Ludwig K. Hilberseimer, directed by Hans Richter.
Television series in 13 parts, half an hour each: 1) Present-day architecture; 2) The house: what it has been; 3) The house: what it is today, 4) The skyscraper: how it became possible; 5) The skyscraper: today's refinements; 6) The growth of a skyscraper, 7) Public buildings; 8) Art and architecture; 9) Grouped buildings; 10) The Illinois Institute of Technology; 11) The Illinois Institute of Technology's School of Architecture; 12) Mies: his method of work; 13) A profile of Mies.
Ludwig Mies van der Rohe has done more to establish new directions and new concepts in the fields of architecture and building than any other architect of his period. He has shown that the new technology and the new materials of our era can – indeed must – become part of modern architecture before our buildings can truly express the greatness of our time. The free-standing wall, the use of glass and bronze as the skin of the buildings, the admission of the steel or concrete bones to be seen and become part of the exterior surface: these and many other Miesian concepts have now become fundamental principles in all modern building. Yet equally important in the work of Mies van der Rohe is his understanding of the beauty inherent in logical simplicity. It is this special kind of order, in partnership with

a brilliant understanding of modern materials and modern technology, which has placed Mies van der Rohe among the leaders of creative architecture. It is imperative that the work, the spirit, and the significance of this creative artist be preserved not only for contemporary generations but also for future generations. As one of many organisations indebted to the work of Mies van der Rohe, the Illinois Institute of Technology has therefore arranged this plan to preserve his work on film and to communicate this story through the media of television and motion pictures.

I think that 'architecture' ... is a terrible word: 'architecture' ... we have such a wonderful word in German and in the Netherlands and in Scandinavia. We call it 'Baukunst', and that is absolutely clear. The 'Bau'... the building ... and the 'Kunst' *[art]* is just a refinement of that building and nothing else.

I think the idea of architecture ... that is what I'm working on ... I'm not working on architecture ... I'm working on architecture as a language ... and you have to have a grammar in order to have a language. And grammar is discipline ... and then you can use it, you know, for normal purposes and you speak in prose. And if you are good at that, you speak a wonderful prose. And if you are really good, you are a poet.

Student: *Do you mean by that, Mr Van der Rohe, that by using the same words you can write a business letter ... or write Shakespeare?*

Absolutely yes. You have to construct something ... you make a garage out of it, or you can make a cathedral out of it. The same structural methods we use for all these things, you know. Architecture starts there where you put two bricks carefully together ... everything that you have to put together should be put carefully together. The structure is the basic grammar, and we use a skeleton on our campus. You should find the right material for the right purpose, and so on ... That is, I think, a moral attitude, you know. That would not be dangerous for an architect to have. I don't want to be interesting ...

I want to be good, you know. I am not a reformer; I don't want to change the world ... I want to express it. That's all I want.

Architecture is not a fashion ... and it is not something for eternity. It is a part of an epoch. And to understand our time means to understand the essence of our time ... and not everything that you see. The trouble is that every architect now tries to find his personal solution instead of an objective solution. Goethe said: you can make mistakes, but you should never build one. If you have not a clear structure, you know, you cannot get a good piece of art.

Now, as to the building at 375 Park Avenue.

It seems to me that a building should also make people happy ... to be in it ... to see it from the street. You hardly see the tall buildings ... you have to be far away from them. A lot of buildings are built without regard for shape or dignity or the pleasure of people. It was explained to me that what was wanted here was not only a practical home for the owner ... but also a noble home. So we came and tried to find out facts. For instance, we wanted to know what it is allowed to build here ... what are the limitations, and so on. And it was not easy because this building code is a very thick thing ... and nobody can read it. But we learned that we can build 25% of the site ... as a tower as high as you want. *[...]*

After we had made sure, you know, what could be built, and then when we got a picture, then we started ... went into details, you know. We had to know what were the requirements for an office building in New York ... what size the offices, and so on. One of the most important things is to synthesise the problems ... to achieve a clarity. This is hard work. We had to find out what the mechanical engineers needed and what I thought. And we had to talk to the structural engineer. Yes, you cannot know everything. I think architects ... they should understand more about engineering ... and engineers should know a little more about architecture. *(Yet to be worked out. The present idea is to use the mullion design as a basis for discussion ... the problem of the size presses available in relation to as simple a solution as possible, i.e. a compromise.)*

I think there are a few real fine materials, and that is stone or marble ... and they last forever. We wanted to have the walls of the building ... where the elevator goes, and so on ... we wanted not just plaster ... but to use a noble material. That is one of the reasons to use marble. And there it is very durable, you know, you do not have to paint it over and over.

We tried in fact many colours. In the end the decision was made for the Italian travertine ... because of the light. It was easy to light that ... and this light material would come out and the building would still be alive in the evening. We used serpentine on the outside because it is the only green material that lasts ... because all limestone ... also green marbles ... they will fade away after a year or two in the air and in the rain. And the serpentine comes from Italy ...

There are behind these serpentine marbles ... sheer walls that are concrete walls ... partly at least ... for many floors.

We could not cover it with glass, but we could have covered it with bronze ... and then we would have made the structure of our building unclear. To arrive at simple things, you have to work very hard. Less, you know, is more ... I think Peter Behrens said that. A skeleton building should be shown as a skeleton building, and if you see a building ... a skyscraper under construction ... you see the building as it is. And to keep that as much as possible, the best thing is to fill it in with glass. The skin can be various materials ... and they make now many of stainless steel. But I think bronze is the most lasting material that we can use in a building. In stainless steel you have this shiny colour, and it will get no patina ... and bronze will have a patina. It is exactly like stone ... a good stone or marble.

They certainly had a lot of trouble with skins because they are new and they have not enough experience. We were interested in every precaution being taken to guarantee that everything is really tight. The shape of the mullions ... that is a very strange affair. I tried many shapes, but the 'I' beam shape was the best. When it is hit by light, by the sun, you don't get only one shadow ... you get two kinds of shadow ... one is the colour shadow and the other is the real shadow ... what the light does. And it was more readable ... you could see it better.

You know, everything is so complicated in a building by now ...

You have to fight and to fight and to fight ... Structure is a philosophical idea. The structure is a whole, from top to bottom, to the last detail ... with the same idea. This coloured glass ... even as little as it is coloured ... has a mellow effect ... it has a mirror effect ... and it closes the building in more than clear glass would ever do. And it reflects and makes the building light and keeps it light. Green glass can have an effect, and I think it has it often ... and that is not a pleasant effect of the glass ... So we wanted to have a warm glass. It is friendlier. And it avoids the glare from inside ... which is very important in high buildings.

... And he started working on it ... and solved it.

82 Interview at Chicago Office: Eight Questions

Published magazine interview (September 1958).
Source: Edward J. Thias, Jack L. Thiess, 'Interview at Chicago Office: Eight Questions', *Construction Record* ('Architecture Mid-America' supplement), September 1958, pp. 4–5.
Also interviewed together with Ludwig Mies van der Rohe were Frank Lloyd Wright and Eero Saarinen.
Republished in Pizzigoni 2010, p. 168; Walter 2022, pp. 176–177.

What or who had the greatest influence on your early work?
I think old buildings with their strength.
What was the first building you designed?
A house for a philosopher *(Riehl House, [Potsdam] 1907).*
What do you think about Frank Lloyd Wright's 'Mile High' Skyscraper?
I have no thoughts about it. I am not a critic.
How do you feel your European work compares with your work in the United States?
I think I would have done the same thing anywhere, but there is greater opportunity for building in the United States.
What do you think about the buildings at the Brussels World Fair?
I am not familiar with them and have no comment on them.
What would you say about the word 'simplicity'?
Simplicity in my work is the elimination of everything that is superficial. Simplicity is honesty!
What would you say about the use of colour?
I prefer using natural materials in my work.
What do you think of urban growth and the cities of today?
The solution lies in planning the cities. I do not think merely tearing down one building and replacing it with another building will solve anything.

83 A Conversation With Mies van der Rohe

Published magazine interview (September 1958).
Source: Christian Norberg-Schulz, 'Ein Gespräch mit Mies van der Rohe', *Baukunst und Werkform*, vol. XI, no. 11, September 1958, pp. 615–616.
Translated from German by Mark Jarzombek.
Republished in Neumeyer (1986) 1991, p. 338; Pizzigoni 2010, pp. 169–172; Walter 2022, pp. 178–184.

Mies van der Rohe is known as a man of few words. Unlike Le Corbusier, [Frank Lloyd] Wright, and [Walter] Gropius, he has never defended his ideas in speech or text; his name only became familiar after the war. But the man behind the name remains as unknown as ever. As a replacement, so to speak, people have attempted to weave legends around him. The opponents of his architecture have discovered that he must be cold and without feelings, a formalist and logician who treats buildings like severe geometry. His adherents perceive him as a distant godhead floating above everything, divulging to his subalterns fundamental truths in the form of short aphorisms in professional journals. These aphorisms contain a certain mystical poetry reminiscent of the medieval mystic Meister Eckhart [Eckhart von Hochheim].
His office in Chicago is full of models of all sizes, very beautiful models of entire buildings, but also of individual corners and details. It is the same in the design rooms of his department at the Institute of Technology. The students work like professional metalworkers and construct detailed skeletons of large proportions. Everything points more to 'building' than to the drawing of 'paper architecture'. The main thing is the model, and the drawings are nothing but tools for the building site. The Institute of Technology constantly gets bigger. Mies is the planner. This way, the students have regular building practice during their courses of study. As you see, we are primarily interested in clear construction, said Mies.

'But is it not the variable ground plan that is typical for your school?' I asked somewhat surprised, for most of those writing on Mies emphasise the so-called variable ground plan.

The variable ground plan and a clear construction cannot be viewed separately. Clear construction is the basis for a free ground plan. If no clear-cut structure results, we lose all interest. We begin by asking ourselves what it is that we have to build: an open hall or a conventional construction type – then we work ourselves through this chosen type down to the smallest detail before we begin to solve the problem of the ground plan. If you solve the ground plan or the room sequence first, everything gets blocked and a clear construction becomes impossible.

What do you understand by 'clear construction'?

We specifically say 'clear' because we want a methodical construction in step with today's demands for standardisation.

Could one say that such a methodical construction should also serve to hold the building formally together?

Yes, the structure is the backbone of the whole and makes the variable ground plan possible. Without this backbone, the ground plan would not be free but chaotically blocked.

Mies then began to explain two of his most important projects, Crown Hall and the Mannheim theatre. Both are large halls formed of roofs and walls suspended from a gigantic steel structure. Crown Hall has two floor levels, one of which is half underground. It houses the workshop of the Institute of Design, while Mies' own Department of Architecture is housed in the upper hall. Malicious tongues have it that Mies has arranged this because he does not esteem the pedagogical methods of the Institute of Design and wishes – quite literally – to keep it down.

We do not like the word 'design'. It means everything and nothing. Many believe they can do it all: fashion a comb and build a railroad station. The result: nothing is done well. We are only concerned with building. We prefer 'building' to 'architecture'; and the best results belong in the realm of 'building art'. Many schools get lost in sociology and design; the result is that they forget to build. Building art begins with the 'careful' fitting together of two bricks. Our teaching aims at training the eye and the hand. In the first year we teach our students to draw exactly and carefully; in the second year, technology; and in the third, the elements of planning, such as kitchens, bathrooms, bedrooms, closets, etc.

Crown Hall and the Mannheim theatre are symmetrical. I asked Mies why so many of his buildings are symmetrical and whether symmetry is important.

Why should buildings not be symmetrical? With most buildings on this campus it is quite natural that the steps are on both sides, the auditorium or the entrance hall in the middle. That is how buildings become symmetrical, namely when it is natural. But aside from that, we put not the slightest value on symmetry.

Another remarkable similarity between the two buildings is the exterior construction. Why do you always repeat the same construction principle instead of experimenting with new possibilities?

If we wanted to invent something new every day, we would get nowhere. It costs nothing to invent interesting forms, yet it requires much additional effort to work something through. I frequently employ the example of *[Eugène]* Viollet-le-Duc in my teaching. He has shown that the 300 years it took to develop the Gothic cathedral were above all due to a working through and improving of the same construction type. We limit ourselves to the construction that is possible at the moment and attempt to clarify it in all details. In this way we want to lay a basis for future development.

Mies is clearly very fond of the Mannheim theatre: he describes it in every detail. He emphasises that the complicated ground plans conformed to the demands of the competition programme, which called for two stages that – having identical technical installations – can be played on independently of each other.

While Mies worked on some projects for months and years, this building was designed in a few weeks of hectic work, in the winter of 1952–1953. Students who helped him recounted how he would sit for hours in front of the large model, in his dark suit, 'as if for a wedding', the inevitable cigar in hand.

As you see, the entire building is a single large room. We believe that this is the most economical and most practical way of building today. The purposes for which a building is used are constantly changing, and we cannot afford to tear down the building each time. That is why we have revised *[Louis]* Sullivan's formula 'form follows function' and construct a practical and economical space into which we fit the functions. In the Mannheim building, the stage and auditorium are independent of the steel construction. The large auditorium juts out from its concrete base much like a hand from the wrist.

There were still many things to ask. Mies suggested continuing the conversation in his apartment over a glass. He lives in an old-fashioned apartment. The large living room has two white walls; the furniture is simple, cubist, and black. On the walls glow large pictures by Paul Klee. The maid serves on a low Chinese table, as if she wanted to arrange a Miesian ground plan.

One is surprised that you collect Klee pictures; one thinks that does not fit your building.

I hope to make my buildings neutral frames in which man and artworks can carry on their own lives. To do that, one needs a respectful attitude toward things.

If you view your buildings as neutral frames, what role does nature play with respect to the buildings?

Nature too shall live its own life. We must beware not to disrupt it with the colour of our houses and interior fittings. Yet we should attempt to bring nature, houses, and human beings together into a higher unity. If you view nature through the glass walls of Farnsworth House, it gains a more profound significance than if viewed from outside. This way, more is said about nature; it becomes a part of a larger whole.

I have noticed that you rarely make a normal corner in your buildings, but you let one wall be the corner and separate it from the other wall.

The reason for that is that a normal corner formation appears massive, something that is difficult to combine with a variable ground plan. The free ground plan is a new concept and has its own 'grammar', just like a language. Many believe that the variable ground plan implies total freedom. That is a misunderstanding. It demands just as much discipline and intelligence from the architect as the conventional ground plan; it demands, for example, that enclosed elements – and they are always needed – be separated from the outside walls, as in Farnsworth House. Only that way can a free space be obtained.

Many criticise you for adhering to the right angle. In a project in the thirties, though, you employed curved walls in conjunction with a free ground plan.

I have nothing against acute angles or curves provided they are done well. Up to now I have never seen anybody who has truly mastered them. The architects of the Baroque mastered these things – but they represented the last stage of a long development.

Our conversation ended late at night. Mies van der Rohe is not the man of the legends. He is a warm-hearted and friendly man who demands only one thing from his co-workers: the same humble attitude toward things that he himself has.

84 [Dedication of Cullinan Hall]

Manuscript and typescript of a dedication speech (10 October 1958).
Source: LoC, Mies, Box 62, Miscellaneous; Box 61 Miscellaneous, 'Dedication of Cullinan Hall'.
Speech given at the opening of the Museum of Fine Arts of Houston, Texas. Republished in Pizzigoni 2010, pp. 173–174; Walter 2022, pp. 185–186.

Honoured guests, this is a very happy day for me. It was a great honour to be asked to design this addition to your museum. Now that Cullinan Hall is finished, I am delighted to have this opportunity to express my appreciation for the help and support I have received from so many of you.

I want particularly to thank Mr Coates and Mr Hudson for their understanding and valuable cooperation at the beginning of this project. And all the way through, for more than four years, the faithful support of Mr Malone and the members of the Building Committee, particularly Mr *[Hugo]* Neuhaus and Mr *[Anderson]* Tood. I have always said that a building could be no better than the client.

I want to thank my Houston associates for their splendid cooperation – especially Mr Howze, who was in charge of this building.

To Mr David Haid, my assistant, I wish to express my warm appreciation for work that was certainly above and beyond the call of duty.

And now – most important of all – I come to Miss Nina Cullinan, whose generous gift made this building possible.

In older times it was the custom when a building was completed for the architect to present the donor the key to the building. Since I have always liked this custom, I have ordered a golden key for Miss Cullinan. I have chosen gold not for its brightness but for the more hidden qualities of this metal – purity and durability. It is my hope that these qualities may find expression in the meaning this hall may have for the community through the years – and in the work that will be done in it.

If these qualities do find expression here, then this hall will be indeed a noble memorial to your parents.

Miss Cullinan, may I now give you the key to Cullinan Hall?

85 [Conversation at the Architectural League in New York]

Unpublished typewritten interview (circa 1958–1960).
Source: LoC, Mies, Box 62, Interview with Mies, 'Architectural League'.
Republished in Pizzigoni 2010, pp. 211–222; Walter 2022, pp. 233–257.

Philip Johnson asked me if I would discuss certain questions with students, with younger architects, and he knew that I would not give a lecture because he knows me too well. And out of this question there came your question if I would come here and give a lecture. That I refused to do, and I said it was understood that that was just a discussion group, very simple, and I would be delighted to do that. And that was accepted by the League. And that it should be absolutely informal. I warn you I am a very bad speaker. I cannot make many jokes like Philip. So I cannot entertain you very much, but one thing I can do: I will answer with all honesty the questions you have. And I hope that we come in the course of this questions period to some problems; they may anyway be of interest to you.

[Why don't you want to prepare a lecture?]
Why don't I want to prepare a lecture? I think … to me it seems ridiculous to come to the Architects' League, where there are experienced architects – and what should I tell them? They know as much … as much as I do. So if you have anything to ask me, I will *[answer]*. You can ask me too … *[Silence]* All right, *[there]* is no question. I will. Maybe this is of interest to you, and it will throw a certain light on the answers I will formulate, just to tell you a little about my thinking about architecture and what was the aim of it. And I must say that in experience … I grew up … from about 1900, and I grew up in the architectural field. I was 14 years old, and in 1900 there was a strange group of very talented men in Europe, this movement of Art Nouveau *[...]* And they tried to develop a new … everything new: life new, dresses new, houses new, and new spoons … everything new. And we thought this was a problem of form. And it didn't last much longer than a fashion, this whole movement. Then it disappeared again. Only a few people, they went on working hard. And they were not the real carriers … this movement, what we call in German 'Jugendstil'. So nothing came out of that. They were most talented people, there were no better in this world. And they still couldn't do it. Then it became clear to me that it is certainly not the task of architecture to invent forms. So I gave that up. Then I tried to understand what … What is that? Why can we not do that? Why is it impossible to have an architecture in our time? And I asked some of these people. I asked Peter Behrens. He couldn't give me an answer. He didn't give any answer, anyway. He hated *[being asked]* that question. But I remembered that I saw some paintings when I was young, in my hometown. They were nothing; they were very simple but very clear. And they were always there, and always the same. And they lasted forever. They were partly medieval buildings, not with a special character, but had been really built. I don't know if the reason that I was impressed by these things was that I had to work in a stucco office. We designed ornaments, any kind of ornaments. And we made 'Louis Quatorze' ceilings. We had to draw that in the morning, 'Louis Quatorze' in the afternoon. A Renaissance ceiling for a dining room, and so on. So I had had enough of these ornaments. Some people ask me what I have against ornaments. I say if you have that for three years, that lasts for a lifetime. But then I came to the Netherlands, where I had to work for Mrs Kröller, and I designed for her a museum *[Kröller-Müller Villa, Wassenaar, 1912]*. And there I *[got to know]* the work of Berlage. And he was a man of straight seriousness. He worked. And he asked for good work. And he didn't accept anything that was fake. And that made it clearer to me that this good work is in fact the basis of architecture. And from there I came to the

idea of structure because he said nothing should be built that is not really clearly constructed. And he did that. And he did it to such an extent that his famous building in Amsterdam, the Stock Exchange, has a medieval character without being medieval. But he used the brick in the way medieval people did. And … but in itself the idea of a clear construction came to me there as one of the fundamentals *[…]*. Now, that is very difficult to do. I can talk about that easily. But to do it, you have to work with people. And they want to have this and that, and so on. But it is very difficult to stick to this fundamental construction and then elevate it to a structure. I must make clear that in the English language you call everything 'structure'. In Europe you don't. We call a shack a 'shack' and not a 'structure'. And by 'structure' we had a philosophical idea *[in mind]*. The structure is a whole, from top to bottom, to the last detail, with the same ideas. That is what we call a 'structure'. I know that is very often misunderstood, so that they think … you know, I just use I-beams because they come from the mill. Nobody has anything to do with it anymore. But that is not the real idea of structure. But there were other … other things of importance. Even if that is right – why was this construction … why even change the construction? And I tried to understand … how that … how that could happen. And I must say that the structure can only be built *[using]* a real construction … *[by using]* a real construction I mean *[using]* a structure of today and not of yesterday or of the past. That brought me then in the end … I was just … a résumé of what I do; you know, when I talk about that, I say it is not all grown in my back yard. I read a lot, and I tried to clarify problems, and I wondered why there are so many ideas that are contradictory, and so on. So I tried to understand what is the time, what is our time. And we see so many things, and to understand our time means to understand the essence of our time, and not everything that you see. Then we came later more and more … I was convinced that technology is a fundamental part of our time and, in addition to that, industrialisation. And then I asked myself what to do with it. Can that be done? Is it worthwhile to try it? And we tried it as good as we could. There's one other thought I still have. I think that 'architecture' is a terrible word – 'architecture'. We have such a wonderful word in German and in the Netherlands and in Scandinavia. We call it 'Baukunst'. And that is absolutely clear. The 'Bau', the building, and the 'Kunst' *[art]* is just a refinement of that building and nothing else. You don't *[throw something over it]*, the construction, and make some funny architecture of it. But I never was able to translate it for you. You should know that.

Could you please explain the Seagram Building?
I will tell you in a few sentences how we worked on it. To explain it would take too long a time. When we got the job, we tried to read the building code. That was impossible. Then we asked for the best office manager. We wanted to know what duties *[employees]* want to have in New York. How do they want to work? How do they want to live in this place? And he gave us some sizes of offices for secretaries, for two secretaries, for the […] the president, you know. So we decided on a unit of four feet, seven. Is that exact? I don't know. Four feet, seven and multiples of that … gave us a skeleton structure. So we have a six-six division and a bay, and this bay was about 27 feet *[27.5 feet]*. And then we made just a roster of 27 feet and put it on this side. And, curiously enough, it worked. It wasn't our … we had nothing to do with it, the site was just wide enough that it really fitted into that …

I'd like to know how you think in terms of the future.
It would be right, but I think it is not right. If there were clarity of what to do … how to work … then you would get in the end a unity. You cannot just command that. You know, there are so many forces in the way. They just make it impossible to do that. You have a wonderful strong man, Mr *[Robert]* Moses, here in New York. He will tell you exactly how difficult it is, you know, to overcome these forces. It is not negative. Those are facts.

I'm wondering why your great interest in technology and structure ... why it does not extend to concrete as we have discovered it works?
Concrete ... I would take that as a technological means too.
You would if you had the opportunity? I mean in shelf form?
That is another question. I would ask myself, you know, is it worthwhile to build the shelves or not.
What did you answer yourself?
No.
I read recently you planned for a piece of sculpture when in Rome [maybe the sculpture planned for in front of the Seagram Building]. Could you possibly discuss it?
That is very difficult. We are working very hard ... We did that mostly to clarify in our minds what would be possible there and what maybe would be good there. That is the main part. I have not been thinking to become a sculptor.
Problem of scale here?
Well, certainly that, and the character, you know ... We don't know yet ...
Why do you use no art, like you did in Barcelona, in your American buildings? Why don't you use more sculpture the way you did in Barcelona?
We don't have in our school buildings, you know ... we are glad to get the money for one granite step. They always tell me, you know, make it in concrete. Nobody sees that if you make it in concrete. I tell them then that if you make it in granite, nobody sees it, but if you make it in concrete, everybody sees it. It breaks to pieces, it is ugly, and so on ...
In other words, there is no money.
We don't have money for that. And then it would be very dangerous if you try to get a sculpture for nothing. Can you imagine what that in the end would be? The administration, they would be delighted to take anything for nothing. It is very difficult ... I am not against sculpture. I am not against paintings at all. But I think our work is so important, I don't think you can solve the architecture problem by putting paintings or adding sculpture to it. That has to be solved in itself.
Staying with the same question about sculpture ... If you have a building ... given choice... would you commission a piece of sculpture for the spot, or would you try to find the piece of sculpture?
I would first try to find it, and if I commissioned somebody, I would be very careful. You know, I really think there is a natural tendency to ... to dicker with things [...], but these things don't solve our problems, and we're still working on our problems. And I'm sure when we have solved our problems, the other things just fall into the right place.
Could you talk a little about what these problems are with reference to the Seagram Building?
I don't think it has anything to do with the Seagram Building. It is just the idea of using a clear structure ... in architecture. And one of the most important things is to synthesise the problems. You know, everything is so complicated in a building by now. So we have to simplify nearly everything in order to achieve a clarity. That is hard work. You have to fight and to fight and to fight. And particularly when there are scientists in the picture. But I [did that] in Chicago, you know.
Mies, while we said that back in the twenties or earlier, you conceded that the task of architecture was not the making of forms, the invention of forms ... it seems to me that it is true that when one reflects on the great architects of the twentieth century, namely Mies van der Rohe, Corbusier, Frank Lloyd Wright, that of these three important figures, the architecture of Mies van der Rohe is one that has not contributed forms, certainly not plastic forms. And yet, in the earlier works of yours that we all know – I'm thinking of the Barcelona Pavilion, [the Tugendhat House], the Berlin Exposition house – the great Miesian invention was the new kind of space. In your work in the United States, while structure has emerged – both the means and the end of building – you have yourself

abandoned, it seems to me, not only the possibility of architectural forms but also inventing the very kind of space that you invented.

No, that is not correct. That is not the case. A clear structure ... gives you all the freedom ... that you cannot, because it is structure, introduce... sentiments in it... As I see it, there are two tendencies going on; the one is a structural one, or you may call it 'objective', and the other is a plastic one, which you could say is 'emotional'. And you cannot mix them ... architecture is not a Martini. You have to be careful if you build a structure ... You have to be very careful what you can put into that structure. It is like a play of chess. There are certain rules, and if you look through the history, all the great epochs, they were certainly able to do anything, but they restricted themselves to a very clear principle, and that is the only way you can make important architecture. I think that is the basis for it. And then architecture depends on an epoch, as I said before. It is not a fashion, and it is not something for eternity. It is a part of an epoch. And it is very difficult to find out what is so important in an epoch because that is a very slow unfolding of a great form. But that is not an invention by me or you or you ... often when we do that, we don't know that we are working on this great form. And when this great form is fully understood, when the epoch is over ... then it is something new. That is how I see ...

Would you comment on Ronchamp? The chapel?

Yah, I think it is a great piece of art, but I would not call it architecture. I think it is ... you cannot ... you have to expect from Corbusier, who is a great artist, that he makes a piece of art. But I would not call it a building. I hate to make walls so big, where you don't need it or where you can [insert] plate glass. And that is my position on this particular building. And I think Corbusier is ... what I call ... a Baroque tendency. You know he painted a lot, and I think he made sculpture too; and he tries to combine these things into an architecture. And there are some people, they proclaim programmes for that. Things, great things, are never made by programmes. They grow. And I don't think that is possible, but I think it is very interesting that if you should attempt to build this chapel here on Fifth Avenue ... then you would see what it is worth. It is wonderful in a nice country. Why should we not do that? I have nothing against it. And when I talk about it, it is just because you asked me.

Would you call the Guggenheim Museum a [masterpiece]?

Yes, certainly I would do that.

Could you comment on it ... a little?

No, I will tell you. I pushed Mr Sweeney very hard to get that thing done. I trust that Frank Lloyd Wright lives until 150 years, but you cannot count on that.

You talked of the thickness of walls in Corbusier's church ... In talking with a client of yours in Chicago, I understand that some of the choice of material, of glass, in your apartments was based on a shortage of bricklayers in Chicago.

No. Not at all.

The same client is now more enamoured of brick in New York. Is that true?

Yes. But he did not get it.

In reference to Corbusier's work, I would appreciate comments on the Marseilles building.

Yah, I think that is a good building, and I think its value is that he tries to find a new way of living. And I haven't seen it, I have only seen pictures, so I cannot say much about it. But that again is something of interest. I am not a reformer; I don't want to change the world, I want to express it. That's all I want. And these ideas, you know, there are sociologists or other people who always tell us what we have to do, and we have to know how to build, and then their programmes or their functions, or whatever you call it, will modify or just colour that a little. But they cannot say it has to be done, and it has to be done, it changes so fast. We were talking about tall buildings versus low buildings. We proposed in Detroit doing both. Now, the tall buildings, you know, we got them mortgaged and everything and they are quite high now. But the low buildings, you know, they are just so expensive. If you take a unit in an apartment building – the same size – and put it on the ground, it costs a lot more, and it is a question … who should pay for it. That is not an architectural problem, you know, that is a finance problem, or I don't know what.

It depends sometimes on the code requirements, does it not? Sometimes when you're working on a low building of just one floor, you don't have to get into a fireproof construction.

Yah, I know. We tried that for a long time, and we are still trying to find a solution, but I became more and more doubtful that it is possible …

Speaking of social aspects, I wonder whether if a very unusual thing should happen, such as the New York housing authority asking you to do a low-cost housing project, would you consider this a challenge to your ingenuity and accept?

Certainly, I have nothing to do even with the cost. You know, they tried to bring it down and we are economy-minded, in spite of the bronze on the Seagram Building, I think it would not hinder me to work very hard to find a good solution for them. But, as I said, we are economy-minded just in another sense. You know we like to do it simple, and so on. You know that … nice and small.

You say you don't believe in applied ornamentation on a structure of any sort. I'd just like to know the function of the mullions on the façade of the Seagram Building.

That is a division where we have to bring the walls, the interior walls in … Then it is a wind bracing. You have to do something to hold the glass.

Well, then why doesn't the Lever Building, for example, feel the need for the same kind of thing as a wind bracing [Lever House, New York, 1951]?

I know they put the steel inside. But that is … you can do either one or the other.

You speak consistently of a clarity of structure; yet in many cases in examining details, I find these details to be rather complex in nature. Is this due to a lack of the technology with which you wish to design, or is the reason in the materials available?

Do I understand you right? You asked me about my own details?

The details …

Why don't you tell me which ones.

Well, let's take the detailing in the Seagram Building since that seems to be the topic of discussion. It seems rather complex at the column intersections there. I think I counted some 17 pieces of …

See, that depends sometimes on the manufacturer. We used in Chicago an aluminium section … That was one extrusion, the window included. Here we were confronted with a press, I think it was 76 inches. And that is what we wanted to have and needed for the mullion. And besides that, I think general [contractors], they are used to doing their work in this way.

So you would say the detail is complicated by the lack of technology in the manufacturing?

Well, certainly. It is always complicated. To arrive at simple things, you know, you have to work very hard.

I think of all the architects I know … who have combined the constructive expressionism of the Gothic with the sensualism, the balanced mathematics of the Renaissance – this is my interpretation. What do you think are the greatest lessons we as architects can learn from the architects of the past, not the recent past, from the earliest times up to the late Renaissance?

Certainly, you cannot learn much structure from the Renaissance.

No, we can learn something else, though, I think. I think you have shown us that we can learn other things besides structure.

Certainly. Certainly. You can learn from the past a lot of things. You know when I do that, too …

How should we search in the past, as modern architects? What should our approach, our attitude toward the past, be … do you feel?

You know, I don't think there is a formula for that. When I was young, I started to read. Since I had to buy the books myself, I read them very carefully

because they were too expensive. And when I came to this country, I had in my library about 3000 books, and I thought they should send them to me. I made a list, about 200, 300 books about. They sent them [to me]. Now I can send 270 of them back. Certainly, these I would not send back, these that I choose. So you see, it is very ... you have to work on that. You have to fight your way through. Nobody can tell you.
What sort of books have you kept, sir?
You are lazy.
I am a bit curious about what prompted the use of the materials, number one, that is bronze for the Seagram Building. Secondly, after this material was determined, why was it not finished to the extent that it would remain in its original form or first lustre?
Well, I'm thinking how to put your question together, you know. No, see, if you ... we used bronze, and I think it is marvellous and would like to have it as a natural material.
I agree with you. But it is rather expensive, is it not?
You [don't] have to pay for it.
... And yet how can you explain that in your own work [...]?
First it depends on the block you have, a city block. You know there is not ... you have no freedom.
I'm not speaking only in regard to the Seagram Building. For example, the Farnsworth House, that's an example where you didn't have anything surrounding you on four sides, and yet you [used] exactly the same theory. I just wanted to know whether you considered that block faithfully honest?
Did you see it?
Yes, regardless...
Did you see it? Did you see the trees around there?
That's just adding something after it's done, I feel, to make up for...
No, the trees [have been] there for 100 years, or 150 years ...
Yes, but to depend entirely upon the trees instead of the resources of the architect ... upon that nature ... I just wanted to know ...

Well, you are talking about the orientation of the building. We moved the building close to the trees so it gets as much shade [as possible] in the summer.
Well, let me phrase it differently ... If there weren't any trees, would you still design on all four ...
It may be. See, we had the building on our draughting board. We didn't have many draughting boards. They made a model out of these things. That is from [steel], and that is glass, but [here] we just cantilevered the roof, so that the building is in the shadow. There are many ways you can do that. But in a tall building you cannot do it. You know, you can just hang your eyelashes out there, and so on ...
But it seems they controlled it fairly well in buildings in South America ... Where you have arrived at a method of controlling most of your sun ...
You haven't been there or you wouldn't say that ...
I'd like to know more ... the great things in the past ... why we appreciate so much ... for then usually architects were also sculptors and artists ... and a man today is also a sculptor and artist ...
I don't know ... if I understand you right ... I'm interested in a cathedral as a structure and not about that ... the things around ... I have nothing against ... but that is a refinement. You know these things didn't ruin the structure. The opposite: I think the cathedral is the clearer structure.
You would prefer, perhaps, the cathedrals without the sculpture?
I have seen wonderful ... they had nothing in it. You can never say ... you still do not believe what I said before, I have nothing against art beside architecture. I have nothing against that. But I would not make it a ... If you have not a clear structure, you know, you cannot get a good piece of art.
Absolutely ... I would wonder whether art would help the architect when he designs the building – the art the architect has himself, not art that he applies afterwards ...
I didn't understand ...

Is there any value in an architect having a thorough knowledge of art – having worked in art himself, so that when he approaches the design of the building, he has at his command ...? I certainly don't approve of adding art after the building is up, after it's been designed ...
You know, I have good advice: do it yourself and see what comes out. That is the only proof you can ... where you really can make an experience.
You were one of the judges on the memorial competition [this competition has never been identified]. This was a most unusual selection. Can you give us some light on how it was picked?
It was picked ... They had a large model, and all the entries, they were made in the same scale, and we put not all of them, but most of them, we put [there] and we came to the conclusion that the smaller the building was, the better. And in the end, you know, we came to the conclusion it would be wonderful if it were a plaza ... nothing [more] ... that is fairly thin and still open. We were uncertain – you know, does it work? We didn't know anything about acoustics and so on, so we telephoned to MIT to find out ...
It seems to me you were trying to bring in one more of the arts after using free architecture ...
That, you know, that was the idea of this man, but for this reason he would not have gotten the prize, not from me. I gave him that for another reason.
Architectural integrity, one of the most important things you can have ... Is it true, or do you feel, that an apartment building such as Lakeshore Drive and a building such as Seagram should have the same outer expression. Don't they serve two different functions? Why should they be treated in the same way?
That is the function: in the one you work, in the other you live. That is the difference.
Well, doesn't one require much more privacy than the other?
I don't know if a businessman would agree with you there. But why is Lakeshore Drive ... why should that not be private?

Well, curtains are just another added thing to combat the architectural intention that if you like windows ...
I think the curtain is one of the finest walls we ever have. You can move it as much as you like, and so on. Why should there not be a curtain? What would you do if you built in brick?
I should say there should be a curtain wall. Living could be just as open in a sense ... I mean ...
Did you live in a building like that?
No, I didn't.
We have been hearing quite a bit about your phrase 'less is more'. Would you tell us what the origin of this phrase is?
I said it ... I think I said it first to Philip ... Oh, I think where I heard it first was from Peter Behrens. Yes. You know it is not original, but I like it very much.
Sir, isn't the architecture of any period in a healthy state when not only can the individual genius design successfully, but the common carpenter and the average builder can produce successfully? How today can we again achieve successful buildings throughout the country? ... We had folk cultures in an earlier period ...
I don't know. But you see, if you have large buildings, then you have to have a very good general contractor, I can tell you that. Otherwise, it just doesn't work. These builders, they build these small houses throughout the country. That is another question. I don't understand why don't they use better design ... Maybe just the way they do it is cheaper.
On the Seagram Building ... The idea of bronze as a building material, how much study went into this? Was there was a great influence ... from there already having been a stainless-steel building, and an aluminium building, and a glass building? ... I'd like to know how much influence these other buildings had on the selection of the materials, as an experiment in a different material, or as a study of the material itself and its qualities as a building material ...
Sometimes there is an influence. For instance, when you ... At 860 Lakeshore Drive, we used steel as it comes from the mill, you know. And it was done by

the American Bridge Company. The next building, you know, we would have used steel, but we would have had to wait 12 months to get it, and then the price would have been higher than for a concrete skeleton. The concrete skeleton gave three floors more for the same height because of the lower floor construction. And there we used aluminium. And the Seagram Building – you know, Mr *[Samuel]* Bronfman, the owner, he liked bronze, and we had nothing against it. *I was in the Seagram Building and noticed first of all the sparse spandrels, how nice and thin they are, enabling you to get nice tall windows, and then I went inside and I saw a lot of ductwork and related things passing through your beams, and it seems to me that each beam had to be specially designed so that all these conveyances could pass through it rather than underneath, allowing for these very nice proportions on the outside. Now, you get as a result, of course, a clarity of structure in spandrels, but in actuality it's accomplished what I thought was a tour de force. I'd like to know what you feel about that.*

No, I think that is so complicated. You know, the mechanical engineers, they had to do something in order that it worked. Do you think we like particularly that they have to drill holes in our beams?

Why wasn't there a space underneath them? Which would have been much easier than to design every beam for these things passing through.

No, I think it would have been much more expensive.

But had there been less glass on the façade, there would have less [need] for so much ductwork … air conditioning …

What would you have used then for that less glass? What kind of material would you have used for less glass? You know if you just close it in, then you need even … you don't need air conditioning, you don't need even a mechanical engineer. Why should we not … A clear expression of the skeleton, I think that is a real modern expression, and the question is not to destroy that. It is an architectural question. And that is why we insist to do it this way.

Isn't there something wrong with our arts and our architecture when the great masses of people don't enjoy it? When you take [out the appeal] of our architecture, don't you lose part of its essence? Isn't a really great epoch one in which the arts appear on every level, the highest and lowest, in which everybody can enjoy painting and architecture?

Yes. But people have a brain too. You know, I had a discussion about that with somebody in Germany, back in Germany, and this man was a Nazi – a top Nazi – and *[making]* trouble for the Bauhaus. He said he studied architecture, he understood perfectly well that *[you]* can cantilever a roof, but he said his feeling was hurt when there was no support under it, you know. I said my brain would hurt if there were one.

But isn't architecture one of the fine arts? And if he were doing the roof, he would put a support under it because that was how he felt; and if you were doing it, you wouldn't.

Under no condition. We wouldn't do that. Whether the people liked it or not.

One of the most important design factors in architecture is structure … I just wonder whether other things such as colour or light could …

When I said … that is … I think it is the most factor … I don't exclude a lot of other factors. I have nothing against the fact that space is well lit or even well painted.

How would you define architecture, Mies? I'm not sure what we've been talking about all evening … I'd like to know what your definition of architecture might be. I don't mean that in a hostile sense at all. But I'm sure your definition would be better than almost anyone's here … I've never seen it in black and white.

… I'll tell it in German. Is too difficult for me: 'Baukunst ist raumgefaßter Zeitwille'. Why don't you write it down and then try to translate it?

We'll let Mrs Marley translate that …

Mrs Marley: 'The art of building is time embedded in space.' Or 'time expressed in space'. Or 'Architecture is the expression of an epoch translated into space.'

Now there are a lot of young people here tonight, and I wonder, Mr Van der Rohe, if you would like to give them some advice. Some of us probably are well along, and maybe we are not going to contribute much to architecture, but these youngsters might like to hear some advice about how they should approach their first commission, or what they should think about – certain clarities that you've mentioned. Perhaps you'd like to repeat them or ...

I think there is one thing that I would do: I would work very hard.

86 [Eulogy for Herbert Greenwald]

Published eulogy (12 February 1959; Greenwald died on 3 February 1959).
Source: published pamphlet, Memorial Service: Herbert S Greenwald at Anshe Emet Synagogue, 3760 North Pine Grove, Chicago, Illinois. Now in LoC, Mies, Box 61, Memorial Greenwald, with drafts.
Republished in Pizzigoni 2010, pp. 175–176; Walter 2022, pp. 187–188.

I am very grateful to Mrs *[Lilian]* Greenwald for the privilege of saying a few words to you at this service for Herb. It will be difficult for me because he was my friend. He was your friend too, and our personal loss is great. Beyond this, the community has lost a true benefactor, and our community is larger than we are. Herb's life was short, but his contribution to life was rich and will be remembered long.

In the many years I knew and worked with Herb, I always found a quality in him that is well expressed in the words of William the Silent. Herb needed no hope to begin, and no success to persevere. He accepted defeat with the same balance and good sense with which he welcomed success. In this he was a real philosopher.

I first knew him shortly after the end of the war – these were his early and most difficult years. Even then, I was astonished at the boldness of his thought and the fearlessness of his action. I saw him in many difficult and even hopeless situations, but to him the difficulty was a source of strength. Herb had an enormous capacity for learning, and he learned quickly. He grew with each new piece of work to an amazing degree.

As you all know, in his very few years he was active not only here but in many of the large cities in this country. All of us in my office liked him so much. He was the friend of everyone who worked with him. We came to depend on his vitality and his optimism – qualities that were a source of real inspiration to us.

We will miss him. We will miss his brilliance, idealism, and his gallant spirit. He was so strongly a man of our age, and yet he held to the best values of all the ages. We have much to thank him for.

87 [Story About the Barcelona Pavilion]

Typescript transcription of a conversation (March 1959).
Source: LoC, Mies, Box 62, Miscellaneous, 'Mies Erects the Glass Walls of the Barcelona Pavilion 1929'.
Republished in Pizzigoni 2010, p. 177.

It was the day before the opening of the pavilion, when King Alfonso [XIII] of Spain was to be received in it by representatives of the German government. The pavilion was ready, except that the glass enclosing walls had not been raised into place. At this juncture Mies had a dispute with the young German engineer who was in charge of the construction and he (foolishly, as he said) fired him. He then proceeded to erect the glass walls himself with the help of some of the people who were working with him on the building. They laboured through the night, and all hands heaved a sigh of relief when, just before dawn, the last section was fixed in place. As the light grew stronger, they stepped back to have a look at the building. To their consternation, they discovered that the large sheets of glass were covered with 'millions of handprints', *as Mies said.*
So, with the king coming just a few hours later, they set to work again feverishly with newspapers, going over every square foot of the glass, cleaning off the hand marks. They beat the deadline, and King Alfonso never knew a thing about it.

88 [Conversation With Architecture Students in Chile]

Transcript of interview (March 1959).
Source: Archivio Histórico José vial Armstrong, Colección Fundadores, Valparaíso: Escuela de Arcquitectura y Diseño Pontificia Universidad Católica de Valparaíso, 2011, Conversación con van der Rohe ['Conversation with van der Rohe'], March 1959.
The original interview given in English is lost; all that we have is a typewritten transcription in Spanish (thanks to Moisés Puente for alerting us to this fact).
Translated from Spanish by John Nicolson.

Arturo Baeza: What did you mean when years ago you said that modern architecture would reach a new level when a new universal material is found?

The new material is the possibility of manufacture by machines. It's now possible to use aluminium, which was also known in the past, but now industry allows its use. I remember many years ago I thought about aluminium, and one day I left a piece of it in the window to see the effects of the weather on it. The role of the architect, however, is not to invent materials but to use materials invented by others.

Bernard Spring: For Monsanto we have made a house type using plastic, and now we're studying a plastic sandwich system that could be used in construction and in creating new forms.

This is one possibility, and there are many. We have to let the industry invent and test the materials, and after they've been tested, the architect must use them. Architects should look at industry as a producer of parts and not of finished units.

A.B. The steel, glass, and bronze that you use presuppose a choice of certain industrial products. They already have a formal purpose. But today industry offers us other materials, such as plastic or concrete itself, materials which do not come in pieces but are homogeneous and continuous and which lead to other possible forms and uses.

Yes, but I like to work with limits and to solve the problems created by these limitations.

A.B. I thought you were referring to a universal material, something like a kind of resistant transparent plastic.

Plastic gives a lot of freedom. Personally, I like having limits. I think that for those who don't have many skills, this would be a great freedom. When you have fewer limits, you have to be a lot more careful. Nervi and Candela, who work with free forms, are very good at designing a roof. But when they go higher, they don't know what to do – because then the only thing that's suitable is the flat roof.

A.B. What do you say about all the floors in this case being identical although at different heights you see different landscapes emerging? How would the height be perceived by the eye?

This is an economic problem. *[Repeating the floor saves money. And that's something that's on many people's minds.]* When I talk about economising, I don't just mean a matter of cost, but that if this represents a possibility whose result lacks strong reality, then it's not worth the effort. Architecture has a social value.

A.B. That's true, but the invention of the car changed many people's way of looking at things. Motorways appeared, along with the things found next to them – signs, parks, etc. – born of the different way that the eye now perceived speed. And this is a challenge for many. Also today, elevators and the technique of building at height have produced different possibilities for looking, and this richness is what we must give. That's also a challenge for many; it has a social value. I think it would be necessary to find another richness for the eye at height, just as speed has produced it in the wake of the car.

And then it doesn't get built. It is more important that the floor plan is free – because nowadays function is variable. But the building is not variable. In the past I would have said that form follows function; today that's not what I think. Sullivan would have said the same thing – due to the speed and changes occurring in the USA. Today, however, the functions of his buildings are changing. There are examples in how his works are used. Flexibility is what I've been working on most recently.

Jaime Márquez: Going back to industry: do you believe in the possibility of creating a prefabricated unit with an architectural content – I mean one that has a finished form just as a car is a finished unit?

At one time we tried doing that in our office. If it can be produced economically, then that's fine. Because today it's all about money, just as a building can be a vision of the Renaissance and not of today. Architecture is an expression of truth, and you can't play with these facts. Today's facts are economic, and the economy is very strong.

Jaime Garretón: What is the limit of flexibility? You talk about it in the horizontal. Why not vertically?

Flexibility is for the individual floor because you don't need it at height. *[I have not needed it.]* But were it to be needed, it would have to be created.

J.G. In this freedom are you happy joining absolutely any functions together – a home with offices, for example?

My house would make a good factory, and I could live in the School of Architecture. I once visited a wooden barrack: the warehouse of Plywood Co. It was a big space with boundaries that were 14 feet high and formed by piles of wood. I would have loved it as a house: it was a simple space.

Ricardo Alegría: What is the new scale you're talking about?

When you travel by car, you don't see the details of a sculpture. A painting should not be put in a hall because people are passing through, they don't stop.

Bruce Graham: But I stop in the hall of the Seagram.

Because you are an architect.

B.G. My brother is a doctor, and he stops too.

It's not the function of a hall to be looked at but to be entered and got out of it as quickly as possible. In South America there is a Baroque tradition, and it's a big problem. Niemeyer does nothing new but Baroque. The Baroque tradition is a good one, but I'm happy not to have it. Here in the United States there is no tradition.

Lautaro Moraleda: Why put up a curtain wall?

If the skeleton is strong, you can use a curtain wall. The 'curtain wall' is the least *[substantial]*.

L.M.: But why cover up the structure?

Steel buildings have to be covered with concrete against fire, but they're made of steel. The steel curtain wall expresses the steel inside.

L.M. Don't you think this concrete cladding is stronger?

No, I don't think it is too strong to express it. In my works you see that buildings in which the steel is not expressed are inferior to those in which it is expressed. That's something you have to see. *[Pause.]* When I went to build the Seagram in New York, the first thing they gave me was a pile of regulations *[gestures with his hands]*. The second thing was a module given me by the economics expert. And with this the Seagram was made. When I start on a challenge, I never have a great idea. I look at the reality and solve it – that's all. I remember, there was a building where construction had already started and an expert came along – and the apartment modules were changed because the need *[demand]* had changed. This can only be done with a neutral module.

R.A. What do you think of the horrible urban landscape that the 'curtain wall' is creating in New York?

Stupidity! You have to find the truths; you have to tell people what the truth is. That one module is good for an office, two for a secretariat, three for an office, etc.

J.G. How do you control the flexibility of the building after it is finished?

If the building has a strong structure, you can do whatever you want inside it. And whatever you want, it won't damage the building. In New York, when they're out of ideas, they move the columns. In this office we spend our imaginative energy on making the structure clear and not on decorations. When I was young, I worked for three years at a stucco-making firm, where I had to design full-scale decorations in the style of the Renaissance, Louis XIV, and so on. A student once asked me, 'Why don't you like decoration?' I replied that I spent three years drawing these details – three years is as good as a lifetime!

What does it say about the orientations of your buildings that they are all the same?

The problem here in the United States is different. There are people who prefer north, people who prefer south, west, and east. In Europe it's a different matter: there isn't much sun, and the orientation is towards the south. And then that scares them, and they cover it up. I always make the smallest orientation to the west. I couldn't close the building to the west either; they put up curtains when they want to open the building and when they want to close it. It's the most advanced orientation.

What do you think about colour?

I prefer the colours of materials rather than the [applied] colours of pigments. Colour is outside in nature, where it reaches a splendid pitch. The 'curtain wall' allows these colours to be reflected. And then white in the interior – a neutral colour; and the white walls are filled with colour and light through the windows. But I accept any colour, so long as it is black or white.

A.B. *I agree.*

So much the better for you. Most people who ask for colour are colour-blind. If you want colour, put up a good painting, and I won't complain. I can't live in a room with lots of colours, but I can live in a white room with a big Picasso.

B.S. *Then why did you put the colours on the fifth floor of the Seagram?*

Oh! Phillip ... *[laughs]* No! But there are some very well-placed colours.

B.S. *But there's one floor that's horribly painted: the third floor.*

I haven't seen that.

A.B. *Better not to see it.*

If you have any other questions, we'll meet again tomorrow.

A.B. *After seeing the buildings in Chicago, one realises that the Seagram is the first Chicago building in New York. And its colour really comes from the materials, and it carries within itself the possibility of use, of time. The changes of colour and the dirt of the city do not affect it: the building takes them into account. This is not the case with the Lever House, for example, which, if it is to be seen properly, must constantly be cleaned.*

The Seagram has already had two more cleanings, but only one will be carried out to protect it from the cement dust from neighbouring buildings, which have changed its texture and colour. After that, though, it will not be cleaned again; the bronze will change naturally until it reaches its final colour.

A.B. *But it is not only the colour of the bronze, but the glass, which reflects the city, like in the Lake Shore apartments, and produces a range of colours due to the transparency of the curtains and the reflections of the exterior, that gives it its overall colour, and this, this colour thing, is something that is never shown or talked about in publications.*

The curtain wall allows the reflection of the colours of nature, which is where the colour takes on a special splendour. I'm talking about the nature of the materials. If you have bronze, glass, and marble, you have everything. *[The Seagram's bronze is a special alloy that has less copper than the bronze used by sculptors.]*

A.B. *The metal profiles of the Seagram were manufactured specially for the Seagram. Are they made of a special alloy, and did that make them very expensive?*

No, it's an alloy that has less copper than the alloy used by sculptors; that's the only difference. Less does not always cost less. But less does more, and this is true economy. *[Pause.]* In my youth I bought 3000 books to read. Because I had bought them, I had to read them – and that cost me more than it had cost to buy them. In my youth there were no teachers, and I had to read 3000 books that were books of culture and not novels. That's why I can now pass this on to my pupils. My habit even today is to spend the morning thinking, reading, studying, and in the afternoons I go to the office. People shouldn't complain that today there are so many pupils studying with teachers.

A.B. But you had to read those books. Today this is free for pupils: they don't have to do this themselves.
Today too they have to read. And today too they have to study, otherwise this costs them nothing and they will just copy.

A.B. And how do you teach at university?
At the university students must: in the first year know how to draw, in the second learn how to build, in the third also to build, in the fourth learn the function of the building, and in the fifth the proportions of a space. You have to teach very simply so they understand the idea.

A.B. Do you give them the idea in the fifth year, or do you start with it in the first year?
What we teach is understanding. Talent cannot be given, but talent does not have half the value of understanding.

A.B. What do you think of your pupils and disciples?
Some understand, some don't. They are as good as any other pupils elsewhere. What I try to give is discipline. I make them draw all the bricks in a wall, because you need this discipline to be able to answer all the questions that arise in architecture. Students have to be taught everything, from cleaning their desks and sharpening their pencils with a knife. The [greatest] difficulty in teaching is when one moves from teaching how to draw to how to build. Because when you start teaching how to build, your pupils start to think, and when they start to think, they become bad draughtsmen. This is the most difficult (and dangerous) stage; you have to insist and insist on drawing. Architecture begins by putting two bricks next to each other 'very carefully'.

A student once asked me, 'How then did you learn so much about steel?' By putting one brick next to another 'very carefully'.

Francisco Schlotfeldt: What were your impressions when you first came to America? And what influenced you?
The worst impression was teaching at architecture schools. The school chiefs told me I would be successful if my students got jobs at architecture firms, and that if I only admitted three students a year, in five years I would have just 15. I replied that to change the architecture of Chicago, five architects would be sufficient.

F.S. Did the architecture of that time [in the USA] influence you?
No! I would like to know if I have changed them. In Germany I would have done the same as here, but the good thing is that there is little tradition here and they let me do what I wanted. In Germany they wouldn't have let me – because of the laws and regulations in the different towns. The bad thing here is that everyone is allowed to do what they want, even the bad guys. The 'yellow' countries and the American continent should do things for themselves, and not use Corbusier for example.

A.B. I think that is very profound. A European can go to a place, discover and identify what is there, give it a form, and take it further. Le Corbusier in India and Brazil. Mies in the USA, with Sullivan ...
It's possible. But I'm not continuing Sullivan's decoration.

A.B. Sullivan is an architect not because of his decoration but because of everything else. I am not saying you are continuing his line. I'm saying you have revealed an order which was latent and ignored.
Yes, but Sullivan was more into ornamentation than anything else. When Sullivan made his benches, which were very simple, you could see that they were made by an architect. But when he decorated, he made some pretty bad buildings. Sullivan and

Wright have the wrong idea of nature; they should read Thompson's book.

A.B. *We have travelled around the south and east of the United States, and we've seen that works of architecture are placed in the landscape without touching it, like in the hollows left by trees. It seemed that nature already possessed order, when in reality it is the architect who must order nature with his work.*

Yes, when I flew from Sao Paulo to Lima, I saw a red city on a plain. It had a lot of order, like European cities.

A.B. *It is the order of the Spaniards that we saw in San Juan de Puerto Rico.*

At one time there was this idea in Europe and everywhere *[that nature possessed order]*. Van de Velde said that the line has force, and I thought a lot about this and realised that Van de Velde was a graphic artist and that's why he thought so. But in architecture this *[the line]* has no importance. *[Omitted from transcript: conversation about Kokura Palace, Japanese architecture, and Farnsworth House. The equal importance of (all) places.]*

A.B. *When one sees your works in Chicago, the Seagram in New York, or the project for Battery Park, the choice of sites seems something very important in your work. The Seagram on Park Avenue with the space of that street and the gap left by the Lever House in front of it. Battery Park as the site of the entrance to New York and Lake Shore at the edge of the lake. These are works in places that are significant for the city. Do you choose these places?*

I participate in the choice of location. I see the possibilities of the places that Greenwald proposes to me. In the case of Battery Park, we chose the land and subsequently got the ordinances changed so that the buildings would open up the sea to the city. Originally it was two buildings, but we're proposing three.

A.B. *In fact, when those buildings are built, Manhattan will have order, just as the Seagram orders the buildings on Park Avenue. The positions that they occupy, like radials: how did you manage this?*

We looked at their orientation in relation to a point in the centre of Wall Street, and we chose that as the centre. The buildings are radial with respect to this point, and also to the brightness they will give with respect to the sun.

A.B. *Are the buildings going to be aluminium?*

I haven't decided on the material yet.

A.B. *They could be marble.*

Glass is a great material.

A.B. *Who will this building be for, and how will its programme be determined?*

I don't know for whom. Probably for the people who work in the surrounding area: Wall Street, the harbour, work involving the sea. The number and type of the flats is being determined by a financial study. There is more economics in my work than you might think.

A.B. *Did anyone from your office go to Cuba when the building for Santiago de Cuba was being designed?*

Yes, me personally. It is a very Baroque city. *[Omitted from transcription: conversation about Van Ersteren.]*

J.M. *You designed some houses in which the car came inside the building. The car was part of the architecture.*

Those houses had curved forms that I don't think I would use today. I realised that living inside those forms would be very tiring. When I set up the architecture school in Berlin, we used an old factory. It was very dirty, and I decided to paint it white. This gave us a big simple white space. Inside it I installed all the students from the different courses, and there was a lot of contact between old and new, which was very beneficial. I once visited Plywood Co.'s warehouse. It was a very simple big space with beautiful proportions: simplicity and proportionality, and inside it you can do whatever you want because this order is strong.

A.B. *How do you teach proportion?*

I only teach the eye to see. Usually students are very lazy, so I try to make their work easier. I once asked my students to place a wall in a house. This they did on a model. The students just cut a wall and stopped at that. So I invented a moveable wall with two pieces of cardboard that moved parallel to one another, allowing for various wall sizes. Another task was to draw a straight line inside a plane. The pupils drew a line and then could not erase it, so I invented cutting a line on black paper and pinning it in different positions to study the problem.

A.B. *What is the point of making models given that they are never complete but only parts, as we have seen in your office, or on a reduced scale? Is this a problem?*

That's true, but a model is better than a drawing.

A.B. *When you designed the Barcelona Pavilion, did you make a scale model beforehand?*

No, just a small one.

A.B. *Would it be possible to build by modifying during construction – to check on site what is not given by drawings and models?*

That could be done in Europe, but not here in the United States. It can't be done here.

A.B. *And would you like to be able to do that?*

I don't think it would be very important. It would be nice, but I don't think it's important.

J.G. *I have thought about building a whole house without plans.*

Yes, that would be possible ... but you would have to decide first. I imagine that if it's a good house, then you'd be happy to make a good drawing of it.

J.G. *A house designed and not built: is that a work of architecture or not?*

Yes, it has value. It clarifies ideas, which is a good thing. I do almost one house a year that doesn't get built. For example, if you have thought of doing a specific project, do one that has to be done and one you don't have to do specifically. And if you live in a specific country, you should do it.

A.B. *Is pre-compressed concrete becoming more important?*

Yes, but it is still too heavy. [It can only be managed on roofs.]

B.G. *An Italian architect said the best thing (in your architecture) was marble.*

He says so because he is Italian.

J.G. *I think flexibility could affect whole buildings too: they could be temporary and then removable.*

I don't think so. That's a theory.

J.G. *I'm thinking of the centre of Santiago: buildings are being put up that will be immovable for many years.*

Instead, they should be building huge halls [inside which you can do anything].

J.M. *What was your aim when you started designing your furniture: what was the challenge?*

I was designing new furniture for every house I built. But then I thought it was better to sell the manufactured furniture; in that case I wouldn't have to argue with every client. It was at the silk exhibition in Germany that I had first had a problem with the furniture. There were those precious silks as beautiful as a Picasso painting, golden yellow, shiny black. Then I saw that the furniture had to be made of steel. The challenge in designing a chair is more difficult than when designing a house: the chair has to be comfortable, beautiful, and not break. I would sit for hours in the chairs we designed, to see how comfortable they were and to try to break them – we ended up with a graveyard of broken chairs. In my office I had my own workshop, which is much more important than a place for the accounting books.

Ivan Godoy: *You talk about giving the building flexibility, but this makes it lose the character it has due to its function.*

The structure is strong enough to support itself; it is the strongest thing. I've been reading a lot lately about integration of the arts. But in architecture the only thing that counts is the structure, and that is for the architect alone to do, without help from either a sculptor or a painter. And if you find a good painting or sculpture, the only thing you have to do is find a good place to put it.

A.B. *What do you understand by structure?*

Construction is what is necessary to support a thing. Structure is the understanding of the construction. The structure is the spiritual value; the construction is just a method. This confusion of words is what prevents many people from understanding me. I must repeat: structure is a spiritual value and construction is a method.

A.B. Ignorance of the real meaning that words have is a serious problem for us.

This problem does not exist in Europe because the words do not mix.

J.G. But if you have a new idea for the concept of structure, will you have to invent a new word?

No, because the content may change, but the word continues to indicate the same phenomenon. The words [still] have the same meaning in poetry. 'Construction is the method of the curious functions of the mind.' That's Beaudelaire. Many people believe that architecture should be an art, but these people have a very funny idea of what art is ... and that's where the problem begins [smiles]. This conversation is making me remember things I thought a long time ago.

I.G. You don't think that character needs to be differentiated in functions such as office, hospital, and room?

The difference should not be that one is different from the other, but only in the scale of values. The difference should be in making one better than the other; it's a hierarchy of values.

I.G. And what would be the scale of hierarchies in the case of a hospital, an apartment building, or an office building?

I don't think there is a difference between these three, but there is a difference between a factory and a city hall. St Thomas said, 'Reason is the first principle of all human work.' Sometimes a house for a person can have merely the value of something to live in; but for another person it may have more significance. But in any case at least it has to have [the significance of] reason. An office building is just a place to work in, and a city hall has more value, so must be better.

I. G. Better in terms of what? Materials?

Materials, space, character; but in any case it must be built with the same method.

I. G. Could the Seagram be a city hall?

No, it's an office building; the municipality should have higher values.

If you still have questions to ask, at least for now you have an idea of what I'm thinking.

89 [Acceptance Speech for the Cross of the Order of Merit]

Typescript and manuscript of acceptance speech (2 April 1959).
Source: LoC, Mies, Box 11, Printed Matter, 'Reply of Mies van der Rohe to Baron [Friedrich] von Lupin's speech at The Arts Club of Chicago on the occasion of his presentation of The Commander's Cross of the Order of Merit of The Federal Republic of Germany'. Speech given at the Art Club in Chicago, 2 April 1959.
Republished in Neumeyer (1986) 1991, p. 330; Pizzigoni 2010, pp. 178–179; Walter 2022, pp. 189–190.

What the Baron said brought to my mind that when I was young, toward the end of the Art Nouveau movement, we began to ask ourselves, 'What is architecture?' We asked everyone. They said, 'What we build is architecture.' We knew better than to ask Peter Behrens. He would have given the same answer. But we weren't satisfied with the answer. Maybe they didn't understand the question. We tried to find out. We searched in the quarries of ancient and medieval philosophy.

Since we knew it was a question of the truth, we tried to find out what the truth really was. We were very delighted to find a definition of truth by Thomas Aquinas: 'Adequatio rei et intellectus.' In modern language: 'Truth is the significance of the facts' *[possibly a reference to Giambattista Vico]*. I never forgot this. It was very helpful and has been a guiding light. To find out what architecture really is took 50 years – half a century.

The idea that architecture belongs to an epoch – whoever agrees has to ask himself, 'What are the sustaining and driving forces of our epoch?' Everybody who is interested in this question will know by now – particularly since *[Alfred North]* Whitehead – that they are science, technology, and even industrialisation. One thing that becomes clearer more and more to us is this peculiar kind of economy. We are soaked in economy as the medieval peoples were soaked in religion.

I have been asked, 'Where do we go from here?' If you accept that architecture belongs to an epoch, there is a long way to go. It took us 50 years to clarify the question of architecture. I think it will take 50 more years to clarify the relationship of architecture to the epoch. This will be the business of a new generation.

I'd like to close with a quotation from Ulrich von Hutten, that gallant fighter of the Reformation: 'It is the dawn of a new day, and it is joy to live' *[Ulrich von Hutten, letter to Willibald Pirckheimer, 25 December 1518]*.

90 Speech on the Occasion of Receiving the Gold Medal of the Royal Institute of British Architects

Draft for acceptance speech and published speech (26 May 1959). Source: LMvdR, 'Presentation of the Royal Gold Medal for 1959 to Ludwig Mies van der Rohe', *Journal of the Royal Institute of British Architects*, July 1959, pp. 304–308. LoC, Mies, Box 61, Speech Notes. Published partially in Pizzigoni 2010, p. 179; F. Dal Co, *Casabella*, no. 800, LXXV, 4, April 2011, pp. 106–107.

(A) London, May 1959 gold medal. I thank the speakers very much for the generosity of their comments.

(B) I wish to thank Her Majesty the Queen, for the great honour She has bestowed on me. And I thank sincerely the Council of the RIBA for proposing my name for her approval.

(1) Search for understanding. Behrens, Berlage, Messel, Olbrich, Van de Velde, Luitgens *[sic; Edwin Lutyens]*, Voisan *[sic; Charles Francis Annesley Voysey]*, Woob *[sic; Aston Webb]*, Bailey Scott *[sic; Mackay Hugh Baily Scott]*, Mcktosh *[sic; Charles Rennie Mackintosh]*: Different directions.

(2) Learned most from Old Buildings.

(3) Architecture must belong to its own time. But what is our time? What is its structure, its essence? What are the sustaining and driving forces?

(4) What is civilisation? What is culture? What is the relation between the two?

(5) In this peculiar year, 1926: Schwarz, Max Sheeler *[sic; Scheler]*, *[Alfred North]* Whitehead.

(6) There is a truth relation. But what is truth? Thomas *[Aquinas]*: Adequatio rei et intellectus. *[Saint]* Augustine: Beauty is the radiance of truth.

(7) Architecture as the expression of the slow unfolding of an epoch. An epoch is a slow process.

(8) Ending: Ulrich von Hutten. [See 'Acceptance Speech for the Cross of the Order of Merit'].

I wish to thank Her Majesty the Queen for the great honour she has bestowed on me, and I would like to thank sincerely the Council of the Royal Institute of British Architects for proposing my name for her approval. I would like to thank too the speakers for their remarks and the generosity of their comments. I am so moved that I can hardly think of anything else to say. I am very thankful and grateful.

I was in this country 50 years ago, on my first and my last trip here, to study the great architects of that time. I studied *[Peter]* Behrens, *[Joseph Maria]* Olbrich and *[Henry]* Van de Velde. I wanted to study *[Edwin]* Lutyens, *[Mackay]* Baillie Scott, *[Charles]* Voysey, and *[Charles]* Mackintosh. Those times were very different from today. There were a few people who tried to do something new and find the way. Everybody went in a different direction, so we had to learn from each of them what seemed good to us and what we liked, but there was nothing clear.

I once asked somebody to tell me what architecture was, and he replied, 'Do not ask silly questions.' But I do ask them. That was all we could get. We had to start. We learned from a great man and his talents, but we did not get a clear direction. I learnt more from old buildings with their fine, simple purpose, their fine, simple construction, their marvellous draughtsmanship and wonderful proportions, and unsophisticatedness. That is where I learned. These old buildings have been a continuous inspiration to me even today.

We had to find our way, and we had to ask hundreds of questions. We wanted to know what was civilisation, what was culture, and whether there was a relationship. We felt that there was a close relationship, but we did not know what was the truth. We had to search among ancient and medieval philosophy to find the answer to that. The best answer to the question of 'What is the truth?' has been given in 'adequatio rei et intellectus'. That is, the whole world.

I have been asked many times, 'Where do we go from here?' To those of us for whom architecture is the expression of an epoch, 'Where do we go from here?' does not make sense. Architecture is the expression of the inner structure of our epoch and the slow unfolding of its soul.

91 No Dogma

Published magazine interview (June 1959).
Source: 'Mies van der Rohe: No Dogma', *Interbuild*, vol. 6, no. 6, June 1959, pp. 9–11.
The following articles make use of a mix of quotation from this text and the text 'Interview Given to the BBC' (see pp. 145–150): Conrads, U., 'Mies van der Rohe. Ich mache niemals ein Bild [Mies van der Rohe. I Never Take a Picture]', *Die Bauwelt*, vol. LIII, no. 32, 1962, pp. 884–885; Conrads, U., 'Mies van der Rohe, Baumeister einer strukturellen Architektur [Mies van der Rohe. Builder of a Structural Architecture]', *Jahrbuch Preussischer Kulturbesitz*, vol. VI, no. 6, 1968, pp. 57–74. Republished in Puente (2006) 2008, pp. 10–27; Pizzigoni 2010, pp. 180–187; Walter 2022, pp. 191–201.

The most stimulating, but for a story-seeking journalist most difficult, factor about interviewing Ludwig Mies van der Rohe, the septuagenarian doyen of modern architecture, is his absolute refusal to be dogmatic. Considered judgement, yes. But no hard and fast rules. Just benign wisdom.
Talking to an Interbuild reporter at his London hotel on May 29 (three days after his moving and much acclaimed appearance at the RIBA to receive the Gold Medal), he maintained a constant demeanour of delighted surprise at the attention he was receiving from pundits, journalists, radio commentators, and television newsmen.
This charming tolerance leaves one indelible impression. To this demi-god of twentieth-century architecture it is not the journalist who is being honoured by being granted an interview. Mies van der Rohe completely reverses the normal procedure. He gives the impression that it is he, not the reporter, who is being honoured.
Opening the interview with a comment on the technique of prefabrication, he said, I do not think it is an advantage to build planned, packaged houses. If you prefabricate a house completely, it becomes an unnecessary restriction. The value of prefabrication is in the units, and it is much better to have single

elements prefabricated and to concentrate on the development of these elements. Thus the architect can use them in a free way. Otherwise, architecture will be terribly boring.

In our last building on Lake Shore Drive (860) we had more than 3000 individual windows but only two different window types. In number 900 we have, I would say, 10,000 windows all of the same type. That is enough prefabrication. But let me not be misunderstood. I think that an industrial process is not like a rubber stamp. Everything has to be put together and, as such, should have its own expression.

But would it not be better to have a standard system of components conforming to a standard dimension?
No. I do not think we need give up our present freedom. Why should not each architect design his own standard? Otherwise, you would have to tell everybody which standard they should use and that, I think, would be an impossible task. Some people, for instance, use seven-foot-high doors and have a plaster space over the top of the door. What I like to do is to make a door between floor and ceiling. So is my standard to be accepted, or the other? I should mention here that we never use a ceiling that is lower than eight feet. Ours are mostly eight feet, four inches.

Has the mixed development concept of your Lafayette Plaisance (Interbuild, May, 1959) project particular significance as a new design approach by you?
We built the lower buildings for people who like to live on the ground. But others like to live up in the air. So here we built for both. People used to say that high buildings are more costly than low buildings, but an interesting fact has come out of this Detroit scheme. The apartments in the tall buildings are much cheaper than the same apartments on the ground. Really much cheaper. So I would not be surprised if, in such town development schemes, we kill off the low house in the end.

But should people live high above the ground?
I think people should live as they like to live. Most people have never lived in tall buildings. But others, and I know many, have lived in them for years and are still fascinated with living there. But if you build high, you must have enough space to live upon – as we have in Detroit. There will be a huge 52-acre park in the centre of the buildings with trees and grass and no streets. Here we have kept the streets out. All access is from perimeter roads which are dead-ends.

Did the authorities ask you to plan this way?
No. We designed it from the start our way, and once we were satisfied the idea was a good one, we made no concessions. We had designed it, and we fully believed in it. We fought for it, and we even said that they must have it our way, otherwise we don't come to Detroit.

Can we always rejuvenate the middle of old cities?
No. Not always. But first you can use up all the slums for new development. In all the cities of the world there are large spread areas of these. Also, you can avoid the spread of these silly suburban houses. Chicago has thousands of them all over the place. Instead of eating up the land, they should have been developed as tall and low buildings in a reasonable way. And I don't say this is only work for architects. I think that the developers could do it also. After all, most of these houses are made by developers and are made by builders. Very few of them are by architects.

But do they understand work such as yours?
Speaking for the Detroit project, I think we will have a great influence on new development. You will see. But generally, I think my work has so much influence because of its reasonableness. Anybody could do that. To do it well, you don't have to have too much fantasy. You should just use your brain. And after all, that is something that anyone can do.

Objective development is a question of education. Things become better and better by example. If there is no example, then people just talk. They talk about things they really don't know about, so they can't judge the difference between good and bad anyway.

Have you always felt this way?
No. I think it was a slow development. At the beginning everything was unclear, and then the pattern and

the answers gradually emerged. The more I searched for a deeper understanding of the problems, the clearer my work became. This development was from within myself. There were no influences in this process from outside.

What happened if you had a fine idea and couldn't get it built?

I can give you an example. I tried these glass skyscrapers first in 1922. That is, I designed them on paper, and they worked fine. Then later, when we started our first skyscraper in Chicago, we had to build in concrete because it was just after the war and we could not get steel. Although I tried to find a solution in concrete, at the same time I designed the same building in steel [*Promontory Apartment Building, Chicago, 1946–49*]. I don't know if you have ever seen this scheme, but after that, we never thought about concrete any more. From then on we built in steel.

Do you often design buildings without a client because you think a site needs a particular building?

That is interesting because most of our designs are developed long before there is a practical possibility of carrying them out. I do that on purpose and have done it all my life. I do it when I am interested in something. I do it just to hope that one day the building will be lived in and liked.

You visualise a scheme when you see an empty site?

Well, not for every site. But for some, yes. Take Chicago for example. I perhaps think in my mind that there should be a large hall for conventions. All right, then we start to design and try the idea out. This is often with no motive but to experiment.

Do you try to influence people to get it built?

Sometimes it happens that they see the scheme somewhere and they come to us to ask us to do the work.

Would you comment on architect/client relationships?

Never talk to a client about architecture. Talk to him about his children. That is simply good politics. He will not understand what you have to say about architecture most of the time. An architect of ability should be able to tell a client what he wants. Most of the time, a client never knows what he wants. He may, of course, have some very curious ideas, and I do not mean to say that they are silly ideas. But being untrained in architecture, they just cannot know what is possible and what is not possible.

But perhaps he would not like the finished building?

That would not matter at all, although I have never had this experience. I may have had many wrangles with clients while a building was being designed, and often while it is being built, but always, in the end, they have been satisfied with the way I did it.

Do you submit alternative schemes to a client?

No. Only one. Always. And the best one that we can give. That is where you can fight for what you believe in. He doesn't have to choose. How can he choose? He hasn't the capacity to choose. No, it is much better to have just one idea, and if the idea is clear, then you can fight for it. That is how you can get things done.

Does any one year have particular significance in the development of the modern world?

I would say that 1926 was the most significant year. Looking back, it seems that it was not just a year in the sense of time. It was a year of great realisation or awareness. It seems to me that at certain times in the history of man the understanding of certain situations ripens. Putting it another way, it seems that a particular situation will be ripe at a certain time and will be understood. That is why great people who may never know each other can talk, simultaneously, about the same things.

Could 1959 be a similar ripening period?

I think there is a lot we do not understand about the mental processes, but if the situation is strong enough, people will become sensitive to the situation and will then work on it. I think that is how it happens, but I am not sure if it is happening today.

Can this awareness be forced?

I do not think so. I think it lies in the nature of things. It takes time. It took me a long time to understand the relationship between ideas and between objective facts. But after I clearly understood this relationship, I didn't fool around with other wild ideas. That is one of the main reasons why I just make my schemes as simple as possible. I have always worked for ordered relationships. Take the buildings on the IIT campus for example. There we drew a net 24 feet by 24 feet over the entire campus, so at all the crossings we could put columns. It is thus possible to connect individual buildings at any point and still preserve the original system.

But your awareness was a long realisation process?
At the beginning it was more of an instinctive drive. Later on, it became more and more conscious awareness. But, again, all this was from within me. Always. In my interview with the BBC I talked of the three other people in Europe who, although I didn't know them, were thinking in 1926 what I was thinking *[see 'Interview With BBC']*. Their business was to get this thing clear in their minds and to write their books about it. In the same way I had to build, and I was very happy with the results.

Can architects work together on major projects?
I do not think very much of this sort of forced teamwork myself. The teamwork in our field is between architect, mechanical engineer, and structural engineer. That is where the teamwork comes in. It is no use working with other architects. What can they do? Who does what? I think it would be better, say, to have five different designs and choose. After all, why should I discuss my ideas with someone else. The most important things cannot be discussed anyway. I would prefer not to work with other people. I work with larger firms of architects in different ways, but I don't discuss with them my ideas. I would never do that.

The same with the structural engineer. We tell him what we want, and he tells us if it is possible. In the field of design the structural engineers, with a few exceptions like *[Pier Luigi]* Nervi, do not know what they are doing.

Can one man have a clear idea of right and wrong. Or is this conceit?
I am with the single man. When an idea is good – and it is a clear idea – then it should only come from one man. If the idea is demonstrated in an objective way, everybody should be able to understand it. But, of course, few people ever do.

Have we moved into a new era of thought, do you think?
I think there is no more difference in the arrival of nuclear fission than there was in the arrival of the aeroplane. People do not, I think, change basically. We can easily become too influenced by what we read in the newspapers. I think this so-called 'space age' is just a technological problem of the universe.

Its existence has no bearing on mankind?
No. I don't think so. It certainly has no bearing on spiritual development. But it does have a strong bearing on the actual facts of life as, for example, the fact that maybe in a short time this atomic energy will be much cheaper and of greater use to everybody. I hope so.

In splitting the atom could we not be near to comprehension of the life force?
Between the ideas and the objective facts I think the problems are always the same. Whatever the objective facts are, these problems will never change. There is a true relationship between these things, and it is the understanding of this relationship that is the challenge to human beings. To become aware of this is a question of deep insight and education.

Many things in life should then be experienced?
Certainly. These inventions, and industrial and scientific discoveries, belong to the objective facts, but they have nothing to do with the relationship of the ideas to these facts. The ideas must be understood if we are to understand life.

But ideas must come first to change facts?
No. The facts are given to *[us]*. We have had them for hundreds of years. When, in the sixteenth and seventeenth centuries, the first modern scientists were

experimenting, they had no idea what would come out of their ideas. They had no influence on the use man would make of them. Now we have science, we have technology, and we have industrialisation. All are accepted as part of progressive existence. The question is what to do with them. That is the human side of this problem.

We must cope then with what we have created?
We have to know that life cannot be changed by us. It will be changed. But not by us. We can only guide the things that can cause physical change. But I would criticise, for example, a nuclear scientist who discovers a natural phenomenon but does not appreciate the consequences of his discovery. Yes. I would criticise him for that. It would be better if he could see. But maybe he can't. After all, he has to do with facts and not with ideas. It is for all men, not just a few, to use all these things for the best for all of us. That, I think, is what we should do with our lives.

92 An Address of Appreciation by HT Cadbury-Brown

Published conference (given on 27 May 1959).
Source: H. T. Cadbury-Brown, 'Ludwig Mies van der Rohe. An Address of Appreciation by HT Cadbury-Brown', *The Architectural Association Journal*, vol. LXXV, no. 834, July–August 1959, pp. 26–39. Conference at the Architectural Association in London, 27 May 1959.
Republished in Pizzigoni 2010, pp. 188–200; Walter 2022, pp. 202–219.

Tonight is a very important one in the history of the AA, because we are here to honour a great architect who is our guest, Mies van der Rohe. [...] We will look now at these slides. Professor Mies van der Rohe has agreed to answer any questions which anyone might have on particular buildings.
This is a view of the German Pavilion at Barcelona. It is very curious how buildings come to pass. Germany had the task of putting on an exhibition at Barcelona. One day I received a call from the German Government. I was told that the French and the British would have a pavilion and Germany should have a pavilion too. I said, 'What is a pavilion? I have not the slightest idea.' I was told, 'We need a pavilion. Design it, and not too much glass!' I must say that it was the most difficult work which ever confronted me, because I was my own client; I could do what I liked. But I did not know what a pavilion should be. Looking back over all these years, I can remember it very well. It was strange. I am sorry that I have not much time in which to tell you about it. If the British and the French had not had a pavilion, there would have been no pavilion in Barcelona erected by Germany.
The photograph now on the screen shows the second of two particular buildings. This is the Tugendhat House in Brno, Czechoslovakia, built in 1930. What always strikes me when looking at this house are the wonderful materials which were used, a quality which I think was really found only in Mies van der Rohe's work at that time. I am thinking of the beautiful marble walls and finishes in everything.

Mr Tugendhat came to me. First, he received this house as a wedding present. He was a very careful man, and he was sick. He did not believe in one doctor only: he had three. He had looked at houses, and he wanted to find an architect. He picked me out for a curious reason. He saw a house which I built when I was very young, when I was about 20 years old [Riehl House, Potsdam, 1907]. It was very well built, and so on. He liked that. He expected something similar. He came to me and talked with me. I went there and saw the situation. I designed the house. I remember that it was on Christmas Eve when he saw the design of the house. He nearly died! But his wife was interested in art; she had some of Van Gogh's pictures. She said, 'Let us think it over'. Tugendhat could have thrown her out.

However, on New Year's Eve he came to me and told me that he had thought it over and I should go ahead with the house. We had some trouble about it at the time, but we can take that for granted. He said that he did not like this open space; it would be too disturbing; people would be there when he was in the library with his great thoughts. He was a businessman, I think. I said, 'Oh, all right. We will try it out and, if you do not want it, we can close the rooms in. We can put in glass walls. It will be the same.' We tried it. We put wooden scaffold pieces up. He was listening in his library, and we were talking just normally. He did not hear anything.

Later he said to me, 'Now I give in on everything, but not about the furniture.' I said, 'This is too bad.' I decided to send furniture to Brno from Berlin. I said to my superintendent, 'You keep the furniture and shortly before lunch call him out and say that you are at his house with furniture. He will be furious, but you must expect that.' He said, 'Take it out,' before he saw it. However, after lunch he liked it. I think we should treat our clients as children, not as architects.

We are now back to 1912, to the Kröller House and the full-scale model of it as built.

Yes, for 50,000 guilders. The client was a rich man, and he wanted to see what he would get. I was in Paris talking to someone who knew about these things one day. I was asked, 'Is it not dangerous to build a model of a real house?' He was right, I am sure. Everything inside – the partitions and the ceilings – could move up and down. However, 50,000 guilders is a lot of money.

The professor was then asked whether it was true, as had been said, that the Kröller House was influenced by the work of Schinkel.

Yes, I agree with that. At that time I was about 22 years old. The whole Art Nouveau movement, what in Germany we call 'Jugendstil', came to an end. There was this old inspiration of [Karl Friedrich] Schinkel, the greatest Classicist we had. I came under his influence, and I studied very carefully. This is the result of that. Certainly, I was influenced by Schinkel, but the plan is not in any way Schinkel's.

This slide shows a design for a brick country house. This was in 1923.

When I made this plan, I made the drawings the night before the exhibition [Grosse Berliner Kunstausstellung, 1923]. I made them the night before in charcoal so that people could see the drawings from a distance and did not have to read blueprints. It did not receive that interpretation in some quarters, but the interpretation placed upon it [that it was influenced by Theo van Doesburg] was nonsense. I just wanted to make it clear enough so that people could look at it.

This is a view of a group of buildings in Stuttgart which was an exhibition of housing controlled by Mies van der Rohe.

You had something similar in this country [in England]. I do not know whether it is still here. Industrialists, artists, and craftsmen worked together in the development. One day we wanted to show new ideas for living quarters – apartments, single houses, and so on. I had the idea just to use about five or six people. The city of Stuttgart said, 'That cannot be done. We have two great architects here.' I said, 'That is just too bad. If one of them had the commission to build an exhibition in Berlin, I would not even ask to be with the exhibition.' In the end they insisted that a few people from Stuttgart should be invited. I decided, 'All right. If it is necessary, then we shall add some more of our choice.' First, I think it was *[Le]* Corbusier, *[Walter]* Gropius, *[Jacobus JP]* Oud, and *[Mart]* Stam. After that, some other people were added. It did not hurt much, but it did not make it better, either. *I think that Professor Henry-Russell Hitchcock used the term 'International Style' as a result of this because, seeing so many architects working together in exactly the same idiom, he felt there must be this very strong connection.*

At that time many people were working together. I think it was unfortunate, in a way, to call it 'the International Style', but we laughed over it.

The professor was then asked to say what materials were used in the external walling.

You could use any materials. My building was a steel building, and we had bricks to fill in the walls. Oud had concrete construction. Stamm had a steel construction. It could be anything. I said, 'Paint it white.' One little building – it is difficult to show it – was painted blue on one side, red on one side, yellow on one side, and black on the other side *[Max Taut House, Stuttgart, 1927]*. I said, 'For Heaven's sake, can you not do better than that?' He said, 'You are afraid of colour.' I said, 'No. You are colour-blind.'

The professor was asked whether that meant that, as architect, he found it difficult to co-ordinate.

It was very difficult. The difficulty came not from the outside people, but from the inside people. We trusted somebody in Stuttgart to be the superintendent. He was the greatest problem. It was terrible. He wrote letters. He should have worked instead of writing letters.

The professor was asked whether the choice of different materials made any difference to the aesthetic character of the buildings.

No. Many of these things we plastered. You could see buildings which were of steel because everything had to be fireproof. It was lighter than if it was built in solid material. We had a wonderful time. I should like to tell you about it. As I was in charge of everything, I asked a friend of mine to be the advertising man, to decide what posters we should have. I told him to find the most terrible material. He came up with a marvellous picture. I approved it, and we sent it out. It was pasted all over Germany. It was the vast living room of Richard Strauss *[Willi Baumeister, 'Wie Wohnen? Die Wohnung', Werkbund Ausstellung poster, 1927. There are two versions of this poster; a similar image is visible in the article 'Two Glass Skyscrapers'. See p. 50]*. That was my first conception of how it should be done. Later, the city wanted to sell. First, they said they wanted to have it, and later, they wanted to sell parts of it. Later, we had to change it, but that was my first conception. It was something like a mediaeval town.

The professor was asked whether he prepared the model before he asked the various architects to design.

Yes. Then I asked these people to come and choose a site. The first man I asked *[Le Corbusier]* promptly chose the best!

This is the house at Krefeld [Hermann Lange House, Krefeld, 1930]. It is made of brick. I think that is one of the first houses in modern architecture to use brick.

I wanted to make this house much more in glass, but the client did not like that. I had great trouble. They were very nice people. We became very good friends. He was the president of the silk industry in Germany, but that was to his sorrow. He drank a lot of wine, and so on. That is what you get.

This is an exhibition house in Berlin, built in 1931 [Exhibition House and Apartment for a Bachelor, German Building Exhibition, Berlin, 1931]. The professor was asked whether he remembered what the people of Berlin who attended the exhibition thought of the building at the time.

The Nazis thought that it should be a stable for horses. Before, in Barcelona, we decided to put in a sculpture. I was an old friend of *[Wilhelm]* Lehmbruck, but he had died previously. I could not find a Lehmbruck. The only sculpture of the right size was that cold-looking figure *['Dawn', Georg Kolbe]*. I put it there. It was really a good sculpture, for all that. The client liked me for the reason that I showed sculpture in space.

Now there is a big jump in time to 1950, the [Edith] Farnsworth House. It is also a big jump in space – from Berlin and Germany to the Middle West.

The floor was travertine, the same all the way through. The kitchen, the bathrooms, and even the utility room were all the same. We thought this would be cheaper.

The professor was asked whether the client was not difficult.

At the beginning, no, but later she was. We got into trouble about the curtains. This is very interesting. I had a great experience with this house. Before you live in a glass house, you do not know how colourful nature is. It changes every day. We had this flooring all the way through, and the wood was very light-coloured. I decided to make raw-silk curtains, in a natural colour. She said, 'Not over my dead body.' She had had a piece of advice from somebody; she wanted a very strong yellow colour. That material cost us about $7 per 1/2 yard. Our silk curtains cost us $2 per 1/2 yard. That decided her. She did not die, but she was furious.

The professor was asked whether he had ever had any difficulty collecting his fees.

Only with this building. It cost $50,000, and the fee was about $5000 or $6000.

He was asked whether the client liked it now.

I have not the slightest idea. I like it still.

We pass now to the campus of the Illinois Institute of Technology. It is a wonderful commission for the entire campus, a job which is still not complete.

It will not be complete because they have decided to give it to a group of other architects. The first president *[Henry Heald]* we had there did not know anything about architecture. When I went there it was a very little school in fact. The president had the idea to really build it up and make it an important institution. He said to me one day, 'Mies, you had better think about a campus.' That was all the commission I had. We never made a contract as long as he was there. I did not think that there was any problem. Then he left for New York University and became the chancellor. Later, he became the president elsewhere.

His followers just did not understand anything, and it was just hopeless. We did not steal money, but they decided that it was better to work with other people and have some local man in the field. They then felt they had made a mistake by doing that, and they asked me to make one of the other buildings. I said, 'No. The campus was planned as a unit and, if it cannot be a unit, I have to be satisfied with the torso.' That is still my position. They always tried to give me a job, but I am not interested in a job. I think they should pay for that. These buildings were the cheapest campus buildings anywhere in the United States.

The professor was asked to say something about the finishing of the steel work in this type of building.

We painted the steel black. I had discussions about that with a great scientist. He said, 'Steel is light.' I said, 'No. Steel is strong.' There we have a first-rate black steel. Somewhere else, we painted the steel white. I would paint steel red, green, or any colour.

The questioner said he was not thinking of the colour but the weathering of the steel.

If you paint once really well, the steel has to be painted about every ten years, but in Chicago normally you have to paint steel every five years.

The professor was asked if he had had much difficulty with the builders in the finishing of the brickwork.

At the beginning, yes, but they learned very fast because we looked after it. They were good bricklayers, but they refused to make careful brickwork. They have to lay 400 bricks a day. We said, 'We want to have it done carefully.' We told the contractors that they had to be careful. I took nearly all the bricks off the first building. As soon as they knew that, they started to be careful. I think bricklayers are bricklayers. You have to ask for good work.

The professor was asked to say something about the layout of these buildings because they seemed to deny the direction that was implied in the model of the Stuttgart housing exhibition.

We were instructed to build the campus. We had about eight blocks in Chicago. My first project was independent of streets. Then I was told, 'We cannot take the streets out.' For political reasons they did not want to do that. So we planned our buildings in the street blocks of Chicago. When we started, I tried to find out what is a classroom, what is a laboratory, and what is a shop. We came to a system of 24 feet, which equals about eight metres, a measurement which is used in Switzerland and in Sweden for school-building. So I drew a network of 24 feet by 24 feet all over the campus. The crossing points were the points where we put columns. Nobody could change that. I had some fight about it, but I stuck to it. So you could connect the buildings at any place, and you still had a clear system.

That is our little chapel *[Robert F Carr Memorial Chapel of Saint Saviour, Chicago, 1952]*. Somebody gave money for a chapel. You know that there are those people who do that. The roof was pitched very high. I do not know what the bishop called it. I had to do something. I said, 'We will do this. We will make just a box.' First, we designed a skeleton with steel, and we must have expended about $60,000. Cost was what was troubling them. So we had to build it in brick and just put the steel beams on the top, with concrete blocks at the back of the altar. We put some very fine raw silk material there. At first, he did not like that at all. Then I talked with him about the problem of truth. He agreed with me. The people – the students and the priest – like it very much. Even the bishop began to like it. He said he could get some money. I said, 'What do you mean by "some money"?' I had an altar. He said, 'Can we not make a veneer?' I said, 'Listen. An altar, in my opinion, is a rock. We have a solid piece of property which cost so much. Ask some more people for money.'

This is the architectural school [SR Crown Hall, Chicago, 1956].

We designed this building. I worked as the architect with all the heads of departments and with the chemistry professor. He told us what to do. This was our own school. I said, 'All right. We will do it our way.' It had to go to the Building and Ground Committee. We made a marvellous model of it in steel. The whole model was perfect. They presented no trouble whatsoever; they were very nice. They said something which I thought was rude; they said that they would have lunch together – not with me, but amongst themselves – and then they would decide what to do. They asked me to come back after lunch. I went to the tavern and took some drinks, strong Martinis. After lunch I went back. They said: 'We do not like it very much. Is it not difficult to paint the steel? Can you not change it?' I said, 'I would not change it for a million dollars.' So I took the model home, and we put it on ice.

Then there came a new publicity manager. He wanted to have money for the building of the campus. You get money only for interesting things, not for stupid things. He knew that. He picked the model up, and he got the money. We built it. It was very interesting to see how the Building and Ground Committee worked. They were old gentlemen. They were more careful about the money of an institution than about their own money. But they were too stupid and too dumb. This young man said, 'I will get the money for that.' He got it, and that is what we did. We proportioned it down, and we lost about a foot. That saved $20,000. The proportions were better before. I think that they are not bad now. Otherwise, we would not have done it. Even this $20,000 would not have made any difference to the committee. They have just to ask people for money, but they are too lazy to do that. They asked us to do it cheaper. They should ask for more money.

I thought that the entrance doors were particularly good because the hinge worked in such a way that the door swivelled on the hinge and the hinge slid out from the frame.

That is a kind of storm door. It is easy to open because the wind goes inside. It is the normal door in the United States.

The professor was asked whether he thought it was necessary or an advantage to be in the IIT building if one was a student of architecture.

I can tell you. I lived there all during the building. I lived there and worked there. It is beautiful. This afternoon a lady was in my hotel. She asked me about how I lived. She asked me if I had built a house for myself. I said, 'No.' She said, 'What would you do?' I said that I would build a huge thing, empty *[see 'Architect of the "Clear and Reasonable"']*. I like to work in this building. There is never any disturbance in the acoustics, only when the professor becomes emotional. He should not do that. Otherwise, we have no disturbances. We work in groups together. I often did not see people.

The questioner said that, in asking that question, he had had in mind whether the professor thought he could teach architecture in an old building.

I would rather teach in a new building. Do you know why? There is this ballast of history anyway. Why put more history or more ballast on the student? I think that when the student went there, he stayed with us in this building. I think that we are really immune against any fancy. The students do not get it, and we do not tell them. When I started to teach, I found in our school that every time a new *[Architectural] Forum* came out, the design changed. I said: 'All right. It is simple. We drop the *Forum*. We have no magazines in future. You have to think and not to look at the *Forum*.'

It was pointed out to the professor that since he had left Europe, he had never once used curved forms but had been content to restrict himself to the right angle. He was asked if he would say something about that decision.

I was once asked by an expert, 'Why should everything be straight?' I told him, 'Why should it be curved?' We built a museum in Jerusalem *[sic; Houston]*, where it was natural to make curves *[Cullinan Hall, Houston, 1958]*. Normally, I think that if you build in steel, the buildings should not be curved. Steel is born in a straight way; it is not curved. It comes out of the mill straight. That is the material you work with.

In some cases we needed two storeys. By putting the workshops for the Institute of Design in a basement I was able still to build a one-storey building. So it pays not to be fireproof. You have to know the tricks. The heating is in the floors and under the periphery of the building. We have cooling by air from the ceiling. It is not actually cooling, but it can be changed easily to cooling. It is not hot in the summer.

The professor was asked how much and in what way he was consciously influenced by Japanese architecture.

I have never seen any Japanese architecture. I was never in Japan. We do it by reason. Maybe the Japanese do it that way too.

Illustrated here are the dormitories on the IIT campus [Carman Hall, Bailey Hall, Cunningham Hall, Chicago, 1953–1955].

That was my first defeat. I wanted to build it in steel and glass. The president of the Building and Ground Committee was the president of Prestige. He visited our building, and he was against it. So we had to build it in concrete.

The professor was asked what he thought of the variations on his ideas to be seen in other parts of America, carried out by other architects.

I do not know. I do it my way. I think architecture should be structure, and I do not like to play with structure. For instance, you could play about with the architect's building inside. You could give any architect the job to build inside, but I would not start playing like that. I think the structure is too serious. Only the clearest structure is good enough for building.

This is the plan of Lake Shore Drive *[860–880 Lake Shore Drive Building, Chicago, 1951]*. There were two similar buildings. In one building we have larger apartments and in the smaller one we had twice as many apartments as in the other.

The professor was asked to say something about the curtaining in these blocks. He was asked how he managed about the windows.

We gave them the curtains. That was the only way to get them to agree to what we wanted to have – for us to pay for them. We were interested in what would happen if there were to be curtains in the next building. The next building across the street has dark glass. I wish all people would love colours, but there is so little that comes true.

The steel of the skin was fabricated. We covered the roof and just lowered it down.

This building was very interesting to me. I was sitting all the time outside on Lake Shore on a bench and just looking at what was going on, looking at the builders and everything. When we were about 12 storeys high, I said, 'For Heaven's sake, why can't we stop? It shows that the system works in any building.' When we put the first few storeys on, I stood back and said, 'We are too happy.' That was the first four of five floors. When we were 26 storeys high, it became very thin.

A slide of 860 Lake Shore Drive under construction is included because to me so many buildings that one sees look much better before they are finished. The last few months are all for the worse. The finished product of 860 is such a wonderful building, and this slide is interesting in that it shows a state of transformation. Evidently the AA has spies who go out and take photographs.

It is very interesting to me to see these pictures again.

The professor was asked whether he had found it difficult to train his structural engineer to let him do these things, or had it been necessary for him to do them all himself.

We tell him what we want to have, and he will tell us if it is possible. Most of the structural engineers, with very few exceptions, do not know what they are doing. They can figure it out, but they do not know the meaning of it. You have to tell them exactly what you want. We had some trouble with the engineer on this building. He wanted to have sheer walls in the building. Normally, we do not use them. Since he was in charge of it, I told him to go ahead and do it his way. That is why you see that in the back of the building there are sheer walls.

I am very happy to have been with you tonight. I cannot tell you how happy I am to be at this very informal but very fine meeting. This is the atmosphere I like. At home we work in the office, we talk and make remarks and fun and jokes, and so on. This is the atmosphere I like particularly. Thank you very much for letting me be with you tonight.

93 Architect of the Clear and Reasonable

Published magazine interview (October 1959).
Source: Graeme Shankland, 'Architect of the "Clear and Reasonable": Mies van der Rohe Considered and Interviewed', *The Listener*, vol. LXII, no. 1594, 15 October 1959, pp. 620–623.
Republished in Pizzigoni 2010, pp. 201–207; Walter 2022, pp. 220–232.

Mies van der Rohe is the most powerful intellectual influence in contemporary architecture. No other architect in this century has sought more deeply to discover what should be first principles in architecture today and none has worked more logically and systematically to develop and purify the architectural concepts built on these principles [...].

You have to realise there are different stages of orders. The real order is what St Augustine said about the disposition of equal and unequal things according to their nature. That is real order. If you compare the architects' building *[SR Crown Hall, IIT, Chicago, 1956]* with the other campus buildings, you can see that. When I put a grid over the whole campus, that was a mechanical help. No one had to speculate where we put our columns. We put our columns on the crossing points of the grid all the way through. In the architects' building I went away from the grid; I took the grid in a larger measure, but the elements are not in the grid any more. The grid was 24 feet in the normal buildings, and here the columns are 60 feet apart. I think the architects' building is the most complete and the most refined building and the simplest building. In the other buildings there is more a practical order on a more economical level, and in the architects' building it is more a spiritual order.

This more fundamental idea of St Augustine, how has it helped your work and your designing?

I would not build a church as a movie palace, and I would not build a factory as a church, so we make a clear distinction what the value of these buildings are. There is not only a hierarchy of values; there is a hierarchy of works too.

But at the same time, in a gramophone record which you made a few years ago I heard you say that there should be the same kind of language for a garage as for a cathedral [See 'Conversation Regarding the Future of Architecture, Part I']. How do you distinguish between these things?

We use the same principles, just as the Gothic men used the same principles for a cathedral as they would use for a barn. And that is what I meant by that.

Your own work has had a big influence all over the world, in Europe and in America. How do you see the effect on the work of other architects?

I think the influence my work has on other people is based on its reasonableness. Everybody can use it without being a copyist because it is quite objective, and I think if I find something objective, I will use it. It does not matter who did it.

Mies not only discards what he discovers to be illogical or confused but severely limits the types of building structure he explores, isolating those he considers most important, like the multi-storeyed glass tower and the single-storey glass hall and subjecting them to an uncompromising aesthetic discipline in the search for the clearest possible architectural expression. To use his own words: We intentionally restrict ourselves to those structures which are possible at the moment and try to work them out in all the details. In this way we want to create a basis for further development. *He can do this because for him architecture is structure and, as such, not something to be played about with. [...] I asked him how he worked with his structural engineers. As I expected, he said that mostly he had to tell them what to do.*

There are some structural engineers, you wouldn't have to tell them – in fact, they go their way alone. But the others know how to figure things out but do not know the meaning of the work, so we have to say what structure is; they know nothing about structure, they know everything about construction.

It seems to me and must seem to many people, I think, that there are not many different ways in which one could live in one of your houses. Even the way the furniture is arranged is something which flows directly from the plan of the building, and the open-planning principles do impose a certain way of living in a house. Could you tell us how you came to this idea of the open plan? Does it, for instance, have any relation to the ideas of Mondrian and the aesthetic ideas of painters like him?

No, it does not: I think that was a mistake that the Museum of Modern Art made. They interpret it this way. But that has nothing to do with it. I never make a painting when I want to build a house. We like to draw our plans carefully, and that is why they were taken as a kind of painting.

But nonetheless, the open-planning idea which you and Frank Lloyd Wright and many architects since have adopted is an aesthetic idea.

Certainly, yes.

There have been criticisms, by people who live in this country in open-planned houses, that they do not find them convenient, that they are draughty, and they have no privacy – that kind of thing.

Yes: I would not like to live in a cubical house with a lot of small rooms. I would rather live on a bench in Hyde Park.

What kind of house, if you were designing one for yourself, would you design?

I would build a simple but very large house, so that I can do inside what I like.

You would like to change things round occasionally, as the Japanese do in their houses?

Yes, something like that.

There have been criticisms of modern architects that they are seeking to impose on people a way of life, a way of living, particularly in houses, particularly through open planning.

Yes: we do not do that. We use the principle of flexibility. For instance, in one of our tall buildings on Lake Shore Drive, Chicago, there are 400 apartments in the building and I cannot remember that two apartments were similar. We cannot help but fix the bathrooms and the kitchens in one place, but otherwise it is quite flexible – we can take walls out or put more walls in.

So you regard open planning in this context as a liberating thing?

Oh, certainly. And the flexibility is in my opinion a vital necessity – for instance, in office buildings.

The most perfect small house you have built is the Farnsworth House; it is a classic example of the open plan – a single space glazed on all four sides, free of partitions, and only a service core with bathrooms, kitchen, and mechanical equipment rising to the ceiling in the centre. Was this not an aesthetic idea imposed on a reluctant client? The Italian critic Bruno Zevi said that this was not a house at all – but a museum.

No, that is not a fact. It was a house for a single person; this makes the problem more simple. I made later a house in glass with five bedrooms and five bathrooms and even a room for a help *[Robert McCormick House, Elmurst IL, 1952]*. That is really a difficult problem, to make an open plan, but it is possible: you only have to work much harder on it. No, the Farnsworth House is, I think, not really understood. I was in the house from morning to evening. I did not know how colourful nature really was. But you have to be careful in the inside to use neutral colours because you have the colours outside. These absolutely change, and I would say it is beautiful.

And you had raw silk curtains, I think, in the same house.

Yes, and a very neutral primavera wood; and the whole floor of the house was Roman travertine, including the kitchen, bathrooms, and the terrace.

That is why, I think, you painted the columns white?

Yes. That was the right colour in the country, you know, against the green. And I like black too, particularly for cities. Even in our tall glass buildings, when you are in an apartment, you see the sky, and even the city, changing every hour. I think that is really new in our concept.

[...] I then took up with him the question of prefabrication. In a modern industrial society based on factory production every serious architect has to make up his mind on what terms he approaches this question. In his own work Mies has always used the individual products of modern industry but never designed completely prefabricated buildings. I asked him why this was.

I do not think it is an advantage to build planned prefabricated houses. I think the value of prefabrication is the value of getting elements which we can use freely, like we have doors and bathtubs. We have many other buildings. In our steel buildings we have about 3000 windows and only two shapes. I think that is the best way of prefabrication. To prefabricate a house or standardise a house from top to bottom is too complicated a process. So I think it is much better that industry should deliver elements which we can use in a free way. Otherwise, it would be terribly boring. And I do not think it will happen.

At the same time there has been in Europe, on a very wide scale now, and in Germany and Russia this use of this 'Groß-Plattenbau' – I think they call it – system: 'large-plate building', or the use of systems of construction involving an entire wall being placed in position by a crane, and so forth. But that does not seem to have interested you. You think this is a limiting factor on an architect, this kind of thing?

Yes, and I think it is not right. When I can build a skeleton where I have really thin columns and they are much stronger than these heavy walls, I would rather use a skeleton and put glass in it, a light material again. Glass is the best material. I have had the chance of drinking wine out of glasses 2000 years old; they were in the ground, and nothing had happened to them; they were discoloured a little, but they were otherwise perfect.

[...] I asked him what other projects and ideas he still hoped to realise as a man of 73.

I am not a businessman as an architect. And there is not much I would like to build. Perhaps a convention hall I designed for Chicago, and some other things, maybe a house for myself.

I think you had news today of a new job?

That is a Federal Court building in Chicago. It has many courtrooms and is a complicated building. We have even to put a prison on the top of it. I am curious what comes of it.

Apart from that, which is an actual commission, what buildings would you still now particularly like to do that you have not done so far?

I would like to build one of these huge halls we designed. I do not know if you remember the design for the convention hall in Chicago? It was 720 by 720 feet without any support inside. And the Bacardi building for Cuba is 65 metres by 65 metres without any support inside. *[The client]* wanted just one large room for his whole office.

Finally, we turned to the question nearest to my own heart as an architect-planner – to the city. First, to the only project in town planning as a co-ordinating exercise he has ever realised, the Weissenhofsiedlung in Stuttgart in 1927. Here he conceived a three-dimensional master plan to guide a collective demonstration of what contemporary architecture could do to produce an environment for a whole community and invited 16 leading modern architects to design individual buildings. Did he regret not having had an opportunity to do this kind of thing in America?

It was an ordeal to do it in Stuttgart, and I can imagine it would be more difficult in America. I do not see the necessity to repeat things like that. In Stuttgart that was a certain hour in history; we could show at once that all these forces were at work but never visible really, and that was the reason we wanted to build this Weissenhofsiedlung, to show at once clearly that there is a new way of building houses and apartment buildings.

What about the future of the metropolis? Many people, as you know, are throwing up their hands in

despair today, saying that it has no future. What is your view on that?
I think we are just at the beginning of changing the cities, but not in a romantic way. I am sure that the economic situation will have a great influence on the way our cities will be. I do not believe that we architects can just plan a city out of the blue sky. There are economic forces so strong we cannot change them. They can be guided; that is about all.
When Mies' own career began, he and his contemporaries had to break away from 'Art Nouveau'. They found to hand in Berlin the Neoclassical buildings built by Schinkel some 80 years earlier.
Around 1910 Schinkel was still really the greatest representative in Berlin. The Altes Museum in Berlin was a beautiful building – you could learn everything in architecture from it, and I tried to do that.
Did you find in Schinkel's work certain key leading ideas or an approach which you have found useful since?
In the Altes Museum he separated the windows very clearly, he separated the elements, the columns and the walls and the ceiling, and I think that is still visible in my later buildings.
Finally, we spoke of the moral idea that a building ought to express its structure. This central idea of the modern monument is expressed in Mies' buildings more than those of any other architect – but it derives from men like Ruskin and Viollet-le-Duc who practised something very different. Mies points to this paradox.
But Ruskin had quite romantic ideas about art. He said, you know, every decoration should be thrown out when it does not support the construction, and look what he did himself. It is very strange that somebody can have a clear idea and work in a different way because he is the son of his time.
But you are the son of yours in the sense that you have based your work on this scientific and objective and rational approach, helped by the philosophers whom you have been mentioning.

Yes, but I learned most from old buildings.
Because they were scientific and rational too?
No, but they were clear and reasonable.

94 [On Value]

Manuscript note (24 December 1959).
Source: LoC, Mies, Box 62, Miscellaneous.
Notes of an informal office meeting transcribed by Jack Bowman.
Republished in Pizzigoni 2010, p. 209.

Value has not to be, but if something should be, it has to be valuable. This is a command.

A thing may have a practical value, an economical value, or a spiritual value. The value of a thing is in its use. A cane, a practical thing, should not be compared with the Parthenon – that has a spiritual value. There is a hierarchy of values.

Structure is the expression of the construction.

95 Famed Architect Enjoys Thinking

Published magazine interview (circa 1960).
Source: AIC, Mies, 1984.2, Box 2, Folder 3. Mervin Block, 'Famed Architect Enjoys Thinking', undated, without indication.
The reporter has written 'v' instead of 'w' to emphasise Mies' accent.
Republished in Pizzigoni 2010, pp. 226–228.

[...] *People from all over the world write to van der Rohe, either to his apartment, 200 East Pearson Street, or to his office, 230 East Ohio Street. Speaking in a thick German accent, van der Rohe lamented recently:*
I vaste a lot of time. They vant to see me. They vant to talk to me. Hundreds. They vant to know everything. High school students, they have to write a thesis. They vould like you to write it for them.
Is he flattered by all this attention? Not at all, replied the 74-year-old architect. I find it terrible. You know, it's terrible burden to be famous.
The question most frequently asked of him, he said, is: What do you think of Frank Lloyd Wright, or Le Corbusier, or Edward D Stone, or ...? Alvays I say the same answer, 'I'm not a critic.'
What did Wright think of van der Rohe? I vas the only architect he liked, *said van der Rohe*, but lately he didn't any more.
Mies (pronounced 'meece') – which is what his associates call him – didn't elaborate. He ended the sentence and stopped, then waited for the next question from his interviewer. In fact, the architect's conversation somewhat resembled his architecture – direct, simple, severe. His apartment, likewise, reflects his philosophy that 'less is more.' The entire six rooms don't have one extra stick of furniture, making the apartment seem almost barren. They also are devoid of carpeting, wallpaper, and frills of any sort. All the walls and ceilings are painted white, a whiteness that is relieved only by paintings and collages. Most are by his late friends Paul Klee and Kurt Schwitters.

When the visitor commented about the paucity of furniture, Mies smiled, his eyes twinkling behind layers of crosshatched skin, and said: It's all vat I need.

The floors in the living room and dining room are covered by heavy grass mats, the type you'd expect to see in a hut in Tahiti.

A typical day for Mies, who lives alone, begins when he gets out of bed about 9 am. He prepares his own breakfast, then heads for the living room.

There, in his pyjamas, he sits on a couch and thinks. For three hours or so he does nothing but think. He may smoke three or four cigars and drink an equal number of cups of coffee, but otherwise he does nothing but sit there, Buddha-like, and think. What does he think about?

Vat is going on in the office, in the world, and new possibilities.

Nearby he keeps a pad and pencil, in case he wants to write down an idea, but he said: I mostly just keep it in my head. I don't make many notes. I don't make many sketches, either. I just think it over, how it should be done.

Mies remarked that he seldom draws any more. A great deal of work is thinking. To draw is relatively easy.

He usually skips lunch. He may read The Christian Science Monitor, *the only newspaper he gets, then get dressed.*

He travels the half mile to his office by taxi, arriving there about 2 pm. He doesn't bother driving his 1954 Oldsmobile to work. Nor does he ever walk there, because of arthritis in his right hip, which necessitates his using a cane.

As soon as he eases himself into his chair, his subordinates begin filing in to consult him about various projects.

What little he says, he says to his three key assistants, architects Joseph Fujikawa and Gene Summers and his personal secretary, Miss Connie McConoughey. [...]

When he came here, he said, his wife and three daughters remained in Germany, waiting until he saw whether he liked it and was able to bring them over. War broke out in 1939, and his family was stuck there.

So far, Mies – van der Rohe is his mother's maiden name, which he tacked on when he was a young man – has acquired four honorary doctorates, the highest awards for architecture from England, Germany, and Italy, plus a slew of gold medals from architectural societies.

Two years ago, during the Jesuit centennial here, he was chosen as one of Chicago's 100 outstanding citizens. He is of Roman Catholic origin but has drifted away from that faith. I'm a religious man, *he asserted,* but I'm not affiliated with any church.

Interestingly, two of the most influential forces in moulding Mies' outlook were St Augustine and St Thomas Aquinas, whose writings Mies reveres. Mies observed: They forced me to think clearer, and I believe I understand the problems better because of my study of them. And that is vy I don't go in funny directions.

Why doesn't Mies live in one of his own glass houses? He has lived in his present apartment for 20 years and has found it comfortable. He had actually made arrangements to move into one of his glass houses, he said, when he was summoned to New York to design the 38-storey headquarters for the whisky-making House of Seagram. He spent about a year there, and, weary of paying rent in three places, cancelled plans to shift to a glass house. (Red tape had to be cut to get Mies a New York license because he lacked the high-school education required for a license and refused to take the prescribed examination.) What does Mies think of Chicago?

I like Chicago. Chicago is a good city to vork in. Vy? I cannot tell you. It is very strange. Chicago has a tradition, the Chicago school. And they're open-minded you know, fellows like *[Herbert]* Greenwald. I think Chicago has a good atmosphere for vorking. It's not so nervous as New York.

Mies sorely misses Greenwald, an imaginative builder, who was killed in February 1959 in a plane crash.

When midnight approaches and Mies has finished the last of his daily dozen cigars, he usually downs three shots of Scotch, which he regards as a sleeping potion. Then he pads into his bedroom – which is kept immaculate by a housekeeper who comes in for several hours every day – and retires.

Is there any chance that he may write his autobiography? No, that is boring to me.

Does he still have a goal? Ve vant to do a good job. That's all.

96 [On Civilisation]

Manuscript note (11 March 1960).
Source: LoC, Mies, Box 62, Miscellaneous.
Republished in Pizzigoni 2010, p. 225.

Architecture should be an expression of the essence of a civilisation. Civilisation comes from certain ideas.

One of the characteristics of our civilisation is its striving for universality. Science, technology, industrialisation, and economy are other characteristics. You could have technology without industrialisation if it were not for economics. A definition of technology, which is an applied science, would be: to use the material forces in the right way.

The architect that has the best expression of our civilisation is closest to the solution.

In architecture you are much more limited than in painting. All individualism is a leftover from the time of Luther when he said, 'Here I stand' *[Martin Luther, Diet of Worms, 18 April 1521]*.

97 [Speech on the Occasion of Receiving the AIA Gold Medal]

Acceptance speech, (21 April 1960).
Source: 'Mies van der Rohe Receives AIA's Gold Medal Award',
F. W. Dodge Construction News Weekly, Friday, 29 April 1960, pp. 3,
31; LMvdR, 'Acceptance Speech Upon Receiving the Gold Medal of the
American Institute of Architects', *Journal of the American Institute of
Architects*, vol. XXXIII, pp. 90–91; 'Wohin gehen wir nun? [Where Do We
Go Now?]', *Bauen und Wohnen*, vol. XV, no. 11, November 1960, p. 391;
LoC, Box 61, AIA Gold Medal., manuscript.
Republished in Neumeyer (1986) 1991, p. 332; Pizzigoni 2010,
pp. 223–224; Walter 2022, pp. 258–260.

Mr President, fellows, and members of the AIA, honoured guests,

to receive the Gold Medal of the American Institute of Architects is indeed a great honour. It is a sign that my work has been understood and appreciated by my colleagues. I am very grateful and very thankful for that distinguished token of esteem.

May I also express, on this occasion, the deep gratitude I have always felt, and shall always feel, that I could come to this country and have the opportunity to teach and to work here.

The teaching forced me to clarify my architectural ideas. The work made it possible to test their validity. Teaching and working have convinced me, above all, of the need for clarity in thought and action. Without clarity there can be no understanding. And without understanding there can be no direction, only confusion. Sometimes there is even a confusion of great men, like the time around 1900. When *[Frank Lloyd]* Wright, *[Hendrik Petrus]* Berlage, *[Peter]* Behrens, *[Joseph Maria]* Olbrich, *[Adolf]* Loos, and *[Henry]* Van de Velde were all at work, each taking a different direction.

I have been asked many times by students, architects, and interested laymen, 'Where do we go from here?' Certainly, it is not necessary nor possible to invent a new kind of architecture each Monday morning.

We are not at the end but at the beginning of an epoch – an epoch which will be guided by a new spirit, which will be driven by new forces, new technological, sociological, and economic forces, and which will have new tools and new materials. For this reason we will have a new architecture.

But the future comes not by itself. Only if we do our work in the right way, will it make a good foundation for the future. In all these years I have learned more and more that architecture is not a play with forms. I have come to understand the close relationship between architecture and civilisation. I have learned that architecture must stem from the sustaining and driving forces of civilisation and that it can be, at its best, an expression of the innermost structure of its time.

The structure of civilisation is not simple, being in part the past, in part the present, and in part the future. It is difficult to define and to understand. Nothing of the past can be changed by its very nature. The present has to be accepted and should be mastered. But the future is open, open for creative thought and action.

This is the structure from which architecture emerges. It follows, then, that architecture should be related to only the most significant forces in the civilisation. Only a relationship which touches the essence of the time can be real. This relation I like to call a truth relation. Truth in the sense of Thomas Aquinas – as the 'adaequatio intellectus et rei'. Or, as a modern philosopher expresses it, in the language of today, 'Truth is the significance of facts' *[possibly, a reference to Giambattista Vico]*.

Only such a relation is able to embrace the complex nature of civilisation. Only so will architecture be involved in the evolution of civilisation. And only so will it express the slow unfolding of its form.

This has been, and will be, the task of architecture. A difficult task, to be sure. But Spinoza has taught us that great things are never easy. They are as difficult as they are rare.

98 [George Danforth Interviews Mies]

Broadcast interview (8 July 1960).
Source: Heritage, programme, WTTW Television Chicago, July 8, 1960.
Recorded in four parts.

In this series of Heritage programmes we are privileged to meet the distinguished architect Mies van der Rohe and his guest George Danforth, director of the Department of Architecture, at the Illinois Institute of Technology. [...]
[George Danforth] *This series of programmes brings to you conversations with Ludwig Mies van der Rohe, architect and educator. Beginning with his earlier formative experiences, influences, and projects, and terminating with his current and his proposed works. [...]*
Hello, Mies.
George.
Mies, the idea of a structural architecture has been a very important one to you. How did this idea develop in your mind?
George, I think it was a very slow evolution of an idea. At the beginning, I liked the structural architecture, but I was not conscious of its necessity. It was later on, when we worked and worked and worked, it became quite clear to me that it is the most important evolution in architecture because it will last, there is no deficiency ...
It is an objective ...
It is an objective idea, you know.
But your early experience was in the building trades, was it not?
Yes, I worked when I left school. I was 14 years old, I became an apprentice in building. There we had to dig a hole in the ground, we had to make our own mortar, we had to carry the bricks around – three, four storeys high.
General tradesman, so to speak.
We did things too, you know. When the plasterers came, we plastered with them, and when the carpenters came, we worked on doors and windows. So we had quite a good experience.
A broad experience. There were no machines then, so this was really something of the hand, right?
Nothing ... everything had to be done by hand.
Your architectural impressions must have had a great foundation in your going to school, at the Cathedral School in Aachen.
It certainly had. We had to go every morning to mass in the chapel, in the octagon of Charlemagne. It was a beautiful building.
I think we have a picture of that [picture of Palatine Chapel, interior]. This is the octagon, is it not?
Yes, it has immense power. And I like particularly that you could see the real stones that it was built of. And later on, the middle renovation of it.
Of the octagon itself?
Of the octagon itself! We saw what it was at the beginning.
At the time of Charlemagne.
But I must say, I liked it better without the renovation.
Without ornamentation, so to speak.
Yes.
Well, the whole cathedral complex was more than this. I heard you say that it was a perfect witness of its time.
[Picture of Palatine Chapel, exterior.] Here are also parts. The main part here, that is the octagon. And here is the huge high choir in High Gothic. It is beautiful. With the highest windows I knew in a cathedral. And then, there were also Gothic chapels, and Baroque chapels, and Renaissance chapels. And this whole thing was one group. Quite a unit.
Yes, this was amazing. What qualities of different periods here do you think have made this 'one thing' even though it was built in different centuries?
I don't know. I think if at any time you do an essential work and put it there, you know, it will be a real expression of this certain time. But all these things fit together, like different churches in the city fit

well together. Cologne is a typical city of churches. In fact, it was once called 'the City of Churches'. And here are Romanesque churches, the Cathedral in Gothic, and early Romanesque and late Romanesque [churches]. And everything was in harmony.
Well, as I said earlier, you recognised that without a unifying spirit there is no real validity and strength in any aesthetic form.
Yes, I think you cannot have unity of action if you have no unity in spirit.
Well, this then must be the clue to another remark I heard you say, that you find it very difficult in our time today to find a spiritual value which might unify.
Yes, I am quite sure about that. We are too much individualists, you know.
And materialists, would you say?
Individualists. Yes.
Would you say materialists too – too much materialists to recognise spiritual values?
That could be a unifying factor. If everybody were that, you know … [smiling]. As you have it in everything, huge factories and so. We all fit together, you know.
Other things in Europe, when you were a boy, must have impressed you? I know you've talked of Leuven, I think we have a picture of that. And then you took a very interesting trip as a very young man. I think it was a gift and a grant from an early client.
Yes, it was my first client I had, when I was 20 years old. Before I designed his house, he wanted me to take a trip to Italy. And I enjoyed this trip. It was for about three months, and we saw a lot. I went with this friend of mine, we saw a lot of things. We started in Vincenza and studied every Palladio …
There is a good museum around Vincenza.
It is wonderful, yes. And then we went down to Florence, where I particularly liked the work of Brunelleschi. The dome of the cathedral and the Palazzo Pitti [picture of Palazzo Pitti]. I think that is one of the strongest buildings …
You've often spoken of that.
I was very much impressed by it.
What did you think were the building's strong qualities?
You know, there is a huge stone wall with windows cut out. And that is that. So, you can see how with few means you can make architecture. And what architecture! I was very much impressed by it.
Then you went on to Rome, did you not?
Yes. We went down to Rome, and there I was impressed, like everybody else, by Michelangelo's cathedral, St Peter's Cathedral. But more, I was impressed by the Roman ruins. You know, no architecture was left …
Just structure.
… Just structure. It is a great monumental …
[Photograph of the Basilica of Maxentius and Constantine.] This is the Basilica of Constantine, I believe, is it not? In Rome.
Yes, yes. I like that particularly.
You found that same spirit and that same straightforwardness in the structural solution in the aqueduct too [picture of an aqueduct outside Rome].
Yes, here you can see a particularly nice one [picture of Pont du Gard].
This one, is it in Spain?
No, that is in France.
Is that in France? I know they built them all over Europe.
Yes, they did that. From the Near East, you know, over the border in Africa. In France, in Spain, even in the Eifel Mountains they had aqueducts to bring water to Cologne.
All of the same character.
All of the same character. Only the forms changed with the situation.
With the geography.
With the geography, yes.
In other words, there was no regionalism involved in the aqueducts at all.
That was really an expression of the empire, you know, of the Roman Empire. As powerful as it was.

This trip with Dr Riehl, I think this was the name of your first client, was quite unusual – that he should have had the perceptiveness to educate a young man.
I think he and his wife were very much interested in young people. That was why I got the job to build the house. They didn't want an old architect. And everything worked out very well, and we were good friends in the end.
You've spoken of Amiens. We have a picture of that which I always felt was a particularly good example of Gothic in the way that the structure is visible [picture of interior of Cologne Cathedral]. This is the interior.
I think that is a beautiful picture. There you can see what a structure is in reality. In this country you talk about structure about everything. If you build a shack, you talk about structure. In Europe we have a different idea about that; we call that a 'construction'. A structure has a meaning; it is the meaning of the construction. So the construction is elevated to structure.
Construction is really just the means by which something is built.
Yes.
The technique, should I say. Well then, your earliest ...
It is a pity that we have not the side ... [Picture of the façade of Amiens Cathedral.] It is most beautiful.
Very early in your life, you worked with Peter Behrens as an architect.
When I finished the Riehl House, I heard that [Peter] Behrens needed people, and he was the leading modern architect in Germany. So I thought that it was a good idea to go there and learn something, you know.
This was the first architect you worked for, isn't that right?
I worked with Bruno Paul, but he was mostly a furniture maker, an interior ... and later on, he came and tried to make architecture too.
But he was very well known and very fine ...
He was an excellent, excellent man. Behrens himself was first a painter, and he built his first house in the Mathildenhöhe [Haus Behrens, Darmstadt, 1901]. It was an exhibition around 1900, you know, in Darmstadt, where the Duke of Hessen gave money to a group of artists so they could build their houses. And Behrens was one of them.
In which they could work and live.
Yes, and he built what was his first house that he built. It was quite interesting, you know.
For himself?
For himself. And [he] finished everything in the inside. You know, it was then almost self-evident to do that. To do the linen, the silver, the china, and often the costumes of the ladies in the house, yes.
Well, this idea carried through, in fact, when he was the architect for the, I think, it was a German electrical company.
Yes, he did nearly everything that he had to do, you know. From the huge factories to lamps, streetlamps, and advertising, printing. He did everything.
It's rather interesting. You said that at one time when you were working with Behrens, you were working on the embassy in Leningrad. And you said that at this time there was some contradiction in Behrens' work. Was this typical of the time?
I think that was typical of the time. We found it natural to build factories in a modern way, but our representative buildings, they were still in the Classicistic ...
Expression...
... Expression. And I think it must be very hard to break a tradition like that. I think that it is a slow process too. We look at this factory, you know. Very powerful too, you know, this huge hall [picture of AEG Turbine Factory, Moabit, Berlin, 1909; Mies worked on this project at Behrens' office].
This was done around 1909, I believe.
Well, yes, 1909. Here is one I like better because it is clearer in the structure [picture of AEG assembly hall for large machines, Gesundbrunnen, Berlin, 1912].
This is the one you worked on, is it not?
Yes. Particularly this part I like better [the short façade].

And done at about the same period?

Yes, when we finished the one, we started with the other.

But were all architects without exception at this time working within a kind of contradiction? Not knowing in quite what direction to go?

Certainly, yes, it was not very clear, you know ... With one exception: Van de Velde. Henry van de Velde. He never was a Classicist, at any time. But he invented his own forms and was very individualistic.

He had a great talent, did he not?

He had a very great talent and great character. I think he was one of the most important people. But I think his influence is not so great because of his individualistic manner.

His work contained too much of him rather than being created out of principle.

Yes. It was too subjective and not objective enough. When you look at a Behrens building, a hall like that could be built today and would be still good. You could not say that of Van de Velde's work.

But you had another important influence, as I guess Behrens did too and a number of you, in the work of Schinkel. Is that not right?

Schinkel, yes. Schinkel was the greatest Classicist we had around the 1800s.

Yes, I believe he died in 1840.

Yes, yes. And he built very important buildings in Berlin. So it was no accident that he had a great influence on all of us. Behrens was influenced by him. The embassy in Leningrad is strongly influenced by him.

Schinkelesque.

We studied Schinkel very carefully and I learned a lot too, particularly in details and proportions. They were just masterly done, these buildings.

And then [Hendrik Petrus] Berlage. How does he come into the picture as an influence?

Yes, Berlage. I didn't know Berlage when I was working with Behrens. But when I left Behrens, I was invited by Kröller-Müller to build a museum for them, to project it. That was in The Hague. [Picture of Kröller-Müller Villa, Wassenaar, 1912.]

The Kröller-Müllers, they were an industrialist family, were they not?

Ship owners.

Ship owners. I see. They were very interested in the arts.

They were very interested in the arts and particularly Van Gogh. They had the largest Van Gogh collection. And for this collection they wanted to build a house large enough that it could be a museum. And they asked me to make a design for it, and Berlage ...

He was also asked.

He was also asked. And I worked for about a year on this design, but at the same time I came into connection with Berlage's work. I was very much interested in it, because of his use of plain, clear, brick construction. And construction as a whole; there was very little decoration. That had a great influence on me. Even so I use these principles, in different ways and with different materials. But the principles are the same – a clear construction. I had a great ...

Now, Berlage, I think I read in some place and I've made a note here, called architecture a 'pure art of utility'. He said one should forget style when designing buildings. Well then, Van de Velde as a man had no influence upon you. Berlage very much so, and in his Stock Exchange ...

Yes. Van de Velde, no.

But Berlage, particularly in his Stock Exchange, you have spoken about great strengths in a statement on that.

Yes. We have here a picture of it in a book. Let me see. That is Berlage. [Picture of Stock Exchange in Amsterdam.]

When you were working with the Kröller-Müllers, you lived with them, I believe, for about a year. This must have been an amazing experience, to live amongst these paintings.

I will tell you *[smiling]*. I worked amongst 51 Van Goghs for a year, and I became an expert on

Van Gogh by the fact that I saw them all the time, you know. And I saw how the Kröllers collected paintings, you know.

Could we see the picture, you have it, of the project you did for the Kröller-Müllers? [Picture of Kröller-Müller Villa, Wassenaar, 1912.] This, I believe you have said, led to a rather interesting development: exposure to the paintings led to you getting to know [Julius] Meier-Gräfe, the critic and writer.

Yes, I wanted to have a critique by Meier-Gräfe for the Kröller house because they were uncertain if it was worth it or not. But I went to Paris and met Meier-Gräfe, and he gave me a critique on it. And, by this time I *[had met] [Wilhelm]* Lehmbruck …

You got to know Lehmbruck's work and you met him?

And I met him. Since then we became friends. So it was early in the war, and he was in Germany, in Berlin. I was a close friend of his.

I see. You have said that from Behrens what you learnt most clearly was his sense of great form. Is that correct?

Yes, that was the great form. And from Berlage I learned what is a sense of construction.

Yes. Mies, at this time, was there any influence felt upon you people in Europe by the work of Frank Lloyd Wright in America?

Frank Lloyd Wright. He had an exhibition in 1910 in Berlin. I didn't see it, but at this time came the publication of his work, which I studied very carefully *[Frank Lloyd Wright, Ausgeführte Bauten und Entwürfe (Berlin, 1910); 8 Sonderheft der Architektur des XX. Jahrhunderts: Frank Lloyd Wright, Chicago (Berlin: 1911); both are in Mies' library at University of Illinois at Chicago]*. And I got a lot out of Wright, *[as did]*, I think, a lot of people in Europe. In fact, it helped us to clarify our ideas.

It offered encouragement too, did it not?

It certainly did that. Yes.

And at any time were you aware of the invention of skeleton construction by the Chicago school of architecture? [William Le Baron] Jenney, who invented the skeleton used in this way?

No, I had no idea about it. The first time I heard about the Chicago school was when Berlage came to America. When he came back, he wrote about that. And I read this little pamphlet. *[Mies might be referring to* Amerikaansche Reisherinneringen *(Memories of a Trip to America),* De Beweging*, II–III, 1912 or to* Neue amerikanische Architektur *(New American Architecture),* Schweizerische Bauzeitung*, LX, 11–13, 1912.]*

So you were not aware of this particular innovation at the time. I see. Well, this then about takes it up to the situation of the First World War. More or less. And I think that includes about everything we were going to cover in this programme. And I want to thank you very much.

[Smiling] Was a pleasure to talk with you.

[SECOND PART]
Hello again, Mies.
[Smiling.] Yes.

After you returned from the war, you went back to Berlin. How did you and your colleagues find the situation in Germany and in Berlin at that time?

Just so you know, there was a revolution. Everything was upside down up there, and not much work could be done. So we had all the time we could wish for, to try just projects we had in mind.

Nothing much was being built at first.

Nothing at all. And the time was very interesting because it was a great liberation. And many forces from the First World War, they became particularly active.

I see.

Painters and musicians, poets too … sculptors and architects too. Sometimes we came together and discussed problems, and so on. It was a somewhat wild situation.

There was no real direction at that time.

There was no direction whatsoever. But we tried to do some work.

You spoke of the Arbeits group at one time. What was this?

That was directly after the war. They came together, these people, it was called the 'Arbeitsrat für Kunst', to discuss what should be done. And often these discussions were very funny. In one discussion it was proposed from one side to build a cathedral. And from the other side to build an amusement park ...

And nothing came out of it.

Nothing came out. There was also another group, the Novembergruppe. It was very active, and very stable, and lasted for several years. I later had contact with these people. And I showed my first skyscraper model in glass [picture of Friedrichstrasse Skyscraper, 1921, view].

This was done for a competition, I believe. Is that right?

It was, and it won. That was the first project after the war. There was a competition in Berlin for a site near the railway station, a triangular site. And I decided to make a design for it. And, without any hope that something would happen, because I knew what I wanted to do.

That was an office building, was it?

It was an office building. And since I found the tall buildings very fine, very good, when they were only in skeleton, when there was no skin attached them, I wanted to do something similar like that, to bring that out, the character of the skeleton. So I decided to enclose it in glass. And, being a triangular site, I just used that, I thought it would be good for the glass too, and that the quality of the glass would come out clearly. And here is the plan of this building [picture of Friedrichstrasse Skyscraper, 1921, plan]. You can see that I even changed from the building line inside and came out again, to give the character of the presence. That you'd see it.

I see.

Yes, that was the main part. That was these three parts of office space which were connected with the core.

I see.

[Picture of Glass Skyscraper, 1922, model.]

Then, after that, I tried a polygonal curve so that I had smaller pieces of glass. And I put them in a curve together to get more reflection and make the whole thing richer.

This was a project that came out of the first as a continuation of an interest of yours.

Yes. And that was the project that I exhibited in the Novembergruppe.

I see.

This plan [picture of Glass Skyscraper, 1922, plan]. First, we tried to make a curve, to design a curve for the building. And then we put the glass together, you know, and there was nothing.

Looked flat.

It was absolutely flat. And then we moved it to the outside of our balcony and put the glass just according to the reflection together, and that was the result of these curves we had.

Just as a consequence.

Yes, just as a consequence.

Now, you mentioned the Novembergruppe. You became in time its director, is that not right?

Yes, but after I made an exhibition, an architecture exhibition, for the Novembergruppe.

I see.

That was never tried before. And I intended to ask my friends to show their plans, their projects. I didn't want to show their buildings. Everybody knew these buildings. I wanted to have new ideas. And it was quite a success. Everybody was very interested in it, and we continued that over a few years. And during this time I became the director of the Novembergruppe.

And you made projects for them nearly each year of that time.

Yes. And that was the next project, an office building in concrete in which I wanted to show the clear structure, the skeleton, and huge glass spans. I was in fact a little inspired by the Palazzo Pitti. [Picture of concrete office building, 1923.]

Which we saw on the last programme.

I showed you then. And I wanted to see if we could

make something of similar strength, with our means and for our purposes.

I see. And then ...

Then I made the plans for the brick house [picture of Brick Country House, 1924]. That was a house on a site near Potsdam, but it was just an idea I had. And there I used brick walls as bearing walls but kept it open. And you could say that is a free plan.

I think this is apparent from the plan. The flowing of the space.

Yes.

Those came a year after the concrete. This was in 1923, for the exhibition of the Novembergruppe.

Yes, that was in 1923.

And then the next year ...

Then they thought I should try a house in concrete, to see the consequences of the material and the different construction [picture of Concrete Country House, 1923].

Now, what came out of this Novembergruppe? How did you develop as far as your work is concerned?

I was connected with the Novembergruppe until 1925. And, then I got work to do; I could not play around anymore as I did the years before. And at this time the Werkbund, that was an organisation of free craftsmen and artists and some architects, got involved too. The Werkbund planned an exhibition in Stuttgart and decided it should be a housing development and should show the modern possibility of living. And I was asked to direct this exhibition. First, I thought there should only be five, six people. You know, Corbusier, *[Walter]* Gropius, and Bruno Taut, maybe *[Hans]* Poelzig, and *[Jacobus]* Oud and *[Mart]* Stam from the Netherlands. But that was not possible because the city of Stuttgart insisted that some architects from Stuttgart should be included. And then I decided to enlarge the group to about 15.

I see. Did not this group also include your former associate at Illinois Tech, Ludwig Hilberseimer? He built a house ...

Hilberseimer built there too, yes. That is the view of the whole exhibition [picture of Weissenhofsiedlung, Stuttgart, 1927, aerial view]. Here there are these different houses, and this is the part of the exhibition hall where we showed new machinery for the building industry.

And your apartment in this was this one here on the back [picture of Apartment House, Stuttgart, 1927, street view].

Yes, it was the main block. You see, here comes out again my love for structure. That was a skeleton building, in steel. But at this time we didn't show the steel because it had to be fireproofed. There are 24 apartments, all different plans in the same building.

Do you think, Mies, at this time in your development, if you could have exposed the steel, you would have? Was this not crystallised in your mind?

I think that was too early. The time has to be right for that, you know. Or you have to be right for that.

This is the back [picture of Apartment House, Stuttgart, 1927, rear].

That is the garden; it's the view to the valley.

Yes. At the same time was there not an exhibition, a silk exhibition at about the same time?

Yes, but we had an exhibition in connection with that.

In Stuttgart?

In Stuttgart, where we showed all objects, you know – from the coffee pot to I don't know what ... you know, what is used, and we tried to find solutions for that, fine objects. There I worked with Lilly Reich, you know. That was the first time I worked with her together. She had a great knowledge about materials and objects, and so on.

Lilly Reich had an architectural training of a kind, did she not?

She had architectural training, yes.

And also, another important period of your time was with her.

See, we made an exhibition room for the glass industry. That was coloured glass, dark-coloured glass, and plain glass, and sanded glass [picture of Glass Room, Stuttgart, 1927].

This was in a large hall, was it not?

That was in a part of a large hall.

Basically, you just suspended the ceiling here to bring it down to scale. Lilly Reich did quite a bit of interior work for you too, did she not?

Yes, she did. But the next thing we did together was an exhibition for the silk industry *[picture of Velvet and Silk Café, 1927].* There we decided to show on large walls different kinds of ... different materials – silk, and velvet, in all different colours, it was quite impressive. We had a white linoleum floor, and that was the first time that I used steel furniture. Because I thought if I used upholstered furniture, it would be too much ...

Oh, the upholstery of furniture would be too heavy.

Too heavy and too much material.

Yes. So this was as a contrast.

This was a contrast, and that is where I started with this chair *[picture of MR10, 1927].*

That is the tubular spring chair.

That is the tubular spring chair. There you have a typical skeleton, you know, in furniture.

Yeah, that was in about 1926.

That was 1926, yes. I used some of these chairs in the Weissenhof exhibition too.

I see. This is another view of it [different picture of Velvet and Silk Café, 1927]. You made the walls, the free walls, just of fabric.

The walls, yes.

There was no other material involved.

Yes, nothing. There was a metal frame, and we used the fabrics over them.

Then you had an opportunity, soon after this, to employ in some actual proposed projects this idea of glass as a skin. Did you not?

Yes, we did. In fact, there was one exhibition, and I was invited to participate at this exhibition for a bank building in Stuttgart *[picture of Bank and Office Building, Stuttgart, 1928].* And that was the first glass building we planned for practical solutions, but nothing came out of that too *[smiling].* Local forces were too strong.

Too revolutionary for the time, was it?

Ja, but not for us, you know.

No, but for them it was not acceptable.

For them, yes. *[Picture of Adam Department Store, Berlin, 1928.]* And that was a department store, the building where we tried to do it in glass and stainless steel. That was maybe 1928.

And then the Alexanderplatz.

That is this solution *[picture of Alexanderplatz Project, 1929].*

Yes.

That was another office building, and that was the office building for the police department *[pointing to the first slab on the square].*

Did you do this alone, or did Mr Hilberseimer work with you on this one?

No, I did that alone.

You hadn't started to work with him at that time.

No, no.

Well, this brings us pretty much up to the time of the Barcelona exhibition.

Yes. See, Germany decided to participate in this world fair in Barcelona. So it came about by itself, you know, that they asked me and Lily Reich to do this exhibition. And first, it was just the exhibition of heavy industry and light industry, airplanes, chemical industry, silk industry, and so on. One day the government called me and explained they needed a pavilion because France and Britain would build a pavilion. It was not clear to me at this time, what the pavilion ... what was the purpose of the pavilion ...

Except as a way of competing with the other countries, maybe.

Yes, it may be. But I started ... I had to go there, we had not much time left to finish. We had to finish the exhibition in May, and it was the end of October. So I had to go there and try to find a site for the pavilion, and I did. And I thought it was a good site for this purpose because the pavilion was a low building and I chose a site close to a huge ... *[picture of German Pavilion, Barcelona, 1929, exterior].*

To a huge wall.

... Art pavilion. That was the hall for art exhibitions. So I tried that.

Well, the entire exposition was placed in an area where there was formerly a slum.

In many places.

Throughout this area?

Yes, that was *[previously]* the slum area for Barcelona. And I think they made this exhibition to get rid of this slum.

And how did you approach the building, then? The idea of the building when you got the commission to do the pavilion, Mies?

Yes, I just thought about it and wanted to build a fine building with really good materials, as good as the money allowed us to do. And that was difficult too, to get these materials because it was in the winter. You cannot take new materials out of the quarries because they are wet, and so we had to choose what was …

Available.

Available, yes.

Well then, it seems to me as I look at your work that in building this building this was the first time that you had a chance to show what you meant by a structural architecture [picture of German Pavilion, Barcelona, 1929, exterior].

Yes, I think that was the first time we just made a skeleton, a number of columns and just a roof plate. And we moved all the walls underneath; they had nothing to carry. They were not meant to carry anything. So we used them only to define the space; you can see the plan *[picture of German Pavilion, Barcelona, 1929, plan]*.

The building was used just for exhibitions and receptions for state purposes.

Not even for exhibitions, just for receptions. You know, the opening took place there with the King of Spain, and also there was a reception for the government.

We might look at some pictures of the interior that show us how you used rich materials, Mies, like you did with the skeleton. You enclosed the columns with a chromium skin, bronze [picture of German Pavilion, Barcelona, 1929, interior].

Bronze, yes, and chromium-plated. And that was beautiful. All the marble was beautiful that we used *[picture of German Pavilion, Barcelona, 1929, interior]*.

Did you have any difficulty finding it?

Yes, we had.

Stored pieces of marble.

We found something. We found an onyx block, a large onyx block, in Hamburg. And I used this onyx block, I had to use twice the onyx block as the height of the building.

In other words, it was the available size that determined the height and proportions.

Yes, it determined the height of the building. And then we developed the whole plan.

It's rather interesting: here you also incorporated …

You see how rich this space is too *[picture of German Pavilion, Barcelona, 1929, interior]*.

Very. And one of these views, I think the next one, suggests what you did with sculpture and art in this building [picture of German Pavilion, Barcelona, 1929, interior].

Yes.

You can see through this glass.

Yes, yes.

The next one, I think, is even more effective. This glass, Mies, was a coloured glass [picture of German Pavilion, Barcelona, 1929, interior].

It was coloured glass.

And was it not the first time you …?

First time I used it as a building material. Yes.

Yes.

Here you can see again this sculpture *[picture of German Pavilion, Barcelona, 1929, interior]*.

How did you select the sculpture?

Oh, I just tried to find a sculpture because we had no time to make one. It is by accident that we found the right size by a good artist.

Georg Kolbe.

Kolbe, yes.

Yes. But your ... as you said, you were trying to, from the industrialised means and materials you were trying to make a good building and take it to the level of art.
Yes, yes. That was all industrially fabricated.
From this, then, you had the opportunity to, in the Tugendhat House in 1931, you had the opportunity to employ some of your concepts of space, free space and free walls, in an actual situation, in this house. How did you happen to get that commission? Did you know the Tugendhats?
No, I didn't know them. They intended to build a house for themselves, and they took a trip through Europe to look at existing buildings, you know. And they saw one of my earlier buildings *[Riehl House, Potsdam, 1907]*, and he liked the quality of the building, so he came and asked me to design a house for himself. When he saw the design, he was shocked *[smiles]*, you know. He wanted to go back to Brno. *[Picture of Tugendhat House, Brno, 1931, exterior.]* And his wife, she was interested in art, and she said, 'Why don't we wait, we'll take these plans with us, stay one week in Berlin, and look them over and discuss these things, and we'll let him know what the decision will be.' A week later, they came and said that they liked the plan and I should go ahead.
This is an interior of the main room, downstairs [picture of Tugendhat House, Brno, 1931, interior].
That is the interior of the main room. See, we had ... Since it was a house for a family, a growing family, we had to separate ... we made this one floor, and ...
You made one floor here, open.
Open, yes. With glass windows you could move into the basement. And you were absolutely in the open there.
I think that we may have to continue with this house in the next programme, Mies. But let's look, as time permits, at the interior of the main floor. This ends at about 1931. [Three pictures of the interior of Tugendhat House, Brno, 1931.]
Yes.

And I think that this ends our programme ...
I think that is ...
For today ...
Enough, yes.
Thank you again.
Thank you.

[THIRD PART]
Mies.
George.
How you do again?
Fine. How are you?
Fine, thank you. Mies, what were the circumstances that brought you to America?
In 1935 I received a letter from John Holabird, the renowned architect in Chicago, *[asking]* if I would take over a school in Chicago, an architectural school. I had no idea what kind of school it was, and so on. And I was not in the mood at this time, you know ...
To leave Germany.
To leave Germany. But not much later, I received a call from Mrs Resor, the wife of the president of Walter Thompson, the advertising company. And she ask me to come to Paris and talk with her about a project she had in mind. So I went to Paris, and we talked with two interpreters because I didn't speak French anymore, and she didn't speak French. And the interpreter, not every interpreter spoke German and English, so we had to make quite an effort to understand each other.
This project was to be in America, is that correct?
Yes, the project was for Jackson Hole, in Wyoming. First, I tried to find out where Wyoming was, and I couldn't find it in the atlas, you know. But at this time I was willing to leave Germany, but it was only for the job in Wyoming. And she asked me, you know, if I would come with her. I agreed to that. I tried to get a passport. And then we came on the same boat. I was, for six hours, in America. In America? In New York, I would say. I was six hours in Chicago, and then out in the wilderness in Wyoming. It wasn't too

wild, as I expected. But we discussed the problems there – you know, what you want to have, what you want to build, and so on. And on my way back to Chicago and to New York, I stopped in Chicago and wanted to say 'hello' to Mr Holabird and President [Henry] Heald, with whom I exchanged letters.
I see. He was president of the Armour Institute.
Yes, he was president of the Armour Institute. Then Mr Holabird said, 'The school is still there. Why don't you take this school?' That was a time, you know, when it was about certain in Germany that there was no work for us left anymore. Even our private practice didn't go on. So there was no difficult decision to make to accept that. So I made my statement, what I wanted to have and that I wanted to have a free hand, and the free hand was accepted.
Some limitations on the financial part.
Some limitations on the financial side, I think. I was not unreasonable, I think, at this time, but they just didn't have money, and they worked enough to do that. So I accepted that under the condition that I could bring two people with me.
Former associates of yours.
Yes. Mr [Ludwig] Hilberseimer, a really excellent city planner, the best one I know. And then another man, Mr [Walter] Peterhans, who was a teacher at the Bauhaus, and I knew his work, I knew his talents, and so on. And I wanted to have men like that with me because I thought it was very important to have people like that, that could teach things like that. We called it 'visual training', but I wonder if they understood what we meant by that. He had to just demonstrate …
When you first came …
When we had just come here. The very interesting thing was that nobody of us three could speak English, you know. I think that happens just in America.
Peterhans just a little, as I remember. Did he not?
But very little, you know. But I remember, I had to use a former assistant of mine, Mr [John Barney] Rodgers, who was a student of mine in Germany. So he spoke German enough that we could understand each other.
He acted as translator.
He acted as interpreter, yes.
Well, the Resor project, when did you do that? After you came back to accept the directorship of Armour Institute, as I was saying?
Since I could not do it at the time that I was here the first time, I was here as a visitor. And you cannot work as a visitor; we didn't know that really. So we had to postpone it until I came back. And then when I was in Chicago, we started at that moment to work on this project.
I see. But the house … You have a photograph of the model of it here, which I think was in an exhibit at the Museum of Modern Art in 1947. Was it not?
Yes, it was. [Picture of Resor House, Jackson Hole WY, 1939, model.] You know, you remember the house. It goes over a stream.
Yes, I do indeed. The stream passing under here.
Yes, yes. And …
In effect, it was one large room.
Was one large room. On one side the kitchen and the maid's room, on the other side the bedrooms.
I see. And you employed the skeleton here; you used it to free the space.
The skeleton, yes, we used it. Yes.
Yes. You have an interior view, I think [picture of Resor House, Jackson Hole WY, 1939, interior]? This is a photograph, is it not?
That is a photograph from the exact … That is the picture you would get [looking] out of the room.
I see. Looking in one direction over the valley.
Looking in one direction: the Grand Tetons, yes.
And then you have a photograph, I think, of a drawing you made looking in the opposite direction [picture of Resor House, Jackson Hole WY, 1939, interior].
Yes.
That is impressive.
That is a picture too.
Yes. When you came to Illinois Tech – it was Armour Institute at the time – you had to create … you had

to develop, let us say, a new programme in architecture. What did you do? How did you approach this problem, Mies?

See, we worked at the Bauhaus, but the Bauhaus itself had different *[programmes]* of education. One, and, I think, the original one, was done by Gropius, you know. Then, there was Hannes Meyer, the second director. He certainly changed a lot, you know. And when I came, I was asked by Gropius to take over the school because they had trouble with the city administration.

This was in 1930, I believe. When Gropius asked you, is that right?

That was in 1930, yes. So my main work was to put it in order again, in shape, you know. *[...]* I certainly did something different than Gropius did. And Hannes Meyer did something different from what I did, there is no question about that. But when I came to this country, I decided to take over the school. I went to other schools to see, in this country, to see what they did, and so on. I wanted to know what is going on in education. And *[...]* It was mostly Beaux Arts education, where they used competition and so on. And I personally was absolutely opposed to that, you know. I think competition is the worst means of education, so we threw that out and started new. And what we put in the curriculum was what I thought a young architect needs to have in order to build a good building. That was about all. There was no mystery, nothing fancy about it, you know. It was just plain done. So we put in the first year mainly draughting, but really good draughting. And in the second year, construction, in wood, in brick, in stone. In the third year we went on with the construction in concrete and steel. But then we started with our ... aesthetic side of our education. With proportions, with space, with scalar problems. We introduced one interesting thing that was the course we called 'Visual Training'.

This is the one Professor Peterhans taught.

Yes, that was that. To teach the eyes, to develop the eyes, to see proportions. It was useless to talk about proportions with a student who cannot see them.

They had not had the experience. I think the value of this course was that aesthetic expression was made a part of the student's experience.

Yes, very much so.

Well, you said you put in the programme what the students needed. [Mies lights a cigar.] And as you have said, what they needed for the State Board examinations. But behind this, there was something more, and this was the physical manifestation of the programme.

The truth of that is it was my conviction about architecture, you know. And since I thought – you know, that is an objective conviction – why should I not put that into the curriculum? I don't like fancy things for myself. I am used to logic, to reason, and it is these things I appreciate most.

And these are the qualities upon which you based your programme.

All our work. My work was based on that.

You know, it is rather interesting. Twenty years ago, when I first started working for you Mies, in your office. I wrote down notes of you talking. What you said about architectural education. And I think it's rather interesting if I may read what you said at the time: 'An architectural curriculum is a means of training and education. It is not an end in itself but depends upon and serves a philosophy.'

Yes.

Then you went on and said, 'the absence of philosophy is not a virtue.' That is the point I wanted to bring up.

Well, certainly, but some people think it is, you know. They think if there is a philosophy, there is a limitation. I think it is the opposite way around.

You went on to say, as a result of this, that you feel it is a weakness not to have a philosophy. That a curriculum without a philosophy is not broad and wide, is not even neutral but nebulous. Then you went on to say, 'Therefore our concern' – meaning at Illinois Tech – 'is with the right use of materials, clear construction, and its proper expression.'

Yes.

I think this next part is a very good ... I don't know whether you recall having said this, but I know you know it. 'Since a building is a work and not a notion, a method of work, a way of doing, should be the essence of architectural education.'

Yes, that is very clearly said. I wonder when I said that *[smiles]*.

Well, that was 20 years ago ... How do you feel about these thoughts here?

Just the same. I would put the same curriculum into ... effect. Yes. Nothing else. There is no reason to change things if they are really based on logic. You know, you cannot change a curriculum in the same college, you don't change it every year. You have to develop it first until you have a good one and then stick to it for heaven's sake, you know.

And then develop it.

Yes, and you can develop it all the time, but you have to have it first.

It's very interesting ... You have read a lot.

Certainly, I did, yes.

What prompted your interest in reading and in what directions have you sought information through your reading? Through what applications, Mies?

See, you know, my ... I had no formal education. That was the reason I learned something – to do *[something]* with my head and to work. But otherwise, I was not really educated. And I had to do that by myself. And, just by accident, I saw things I was interested in. In magazines, a weekly magazine, it was called 'The Future', very good name by the way.

A philosophical magazine?

No, a political and a cultural magazine. Then I found one day on my draughting board a pamphlet about the Kant-Laplace theory. It was a cosmological thing. And so I became interested in that and started to read. I mostly read wild things at the beginning, you know, but *[then]* selected more and more.

I remember your story about your first client, Dr Riehl, who was a philosopher. You mentioned him in an earlier programme. When he came to your office the first time, he was amazed. He said, 'For heaven's sake, who advised you on your library?' You had a lot of books there.

He couldn't imagine that it was me *[smiling]*. But that was just because I did it myself, and I had to go through all this. That was a hidden Mies method, you know ... to start and so on. But I think I came out very well.

I think you did indeed. Often you speak of and show in your work an idea of order. What do you mean by 'order'? Speak of that a little bit if you will.

See, that belongs to the philosophy of values, you know. There are things that have higher value than other things. And, let us say, the most primitive values are the values where you achieve years of purpose. And, little by little, you come to a higher stage, you give things not only a function but a meaning. And in the end, you know, in the highest stage, like in a cathedral, there is only meaning. You can hardly talk about the purpose there.

This is what you mean by your 'hierarchy of values'.

That is the hierarchy of values. And there is not only a hierarchy of values, there is at the same time a hierarchy of works. It is different if you have to build a factory or if you have to build a movie *[palace]*, or if you have to build a city hall or you have to build a cathedral. That is what we are trying to tell the students, to make a real difference. If you build a cathedral like a factory, it certainly would be wrong. But *[it would also be]* wrong if you build a movie *[palace]* like a church, or a church like a movie *[palace]*, you know. I think it is very important that people know about this hierarchy of values.

What effect, should I say, has your teaching had upon your work?

I think the most obvious effect was that I was forced to clarify my ideas in order to teach them to my students. You know, if you have not to teach, you can have some ideas *[...]* and you don't care if they are right or wrong. But the students, they perforate you with questions. So *[the ideas have to]* be strong enough. Otherwise, the students, they would laugh at you.

When you work, then, you have the opportunity to make manifest these principles.

The work ... The value of the work, besides a lot of other things, is to prove the validity of the ideas.

Well, in this country you had your first opportunity to do this, on the same campus in which you would later become head of department ... A little of that story. How did this come about? Mr Heald approached you?

You know, Mr *[Henry]* Heald was a wonderful man, is still a wonderful man. But he was so nonchalant, yes, and, he just came and said, 'Mies, I want to make out of the Armour Institute a very important mid-western technological institute. You better think about a campus for us.' That was about all. That was my first project for the campus *[picture of AIT campus, 1940, aerial view]*. So what I did, and what was absolutely logical to do, I took all unnecessary streets out of the campus, so there was no traffic.

It was the openness of open areas and ...

There is one street which went through, and I was told that cannot be moved *[33rd Street]*.

So you created another programme then.

Yes, we had to ... *[We were told]* this cannot be done, you cannot close these streets. So we made another scheme, yes, in which we kept the streets open and built just to make our composition in the building blocks *[picture of IIT campus, 1947, aerial view]*. Now all the streets are closed. Nearly every street is closed.

You found the module within this scheme, which came from the needs of an office, a classroom, and so forth.

We started with the classroom. And we found out that a good size for the classroom was 24 by 24 feet. And we thought, you know, multiples of it would make a good draughting room, or a good laboratory, or a workshop, and so on. So we accepted this module of 24 by 24 feet, and we threw a net over the whole campus area and designed in this net.

The crossing points of this grid were columns points in our buildings.

This is the dimension of unification ...

Yes, that was very important because ... If you have to make a walk, a connection from one building to the other, *[it was important]* that it was in the right place, that you could do that. Otherwise, you ...

Would have a lack of unification.

Yes.

The Metals and Minerals Building was the first building – built in 1939, as I recall [Mineral and Metals Research Building, IIT, Chicago, 1939]. That must have been a very important decision, even deciding what would be the character of the first building, which would establish the rest of it.

Yes. The main decision came when I was asked to build on the campus. What kind of architecture should it be? I knew it would take about 15 years to build a campus, and 15 years is a long time when you see that today ...

From that end of the line, yeah.

... Today people change their architecture every year, you know. So I wanted to have a principle which would last and not be outmoded.

Yes. This, I think, is a good example of the character of the building, the architecture ...

Yes. That was our original idea about architecture, how to build things. So, like these things, you know, this technology and the designs that are the foundations of our civilisation. And that is what architecture has to be.

And this is, I think, very clearly shown in your work on the entire campus.

Yes, we tried to stick to that.

We will not have enough time to see the rest of the buildings now, but I think it's important to show one or two in the next programme.

Yes, we can do that.

And, I think, this is the time for me to thank you for the pleasure of being with you in this programme.

Always *[smiling]*.

[FOURTH PART]
Hello, Mies.
Hello, George.
Mies, last time we didn't have a chance to finish talking about the development of some of the important buildings on the Illinois Tech campus. Which, as you pointed out at the time, was the opportunity in America to prove through buildings the validity of your architectural ideas and those which you made a basic part of the school programme.
Yes. Why don't we look at this ... Thank you. You may remember this first administration building [picture of Library and Administration Building, IIT, Chicago, 1944, exterior] ...
I do indeed, very well.
... where we had a huge steel construction filled with brick and glass.
Yes. I think this detail shows very clearly what you did and how you used ... [picture of Library and Administration Building, IIT, Chicago, 1944, corner detail].
Oh, the stone. Yes.
...the structural members as an expression. This is the building, I think, which you mentioned at one time as violating the 24-foot bay pattern as far as the span is concerned. [It has bays of 24 by 64 feet.]
Yes.
Now, as for the early buildings on the campus, this is an example, it's the Alumni Memorial Building [picture of Alumni Memorial Building, IIT, Chicago, 1946, exterior]. Built, I think, in about 1945 or 1946, it shows again the idea, as carried through the last programme, in which you showed the Metals and Minerals Building, where you had this problem of establishing the character.
Yes, still we kept going, at least in the same spirit. Sometimes we were forced, for certain reasons, to change something. But in general we kept the spirit of the other buildings, you know.
This is a detail of a typical corner [picture of Alumni Memorial Building, IIT, Chicago, 1946, corner detail].
That is the corner of ... the other building, yes.
... Leaving this expression of the structure was to ...
The steel was hanging.
Non-structural steel.
It was hanging on the construction. So there was no reason to ... make the impression it was sitting on the ground.
Yes. This is a detail you used to qualify that. I think probably the most distinguished building, architecturally, on the campus is the one which houses the Department of Architecture [picture of SR Crown Hall, IIT, Chicago, 1956, exterior].
Yes, we could do that because I was head of the department, and the heads of the department decided the programme for their departments. So I wanted to have a huge hall for all the students in the department, from the freshmen to the graduate students. And we needed a huge hall for this purpose. And we constructed it in a way ... Let me see if I have this construction here [picture of SR Crown Hall, IIT, Chicago, 1956, during construction]. We constructed it in a way ... These girders, they carry the roof beams, which hang underneath the girders.
Which allowed you complete freedom within this space.
Absolute freedom in this space. That is a huge space, 120 by 210 feet.
Well, isn't this something consistent with your idea that functions over periods of time may very well change.
Well, certainly. That is one of the principles we used. The principle of flexibility. I think that is a modern principle.
This is a very good picture of the interior [picture of SR Crown Hall, IIT, Chicago, 1956, interior].
That is the interior, yes.
It shows the character and quality of the space.
And it is wonderful to work in.
Yes, I can attest to that.
We tried that out over many years, you know.
Well, there were other buildings on the campus, but I think this one gives an idea of those important

buildings, or those characteristic ones. After this, or during this time, you had your first commission to do a building in Chicago, outside the campus development. This was Promontory Apartments. How did this come about? How did you get this job?

A student and friend of mine brought me together with this developer, Mr Greenwald.

Mr Herbert Greenwald.

He was a young, really aggressive developer with a lot of courage, so we could do about what we wanted to do, you know. We had here at the beginning some problems with steel. It was shortly after the war. We couldn't get steel, so we were forced to build it in concrete. But at the same time we tried to find a solution for a steel building, on the same site, just to find out what it would look like. And, then we used the same principle in our 860 buildings *[picture of 860–880 Lake Shore Drive Building, Chicago, 1951, during construction]*. When they came up, we never talked about concrete, we talked about steel: what would we do with steel? And we worked on models, and you can see how light the whole construction is. We took all the weight out of the building to make it as light as possible. Sometimes people think, you know, the building needs its heaviness in order to be strong. That's wrong. It's just the opposite, you know.

Which is the contradiction of the idea and adjusts it on itself.

Adjusts it, yes.

You always felt more strongly, of course, as we know from your work, towards steel than towards reinforced concrete.

I like steel particularly. I think it is a fine material, and it's a material we have in this country a lot.

Talking of 860–880 Lake Shore Drive, Chicago, that earlier picture showed the building under construction. It is more or less as it appears today [picture of 860–880 Lake Shore Drive Building, Chicago, 1951].

Yes, yes. Without these …

Construction elevators.

… construction elevators.

I think it is very important to point out in these, though, how the character of the structure has not really changed from that earlier picture … The integrity of how it's built has been retained.

We try to express the essence of the buildings. *[Picture of 860–880 Lake Shore Drive Building, Chicago, 1951, during construction.]* Here you see how it is constructed. The building was constructed to the roof. At the top of the roof there was a workshop to make parts of the …

The skin.

… of the skin. Here the skin is held at the top, and then it is lowered in this part here, you know. That is the way modern construction works, and that has an influence on the expression of the building.

These were prefabricated before they came to the job, isn't that right?

No, they were fabricated on the top of the roof.

I see. This is the group of buildings immediately north of 860 [picture of 900–910 Lake Shore Drive Building, Chicago, 1956].

See, that is a building that is concrete skeleton and aluminium skin. At this time we couldn't get steel, or it was too expensive – something like that happens all the time. Yes, we couldn't get the material, but we got all the aluminium that we wanted. So we had to translate our steel solution into an aluminium solution.

I think this was interesting to show although, you know, you are always being attacked for designing buildings that all look alike.

What are they saying?

You know, that the skeleton always looks the same. I think this is an interesting example … that it doesn't.

No, that is nonsense in itself.

The same principle as the other. I think I feel …

I should … I differ very much. Because it's the same way of doing things, you know.

I think in an earlier remark that you made, when I was taking notes in your office, notes that I read in the last programme, you said that construction is the truest guardian of the spirit of the time

because its objective is ... not affected by personal individualism.
Yes, yes. And fancy [smiling].
Yes, Fancy. These two, which were built about the same time, I think they were almost built concurrently. These two here up on Diversey and Lake Shore. Same idea, but its skeleton is natural aluminium.
Yes, yes.
Here in black.
That is black aluminium.
Then in the residential field in this country, in about 1950 you did this residence in the Fox River valley, to the west of Chicago [picture of Farnsworth House, Plano, Illinois, 1951].
Yes. That is a steel building, you know. Plain steel, the clearest construction that you can think of.
It's a very pristine example.
Yes, and that its importance, in my opinion. You cannot make it better.
You have raised the floor level above the ground.
Because once in a while the river goes a little over the bank.
I see. It overflows.
It overflows, and we wanted to have [the floor level] high enough so that nothing would happen to the inside.
This is a different and closer view of the building.
Yes.
The idea of creating a large uninterrupted space came ... You first showed this idea in this project. When is it? About 1947 or 1948? [Picture of Cantor drive-in restaurant, Indianapolis, 1946.]
Yes, yes. That was a drive-in restaurant.
Ah, yes.
And we wanted to have something fancy so that people could see it from far away, you know. And I said, why don't we put the structure on the roof, and then they can see that. Not everybody does it, so you will be known by that. That can be your trademark, you know.
This is the way you guided him from ...
Yes.

... from fantasy to reasonable art.
Suspended, I think. 150 feet was the span. And the kitchen was in the back, and that was the dining room, and outside parking lots for ...
And within this suspended plate ...
In this, yes.
You had the lightning equipment. This is the same idea and principle you used when suspending the ceiling from Crown Hall, that we showed at the Illinois Tech.
In principle, the same idea.
The same idea.
But they are always the same ideas, you know. We don't go far away from that. There was the opera house in Mannheim, in Germany. That was a competition. [Picture of National Theatre, Mannheim, 1953.]
You were invited to submit a scheme for this project.
Yes, yes. A theatre and an opera house in the same building. So we built a huge hall and then put everything in it. Then, you notice again, we brought the steel out without any fireproofing since we fireproofed everything inside.
I see. This is the entrance detail [picture of National Theatre, Mannheim, 1953].
This is the entrance detail, yes.
This is quite a tall room, quite a large room.
Yes, quite a large room, and the auditorium was like [hanging] free in the room, you know. You could go underneath it, and it was a cantilevered shell, where you could see that.
And you entered below it.
Yes.
This is another view of it.
If you look, you can see the shell here of the auditorium.
And an even larger enclosure of space was this one [picture of Convention Hall, Chicago, 1954].
Yes, we never did the really large hall. I was very interested when Mr Spade – he was the president of the South Side Planning Board – when we heard that we needed a convention hall in Chicago. He came to me and said, 'Why don't you make one in the South Side?' I said,

'First it has to be in the right place, not on the South Side.'
They were more specific than that.
Yes, but he thought more about the South Side. But we tried to choose a place, very well situated, and very good for the traffic. We developed then this hall, it's a huge hall, 720 by 720 feet without any inside support.
That's a tremendous size. I think that is longer than the downtown, north, and south loop city blocks.
It is, oh, yes. Most certainly, yes, yes. [Picture of Convention Hall, Chicago, 1954, first proposal.] That is the first construction scheme; we changed it later a little.
To accomplish this, you had a three-way truss space frame.
Yes, a two-way truss.
Two-way.
Two-way truss, yes. And that is the elevation of it [picture of Convention Hall, Chicago, 1954, exterior]. That indicates the structure of it. And these huge triangles here, that was to take the wind load off the building.
Well, your idea of changing values here was in this colour, that we see in this grey. Was it to try as the skin again different ideas for the fill? Is it marble?
Yes, you can fill it in marble or in glass or in metal, it doesn't matter how you fill it, you know. [Picture of Lafayette Park, Detroit, 1956, model.] This was a development for Detroit. We developed …
Lafayette Park, I believe it's called.
Lafayette Park. It's 52 acres, and I did it [...] with Mr [Ludwig] Hilberseimer. I thought it was big enough that a city planner should work on it, you know. And he made the plan of the development.
This scheme shows the full possibility …
The full possibility. We built this part here.
That has been built now, yes. I think that has been published just recently. These are views of the actual site [picture of Lafayette Park, Detroit, 1956]. Your use of something like townhouses …
Yes, those are townhouses in fact, you know.
This is exposed steel, and this again is a scaffolding in aluminium on the outside.

Yes, this is aluminium.
It's interesting: back in 1933 and 1934, you did some projects for courthouses in which the plot was surrounded by a wall. And there were houses within that. You've employed that to a degree in this project, I think?
Yes, but not really. We tried to do it, you know. And then they became too expensive, so we didn't have enough money to do that. That is the Seagram Building [picture of Seagram Building, New York, 1958].
You might say this is your 'pièce de résistance.'
You could say that, yes [smiling].
It's a very elegant building. How did this come about? How did you get this project, Mies?
There is a story. The owner [Samuel Bronfman] got a plan for a building and published this building, and his daughter [Phyllis Lambert], who lived in Paris, saw it, and she telephoned to her father, 'Don't build that [...] I'll come directly back to the United States and I will find you an architect,' and so on. And then she talked with the Museum of Modern Art, and they proposed that a group of architects should … one out of this group … should be considered, yes. And she went around and looked at their buildings, you know. And then she came back and decided that I should do it. She proposed that to her father.
And this is the result.
That is the result of it. That is …
That is bronze.
… A bronze skin, yes. Not aluminium anymore. That will last forever – bronze and glass. Nothing will happen.
As you, I think, were quoted saying, you feel, and felt here, that bronze is a very noble material.
Yes, certainly it is.
That the quality of it is something … you were willing to have. This is a detail of one of the side entrances I believe [picture of Seagram Building, New York, 1958].
Yes.
Now as to your projects which are as yet unbuilt, Mies. This one you worked on is for Cuba, on

Santiago, near Havana [picture of Bacardi Building, Santiago de Cuba, 1957].
Yes, that was a project for Bacardi.
Bacardi Rum.
He wanted an office building. He saw the publication of Crown Hall, this huge room. And he said, 'That is an ideal office for me.' We couldn't do it in steel; we had to do it in concrete. But it is the same principle again. Here we have a huge slab, and we supported it on eight columns ... outside, yes. Nothing is inside, you know, only free-standing partitions.
With the glass lines set well back, I noticed, because of the orientation problem with the sun.
Yes, the sun.
The site seems to be a little low, and you put ...
It is. On one side it is two storeys high.
So, in classic tradition, you put it on a pedestal.
Yes, something like that. That was the design for the inside of the office. The way it would look. You see the natural site here used in the picture.
You are doing – this is being [kept under wraps] at the moment – but you are doing an office building for Bacardi in Mexico City now in steel, right?
Yes, that is in steel. There we could get steel.
And this project [picture of Battery Park City Apartment Buildings, New York, 1959]?
That is on the tip of Manhattan. Huge apartment buildings, 40 storeys high. We wanted to build 40 storeys high so that we could bring these buildings far enough apart that you could look from the centre of Manhattan through them and see the river.
This is a very imposing site.
That is very ...
Looking over in this direction towards Brooklyn.
A fantastic site.
It is interesting, Mies, that in these buildings you have made extensive use of this idea of the skin composed of glass, or whatever you want to put in. Yet the structure of the skin is the I-column or the H-section column. People have said – I think that it would be interesting to hear what you think about this – they've said, 'Oh, they all look the same, use the same idea.' How do you feel about this?
First of all, whether they should look alike, as they do. Why should we change this – it's a good solution, you know. And if you change it, the interesting part is that the site plan of the buildings, the grouping of the buildings, becomes very much more important than the buildings themselves.
It is a quality that many forget.
Certainly, they don't realise it even.
Yes. I think that's rather a succinct statement of how you feel about it. You've spoken about architecture being a part of civilisation and an integration of it, and there is a technological, a strong technological quality to our civilisation today.
Yes, I made that very clear, you know.
You wrote this. And then presented it here in Chicago in 1950. I wonder if you wouldn't mind reading it in the last few minutes of this programme.
Oh, I will do that. 'Technology is rooted in the past, determines the present, and tends into the future. It is a real historical movement. One of the great movements that has shaped and represent the epoch. It can be compared only with the classic discovery of man as a person, the Roman will to power, and the religious movement of the Middle Ages. Technology is far more than a method; it is a world in itself. As a method, it is superior in almost every respect, but only where it is left to itself, as in gigantic structures of engineering where technology reveals its true nature. There it is evident that it is not only a useful means, that it is something, something in itself. Something that has a meaning and a powerful form, such a powerful impact that it is not easy to name. Is that still technology, or is it architecture? That may be the reason why some people are convinced that architecture will be outmoded and replaced by technology. Such a conviction is not based on clear thinking. The opposite is happening. Whenever technology reaches its real fulfilment, it transcends and becomes architecture. It is true that architecture depends on facts, but its real

field of activity is in the realm of significance. I hope you will understand that architecture has nothing to do with the invention of forms. It is not a playground for children, young and old; architecture is the real battleground of the spirit. Architecture wrote the history of the epochs and gave them their names. Architecture depends on its time; it is the crystallisation of its inner structure, the slow unfolding of its form. That is the reason why technology and architecture are so closely related. Our real hope is that they grow together, that someday the one will be the expression of the other. Only then will we have an architecture worthy of its name. Architecture is the true symbol of our time.'

Mies, with that statement of yours, we'll end this fourth programme of the series on your work and your thinking. I want to thank you for it and express my appreciation for being with you.

It was very nice to be with you.

99 [Interview With Peter Blake]

Unpublished typewritten interview (May 1961).
Source: Columbia University, New York. Partially published in 'Programme', Columbia University, School of Architecture, spring 1961, pp. 44–46.
A conversation between Mies and Peter Blake on the occasion of the 'Four Great Makers of Modern Architecture' symposium at Columbia University in New York.
Republished in Blake 1970, pp. 93–104; Punete (2006) 2008, pp. 29–47; Pizzigoni 2010, pp. 229–249; Walter 2022, pp. 261–262 and 279–292.

I think that the questions I want to ask you don't necessarily reflect any opinions in mind; they are just meant to elicit answers from you about a number of things concerning your work. One of the things I wanted to ask you was this: it seems to everyone that the principle of discipline in your work is structure. Today a great many other things are important in building – mechanical equipment etc. Some people have suggested that maybe you are over-emphasising the structural discipline and under-emphasising mechanics, air-conditioning, heating, planning, etc.

I don't think that's right. In certain buildings, for instance 860, we proposed to air-condition the buildings, but the owner said it has to be a building with apartments in the class of the Chevrolet, not the Cadillac *[860–880 Lake Shore Drive Building, Chicago, 1951]*. He wants to have a reasonably cheap grade for the apartments. He proposed, indeed was convinced, that that was what his last building *[900–910 Lake Shore Drive Building, Chicago, 1956]* should be.

Now some people suggest again that the preoccupation with glass, with glass-walled buildings that are very good at revealing structure has created so many problems in other ways that maybe this was the wrong direction in which to go.

I must confess that, for instance, the Seagram Building, I didn't hear one word about the heat or the trouble or anything like that. I think people like the building … I think that there are just questions in people's minds. We have questions too, you know. *Why is it that you are so principally interested in structure? It is your background?*

During my life I have been thinking about architecture: what it is, and how it could be gone in our time. I think that a clear structure is a great help to architects. I am old by now, you know, and I cannot do anything that is not clearly conceived. I don't play with emotions in my buildings.

But still at 860, for example, and the Seagram Building the structure that is shown, that is expressed on the outside, is not really just structure. It is emotional, if you like.

I don't know. No, I don't think so. At least, that is not the driving power in the design of the building. I think it's impressive because of the height.

And the applied mullions emphasise the height and the sculptural discipline.

You have to use mullions, you know, whether you put them inside or outside, there is no difference, you know. If you put them inside, you cannot see to the outside. If you put them outside, you know, it is an architectural limb … You have … columns and mullions too … I think we talked once before about that, certain reasons for doing that. It was very good that we did it because the process of building was [to] put together on the roof [the façade] in a two-storey [piece]. We had to lower down it from the roof, and then clip it onto the skeleton. And even though we used these heavy mullions, it moved very much, like a piece of paper. The mullions, the steelwork, you know, that is not so [firm until] it is in place.

This brings up another question that I should like to ask. The kind of work you do requires a great deal of precision and very fine workmanship. In many parts of the world today this kind of workmanship isn't really available, and even in America it is sometimes difficult to get it. Do you think that the kind of craftsmanship that your building demands is perhaps ahead of its time.

I don't know if it has anything to do with being ahead of time. I think certainly with these new materials [there is] the demand for certain techniques and certain experience from the people who do the work. We are not especially interested in just the science of craftsmanship; but good craftsmanship, it should be there anyway.

What I was thinking of was, you know, in the last few years Corbusier has been going in the directly opposite direction of making buildings more crude. There are almost no details in his buildings at all any more. They are crudely done, and deliberately so. Do you think that that is the wrong direction to take today?

I would not say the wrong direction. Corbusier, when he made his buildings, he had to work with these primitive people too, and I think it is one of the reasons why he could do it. It was in France, outside of the city. What would you think of one such a rough building on Park Avenue? Where people don't really rest, they go into the building and out of the building, etc. Our arts, it seems to me, use technological means.

You know, would you say that the kind of work you've done since you came to America has been very much influenced by the possibilities of American technology in this respect?

I think I did here what I have done in Europe too. I must admit that here I have more possibility to do it. You know, people accept things more easily here than they do in Europe. Here nobody is handicapped by tradition. In Europe the tradition can be a good thing, but only on one hand. You know, you can learn something from these old buildings you find at any street corner in Europe. But it is a handicap for the new buildings.

What would you say you have learned from the old things in Europe? A lot of people when describing your work refer to [Karl Friedrich] Schinkel and even to the Renaissance.

When I came as a young man to Berlin and looked around, I was interested in Schinkel, and Schinkel was the most important builder in Berlin. There were several others, but Schinkel, he was the most important man. His buildings were an excellent example of Classicism ... The best I know. And certainly, we became interested in that and studied it carefully and came under his influence too. That could have happened to anybody. I think he has wonderful constructions, excellent proportions, and good detailing.

What about the way he places his buildings, you know, on pedestals etc.?

I think that is a good way of doing it, in spite of the fact that it is a classic way of doing it. I think that we have this influence of history on us and that we still ... I would not deny certain influences, but ...

In your very early work there was a tremendously sudden break, where you had been working very much in the Classical tradition up to the beginning of World War I and then suddenly in 1919 you seemed to have broken completely with everything you had done before.

I think the break started long before. The break started when I was in the Netherlands working on the problem of the Kröller museum *[Kröller-Müller Villa, Wassenaar, 1912]*. Then I saw and studied carefully *[Hendrik Petrus]* Berlage. Then I read his books, and his theme that architecture should be construction, clear construction. But *[...]* his architecture was in no way medieval ...

Do you feel that you have come to your kind of architecture through construction and through knowing about how things are built, rather than through theory?

I think that ... that goes together. I thought about architecture, and then I tried architecture to prove it. And often the experience showed that my thoughts were in no way right, but many times the experience proved my thoughts correct.

You know, people who refer to your work now as being Classical in spirit also say that the tradition of architecture in America, at least in the past 100 years, has been romantic and anti-Classical; organic in the case of [Frank Lloyd] Wright and quite romantic in the case of [Henry Hobson] Richardson, etc. Do you feel that your architecture is in any way in conflict with the basic motives of American architecture, that it is a stationary kind of thing as opposed to a moving kind of thing, which seems to be the American theme?

I never think about it in these terms. And I think it is quite dangerous. You know, we had in Europe and England, *[William]* Morris, some Arts and Crafts people, and we had people in Germany. We were quite romantic ... I think that is the main difference, but also I think that in the nineteenth century there was a great confusion. You could say that is a phase of democracy too, with everybody, but democracy does not have to be confused.

If you compare the Barcelona Pavilion with the first building at Illinois Tech, the Barcelona Pavilion had a very strong sweep. It was almost a building in motion – at least that is the way it looks in photographs. The buildings at Illinois Tech were very stable, very clear. They were objects that were standing there and were completely enclosed within themselves. Don't you feel there was quite a change between those two buildings?

No. If you remember, I made one design for the campus, it was not built, where I removed most of the streets so that I could move the buildings freely there. And then I was told by Henry Heald, the president, that it could not be done at the moment. They would not permit me until much later to remove the streets. And so I was confronted with the past, to develop a plan in just normal block pattern, and I did that. You cannot do much about it. And that is another question too – to make things particularly moving or something ... is that not a handicap to modern architecture, and to buildings? We had to build, for instance, classrooms. We didn't know often for what they would be used. So we had to find a system that made it possible to use these buildings as classrooms, as workshops, as laboratories, etc.

Now this brings us back to what we said before. The fact that maybe democracy does mean a certain amount of chaos. As I understand it, your buildings are designed to be very flexible within so that almost anything can be done within them.

That is the way I see it as a possible solution. I don't believe that democracy is just politics. I think democracy in the real sense is the highest form of all.

Do you think that this idea of creating a free order within architecture, that this has worked out in practice in your buildings?

At least, I try. I think it has worked out.

You mentioned the many different apartments in 860 Lake Shore Drive, and this is one example where a great many things have been done by each of the tenants, etc.

Yes.

You mentioned Wright a little while ago. It seems to me that in some of the early buildings, like the Barcelona Pavilion, there are traces of Wright's principles. Certainly, they don't look like any Wrightian building, but there are some traces of those principles. Would you like to say something about to what extent Wright has impressed you and influenced your work.

See, I think that I wrote that down in Philip Johnson's book – I wrote about Wright and the influence he had on us in Europe *[Johnson (New York, 1947), pp. 195–196]*. Certainly, I was very much impressed by the Robie House and by the office building in Buffalo *[Larkin Administration Building, Buffalo NY, 1906]*. It came to us at a time when *[Peter Behrens]* built office buildings for the rubber company in *[Hannover] [Offices for Continental-Caoutchouc und Gutta-Percha Compagnie, Hannover, Germany, 1914]*. You know, *[a lot]* of glass. He was a great lift. I was certainly impressed by Wright's work. Who couldn't be impressed? I think he is certainly a great genius. There is no question about that. But I don't believe that he had a very great influence in general. You know, it is very difficult to go in his direction. You sense that his architecture is based on fantasy. You have to have fantasy in order to go in this direction, and if you have fantasy, you don't go in this direction, you go in your own.

In other words, you don't think anyone would copy the Guggenheim Museum very successfully.

No, I don't. You see, Wright had a great influence, but very late in his life ... About, you know, in the thirties he started that, the early thirties. Then he built 1000 or 1200 buildings or houses. But his influence on the face of America is quite modest.

What would you say – I know this is a difficult question – is the main problem of architecture in America? What can architecture do to change the American scene as it looks now, and how should architects go about it?

That is a question I am very much concerned with: not only what should be done in America, but what should be done anywhere. I come more and more to the conviction that architecture is related to a certain kind of civilisation, and you have to agree to that or nobody can talk about it. You know, if somebody says it doesn't, there isn't any use talking about it. I personally really believe that it is. And that seems to me to be the main task we have. To build an architecture which expresses this kind of civilisation we are in. That is the only way I can see to overcome any chaos.

Well, of course, one could argue that our time in every other field, politics etc., is so chaotic that maybe the way our cities looks is a real ...

Still, still there is a lot of what is, you know, the real fact. That our civilisation depends largely on science and technology, to a great degree, that is a fact, you know. Everybody should see that. The question is how far can we express that? You know, the architects ... we are in this peculiar thing. We should express the time and yet build it at the same time, develop it at the same time. But in the end I really believe that architecture can only be the expression of this civilisation.

To a great many artists, including some architects, the natural reaction to our time, which tends to create a lot of sameness, is to revolt and to be different. Do you think that it is excusable for an architect to react to his time by being different from his time?

No, I think it isn't. I believe he cannot. So that makes it hopeless to try. But I don't believe that everything has to be the same. But there must be, and I am sure there are, certain fundamental principles we are given. We are not ... We are ... to a very small degree, craftsman. We build these machines. We use them. More and more, buildings are becoming the problem of machine products.

Would you – to come back to a point we talked about earlier – say our buildings are a product of machine technology? If you were building in India today, as Corbusier is, how do you think you would build?

As simple as possible. If I cannot use any technological means, then I would have to do what they did in former times. Work with the hands.

You know, you brought up the question of democracy requiring discipline and order. Do you think that in a free-enterprise democracy where everyone is free to do just about what he wants within very slight limitations, it is possible to create architectural order?

Yes, I think it would be an order in freedom.

But you think that it requires, perhaps, discipline on the part of the architects before it could work, or how would you put it?

I think, certainly, you need discipline for any kind of work. I think even Wright needed a lot of discipline for his work.

Wright's buildings in cities, at least his buildings in the last 20 years or so in cities, seemed to have been very antagonistic towards the city.

Yes, certainly. I do not share this position, you know. I believe that you have to accept the reality. I don't think anybody can change it by a theoretical formula or something. I have seen that too often, and it's gone to pieces. I would accept it, and then do something with it. That is the problem, you know. People often think I have a formula when I talk about structure. They think that I am talking about a steel beam. I'm not, you know. That has nothing to do with it. You can build in concrete. But if I had to build in concrete, I would not build these Wright things. I see no reason for that, because I believe that these Wright things don't belong to our time.

One of the things that is sometimes suggested about your idea of a universal space, a building that might be used for one thing today and something entirely different ten or 20 years from now, is that the American economy depends upon rapid ... some kind of obsolescence of buildings, so that they can be replaced and people can be kept at work and so on. Do you think that the idea of a universal kind of architecture which is infinitely flexible is a threat to the idea of some kind of accelerated obsolescence?

First, let me say that I think that the idea of rapid obsolescence is a very funny idea. I don't even think it is a good idea, and I don't think it is there. You know, if you look here in Chicago and around, you find all this pulling down of houses. There is no possibility of replacing them. I think that is just something we ... it is a kind of excuse. I don't think it is a real fact. You know, there are things that don't have to last for a lifetime. This suit for instance. In some older times we had one suit when we married, and we kept that all the time, for good. And otherwise, we had only working clothes. That is not necessary that it lasts forever. There are things that can be replaced and by necessity will be replaced, but I wonder if the buildings will be replaced. I always thought we had some buildings on our campus that we got from the armies. You know, the army barracks. Oh, they say it is just provisional, you know, but they last forever. I think on any campus you can find these things now. The war has been over now for 15 years, and they are still there.

In Washington they still have buildings from the last world war ...

Yes, there you see ...

Temporary buildings!

No, I think it should be reasonable. You know, you don't have to build like the *[pharaohs]*, to last thousands of years. But *[a building]* should live as long as it can live. There is no reason to make it just provisional. Then they should build a tent, you know?

I'd like to come back to something you said a while ago. [...] Now, if we are today going to have these very complex mechanical systems in buildings, the way that [Louis] Kahn and [Paul] Rudolph are doing today, shouldn't we dramatise those rather than the structural elements which seem to have become a little subsidiary, at least in terms of cost and in terms of size?

I think these structural elements are very essential elements, and I think that pipes are not. The structure can be integrated into architecture, but I don't think that pipes can. Well now, we can [move] the pipes – we do that in our buildings – in fact we move the pipes to where they belong, you know.

Well, Corbusier, has in some of his buildings dramatised the mechanical parts, on the roof for example, into very strong sculpture, so maybe there are ways of elevating pipes into architecture too.

That is possible, and I think Corbusier did it well. You know, we can do that, but not everybody can do that, and I see no reason why everybody should do that.

Isn't it true that you really believe that structure is a kind of ethical basis of architecture?

You know, to me it is something like logic. It is the best way to do things and to express them. I am very sceptical about these emotional expressions – I don't trust them, and I don't think they will last for long.

When you talk about structure, I think most of the time you still talk about rectangular structures because they are the most reasonable, practical, and economical. But now it's possible at least to have very fluid structures take over from the simple rectangle.

I don't think that would happen, that they would take over ... I think those fluid structures, like shells etc., have a very limited use. They are in fact open structures. You know, you can say they are also fluid structures, but nearly everything we have to do, what we have to build, you know ... we have to build a one-storey building, and you can do about what you like with it, maybe a two-, even a three-storey building – you are to a certain degree free. But then it ends. What would you do with a tall building? I'm not answering the question ... I know.

I think most things we do, we need space, living space, working space, and ... If there is no reason for it, why make them fluid? I think a rectangular space is a good space, maybe much better than a fluid space. With a fluid space, if you have something that is fluid inside, you know, or some particular function, I think it is a good idea to make it curved or something like that. But to make an office space a geometric form or such just for aesthetic reasons ... you can do it if you have a theatre or a single building or a side where you can be free-moving. But most of our buildings are quite patterned to the city ...

Now, some people who are very much interested in these fluid structures think that if you were to do a whole city, that it would be a rather dull place, that the buildings would be very much alike – the buildings would be of different heights, but there would be no variation in the forms, and maybe there is some need for variation here and there.

But see the medieval cities, that is a good example. Are the houses really the same? Are the plans really the same? Who could afford it put in a fine entrance hall. Who could afford a fine knocker, he put that on. And if somebody could afford a bay window, he did that. But the plans are the same, and how rich is the medieval city!

Well, the medieval city also had a cathedral, and what is the cathedral today?

But there are medieval cities without real cathedrals. They had churches, yes ... but ...

But what would be the cathedral today?

I don't know ... I once said, 'We will not build cathedrals' – that was in 1924 or 1925 – and everybody cried, 'We need a cathedral for architecture etc.' And I said, 'We will not build cathedrals,' and some people, they were furious at me because I said that. But a cathedral was the expression of a civilisation which was drenched in religion. And we are not. We may build large churches, but that is not a cathedral. The cathedral had an absolutely different meaning to these people. People today, they hardly go to church.

In the medieval times every day, every hour was built into this religious system. You know, at noontime, the bells were ringing, they gave you the time. You had to go to the church every morning and often every evening too, etc. I think that is an absolutely different consideration. You know, it is what I said about civilisation. We have a different civilisation. I cannot tell you what is the most important building today. Maybe we don't have that anymore. We have a lot of other things. Even the town houses are not much today, when compared with the medieval town house.

You know, some of the other architects of this century, like Le Corbusier, Walter Gropius, and Frank Lloyd Wright, have been interested in developing a complete philosophy about society, about life, about all aspects of life, as well as working as architects. And it seems in your work you have concentrated very much on architecture and, within architecture, almost on a rather limited area of architecture. Are you at all interested in the other factors – politics, sociology, etc.?

I am interested, but I don't think that is the business of architects. You know, you can invent any kind of system, any kind of sociology. Talk with sociologists. You know, I studied a lot of sociological theories, and everybody thought, this one is the right one, to be followed. But it is like a tapestry, it works together, it is the work of the many.

But still, one of the things that is interesting about you, at least to those of us who know you today, is that you seem rather conservative in many ways – in your building, in your work, in your preferences, etc., and yet in the early twenties and right after World War I you must have been a wild radical and you were involved in very radical movements at the time. How do you account for the change?

I don't think there is a change. I think there is a natural development. In the early twenties I tried to understand architecture, and I tried to find possible solutions, and I am still doing that, you know. I think I am mostly interested now … you know, I don't construct sociological systems, but I am very much interested in the question of civilisation. What is it? What is going on? This is not a system or a work of one, it is the work of the many. I believe in many cases that it is given to us from the past, and all we can do is to guide it. I don't think we can change it fundamentally. The only thing is that we can guide it and we can do something with it, in a good way or in a bad way.

I'd like to ask you some things about how you started, how you became an architect, about your life in the twenties and the thirties, before you came to America. Would you just like to talk a little bit about the beginning, when you were an apprentice on certain projects and so on.

You know, as a young boy I went to the cathedral school in my hometown. That was a Latin school, and it was a Catholic school, but I was not very good, and my father decided I should do some practical work and for this reason sent me to a kind of vocational school, but not really a vocational school. It was between these things a little. But it was a very practical kind of school. When you went there, it was a course of two years, and when you went through that, you knew something about physics and chemistry, you learned something about draughting, and the language, and we had French beside our German; but it was a good education for people for business or in factories. We were not engineers, but we were not craftsmen either. We were somewhat between. After I finished this school, I went as an apprentice on a building. There we had to do harder work in the beginning. We had to dig a hole in the ground, and we had to make our own mortar. At the beginning we had to carry the stone and the mortar to the bricklayers, and later on, you could work in the role of the bricklayers, and later on, you could even put up a corner of the building. So we did all kinds of work until it was finished. People came and put a roof on, and we worked with them; but a good deal of the work was to boil coffee water for the bricklayers for breakfast and *[cut up]* small pieces of sausage and cheese. Then we had to clean the building every Saturday perfectly. Then, when the building was finished – I remember it was an apartment building – the architect called me into his office, and I had to make signs in all the windows – 'four-room apartment' and 'three-room [apartment]'. It was primitive, you know. We didn't use ink, we had to make it with a piece of Chinese ink. We had to rub it, and we didn't spend one cent on the advertising for the rooms. Then I asked him if I could not have some money, because, you know, I was working for him. I received some money, but only ten [German marks] a month. But 'No,' he said. So then I decided to take another job I had heard of, and it was in the stucco business. I worked in [an] office, and I had to write addresses, and nobody could read my handwriting ... and I pasted stamps on cards for the government. One day the top man there, he had to go into the army, and everybody in the office moved up one step. That brought me into the design department of the stucco business. There we had to work on stucco decorations. First, we designed on a smaller scale, but then we had to make full-sized details – a quarter of the ceiling, in any style, Louis XIV or Renaissance, Gothic for a dining room, etc. ... There I learned really how to draw. We had to make these details on a flat wall, and you did not dare to ... From there I came to an architect who was ready to build a department store in my hometown. We had a lot of ornaments on the outside on the façade, and nobody could draw the ornaments, so he asked me if I could come there and draw the ornaments. He said it was an enormous job, you know. I said, 'When do you need it, tonight or tomorrow?!' It was nothing to us! And then from there I went to Berlin because somebody who was working on these apartment buildings said, 'You should go away from here, to Berlin.' So I tried to get a job; they advertised open places in larger offices, you know. I went to a place that was a suburb of Berlin, and they were building a city hall. They gave me a job. I was to design the concert chamber ... They wanted to have it in wood. Now, I knew everything in brick and plaster and stone, but wood I didn't know. I worked there for a while, and then I decided that I had to go and to learn to work in wood. Then I went to *[Bruno Paul]*. I worked there for a year, and then I built a house for a philosopher *[Alois Riehl]*. It was a little difficult because he wanted to have a young architect do it for him. He didn't want to have a known man. So I was the only one ... I was not known. But in the end *[they]* were a little afraid, you know, about my experience. And this woman *[Sophie Riehl]* asked me if I had built houses. I said, 'Not by myself,' and she said, 'Is that not dangerous? We cannot be *[a test]*.' I said, 'Listen, if somebody would answer me that until I am 60, what would I do?' And then they said, 'Go ahead.' And then I built this house *[Riehl House, Potsdam, 1907]*, and when that was finished, I went to *[Peter]* Behrens' office, just to work on these huge structures for the electrical industry in Berlin *[AEG]*. And later on, I was in charge of the embassy in Leningrad *[German Embassy, St Petersburg, 1913]*. Then from Behrens I went to Kröller in The Hague. There I really designed their house *[Kröller-Müller Villa, Wassenaar, 1912]*.

How come that house was built as a full-scale model?
They wanted to see it. And I remember *[a friend]*. I showed him that when I went to Paris; I wanted his ideas about it, what he thought, and I told him that we were going to build a model in full size. He said, 'That is very dangerous. You shouldn't do that. Even if you build it carefully, it is still just canvas, you know, and a wood structure. Not real material.'

This house was never finished.
No. *[Hendrik Petrus]* Berlage made a plan for it too. They gave him the job. But later on, they decided to move the museum – it was a house as a museum – and *[they]* moved it to the centre of the Netherlands, away from the city, because *[they]* were afraid that the city, The Hague, would expand so much there and we would be *[no space in the]* neighbourhood.

This was just about before World War I, wasn't it?
Yes, it was in 1912–1913.

You were in the army ...

Yes, in the army I was in Romania mostly – for two years, anyway.

Were you building things with the army engineers? Or what were you doing?

No, I was with the railroad engineers. We built things we needed, but mostly we had a lot to do with telephones and ...

Now, after the war was over, you went back to the Netherlands?

Yes.

And did you start to work on your own? Did you have your own office?

Yes, yes ...

How did these first glass skyscrapers come about?

There was a competition. Somebody, you know, a real-estate man, somebody like Mr *[Herbert Greenwald]*, he wanted to build next to a railroad station, there was an empty place. He wanted to build an office building there. The site was triangular. Very triangular. And since it was a competition, it was easy to have a lot of courage! I didn't think I would win it and would build it. So at least I could do what I liked. And then I thought I would do it in glass because I saw these American skyscrapers, and they were all good and it was only a skeleton. So I picked out *[glass]*. But then I was a little afraid to use such enormous areas of glass because I found, when I looked at glass areas, that they were sometimes absolutely dead and sometimes just clear. So I thought it would be good if I could take some part of the façade and change the angles a little bit. To at least break that up, so it wouldn't really be dead ... so that something was there. And on the second skyscraper I thought maybe it would be a very rich building if I built it going around a curve, so that each glass piece or strip had a different light.

Now these were designed in models ...

Yes, we made models about five or six feet high. And in glass strips, to show it as it was.

Were you working alone then, or did you have some assistants or a draughtsman?

No, at that time, I think I was alone.

Did you do any other buildings ... How were you able to support yourself? Did you do any small houses at that time?

Yes, we had to finish one house – the *[Urbig]* house *[Potsdam, 1917]*. We started that in 1914 and we had to finish that after the war. And then we got one other building. But mostly private houses. For rich people, for bankers.

How was it that they came to someone radical?

We didn't know that it was radical on this side. They knew my first house, and for this reason came to me. Even the *[Tugendhat]* house, *[Fritz Tugendhat]* came to me because he saw one of my early houses *[Riehl House, Potsdam, 1907]* and he found that it was very well built, and for this reason he came to me. And he was shocked when I showed him my design for the *[Tugendhat]* house. He thought it was wrong. But his wife said, 'No, let us take it with us and study it a little.' A week later, he said, 'All right, go ahead with it.'

In the early twenties you were bringing out a magazine, and you were also involved with a group of artists which put on exhibitions etc.

Yes, yes ... that's because ... That was really funny ... Gropius had a Bauhaus *[exhibition]* in Weimar, after five years of existence. He wanted to show what was going on. We went there with friends; a lot of people came there, not only architects, you know, painters too; and ... we were in agreement with what the Bauhaus was doing.

Why was that?

Because it was quite different. The architecture ... and the objects they made. So we got started in Weimar to make a magazine that we called 'G'. The first letter of *['Gestaltung' (arrangement)]* is a 'G', so we called it 'G'. That was in protest.

How would you translate ['Gestaltung']?

To be formed. That's not a good translation because 'Gestaltung' is not in fact formalism. This is just directed to the other end, you know. To break out ... the essence of things, to be only concerned with the essence of things.

And this also involved exhibitions etc. This same group of the magazine.

No, that had nothing to do *[with it]*. We had no exhibition at this time. That was a separate group, the Novembergruppe. I came to the Novembergruppe because a friend of mine knew that I had this modern glass skyscraper, and he said, 'You should show them in the Novembergruppe.' I didn't know what the Novembergruppe was. It was a group of radical artists, and they showed every year in a large exhibition building. They showed their work, that was the main exhibition. Then they asked me to be a member, and then very soon they asked me to be the president of the Novembergruppe. And that was very typical of this time too. You know, it is something that people *[don't]* understand today. They said, 'We should not just show our work every year.' So I said, 'All right, what would you do?' 'We should do some*[thing]* great, something important,' they said. 'If we could only do something important, something big.' Their exhibition was always the centre. But then I brought architecture into these exhibitions. I asked *[Peter]* Behrens, I asked *[others]*. You know, about ten people. I *[wanted]* to have ideas from them for an exhibition. Most exhibitions, they wanted to show executed buildings. No, I *[wanted]* to have ideas. And it was quite a success. We kept it going. Each year there was at the same time an architectural exhibition. At least, as long as I was president.

How long did that last?

I was president, I think, for about five years. Many of these things I did … I did for these exhibitions. You know, the brick houses, the concrete office buildings, and the concrete country house, that was for these exhibitions.

Mies, you were talking about the Novembergruppe, and I was interested in knowing how you came to design and build the monument to Karl Liebknecht and Rosa Luxemburg. It must have been about that time.

It was about that time. It was very strange. You know, I built a house in 1911 for a man called *[Hugo]* Perls *[Perls House, Berlin Zehlendorf, 1912]*. He was the father of *[Klaus Perls]* and was very interested in art. He was a friend of *[Theodor Wiegand]*, director of the museum in Berlin, and when I built this house, I intended to make the dining room like a fine Schinkel room. One day he had just ordered *[Max Pechstein]*, the Expressionist painter; he said to him, 'Why, don't you paint these ceilings?' *[Pechstein]* put canvas around and started painting in no time. In a few days he had the whole room painted. With trees and landscape etc. … Then after the war he worked in the government, and more and more he became interested in art and became in fact an art dealer. One day he sold his house for *[five paintings by Max Liebermann]* to a man; his name was *[Eduard]* Fuchs. Fuchs, he was a collector of Chinese art and of Daumier etc. … He had a very good collection. And he intended to add to the house an exhibition building where he could hang his pictures. His whole house was full of pictures and pieces of sculpture, mostly Chinese sculpture. And so Fuchs told my friends that he would like to meet me and to see me. So one day *[Ms …]*, who knew my work, she was in Berlin, and she visited me one afternoon, and she said she had to go to *[Eduard]* Fuchs because she was a friend of his father. And I said, '*[Eduard]* Fuchs, he asks me all the time why I don't come and see his house and his collection etc. … Why don't we call him up?' And we called him up, and he said, 'Why don't you come to dinner?' And then we went there for dinner. And after dinner he said, 'I would like to show you something.' And he showed us a drawing of a monument. It was a monument with Doric columns, porticos, etc. And he said that this was a proposal for a monument for Karl Liebknecht and Rosa Luxemburg. I said, 'You must be nuts. You know, I tell you, these people, they *[died]* in a bank, you know, or before a brick wall. Why don't you build a brick wall. *[But that,]* that is something for a banker. Mendelsohn or any of these rich bankers' *[Mendelssohn & Co. was a big German private bank]*. He was a little disturbed, but he didn't say much. The next morning, when he got me up, he said, 'I would like to see you. You know, you disturbed me a little with what you said.' Then he told me that he was responsible as the chairman of a committee to build this monument. Then I said, 'I knew Liebknecht in Paris. So I knew him. I never met Rosa Luxemburg, but Liebknecht was very familiar. He was a very fine so-called "Edelkommunist" (idealistic communist). He was a very fine communist. He was not an "Edelkommunist". He was a very practical communist.' 'Why, don't you decide on this monument,' he said. I said that I didn't know if I *[could]*. 'I told you, build a brick wall. I can't do it.' But he worked a little, and I said I would try. Then I showed him my design, and he seemed to be satisfied with it, and the people on his committee seemed to be satisfied with it. Then I had a problem about the brick. What kind of brick should be used? I wanted a very rough brick. Then I found out that there were no rough kinds of brick at all. We tried to find some. I was in Hamburg at a huge brick factory. And they showed me a mountain of junk that they had. Bricks that were baked together etc., and I said, 'I think that will do it,' or something like that. And then I said, 'How much does it cost?' And they said, 'Oh, you can have the whole mountain. We are glad to get rid of it. It cost nothing.' So then we started to do that, and I sent these bricks to the cemetery, and that was the end of that. The communists? They went there and looked, and they were upset by these terrible bricks. But that is how I *[wanted to]* do it.

How did it come about that you were appointed to be head of the Stuttgart exhibition?

You know, back then, I think it was in 1925, we had a series of talks for the members of the Werkbund and I gave one of these talks. They were very much impressed and asked me to be an officer of the *[Deutscher Werkbund – German Association of Craftsmen]* exhibition, and then at the next meeting we talked about this exhibition at Stuttgart. And there was a man with the name *[Gustav]* Stotz. He was the secretary of the Werkbund in Württemberg. He came with a proposal to make an exhibition in Stuttgart. He wanted to call it *[...]*. He proposed that I should be the director. He decided on that.

And then you began to invite a number of architects ...

Yes ... I thought about what to do. And I thought that the best people that were interested in the problem of modern living ... they should be invited. I thought about Corbusier and Gropius and *[Oud]* and *[Stam]* and a few others. But the city of Stuttgart insisted that some from Stuttgart should build there too. So we took some harmless people in, but we had to enlarge our group too. It would have been a fantastic contrast. The whole affair was not easy to do. This Stuttgart was the centre of a certain architectural school. Somewhat like regional architecture. And we were fought by both of them, very much. I talked one evening with one of them – I'd met him somewhere – and I said, 'What do you have against the fact that we build here? If it is good, you have a wonderful example to show your students, and if it is bad, you have a wonderful example to show them too.'

After the [Weissenhof] exhibition you were picked to do the German Pavilion in Barcelona, is that right?

Yes, that was *[a chance]* that I should do that. He *[Peter Behrens]* was then building a huge building in Frankfurt *[the Technical Administration Building, Frankfurt-Höchst]* for the chemical trust *[IG-Farben]*. One of the top men of the chemical trust was in charge of the exhibition in Barcelona. So he proposed that, and I did it with little *[information]* about the whole exhibition.

You know, a lot of people take the example of the Georg Kolbe statue in that court as a wonderful demonstration of collaboration between sculptors etc.

Yes. Well, I will tell you ... You know, I was thinking then about a sculpture by *[Wilhelm]* Lehmbruck, but I couldn't find one that was large enough. I had no particular preference, you know – *[Kolbe]* or anybody else. But *[Kolbe]* had a sculpture done many years ago that was just the right size. That was how we asked him to send it, and we put it up.

I'd like to ask you something quite different. Which modern painters and sculptors interest you most and why?

I was particularly interested in *[Paul]* Klee, in *[Piet]* Mondrian, in *[Georges]* Braque, in *[Pablo]* Picasso. Then, when I had to work in the Netherlands for Kröller, I saw how a collection is put together. You know, he had the largest collection of *[Vincent]* van Gogh. And I saw that when Mr Kröller came from Paris, he always brought one or two Van Goghs with him. During the time I was with Kröller I became interested in art particularly. Later, when I went to Paris, and I met Lehmbruck, we became friends, and when he came to Berlin, I saw him every day. Mostly for dinner we would get together and talk about everything.

This was before World War I?

That was before, yes.

A lot of people, art critics etc. claim that your work is very much influenced by De Stijl, Theo van Doesburg etc.

No, that is absolute nonsense, you know.

Why don't you explain why?

Doesburg, he saw these drawings of the office building, and I explained it to him and said that this is skin and bone architecture, and since then he calls me an 'anatomical architect'. I like Van Doesburg, but not as though he knew very much about architecture. He made some architect's solutions to houses or buildings with *[Cornelis van Eesteren]* together, the city planner, you know. But mostly he was interested in his particular kind of art. Like Mondrian, you know. Once in Düsseldorf he proposed the dictum that everything should be square. But there is no influence. The same people claim that I was influenced by Mondrian in the first building for the campus, the *[Mineral and Metals Research]* Building. This one wall they say looks like Mondrian. But I remember very well. Everything was given for this whole building. The site had 64 feet to the railroad from the sidewalk. Then somebody gave the *[crane]* for the hall, the 40 feet. And we wanted to have laboratories. We took the 40 feet for the *[crane]*, so we needed 42 feet for the hall, from column to column, or from centre column to centre column. The rest was laboratories, you know. Everything was there; we needed steel bracing in the wall, the brick wall. It was a question of the building code. You can only make a six-inch wall so big, otherwise you have to reinforce it. So we did that. Then, when everything was finished, the people from the building, the engineers, they came and said, 'We need here a door.' So I put in a door. And the result was the Mondrian.

What about the Constructivists – the Russian Constructivists? Were you interested in their work?

No, I was never interested in formalistic ideas. I felt that very strongly. Even Malevich, you know. Very Constructivistic. I was interested in construction, but not to play with forms.

Tell me, to come back to the twenties and the thirties, when did you became head of the Bauhaus, and how did it happen and what happened after that?

That was some day in the thirties. One morning, Gropius and the mayor from the city of Dessau *[Fritz Hesse]* came to me and told me that they had talked to *[Hannes Meyer]* – he was a follower of Gropius in the Bauhaus – and that the students had become too wild, they were in the hands of young Communists etc., and the city was a democratic city, and they didn't want to spend money for this Communistic affair. And he said you are the only one who still has credit to convince the city fathers to take over the Bauhaus so they would finance the school. Then I said, 'Yes, I would do that.' I didn't know what trouble I would be in in a short time!

What happened when you got there?

Oh, they made a lot of trouble. First, they asked me to make an exhibition of my work. They wanted to see what I did. They wanted to criticise it. Then I told them that that is what I don't do. I don't let the students tell me what I should do. I will tell the students what they should do. And I can tell you that in two words, you know. Whoever doesn't work here I will drop. There is no room for big talkers. Nearly every day we had a large meeting when I came there. At the beginning we had faculty meetings, with students together, oh, every second day. So I stopped that. And then we had trouble. The students started to strike, and they wouldn't work. So I got the faculty together and said, 'Tell me, what do you think. Is that a normal situation for the school?' I asked every faculty member to answer. Some were a little hesitant, but I said, 'You have to answer me. Do you think that is normal?' Then they said, 'No'. And after I had asked everybody, I picked up the phone and called the mayor and said, 'I would like to close the Bauhaus for four or five weeks.' He said, 'Why?' And I said, 'This strike of the students. I have the impression that the students don't know their rights and responsibilities, and I don't think the faculty know that either. And we have to make a new constitution for the school. And for that reason we have to close the Bauhaus.' He accepted that with some hesitation, but he accepted it. And then we made a new constitution for the Bauhaus. The so-called 'Edelkommunists' left, but the real Communists stayed. But by then they knew that I meant *[it]*, and they worked.

What happened when the Nazi influence began to make itself felt?

[Free State of Anhalt] was the first state under Nazi rule in Germany. And we knew that was about the end. But the mayor asked to come with some experts and to visit the school and to look at what we were doing. And he said, 'I could understand it if you would like to take a vacation during this time.' And I said, 'No, I don't, I would like to see the progress.' Not that I was convinced that I could convince them about what we were doing, but at least I wanted to stay and see whether they ... So they came, and the top man was *[Paul]* Schultze-Naumburg, a man from Weimar or the neighbourhood of Weimar. Around 1900 he wrote a group of books he called *[Deutsche Kulturarbeiten]* – you know, 'Ideas about Culture'.

He wrote about how to build in the country and how to build in the cities and how to live and about dress for women, etc. He came with a group of other people, and I showed him an excellent, excellent *[exhibition]*. I insisted on that. Then he told me what there was here about the building, you know. 'You heat the universe, you know? You heat the universe, you know? With these huge classrooms that Gropius built and the shops.' And I said, 'Oh no. In the winter it is perfectly all right, you have just to heat it enough. But you should come in the summer. Then it *[gets hot!]*.' Then we talked about flat roofs. They are not tight, etc. And I said, 'I know that there are some difficulties. I once had to fix one of yours!'

What happened after the Bauhaus moved to Berlin? [See 'The End of the Bauhaus'].

We moved to Berlin where I designed *[sic; in fact, rented]* the factory. The former telephone factory. We painted everything white inside, and people and the students were very happy with it. It looked rotten and everything from the outside, but the inside was nice, and we started to work and have a good time there. And then in the early spring in 1933 ... in '33 the Nazis came into power all over Germany, and in the spring of '33 they came and tried to find documents against the mayor of *[Dessau]*, documents about the foundation of the Bauhaus, how that was done, etc. They thought we would have that. I knew we didn't have it. But they worked there, and they told me later that they worked there all night, just to find out if we had told the truth about it. Then they didn't find anything. And there were Gestapo people, you know, soldiers etc. with their bayonets living there. And they got angry and telephoned to the headquarters, and they said, 'We have no time now. We have more important things to do than this. Close that thing and come home.' So they had it closed. Then I called Karl *[in fact, Alfred]* Rosenberg. He was the philosopher, the philosopher of the Nazis. I called him and said, 'I would like to talk with you.' And he said, 'I am not free, I am so busy, you know.' Then I said, 'I would really like to talk with you. They closed the school for no reason.' And he said, 'All right, you can come. Eleven o'clock in the evening.' And my friends said, 'You will not really be so dumb and go there and never come out anymore'. And I said, 'I will go there.' And I talked with him for an hour, and he told me he was a diploma architect from *[Riga]*, from the Baltic states. And he couldn't understand certain things in modern architecture; for instance, he didn't like cantilevered things. He said, you know, 'my feelings ask for the support there …' And I told him, 'There is nothing you can do. If I put a column under a cantilevered roof, my brain wouldn't work anymore.' So we talked about a lot of things – what the Bauhaus is about, and he said, 'Why didn't you change the name at least, when the Bauhaus came to Berlin?' And I said, 'The best thing that Gropius did was to call it "the Bauhaus". Why should I change that?' And then he said, 'All right, I will see what I can do.' But nothing happened. So I went to the Gestapo myself and wanted to talk with the head of the Gestapo. That was *[…Tapler?]*, a young man from Cologne. I couldn't get him for weeks. I went there every single day. So I never met him. But one day I did. And he said, 'Oh, come in, come in … etc. I would like to talk with you. I am interested in architecture, and in the Bauhaus and what you are doing there.' And he said, 'I will see, I will propose to *[Hermann]* Göring that you can open it again. But one thing is certain. You cannot have *[Kandinsky]*.' I said, 'Why not?' He said, 'He signed a petition for the League of Human Rights for union men in China.' I started to laugh, and he asked me, 'What are you laughing about?' And I said, 'These people came to me, and I said, "Why should I sign that? How do I know that there are people like that in China?".' And then he said, '*[Kandinsky]* is out. Convince me. We don't know anything about him.' And then I told him that very early he wrote a book about the spirit in art. And I said, 'That doesn't sound very *[Communist]*.' And he said, 'That is your responsibility. But I warn you, these people are very clever. You think that they are very harmless, but that is just when they are the most dangerous.' And then I said, 'All right, I'll take the responsibility for him.' And he said, 'All right, *[I'll]* see that I talk with Göring.' And one day we got a paper that we could open the Bauhaus again with the condition that we should talk with the Ministry of Education. But I knew these people there. When I got this letter, I got the faculty together and said, 'Here we have this. Now we can open. But I propose that I write them a letter that the faculty decided to close the Bauhaus.' I wanted that. I wanted that we take this step. And that was the end of it.

Mies, you mentioned earlier that you had been thinking a great deal about the relationship between architecture and civilisation. Would you like to add something to that?

Yes, I think that it is in fact the most important question … You know, if somebody doesn't agree with me that there is a relation, that architecture is only possible in relation to civilisation, then there is no use talking about it. But if somebody accepts that, then we can ask ourselves: What kind of relation is there, and what is our civilisation like? Everybody talks about it, but it is really difficult to define it. Since civilisation is a process partly in the past and partly in the present and partly open to the future. So it is really difficult to find in this moving process the characteristic of civilisation. But I think it is not enough that somebody has some ideas about architecture. To just say these things are architecture or just say that is what I like to do. We had that when I was young. I listened to these great people, around 1900. We were talented, we had everything you could ask for to work in the field of architecture, but we were just subjective, in my opinion, as most people are subjective today. I think we can move on only if we really find some ground to stand on. Architecture, in my opinion, is not a subjective affair. It wears a subjective characteristic, but the tendency should be in an objective direction.

Mies, you read a great deal of philosophy etc. What philosophers interest you most ... and historians.

You know, I have been interested in architecture, all my life. And I like to find out what was sick about architecture. I tried to find out what influenced architecture. We were quite dumb ... I have the feeling that architecture belongs to certain epochs and is the expression of these epochs. In the successful epochs it expresses the real essence of these times. That is also the question of truth. How can we find out? We know, or we felt, that it was a question of truth. But at this time it was very difficult for us to say what is the truth. And to understand the truth. What I say is the result of a lifetime of work. It is not a special idea I have when I talk when I say that architecture should be the expression of the structure etc. But the interrelation of these things was not clear at this time. So all my reading was at least a lot about what can influence architecture. When I read about sociology, I wanted to know what ideas were there that would be an influence on our time. I didn't want to change the time; I wanted to express the time. That was my whole object. I didn't want to change anything. I really believe that all these ideas, the sociological ideas and even the technological ideas but particularly the sociological ideas, they would have an influence on architecture. But it is not architecture itself. What we really need is to know how to build, with any material. And that is what is missing.

You know, I have just one more line of questions that I would like to ask you, and that is about education. Most of your own education as an architect has been very informal. At the same time, though, people have said that Illinois Tech, which is the expression of your ideas on education, is perhaps the most rigid and formal school in America today. What motivated you to make Illinois Tech what it is, and what do you expect the students to get out of the school?

You know, when I came here to the school and had to change the curriculum, I was just thinking to find a method which teaches the student how to make a good building. Nothing else. First, we taught them how to draw. The first year was spent on that. And they learnt how to draw. Then we taught them construction in stone, in brick, in wood, and made them learn something about engineering. We talked about concrete and steel. Then we taught them something about functions of buildings, and in junior year we tried to teach them a sense of proportion and a sense of space. And only in the last year we came to a group of buildings. And there I see no rigidness in the curriculum at all. Because we try to make them aware about the problems involved. We don't teach them solutions; we teach them a way to solve problems.

Are they given any design problems at all? Are they given any buildings to design?

That starts, I think, in the junior year with a skeleton problem. But later in the senior year they design buildings. But we didn't like the word 'design' at all. We 'develop' a building.

Do they build any structures?

No, we tried that in the early times, to do some work, but it was very difficult here in Chicago. So we sent them mostly in the summer during the vacation to a building *[site]*. Usually they are just a timekeeper or something for a month. But we thought that was still better than nothing. At least they see that a building is different from a piece of paper.

How long were you head of the school of Illinois Tech? About 20 years?

Twenty years ...

What happens to students who have graduated from Illinois Tech? How long does it take them to become architects in their own right?

I think what they had to do and what most people did was to go from our school and work in offices, and very often large offices. It would take them a few years to get enough experience. You know, we didn't think that a student had to be ready after leaving the school to design huge structures. Why don't the owners of

the offices do that themselves? But they are very well prepared to help them.
Is there anything else that you would like to talk about before we finish this tape? Any other subject you have in mind?
I don't think so.
Good. Thank you very much.

100 [Speech on The Voice of America]

Radio speech (between 27 March 1961 and 9 July 1962).
Source: LoC, Mies, Box 62, Miscellaneous.
Republished in Neumeyer (1986) 1991, p. 333; Pizzigoni 2010, p. 250.

I would like to take this opportunity on 'The Voice of America' to thank my German friends for remembering my 75th birthday. I not only think on this day of my friends but of my hometown, Aachen, within whose walls I spent my youth. Then of the city of Berlin, where I lived and worked one quarter of a century. The city with the great buildings of an *[Andreas]* Schlüter, a *[Hans Georg Wenzeslaus von]* Knobelsdorff, and a *[Karl Friedrich]* Schinkel, and where I found my first great teachers in Bruno Paul and *[Peter]* Behrens. Then of the work, together with people of the same kind in the German Werkbund.
I remember also the rich and grand time of the twenties, which made such a great contribution to our Western culture and ended with the fight for the Bauhaus.
All this was for me of great significance for my later work in America.
All this I will always keep in grateful memory.

101 [Speech at Aachen Industrial School]

Speech (26 January 1962).
Source: LoC, Mies, Box 62, Miscellaneous.
Speech at his old school: the Gewerbeschule der Stadt Aachen, 26 January 1962.
Translated from German by John Nicolson.
Republished in Pizzigoni 2010, p. 251.

I would like to send my old school my warmest wishes on the occasion of its 75th anniversary *[Aachen Gewerbeschule was established in 1887].*
I have often thought of the school with great gratitude during my long, busy life. For me, as for many others, the trade school meant the first step towards a free profession. Without it I would probably have entered my father's workshop and become a stonemason. I have always wondered at the common sense of the school's director, Herr Spennrath, who saw the need for a step between elementary school and the higher institutions of learning and who implemented this by creating the trade school. He thereby released numerous energies and made it possible for thousands of young people to set out on the path to a freer life. For that we want to thank him today.

102 An Architect for His Time

Published interview (October 1962).
Source: 'An Architect for His Time', *Show. The Magazine of the Arts*, vol. 2, no. 10, October 1962, pp. 56–57, 134–135.
This text contains quotes from different sources.
Republished in Walter 2022, pp. 263–275.

A few significant years ago, Mies van der Rohe, an architect from Aachen, Germany, began to apply the borrowed aphorism that less is more in an American building or two. Buildings have a way of influencing their eras as well as reflecting them. And in a celestial twinkling, a salesman in Duluth discovered that he could no longer buy a tie wide enough to cover his paunch.
However indirectly this generalisation is applicable, it is indisputable that the genius of Mies van der Rohe has reached deep into American life. It was inevitable that an architectural statement of such powerful clarity would cut giant swathes through the tenacious rococo cobwebs of many American artistic attics, architecture's especially. I have tried, Mies says, to make an architecture for a technological society. I have wanted to keep everything very simple, to have an architecture that anybody can do.
Mies has done this precisely. His architecture is a pure expression of his time. It reflects the simplicity of logic. And, of central importance, its elements can be taught.
Most of Mies' professional life has been spent in teaching it, and his methods have been as unique as his results. They make such simple good sense that the layman wonders why architecture is still taught any other way. And they are the certain clues to the personality which animates them.
For 20 years Mies was director of the Architecture Department of the Illinois Institute of Technology in Chicago. George Danforth, his successor, is a former

pupil and a disciple; as a result the programme at IIT remains essentially as Mies created it. When I first came to Chicago, *Mies says*, I found all schools in this country following the Beaux Arts tradition, which I thought was absolutely ridiculous – at least, if your purpose is education – because it means that everything about it is accidental.

In the Beaux Arts school a freshman was already designing something. This is silly. In the first place a student must have the basics – something he can stand on. First, we taught students how to draw very exactly.

Next we taught construction: what is a stone construction; how to work with brick or wood.

Then we taught proportion. This is something hard to talk about. Proportion, whether it is good or what makes it bad, is something for the eyes. You must see it.

So we had a course in visual training because I found that the students couldn't see. They had to learn to use their eyes.

And then we talked about a building, and what you must have to make a good building.

And in the last year, we worked on groups of buildings, how they were related to each other.

We tried to depend entirely on reason. Everything which did not come from reason was out.

To the layman none of this sounds unusual. But in the teaching of architecture it was revolutionary.

On the streets of every American city is evidence that American architects of the first half of this century have approached architecture as caprice. Says Mies of Chicago, You look at Michigan Avenue from the bridge to the station. It looks exactly like a woman's hat shop! *And it does.*

My idea, *he says*, was for a structural architecture. In Germany, Holland, Scandinavia we say Baukunst. First comes the building. And only afterwards the art, the Kunst, which is the refinement that comes from a good building.

In 1950, in an address at IIT, Mies, said, Architecture has nothing to do with the inventions of forms. It is not a playground for children, young or old. Architecture is the real battleground of the spirit. Architecture wrote the history of the epochs and gave them their names.

For most of the first half of the twentieth century, from Louis Sullivan to Mies van der Rohe, American architecture was assigning no names to its time. There were architects, like Wright, who were signing their personal signatures. But as Mies has said, the architecture of an epoch is principally impersonal and anonymous. For the most part, the Americans were building an early Disneyland of types and styles.

Mies points to genuine Greek temples, Roman basilicas, and medieval cathedrals as creations of a whole epoch, *structural because, when they were built,* architecture was a problem for which a solution was found. You have it not only in Europe. In New England are buildings, barns and such, that are perfect. You could not improve on them.

It is Mies' point that there is then no need to try to improve on them. He takes that same attitude towards his own work. We feel, *he says*, that if we have something that is as good as we can do, then there is no reason to change it. *He has said that the day will come* when others, who have something important to give, will do what we could not do.

Just as his buildings tend to strike the inexperienced observer as cold, so has Mies' personal façade seemed, especially to his competitive colleagues, to be icily cerebral and remote. His longtime friend and associate, Ludwig Hilberseimer, who followed Mies from Germany to IIT, explains this aspect as a disinclination to 'make propaganda'. Recently, despite this quasi-misanthropy, despite advancing age (he is 76) and the fact that he is confined to a wheelchair because of crippling arthritis, Mies has become somewhat more accessible, though to await his arrival in his offices can be an uncomfortable experience for an outsider.

The premises occupy an entire floor of a former warehouse east of Michigan Avenue in Chicago. On the opaque glass door is his name in black letters – all that need be explained about the activities within.

The area is spare and austere. Mies' personal office, enclosed at one side, contains an oversize desk on steel legs, several steel chairs of his own design and a presentation model in a glass case. On one wall is his 1919 drawing for a glass skyscraper in Berlin. The walls are painted flat white. The floor is black. In one corner stands a steel wheelchair with black fittings. The remainder of the floor houses 20 staff architects and two administrative assistants in spacious communal proximity. An extensively equipped wood-working shop at the rear is segregated by partitions.

Mies has always stood for this kind of unencumbered space. His home is an apartment on the third floor of an old-fashioned building not far from his Lake Shore Drive apartment buildings. He has lived there for 20 years and, though he considered moving to one of the Lake Shore buildings, he decided he was too old to go to the trouble. His apartment is old-fashioned only on the exterior. The large, airy rooms are painted white. The furniture, almost entirely in black, includes MR chairs in the dining room. Mies' valuable Klee collection is on the walls. There are blinds at the windows but no curtains. Everything is scrupulously clean.

Though Mies' personality is widely advertised as 'reserved and withdrawn', he can be extremely affable and will converse with great warmth and enthusiasm about his childhood and early working years. Aachen, where he was born in 1886, was the first capital of the Holy Roman Empire and before the Second World War had many buildings from the early Middle Ages. Among Mies' childhood recollections is that his mother took him each morning to the Chapel of Charlemagne and that he loved to pass the time counting the stones in the walls instead of at his prayers.

Mies attended the cathedral school founded by Charlemagne, then spent two years at a trade school, which concluded his formal education. But he knew he wanted to be an architect, and the education he pursued for himself is the prototype for the teaching methods he later devised.

He began by learning materials. His father was a stonemason, and Mies often helped in the family stonecutting shop. He was apprenticed to a local builder, where he was exposed to other materials, but the fact that he got no wages interfered with his appreciation of that phase of his education.

At the age of 14, Mies was at work, at a salary, for a firm of specialists in stucco decor. We made stucco panels, in detail, full size, *he recalls.* We made them in Louis Quinze, Louis Quatorze, Empire, everything. It wasn't long before I was fed up. That was enough for me of decoration. I wanted to find out what really is architecture.

In 1905, when he was 19, Mies went to Berlin. In those days, as he says, we were looking for a master who could show us the way. There was none. *But Mies managed to learn: about wood from Bruno Paul; about proportion from Peter Behrens (Behrens had a great sense of form); and about integrity of design from Hendrik Berlage (Berlage ... would not accept anything that was fake).*

While Mies sought to know what architecture really is, he planned many buildings but built few. These were praised for a sure sense of quality, but they were solidly traditional. He kept searching for better answers.

We searched in the quarries of ancient and medieval philosophy. Since we knew that it was a question of the truth, we tried to find out what the truth really was. We were very delighted to find a definition of truth by St Thomas Aquinas: 'Adequatio intellectus et rei' or, as a modern philosopher expresses it in the language of today, 'Truth is the significance of fact.' I never forgot this. It was very helpful and has been a guiding light. To find out what architecture really is took me 50 years.

[...] Mies' other internationally known work of this period is the Tugendhat House, which was built in 1930 in Brno, Czechoslovakia. It was built as a private house but has not been used as such since the beginning of World War II. At first, says Mies, *it was*

a Nazi high command headquarters, then the Russians stabled horses on the lower floor. Now I understand the Communists use it as a dancing school.

The vicissitudes of the Tugendhat House are typical of the hard times which befell architecture and Mies and all free expression in the years that followed its construction.

In 1930 Walter Gropius and the mayor of Dessau asked Mies to take over as director of the Bauhaus. What happened is best told in his own words.

You see, *said Mies*, the Bauhaus was state-supported. And our students were driving the Nazis wild. So I went to the students and I said, 'Look, I don't care what you think. You can think what you like. You can be a Communist or a Catholic or something else you want. But here you work.'

But then the state under the Nazis decided to give no more money. So I moved the school to Berlin, as a private school. We found a factory there, painted it white, you know, and for a time we were very happy. But then the Gestapo closed us up, locked us outside on the street. We couldn't do anything.

So I went to the Gestapo. I would wait hours there, day after day, because I wanted to see the head of the Gestapo, that was not yet Himmler, that was then a young man from Cologne. When I saw him at last, he told me he was interested in the work we were doing. That was really so. He was a Nazi but they were not all alike. So he said he would like to help us to continue but there were some problems.

He told me, 'You can't have Kandinsky unless you will be personally ... *[the continuation is missing in this article; see text 62, 'The End of the Bauhaus']* Rosenberg, who was the great 'philosopher' of the Nazi Party. I had to see him at 11 o'clock at night because he was so busy. People said, 'Listen, you better not go there. You will never come out.' But I went, and Lily Reich, who was working with us then, sat in a restaurant across the street to see when I would come out again, or if ... Rosenberg told me he was a doctor in architecture from the university in Riga. But even so, he couldn't understand me. He was completely irrational. He asked me why I didn't change the name when I took over. He said it would have looked better. I said, 'Why should I change the name from Bauhaus? That is what it is.' He said he knew you could cantilever a roof but why would you want to do it. He said that to see no base underneath hurt his feeling. I said that the other way hurt my reason.

I said, 'Look at the desk where you are sitting. It is so terrible I would open that window behind you and throw it out.'

'Why?' he asked, and he was astonished. 'What is wrong with the desk?'

I said, 'What is wrong is that you don't know.'

Somehow, in spite of all this, the Gestapo chief did give me a paper with the conditions under which I could keep the Bauhaus open. I went home and called a faculty meeting and said, 'Now you see why I have been going so much to the Gestapo. Here is the little piece of paper that means we can keep the school open, and here are the conditions. Personally, my recommendation is to close the school.' And that is what we did.

In 1935 Mies began receiving feelers from the Armour Institute (later IIT) in Chicago, but at the time relocation there seemed a remote and outlandish possibility. However, in 1938 Mies had a phone call from Mrs Stanley Resor, whose husband was then president of the J Walter Thompson advertising agency. She was in Paris and asked Mies to come there.

She told me she wanted to build a house in Jackson Hole, Wyoming, and asked me if I would go back with her.

Just before this, Hitler had opened the Haus der Kunst in Munich, and in a speech he said exactly what he wanted. I knew there was no use staying any more in Germany. Now, with Mrs. Stanley Resor's offer, I could go.

I had six hours in New York, six hours in Chicago, and the next thing, I was in Jackson Hole.

Mies' plan for the Resor house (never built), set as a bridge across a mountain stream in spectacular surroundings, was his first work in or for the United States. When he left Jackson Hole, he stopped in Chicago to visit Henry Heald, then president of the Armour Institute.

And once again he said, 'Look, the architectural school is here. Why don't you take it over?'

I said I would have to have a free hand with the curriculum, I would want to bring maybe two other people, and I would want $10,000. Heald said to me, 'We only have $8000, but you can have an absolutely free hand.' So I said that was a fine bargain.

As it happened, it was a fine bargain for America as well. Today Mies van der Rohe's buildings refresh city architecture throughout the United States and inspire a clean and reasoned approach in his disciples and his imitators alike. In Mies' own buildings there is economy when it is necessary, but there is nothing shoddy.

[...] A recent commission is the new Headquarters Administration Building for Friedrich Krupp, near Essen. This is Mies' [only] European work in almost 30 years. It will be a huge structure of three storeys, built of white steel and gray glass, situated on a hilltop with industrial Essen visible on one side and a plot of pastoral Deutschland spread on the other.

Those who live and work in Mies' buildings respond variously to the experience. They may hate it or love it, but the reaction is rarely tepid.

He has been called a fascist for imposing environment on the occupants of his buildings. Hilberseimer denies this. 'He imposes nothing,' he says. 'If you live in a Frank Lloyd Wright house, you do not dare to add a single picture to a room because it is all Wright. With Mies, you are given space. After that it is entirely up to you.'

A resident of a 23rd-floor apartment in one of the Lake Shore Drive buildings recently noted that Mies had given him 'sky and horizon, a whole feeling of space'. Agoraphobes find that feeling terribly uncomfortable. But as one teacher of design tells her students, 'To live in a Mies van der Rohe building, you must be ready to meet the twentieth century. You must be ready to face space.'

103 [Eulogy for Rudolf Schwarz]

Published eulogy (14 April 1963; Schwarz died on 3 April 1961).
Source: R. Schwarz, *Gedächtnisausstellung des BDA Köln* (Heidelberg: Akademie der Künste Berlin, 1963), p. 5.
Translated from German by Mark Jarzombek.
Republished in Neumeyer (1986) 1991, p. 333; Pizzigoni 2010, p. 252; Walter 2022, p. 278.

Rudolf Schwarz was a great building master in the full sense of the word. His entire life – not only his activities but his incomparably profound thinking – was a constant effort to achieve clarity, meaning, and order. Rudolf Schwarz was a thinking building master, and building art was for him a form-giving, meaning-imparting ordering.

Whatever challenges in life confronted him, whether giving meaningful organisation to a training school or an academy or the planning of new villages or entire landscapes or the exquisite plan for rebuilding of Cologne and particularly its many beautiful churches, his thinking penetrated the task and set about its ordering work.

Basic to his accomplishments were his thoughts – carefully unfolded – in his wonderful writings.

Thought and work prove the unique greatness of a dead friend.

104 Acceptance Speech at the Presentation of the Gold Medal in Architecture

Published speech (22 May 1963).
Source: LMvdR, 'Acceptance Speech at the Presentation of the Gold Medal in Architecture at the Annual Ceremonial of the National Institute of Arts and Letters in New York City', *Proceedings of the American Academy of Arts and Letters*, vol. XIV, no. 14, 1964, pp. 331–332; LoC, Mies, Box 61, National Institute.
Republished in Pizzigoni 2010, pp. 254–255; Walter 2022, pp. 307–308.

Thank you, Gropius, for your act of friendship. Mr President, members of the Institute, it is with deep gratitude that I accept the Gold Medal for Architecture from the National Institute of Arts and Letters. I sincerely regret that I cannot be there in person.

Since you are bestowing this award for my lifelong work, I would like to say a few words on this occasion about the ideas which have impelled me to do what I have done.

The beginning of my working life, around 1910, at the end of the Jugendstil and the movement of Art Nouveau, was a time of great architectural confusion. Nobody could or would answer the question, 'What is architecture? What is the art of building?' I had to ask this question of myself.

All around me, profound changes were taking place in technology. New materials and means and processes were emerging, but they were not thought to have any relation to the arts. I came to believe it should be possible to make architecture with these new means and materials. I wanted to prove that they could be endowed with the same values for architecture as the old means and materials. I felt that a harmony could be found and established between the new forces in our civilisation and the ancient art of building. Each building I built was intended as a demonstration of these thoughts, a step forward in the process of my own search for clarification. A conviction was growing in me that the means being developed by science and technology were the unique means for the art of architecture in my time. This conviction has never been shaken.

Today, as always, I believe that architecture has little or nothing to do with the invention of interesting forms or with personal whims. I believe architecture belongs to the epoch, not to the individual; that at its best it touches and expresses the very innermost structure of the civilisation from which it springs.

105 [Acceptance Speech for the Munich Cultural Award]

Acceptance speech (June 1963).
Source: LoC, Mies, Box 62, Writings Mies General, 'Dankadresse anlässlich der Verleihung des kulturellen Ehrenpreises der Stadt München [Address of Thanks on the Occasion of the Awarding of the Cultural Honorary Prize of the City of Munich]'.
Translated from German by John Nicolson.
Republished in Blaser 1977, pp. 5–6; Neumeyer 1991, p. 335; Pizzigoni 2010, pp. 256–257; Walter 2022, pp. 276–277.

Highly esteemed Mr Mayor, esteemed members of the city council, esteemed guests,

To receive the Cultural Honorary Prize of the city of Munich is indeed an especially high distinction for me, and I accept it with profound gratitude. I am sincerely sorry that I am unable to be present today in your venerable and epoch-rich city to accept this distinction in person and thank you for it.

Since I probably rightly assume that this honour is due to me for my efforts over many years to create a contemporary art of building, I would like to use this opportunity to briefly set out the ideas and thoughts which have guided me in my work.

My conscious professional career began around 1910. The Jugendstil and Art Nouveau had come and gone. Representative buildings were more or less under the influence of Palladio or Schinkel. The great achievements of that period, however, were to be found among industrial buildings and purely technological structures. It was in fact a confused time, and nobody could or would answer the question as to the nature of the art of building. Perhaps the time was not yet ripe for an answer. At any rate, I posed this question and was determined to find an answer to it.

It was only after the war, in the twenties, that it became increasingly evident how much technical developments had begun to influence many aspects of our lives. We began to realise that technology was a civilising force that could not be ignored.

In the field of building the evolving technology furnished new materials and more practical work methods that very often stood in stark contrast to our traditional concepts of building art.
Nevertheless, I believed in the possibility of developing a building art with the help of these new means.
I felt that it should be possible to bring the old and the new forces of our civilisation into harmony with each other. Each of my buildings was a demonstration of these thoughts and a further step in my own search for clarity.
I became increasingly convinced that these new scientific and technical developments constituted the preconditions in fact for a building art of our time.
I have never lost this conviction.
Now, as for a long time, I believe that the art of building has nothing or little to do with the invention of interesting forms or personal inclinations.
True building art is always objective and expresses the inner structure of the epoch out of which it arises.

106 Building Details

Published journal statement (October 1963).
Source: LMvdR, 'untitled', *Architectural Record*, vol. LXXII, no. 10, 1963, p. 149; LoC, Mies, Box 62, Writings Mies General (the typescript has the title 'Building Details').
Republished in Pizzigoni 2010, p. 253; Walter 2022, p. 298.

Construction is the truest guardian of the spirit of the times because it is objective and is not affected by personal individualism or fantasy. The idea of a clear construction is one of the fundamentals we should accept. We can talk about that easily, but to do it is not easy; it is difficult to stick to this fundamental construction and then to elevate it to a structure.
Architecture begins when two bricks are put carefully together. Architecture is a language having the discipline of a grammar. Language can be used for normal day-to-day purposes as prose. And if you are very good at that, you may speak a wonderful prose. And if you are really good, you can be a poet. But it is the same language, and its characteristic is that it has all these possibilities.
The physicist *[Erwin Rudolf Josef Alexander]* Schrödinger said of general principles, 'the creative vigour of a general principle depends precisely on its generality,' and that is exactly what I mean when I talk about structure in architecture. It is not a special solution. It is a general idea. And although each building is a single solution, it is not motivated as such.

107 [Conversation Regarding the Future of Architecture, Part II]

Published interview (1964).
Source: John Peter, 'Conversation with Mies', in J. Peter, *The Oral History of Modern Architecture: Interviews with the Greatest Architects of the Twentieth Century* (New York, 1994), pp. 154–173.
Mies was interviewed at his apartment in Chicago. Published together with 'Conversation Regarding the Future of Architecture. Part I' (see pp. 139–142). Republished in Punete (2006) 2008, pp. 49–87; Pizzigoni 2010, pp. 262–272; *Casabella*, no. 800, 2011, pp. 120–123; Walter 2022, pp. 364–388.

What first interested you in architecture?
I learned from my father. You know, he was a stonemason. He liked to do good work. I remember in my hometown in Aachen was the cathedral. This octagon was built by Charlemagne. In different centuries they did something different with it. Sometime in the Baroque *[age]* they plastered the whole thing and made ornaments in it. When I was young, they took the plaster off. Then they hadn't the money to go further, so you saw the real stones. When I looked at the old building that had nothing on it, just fine brickwork or stonework, a building that was really clear and with really good craftsmanship, I would have given all the other things for one of these buildings. Later they covered it with marble again, but I must say it was much more impressive without the marble.

Tell me, were you influenced in your thinking by things other than architecture – music or painting?
Yes, it may have been later. But not when I was young, you know. I didn't have any relation to other arts particularly.

Did reading have anything to do with your thinking?
Yes, quite a lot. You know, I left school when I was 14 years old. So I had no education. I worked for an architect. When I came to his office, he said, 'Here is your table.' I cleaned it up and looked in the drawer ...

What I found there were two things: a magazine called 'Die Zukunft *[The Future]*'. It was a weekly magazine. It was a very interesting magazine. It was partly a political magazine, but in the way that *[Walter]* Lippmann would talk about politics, not a party affair. It was a cultural magazine, let us say that. It talked about music. It talked about poetry. It talked about architecture, but very seldom. That was one thing.

Then I found another pamphlet about the *[Pierre-Simon]* Laplace theory. That was these two things, you know. From then on I started to read this magazine, *Die Zukunft*. I bought it every Sunday morning and read it. Then I started to read.

A few years later, when I came to Berlin, I had to build a house for a philosopher *[Riehl House, Potsdam, 1907]*. It was at the university in Berlin. There I met quite a number of people, and I started to read more and more. When this philosopher came to my office the first time – I had an office in my apartment; my books were lying on a huge draughting board, about a foot high – he looked around, and he saw all these books. He said, 'For Heaven's sake, who advised you on your library?' I said, 'Nobody. I started to buy books and read them.' He was very surprised, you know. He saw no discipline in it or anything like that.

At that time, we were working for *[Peter]* Behrens. There were other architects in Berlin. *[Alfred]* Messel, he was a very fine architect but a Palladio man or something like that.

I was interested in what is architecture. I asked somebody, 'What is architecture?' But he didn't answer me. He said, 'Just forget it. Just work. You will find that out by yourself later.' I said, 'That's a fine answer to my question.' But I wanted to know more. I wanted to find out. That was the reason I read, you know. For nothing else. I wanted to find out things; I wanted to be clear. What is going on? What is our time, and what is it all about? Otherwise, I didn't think we would be able to do something reasonable. In this way I read a lot. I bought all these books and paid for them. I read them in all the fields.

Do you still read?
Yes, I do. And I read very often the old books. The New York Chapter of Architecture once had some affair going on. I said, 'When I left Germany I had about 3000 books. I made a list, and they shipped me 300.' I said, 'I could send back 270. Thirty is all I wanted to have.'

I was interested in the philosophy of values and problems of the spirit. I was also very much interested in astronomy and natural sciences ... I asked myself the question, 'What is the truth? What is the truth?' until I stopped at Thomas Aquinas, you know. I found the answer for that.

So, for other things, what is order? Everybody talks about it, but nobody could tell you what it is. Until I read Augustine about sociology. There was a mess as great as in architecture then. You could read a lot of sociological books, and you were not wiser than before.

Do you feel that the thinking of people who sought truth in other periods is applicable today?
Oh certainly, I am sure. There are certain truths. They don't wear out. I am quite sure of that. I cannot talk for other people. I just followed what I needed. I want this clarity. I could have read other books, you know, a lot of poetry or others. But I didn't. I read these books where I could find the truth about certain things.

Did your father or mother influence you in thinking this way?
Not at all. No. My father said, 'Don't read these dumb books. Work.' He was a craftsman, you know.

[Break]
If I were subjective, I would be a painter, you know, not an architect. There I could express anything I like, but in buildings I have to do what has to be done. Not that I like it particularly. Just what's best to be done. I have often thrown out ideas I was in love with, but when I thought it through, I just had to throw them out. That is the difference. It is not so much the function. You cannot be really subjective; it looks funny in buildings. You have to be good, a stonemason or a timber man. There is nothing funny about that.

In painting you can express the slightest emotion, but with a beam of wood or a piece of stone you cannot do much about it. If you try to do much about it, then you lose the character of your material. I think architecture is an objective art.

What was the Bauhaus? Why did you associate your own name and talents with it?
I think *[Walter]* Gropius could answer this question best because he was the founder, and to me that is the Bauhaus. He left the Bauhaus and gave it into the hands of Hannes Meyer. At this time it became more a political instrument or was used not so much by Hannes Meyer but by younger people. Hannes Meyer, in my opinion, was not a strong man. He was taken in by these young people. I can understand that, too. But there was a certain difference. You could say that was the second phase of the Bauhaus, quite different from Gropius' phase. The Bauhaus from '19 to '32 was no way one affair. It was quite different.

I came to the Bauhaus when the Bauhaus had trouble for political reasons. The city, which was Democratic or Social Democratic, had to pay for it. They said, 'We will not do that anymore.' Gropius and the mayor of Dessau came to me. They explained that to me and asked me to take it over. They thought if I did not do it, it would be closed. I went there and made it clear to the students, as clear as I could: 'You have to work here, and I can assure you: who doesn't work I will throw out. I have nothing against any political idea that is here.' I spent my time teaching them something, and they had to work on it. But I was not so involved as Gropius was. That was his idea. We were working in the same direction.

At Gropius' 70th birthday I talked about the Bauhaus *[see pp. 136-137]*. I said that I didn't believe that it was the propaganda which made it known all over the world, but that it was a new idea. Propaganda would never be so strong as to do this work. But I think Gropius can tell you more about it than I can.

Would there have been a Bauhaus if there had been no Gropius?

No, I think there would not have been a Bauhaus. There would have been another school. The school was there when it was in Weimar. If I'm not mistaken, I think that Gropius was proposed by [Henry] Van de Velde, who was the head of the school in Weimar. When he left Weimar, he proposed Gropius as his successor.

Getting the different people was Gropius' doing. There is no doubt about that. He brought these people. He must have seen that these people were driving in a different direction, too. But that they were good people, that was Gropius' doing.

How important to the Bauhaus was the climate of the [Deutsche] Werkbund?

That may have had an influence. Gropius was one of the leading people in the Werkbund, particularly so, say, after 1910. There was this Werkbund exhibition in Cologne where he built one of the important buildings *[office and factory buildings at the Werkbund Exhibition, Cologne, 1914]*. I think his building and Van de Velde's theatre were the real buildings there. He certainly was very active in the Werkbund. There were other people – not often architects, but craftsmen. They tried to use good materials. They had a sense of quality ... I had nothing to do with the Werkbund then. I came much later. It was in '26 when I came to the Werkbund, when they gave me this job to do, the Weissenhof exhibition.

Has working in America changed what you think or what you do?

I think you are always influenced by your environment. There's no doubt. I think that teaching helped me a lot. I was forced to be clear to the students. You know, students are funny people. They perforate you with questions. You look like a sieve. You have to make it really clear, and you cannot fool them. They want to know, and you have to be clear. That forces me to think these things clear through so that I can answer them. I think teaching had this influence. It was in the direction I was going anyway.

So that was not a waste of time as far as you were concerned?

Oh, no, no, the opposite, I think it was really good. I don't think you have to build 1000 houses or 1000 buildings. That's all nonsense. I can make a statement about architecture with a few buildings. If I would do nothing else, that would make absolutely clear what I mean.

I remember the greatest impression I had the first time in New York – that an elevator could take you up in no time, fifty storeys high, and really hit it on the head. I was very much impressed by that.

You once mentioned the Pennsylvania barn.

Yes, the good Pennsylvania barn, I really like better than most buildings. It's a real building and the best building for that reason that I know in America.

The Washington Bridge, I think, is a fine example of modern building. It's direct to the point, you know. Maybe they had ideas about these towers, but I'm talking about a principle and not about that. But to go in this simple straight line from one bank of the Hudson to the other, this direct solution, that is what I am driving at.

There's something else. We use in German the word 'Baukunst', which is two words, 'building' and 'art.' The art is the refinement of the building. That is what we express with 'Baukunst'. When I was young, we hated the word 'architecture'. We talked about 'Baukunst' because architecture is *[when]* you form something from the outside.

Would you say that a characteristic of 'Baukunst' has always been a certain reasonableness?

Yes, at least that is what I like in 'Baukunst'. Even though we had to make a lot of Baroque things when I was young, I was never much interested in Baroque architecture. I was interested in structural architecture, I was interested in Romanesque, I was interested in Gothic architecture. They are often misunderstood. You know, the profiles of a pillar in a cathedral, that is still a very clear structure. The refinements were to make it clearer, not to decorate it, but to make it clearer. People think, when they see one of these buildings, they say it is too cold. But they forget what they are asking for because they think that is too strong an order. They have it on Michigan Avenue, on the lakefront, everywhere. That is what they really ask for. They are not clear about it. They ask for chaos. But there can be a richness. It has not to be a chaos. I think you can use clear elements and make it rich. Any medieval city used the same plan all over. What was the difference was the doorknob or the bay window, and that depended on the money they had. But the plan was *[more or less]* all the same. They had the stable culture.

[Break]

What about technical developments?

People are surprised that I used construction in different materials, but that to me is absolutely normal. In the one case the roof plate is a real plate and has to be supported. It doesn't matter if you build it in steel or in concrete. Nearly all the cathedrals have the same structural principle. What is wrong with that? You can change. You need not copy it really, but you can use it as a structural principle.

That was, in fact, our idea when we started to work. We wanted to develop new structural solutions which could be used by anybody. We were not after individual solutions. We were after good structural solutions. We are not hurt if somebody uses them. We are hurt if somebody doesn't use them well. There are certainly many more unknown students of mine than direct students. But certainly, I am not hurt at all. On the opposite, that is what we tried to achieve, and we did it. There is no doubt about that.

And your sketches for the glass skyscraper?

That was another problem. There I was interested in glass and what can be done with glass buildings. I tried to avoid a certain glare or a dead front. So first, I bent these large pieces so that they had the character of a crystal. Under no circumstances was it a dead solution. Then later, I thought that maybe it would be much richer if I made it fully curved. But these were just studies in glass. I was thinking about a building all right, but that was a particular study in glass.

As for the buildings you now build, are they more characteristic of steel or of glass?

Some people say the Seagram Building is a bronze building. They don't talk about a glass building because there is so much metal there. I think that they are glass buildings, but that is when one works the problem through.

When you use concrete, you waive the plasticity of concrete?

The plasticity of concrete, that is very funny. The plasticity of concrete is not necessarily the best way to use concrete. I think I use concrete, if I use it, in a structural manner. What I call a structure. I know you can use it in another way, but I don't like the other way. I still like it for building a clear structure. I don't care about the plastic solutions, I just don't.

Even in your chairs?

See, that is the same. The chair is an arc chair with this half circle in front of it *[MR10, 1927]*. That is a skeleton structure, you know. Even the Barcelona chair is still a skeleton structure. I made some designs in plastic chairs. I didn't follow them up. There I used the mass, you know. If you want to use a plastic material, then you have to use the mass. But because you can form the concrete, it is not necessary to form it in a plastic manner. It's just because that is a possibility, you can do it. You see, when we used aluminium, there you can use extruded materials. When we used it for the first time, we tried it for our mullions. Then we hung it on the roof of 860 to see how it reads *[860–880 Lake Shore Drive Building, Chicago, 1951]*. I tell you that the simple I-beam worked much better. That is why we used, even in aluminium, the I-beam structure. It reads better. It is much clearer.

You say 'clear'. Do you think there's a relationship between clarity and goodness?

Yes, to me, certainly. Yes, I'm quite sure about that.

If you had lived in another period, might you have used …

Oh, certainly, if we didn't have other materials, but we have steel. I think that this is a fine material. By 'fine', I mean it is very strong. It is very elegant. You can do a lot with it. The whole character of the building is very light. That is why I like it when I have to build a building in a steel construction. What I like best is when I can use stone on the ground and then come up a little.

Do you like steel because of the factor of economy?

It is an economy factor, but it is not an architectural factor. It is a factor here in our country. When you have to build something, you take a sheet of paper and write down what the site costs, the architect's fee, the engineering fee, and God knows what we get back. If that is not 12 percent or 15 percent, it will never be built. That is the economical question you were talking about. Even the greatest idea will not be built if it is not economical in this sense ... I am not talking about this economy. I am talking about a spiritual economy, the economy of means. The clearest sentence is, to me, economy. It is the economy that has an influence on architecture.

You can build in concrete. There are the *[Robert]* Maillart bridges in Switzerland that are wonderful bridges, very clear. I have nothing against that. But if you build in steel, it gives you a lot of freedom inside. People say, 'Ah, that is cold.' That's nonsense, you know. Inside you can really do what you like. You are free to do something. But you are not free outside.

You have to remember: in an enclosed building you have a few floor-plan possibilities. When you really work in one of our buildings, you will come to the conclusion there are only a few good solutions. They are limited, even though you could do anything you like.

However, if the use of the building changed, say the museum building became for some reason a century from now ...

Yes, it could be something else. I would not hesitate to make a cathedral in the inside of my convention hall *[Convention Hall, Chicago, 1954]*. I see no reason why not. You can do that. So a type, like the convention hall or like the museum, can be used for other purposes just as well ... This is not anymore that the form follows function or should follow function. I am, anyway, a little dubious about these statements, you know. There was a reason when somebody *[Louis Sullivan]* said it. But you cannot make a law out of them ... You could very well make an apartment building form an office building. They are similar in the fact that you have 20 or 30 floors one on top of the other. That is the character of the building, not to talk about what is inside. In an apartment building you may use, for economical reasons, smaller spans or something, reduce the size, but you could very well live in an office building with the large span and have a fine apartment in that.

The sociologists tell us we have to think about the human beings who are living in that building. That is a sociological problem, not an architectural one. That always comes up, you know. But that is a sociological question. I think the sociologists should fight that out. That is not an architectural question.

And it can't be solved architecturally?

No. It could be solved if they would give us a programme. But first, they have to prove that their idea is a sound one in the sociological field. They would like to make us responsible for that, you know! No, not with me!

When I look at these projects, I am struck by the fact that there is a sense of continuity in your work. Is there a relationship?

It is always the same problem. It is only that in one case you have just, say, walls to work with and, in this group of buildings, you have buildings to work with. But it is the same problem. You find a good relation among them, you know. It's always the same. It is a very simple problem. We had in our school a space problem which every student had to go through and work on, and that is the same for a small apartment as it is for a hotel or a bank lobby. There is no difference in these. It is the same problem.

Is it the same for a city plan, almost?

I would say yes. You know, in city planning you have the traffic problems, but in itself it is the same problem. It is a very simple problem of the good relation of one to another. In some we had first a free plan and then we were bound by streets, so it became a geometric plan, not a free plan *[plan for AIT campus, 1940 and plan for IIT campus, 1947]*. But you can make a free composition or a geometrical composition just as well. In principle there is no difference in it.

But the fact that streets are a gridiron, does this tend to suggest a …?

Certainly, to me it suggests a geometrical solution. Not that I am for it out of principle, but that is what I have to work with. That is a material to me, you know. I can make a building or a group of buildings. I can make it symmetrical, or I can make it asymmetrical – that is just what the problem is about. Some people think it has to be asymmetrical. That is not the case, you know. Maybe they are tired of a lot of things, and they just try something else.

I remember when I made the symmetrical solution somewhere, and I was told, 'Now we have to learn again that there can be symmetry.' But the symmetry was the reasonable solution, not that I particularly liked it or did not like it. That was the reasonable solution for this purpose. I would not hesitate to do that, you know. I think that is more an aesthetic speculation. I don't care much about these things.

In regard to your buildings, the Krupp office building, for instance … [Friedrich Krupp Administration Building, Essen, 1963].

The Krupp is an enormous skeleton building. If you use a skeleton, you will come to a similar solution. You can do something that is not similar but the form is the same. The skeleton is just a skeleton.

The Duquesne is a laboratory *[Mellon Hall of Science, Duquesne University, Pittsburgh, 1962–1968]*. Since we did not know what would be inside, we thought we would give a possibility to let the pipes go wherever they wanted to go. We made the first lab building in Chicago – the Metals Building *[Mineral and Metals Research Building, IIT, Chicago, 1939]*. That was kind of a laboratory, but it was not a chemical laboratory. There we used glass on the outside.

Do the plans for Montreal, Toronto, and the Chicago Federal buildings have something in common [Westmount Square, Montreal, 1964–1967; Dominion Center, Toronto, 1964–1969; Federal Center, Chicago, 1964–1974]?

We put the buildings so that each one gets the best situation and that the space between them is about the best we can achieve. They all have that in common. Even if I would build a group of single houses, I would use the same principle there. Only that the space between them maybe would be smaller.

[Break]

You set the Seagram Building back at a time when nobody else set buildings back.

I set it back so that you could see it. That was the reason. You know, if you go to New York, you really have to look at these canopies to find where you are. You cannot even see the building. You only see the building from a distance. So I set it back for this reason.

Why was the material bronze?

We used bronze because of the client. Just in the talk we had, he said, 'I like bronze and marble.' I said, 'That's good enough for me!'

In designing your building the way you do, somehow the Seagram respects other buildings, like the McKim, Mead, and White building across the street [Racquet and Tennis Club, New York, 1916].

Oh, certainly, yes. The Lever House was there when we started. When we moved the building back, we didn't know what would happen on each side of it. After the Seagram Building was finished, there you had the Lever House and the Seagram Building, so it was quite easy to set back the next building that is right between them *[399 Park Ave, New York, 1961]*. But they didn't! That was so funny. That was a great help for any architect, but that is just what happens, you know.

Compared to the Seagram Building, the two Bacardi buildings posed different problems [Bacardi Building, Santiago de Cuba, 1957; Bacardi Building, Mexico City, 1961].

Yes, it was certainly a different *[kind of]* site. The first building was in Cuba. The client wanted to have a large room. That is what he liked. He said, 'I like to have a desk in a large room. I like to work with my people. I don't need a closed office because I work more than anybody else, so it doesn't hurt me that they see me.' We tried to solve that.

But in Mexico there were two factors which changed the character of the building. One was that the highway is higher than the site. So if we built a one-storey building there, you would see only the roof. That was the reason why we made a two-storey building there. It was a more normal office building because the leading people insisted on separate offices.

How important are historical influences in your opinion?

I am not interested in the history of civilisation. I am interested in our civilisation. We are living in it. Because I really believe after a long time of working and thinking and studying that architecture has in fact only to do with this civilisation we are in. You know, that is really what architecture is about. It can only express this civilisation we are in and nothing else. There are certain forces that are in contrast to each other. But if you really look at it, you'll find leading forces, sustaining forces, and you'll find superficial forces. That is why it is so difficult to give a definition of civilisation and to give a definition of our time. In older civilisations the superficial forces are gone. Only the deciding forces become historical forces, the exceptional forces.

Often you cannot make a definition of something. But then you see something that strikes you in the bones. You know that is it. You cannot express it, but that is it. It's like when you meet somebody who is healthy. What could you say, but you know when somebody is healthy or not. That is what I find so important, particularly in the time we are now when this Baroque movement is going on. You call it 'Baroque' or whatever. But I think it is a form of Baroque movement against the reasonable, the direct. In particular, in a time where there is confusion what should be leading if not reason? That is why we were trying so hard from the twenties, the early twenties, to find what is a reasonable way to do things. There were people who had a lot of fantasy and sculptural interest in the Jugendstil and the Art Nouveau period. They all were, more or less, fantastic. But very few were reasonable then. I decided when I was quite young to accept this reasonableness.

108 [Architecture Is Not a Martini Cocktail]

Excerpts and paraphrasing of interviews (1964).
Source: Peter Carter, 'Mies', *20th Century*, vol. 172, no. 1021, spring 1964, pp. 138–143.
In his texts Peter Carter often uses quotations from Mies taken from different sources. See also P Carter, 'Mies van der Rohe. An Appreciation on the Occasion this Month of his 75th Birthday', *Architectural Design*, vol. XXXI, no. 3, 1961, pp. 95–121; P. Carter, 'Mies van der Rohe', *Bauen und Wohnen*, vol. XVI, no. 7, 1961, pp. 229–245.
Republished in Casabella, no. 741, 2006, p. 3; Pizzigoni 2010, pp. 273–276.; Walter 2022, pp. 299–306.

Mies van der Rohe would agree that his architecture is both conservative and radical. Conservative – in that it is based upon the principles of order, space, and proportion common to all the great architectural epochs. Radical – in that it uses the scientific, technological and sociological forces of our time as prime determinants. I have tried, *he has said*, to make an architecture for a technological society. I have wanted to keep everything very reasonable and clear; to have an architecture that anybody can do.

To clarify his attitude, he has often used the analogy of language. A living language is disciplined by grammar, and architecture, Mies believes, should likewise be disciplined – in his opinion, by structure. Language can be used for normal day to day purposes as prose, *he has said*. If you are very good at that, you may speak a wonderful prose. And if you are really good, you can be a poet. But it is the same language, and its characteristic is that it has all these possibilities.

During his 25 years in Chicago Mies has developed the structurally oriented architecture upon which he was working in Europe during the 1920s and 1930s. I have always wanted to express a building as it really is; I don't want to hide its structure, *he says. Because of this structural concept of architecture, Mies' work shows that it is possible to realise a range of building types extending from a 50-foot-by-50-foot house to a 720-foot-by-720-foot convention hall from the same fundamental ideas. Today, when numerous functions have to be accommodated within the architectural canon, the values of a general approach based on universally tenable ideas are becoming more and more apparent …*

Whenever I talk with students or young architects, I make a point of encouraging questions of a general nature because I think that an architectural development depends upon how seriously such questions are stated and how clearly they are answered. I feel that these questions should probe deeper and deeper and be directed more and more towards the essence of things. We must get at the kernel of the truth. Questions concerning the essence of things are the only significant questions; and the answers each generation finds to these questions will be its contribution to architectural development.

Mies, you have often spoken of the close relationship between architecture and the ethos of a civilisation or culture. Before asking you to take up this point, would you first define 'civilisation' and 'culture'?

My definition of civilisation is an order in the material realm; and culture is the order in the spiritual realm – or rather the harmonious expression of order in the spiritual realm … We speak of Roman 'civilisation' and Greek 'culture'; and this is how I see it. Anthropologists look differently at these things: for them 'what is' is civilisation. I do not agree with this. I think that you can only talk about civilisation when you have order in the material world.

To achieve this order, there has to be a unity of action, and there cannot be a unity of action without a unity of creative thought. In this respect I am convinced of the need for clarity in both thought and action. Without clarity, there can be no understanding. And without understanding, there can be no direction – only confusion, which is where we find ourselves today. Today there is no order, not even in the material sphere; the chaos we have in the architectural field shows this quite clearly.

What would you say are the factors which have determined our particular epoch?

You know, the structure of a civilisation is not easy to define because it is in part the past, in part the present, and in part the future. The past, by its very nature, we cannot change. The present we have to accept and should master. But the future is open – open for creative thought and action, and I believe that the real acceptance of the present will be the basis for the future. A civilisation is not made by one man – it is the work of many, but not of all of them. Around 1900 nobody could be sure what the character of our epoch would be. An epoch has to be developed to a degree before its particular identity is made clear – you cannot just guess at it.

In my opinion only a relationship which touches the essence of the time can be real. This relation I like to call a 'truth relation'. Truth in the sense of Thomas Aquinas, as the 'adequatio rei et intellectus.' Or, as a modern philosopher expresses it in the language of today, 'Truth is the significance of facts.' Only such a relation is able to embrace the complex nature of civilisation. Only so will architecture be involved in the evolution of civilisation. And only so will it express the slow unfolding of its form.

Mies, you once said that we are 'not at the end but at the beginning of an epoch.'

Yes, I am absolutely convinced that we are at the beginning. It would be a very short epoch indeed if that were not the case. Most of the important developments were initiated in the 1920s and 1930s – and not only in architecture. One of the characteristics of our epoch is its striving for universality. The forces of science, technology, industrialisation, and economy are other characteristics. Everything that does not take these realities into account will be unimportant.

How can these characteristics be assimilated into and expressed by our architecture?

Thomas Aquinas said that 'reason is the first principle of all human work.' When you have grasped that once, you act accordingly. So, I would throw everything out that is not reasonable.

I think that 'construction' is the truest guardian of the times because it is objective and is not affected by personal individualism or fantasy. If we use the word 'Baukunst', we get a more exact meaning across of our idea of architecture: the 'Bau' is the clear building construction, and the 'Kunst' is the refinement of that and not anything else.

I had the idea of developing a structural architecture because I thought that it would at least be reasonable. I do not think it has excluded anything that is fine and valuable – 'that' is just refinement of the structure.

I must make it clear that by 'structure' I have a philosophical idea. The structure is the whole, from top to bottom, to the last detail with the same ideas.

The physicist Schrödinger said of general principles, 'The creative vigour of a general principle depends precisely on its generality,' and that is exactly what I mean when I talk about structure in architecture. It is not a special solution. It is a general idea. And although each building is a single solution, it is not motivated as such.

I decided to stick to a structural architecture because I felt that it would be the safe way. If you don't do this, you may go astray, and that would slow down architectural development – or even make it impossible.

How do you think architectural education can meet the specific needs of our epoch?

The function of education is to lead us from irresponsible opinion to truly responsible judgment. When I came to Chicago in 1938 to direct the School of Architecture at the Illinois Institute of Technology, I found that all architectural schools in America were following the Beaux Arts tradition, which I thought was absolutely ridiculous – at least if your purpose is education – because everything about that tradition is accidental. In the Beaux Arts schools first-year students were already designing; I did not think that was realistic because a student must first have the basics – something on which he can stand. This is not a new idea. The master builders of the medieval times progressed from the craftsman level; they knew just about everything about the job of building by the time they became masters. Every student can be a good draughtsman if he will work, and many can learn to be good constructors. But it is only one student, every year or two, whose discipline and experience entitle him to use his fantasy.

I believe that an architectural curriculum is a means of training and education; it is not a thing in itself: it depends upon and serves a philosophy. The absence of the philosophy is not a virtue, although some people think it is. It is a weakness not to have a philosophy. A curriculum without a philosophy is not broad and wide, not even neutral, but nebulous. Since a building is a work and not a notion, a method of work, a way of doing, should be the essence of architectural education. Two things should be covered by the curriculum. One is training – in order that the student be provided with the basic tools for his work. The other is a general education – in order that science and technology, and the other significant forces of our epoch, should be understood.

Architecture in its simplest form is concerned primarily with the useful. But it extends from the almost purely practical until in its highest forms it attains its fullest significance as pure art. This relationship should lead to a curriculum which makes clear, step by step, what is possible in construction, what is necessary for use, and what is significant as art.

As you know, it is my opinion that everything should be guided by reason – in order that one is kept on the right track. Some people do not think of reason in connection with architecture. They forget that a brick wall is a very reasonable affair. At our school we tried to develop a system of training in which everything leads to reason; I thought that if there were nothing in the course against reason, the student would attack everything with reason.

How have over 20 years of teaching affected your own architectural development?

I think that the most obvious effect teaching has had on my work is that I was forced to clarify my ideas in order to teach them to my students. If you do not have to teach, you may have some ideas and you may not care if they are right or wrong. But when students perforate you with questions, your ideas have to be strong enough to stand up to this; otherwise, they would laugh at you.

Mies, you have implied that form in architecture is a consequence of the structure and not the reason for the construction. Since modern technology makes it possible to construct almost anything, does this not give us the possibility of inventing new forms?

As I see it, there are two general tendencies today. One has a structural basis, and you may call it the more objective. The other has a plastic basis, which you could say is emotional. You cannot mix them. Architecture is not a Martini.

I really believe, more and more, that architecture is closely related to the driving and sustaining forces of an epoch and can, at its best, be nothing more than an expression of these forces. It is not a fashion, nor is it something for eternity; it is a part of an epoch. To understand an epoch means to understand its essence and not everything that you see. But what is important in an epoch is very difficult to find out because there is a very slow unfolding of the great form. The great form cannot be invented by you or me, but we are working on it without knowing it. And when this great form is fully understood, then the epoch is over – then there is something new.

But some people think that you should always be doing something new; they ask for more and more novelty – not essential things. The essential is what architecture is about, and we should not be afraid if that gets a little boring.

Architecture is an historical process. Since I understand that, I would not be for fashion in architecture. All individualism is a leftover from the time of Luther – when he said, 'Here I stand.' I would look for more profound principles. And since I know that we are under the influence of science and technology, I would ask myself what result comes from this fact.

Can we change it, or can we not change it? And the answer to this question gave me the direction which I followed. I find that I often throw things out that I like very much. They are dear to my heart. But when I have a stronger conviction, a clearer idea, I follow the clearer idea.

The great historical epochs restricted themselves to very clear principles, yet they were certainly able to do anything, and I think that that is the only way you can make important architecture.

109 Meet Mr Mies van der Rohe

Published newspaper interview (early 1964).
Source: Dorothea Kahn Jaffe, 'Meet Mr Mies van der Rohe', *The Christian Science Monitor,* LoC, Dearstyne, Box 11, Mies Printed Matter.
Republished in Pizzigoni 2010, pp. 258–261; Walter 2022, pp. 293–297.

A man who stands among the world's 'greats' for his influence upon modern architecture looked back over six decades of work and study and more work and remarked humbly:

Even since I was young, I have tried to understand architecture. I am still doing that today. Step by step, I come closer to understanding what architecture is about. Architecture must be closely related to the civilisation we are in, or it is nothing.

[…] *Seated at his desk, Mies smiles a friendly welcome and strives to give clear and honest answers to this reporter's question.*

I am not a literary man, *he explained as the interview began*, I am not good at words. When I speak it is as if I am translating …

This was an overly modest estimate of the architect's power of verbal communication. He speaks deliberately, with a vestige of his native German in his sentences, but his expression has the clarity and coherence of his buildings.

The driving force of our times is economics. The sustaining forces are science and technology. These are essential to our civilisation and should be expressed.

Mies began his career in a far different kind of society, he recalled. As a lad in Aachen, Germany, an ancient Carolingian city, he lived among historical monuments. All around him were eighth-century buildings of Charlemagne's time, still in use, and those of succeeding architectural periods.

So many styles – I had to count them on my button-holes. Some were not good. I felt the healthiest buildings were those of old farmsteads, house and barn combined, built centuries ago and still good. They had no style – nothing but good construction – but they had a character of their own, which didn't change over the centuries.

[...] *The Mies philosophy of architecture is that a building should be* a clear and true statement of its times. *Every great architecture of the past expressed its period, he says. Today's building should do the same. Mies thinks the George Washington Bridge in New York City is an outstanding example of a structure expressing its period. He says he goes to see it every time he comes to New York.*

It is the most modern building in the city.

He admires it because it is beautifully proportioned and does not hide its structure. Mies likes to see the steel, the brick, the concrete of buildings show themselves as they are. He shuns decoration, convinced that a building should achieve beauty through the character, proportion, and arrangement of its structural elements. With his gift for pithy expression, Mies calls his work 'skin-and-bones architecture'. The bones are the structure; the skin, the covering of glass, aluminium, bronze, or whatever else may be used to shut out the elements.

To many people, accustomed to the architecture of past epochs, this architect's buildings seem too angular, too severe. They prefer the traditional styles with adornment. Mies is aware of this, but he is convinced that most people will come to like the modern structures as they get used to them. Americans especially, not so bound to their historical heritage as Europeans are, will accept good, reasonable, modern design. If they are educated rightly, many will accept the present, he said.

He sees today's architecture as fitted to their needs.

Change is a characteristic of our time, *he continued.* People move from one place to another, change their occupations, get new hobbies. They should be free to do what they like with their homes. So I make the plan open enough for them to do what they want, to change the arrangement of space.

The walls in his buildings – houses, schools, skyscrapers – are not load-bearing, and partitions can be moved to suit changed needs.

Mies is essentially a city man, and he hopes and expects to see cities become better.

Largeness should not disturb us, *he said, speaking of population growth.* The great buildings of the past are found in cities – the Acropolis, the cathedrals. To*day urban renewal, he thinks, offers great hope.*

I would say it is a pity our renewal projects are not better than they are, but they are making our cities much better than they were before.

Most of Ludwig Mies van der Rohe's important works have been buildings in the central city. Downtown New York bears his imprint in the 38-storey Seagram Building, done with Philip Johnson, and now threatened with additional taxes because it is 'monumental,' and monumental buildings come higher on the tax rolls. [...]

Mies has a reputation for economy in building. His most noted skyscrapers cost less per cubic foot than average buildings of their kind. But he doesn't put value on economy for its own sake. If money is saved on construction, he said, it can be spent for better materials than could otherwise be used. *For Mies is not a cold utilitarian. He uses onyx, glass, marble, steel, chrome, and bronze in his structures with an artist's feeling and achieves beautiful proportions with an artist's touch. In saying that today's buildings must express the technical and scientific nature of today's civilisation he is not banning beauty. Each epoch, he believes, has its own way of expressing the fundamentals of order, proportion, and imagination. And the present is no exception.*

110 [Mies Speaks in Berlin]

Typescript of a radio interview (given in October 1964).
Source: LoC, Mies, box 62, 'Mies Speaks', interview with Mies. Published with omissions and rephrasing in The Architectural Review, vol. CXLIV, no. 362, 1968, pp. 451–452. Partially available as 'Mies in Berlin', a gramophone record, 'bauwelt in der Ullstein Gmbh', Bauwelt Archive. Radio interview for Rundfunk im amerikanischen Sektor (RIAS; American Radio in Berlin).
Republished in Pizzigoni 2010, pp. 277–286; Walter 2022, pp. 328–340.

I never start with a preconceived image if I want to build a house, *Ludwig Mies van der Rohe once remarked. Architecture is not a cocktail – absolutely nothing should be mixed into architecture, whether it be image, preconception, or subjective wish. The slightest blurring of the architectural idea hurts a building's general validity, hides its structure. For Mies van der Rohe the art of structure in its unbroken purity is the goal, the 'idea' of his building, the general principle which a building must obey from top to bottom, down to the very last detail.*

No architect of our time is as self-disciplined as Mies. No one else has worked a whole lifetime in order to find the relation between ideas and objective facts. No one has searched with such unbroken persistence for the point – the ultimate point at which a building's factual order becomes identical with its spiritual order. This is the objective idea of his architecture; this is his goal. Since he recognised this fact, his designs have become simpler, as simple as possible; they are pure structural architecture.

Please do not confuse the simple with the easy; there is a great difference. I love simplicity for the reason of its clarity – not for easiness, [cheapness], or anything else. We do not even consider this when we work. Certainly, we try to find new possibilities. We even search for them, but if there is no real new solution, then we are not afraid to stick to the old one which we found before. I do not make every building different; I would not even dream of doing so. Only if the programme or the real purpose asks for something new, then we work in that direction, but not to dream up new effects – we just don't do that.

Mies van der Rohe is with us. We are talking about his first post-war building in Germany, the new Nationalgalerie in Berlin, which will be completed within two or three years.

It is a beautiful morning in Berlin. Our view overlooks the old diplomatic quarters on the south edge of the Tiergarten. If Mies van der Rohe's building were completed, one could probably see it from this room at the Hilton Hotel. One would see sharply and clearly the large glass enclosure covered by a floating roof supported by only eight columns. The ground, however, was broken only recently. We already know the plans, and we have seen the model.

Professor Mies, if one studies your buildings, including the design for the new Nationalgalerie, one becomes aware of their clarity; one can almost see the rationality and also the simplicity of your buildings. You only use steel and glass, and it almost looks Japanese.

I don't really know why – people have often said this about my buildings. I have never been to Japan although I have been invited many times, but, you know, I don't like to travel.

Even if Mies were not to be 80 years old next March and we did not know of his arthritis, which makes every step he takes very painful for him, it would be natural to believe that he doesn't like to travel. The way he is sitting with us, he is completely relaxed but at the same time wide awake; he gives the impression of someone who doesn't need the world to create a world. Whatever subject we touch in our discussion, nothing is unclear, the problems are defined, examples are established – this is the very masculine quietness of someone who has relied upon himself during his entire life. Again and again, one looks at his hands, these almost transparent, sensitive hands which have drawn so many times the one clear line, which has been so important in his life, these hands which have given form to the self-evident or self-evidence to the form.

I am interested in clear structure, whether it is done with plasticine or whatever, I do not care. The fact that concrete can be used for anything that people dream up makes it so dangerous. But this is really not the case. If you want a clear structure, you have to really use it structurally. Of course, you can use it also differently, but I would not do that. I want to have a structural architecture because I find it to be the only possibility for a true expression of the essence of our civilisation.

Is that the reason why you prefer steel and glass – because they show the structure more clearly?

Yes.

And then Mies van der Rohe begins to talk about Hugo Häring, his friend and opponent, who in 1958 died alone and almost forgotten in Biberach [sic; in fact, Häring was born in Biberach and died in Göppingen], Germany. At the beginning of the 1920s Mies gave Häring a draughting board in his office. They did not work together and never agreed with each other's ideas, and yet this meeting was very significant for both. This was a clash between the concept of what Häring called 'Neues Bauen' [New Construction] and the concept of 'Neue Architektur' [New Architecture] – between organic building and rational design.

I often fought with Häring about this question; of course, we remained friends. I used to tell him that his organic building, as he called it, is nonsense. You shouldn't call it 'organic'. You cannot say that the Parthenon is not organic; you have to use another word for it. Then he called it 'organhaft' [organ-bound]. At the same time, I told him that our beams are born straight and that you really have to try hard to bend them.

Mies van der Rohe has never tried very hard to bend steel beams. He has used the materials as they came. He has never forced them into a certain shape; he has listened to the steel, so to speak, or to the glass or the concrete. He has searched for possibilities, for the structural form of the materials in order to subject them to his idea of form – not by reshaping them but by using a construction appropriate to these materials. Mies calls this 'a clear structure'.

Mies van der Rohe's most beautiful building, a structure which symbolises a whole epoch, although it was torn down after a few months, was the German Pavilion for the International Exhibition in Barcelona in 1929. This exhibition building was the most perfect architecture yet seen in this century. It became a symbol of the new architecture.

Who would think that its dimensions were derived from the size of a stone block which Mies van der Rohe happened to come upon in the winter of 1928 in a marble yard in Hamburg.

Of course, I already had an idea of what I wanted for the pavilion, but it was not yet fixed and was still a little unclear. Then when we visited a marble yard in Hamburg, I asked, 'Don't you have something really different, something really special?', and I was thinking of this freestanding wall which I had inside the pavilion. And they said, 'Yes, we have this huge block of onyx, but it is sold to Norddeutscher Lloyd for one of their new ocean liners; they want to use it for two large vases in one of their dining rooms.' And I said, 'Why don't you show me this block?' But they shouted immediately, 'For heaven's sake, we can't even touch this beautiful stone.' I said, 'Why don't you give me a hammer, and I will show you how we did this at home.' And then somebody brought a hammer, and they were very curious to see if I would knock a corner off the block, but instead I made a very hard stroke in the centre of the block and got a hand-sized slice, very thin, which they polished so that I could see it. And then we decided to use this material. We determined the quantities, and we bought the stone.

And the dimensions of this block of onyx determined the dimensions of the legendary pavilion. The structural order grew to fit the block's dimensions. The order of a pure, absolute architecture. As Mies recalls, At the end of the meetings about the purpose of this pavilion, it was concluded that it should only be a representation space without any special purpose. It should not contain any objects – nothing. Of course, we had to put some furniture in it, and as we did not want to have any ordinary living-room furniture, we designed the Barcelona chair with its cushions covered with white kid leather. And then we had some stools. These things were never, in fact, used; even during the opening ceremony nobody sat on them.

For the first time, this was a building in which the roof was supported by columns, (chromium-plated steel columns) and the walls were non-load-bearing. You seem to get great pleasure in using valuable, interesting materials and in details?

Yes, certainly, why should something not be as good as possible? I cannot understand why people say, 'This is too aristocratic, this is not democratic enough.' I can only answer, 'What is this?' For me this is a question of value, and I make everything as good as I can.

You could say that the Barcelona Pavilion was almost architecture without function or that the function was kept to a minimum. Spiritually, was this the beginning of a new concept for your future concept of architecture?

Here we have to consider some of Mies' other buildings, especially some of the large structures – for instance Crown Hall, designed for the Department of Architecture at the Illinois Institute of Technology in Chicago and built in 1952.

Throughout his time teaching in Chicago, Mies van der Rohe repeatedly gave his students an assignment to design a large space in which almost any function can be accommodated relative to the magnitude of the space. Was this related to the idea of the Barcelona Pavilion, which became a sort of milestone in the history of architecture?

I don't know whether all this was done consciously. I always liked large spaces because I could do in them whatever I wanted. I often discussed this question with Häring. He wanted to realise this 'Leistungsform' *[performance shape]* as he called it. I told him, 'For heaven's sake, why don't you plan the building big enough so that you can walk freely and not in just one predetermined direction? We don't know at all if people will use it the way we would like them to. First of all, the functions are not clear, and, secondly, they are not constant – they change much faster than the building. Our buildings last for several hundred years. What will wear out is the elevators or the heating system, etc., but the structure will never wear out.' These things, I believe, are at first not conscious, but they become clearer and clearer, and then one day, one expresses them as theory. But actually the thoughts unfolded themselves – little by little.

Ludwig Mies was born in Aachen in 1886. Van der Rohe is his mother's maiden name. He attended the cathedral school in Aachen and then went to the local trade school for two years.

Why did Ludwig Mies become an architect? Here is his explanation in his own words:

This was not a difficult decision. Actually, it came about all by itself. My father was a stonemason, and we were always having to deal with buildings. As children, we were allowed to take part in everything, but our main job was to buy water for coffee, a little pot for two pennies, or sausage and cheese for five pennies for all the bricklayers, and once in a while they would allow us to lay a brick, and later they even let us do a corner. But this was already a master's work and therefore very seldom. Of course, they had no confidence in us.

Thirty years later, the apprentice became a master of corner solutions, a master of details and of the use of materials, a magician of the architectural discipline. Mies does not like to hear that in his life there is no break – everything evolved step by step.

After my practical apprenticeship, I went to a stucco firm where I really learned to draw. There one had to draw full-size details on vertical walls. Maybe a quarter of a ceiling. Louis XIV in the morning. In the afternoon: a Renaissance ceiling for a dining room or a ceiling in the Gothic style for a library. And sometimes one invented new ornaments: modern chestnut leaves with burst chestnuts. There one really learned to draw; one worked very freely. After that period, I could draw everything, it did not matter what it was. When I told my students about this, I often turned around, took a piece of charcoal, and made a drawing on the wall without even looking. You see, this is like learning to skate – you can do it all your lifetime, you will never forget it.

When Mies van der Rohe came to Berlin in 1905, he knew everything there was to know about load-bearing wall construction. He knew how to use natural stone, bricks, knew the plastering process, knew stucco, knew how to draw and to design ornaments. He enjoyed working on details, appreciated careful work, but his first job was unfortunately to design the interior of the conference room for the new City Hall in Rixdorf [today: Neukölln], a suburb of Berlin, in wood.

And I knew nothing about wood. I tried for two or three years but finally decided to go to Bruno Paul and learn something about furniture details.

At that time Bruno Paul was considered one of the leading furniture designers in Germany. He participated in all large furniture exhibitions, such as the Exposition Universelle *in Paris in 1900 and the arts and crafts exhibition in Dresden in 1906, to name just two. His style was a kind of new Biedermeier: very solid, very Prussian. At Paul's office Mies got to know wood as a material. Afterwards, however, he did not return to Rixdorf but instead built his first house – the Riehl house in Neubabelsberg. Mies had met the Riehls through a friend who worked with the painter Emil Orlik.*

The Riehls had decided to build a house, but they wanted to have a young man do it, not a celebrity – and young I was then. I believe I was 20 years old when my connection with the Riehls began.

I left Bruno Paul's office and worked on the plans for the building. It was not really a villa; it was more in the character of the Margraviate of Brandenburg, similar to the houses in Werder *[a town to the west of Berlin]* – very simple roof shapes with gables and a few dormer windows, mostly curved.

This was 1907. A year later, Mies van der Rohe was to be found in the office of Peter Behrens, working for the man who, more than anyone else of this generation, became the ideal of an architect – not only in terms of what he built but also in determining to a great extent the forms of modern industrial society.

When Mies came to Behrens, Behrens was working on his famous AEG lighting fixtures. He was also doing the advertising for AEG and building the large new turbine hall in Moabit. Here Mies van der Rohe encountered a modern architecture with a Neoclassical simplicity of means, purity of form, perfection of proportions, elegance of detail, and dignity of expression. Soon afterwards, Behrens received a major commission to build the German Embassy in St Petersburg. Mies supervised the construction on site. It was his last assignment before he left Behrens after three decisive years. The first design for the Petersburg embassy was submitted to the Russian emperor for approval.

Actually, this was palace architecture, Palladio or something like that. However, later, Behrens decided to use granite from Finland, and all the classical details then disappeared and the architecture became similar to *[Carl Gotthard]* Langhans' Brandenburger Tor, somewhat in the Berlin character, which fitted into St Petersburg rather well.

Did you meet Le Corbusier at this time?

Yes, I met him briefly. He was just leaving the office when I entered it *[in 1910]*. Only Gropius was there; he was an assistant to Behrens.

Can you tell us what you learned from Behrens?

Yes, to summarise it in one sentence, I learned the 'Great Form' from him.

Couldn't one almost say, 'the Monumental'?

Yes, certainly.

Behrens' architectural 'Great Form' also governs the design for the house and gallery of Helene Kröller, the owner of the famous Van Gogh collection. For this project Mies was sent by Behrens to The Hague, where he built for Mrs Kröller a full-size model of the entire complex from wood and painted canvas. But the client was not satisfied. She instead commissioned Hendrik [Petrus] Berlage, the Dutch architect who became famous after building the Stock Exchange in Amsterdam in 1903. Mies agreed to assist Berlage with this project.

I was shown around Holland for several weeks to get to know the country, which I knew only a little from [my time spent at] the border near Aachen. And then one day, Mrs Kröller said that she had discussed with her husband asking me to submit my own design. So I never really worked with Berlage.

They gave me a large hall to work in, which contained at the time approximately 50 Van Goghs. Unintentionally, I became a Van Gogh expert – one could not avoid looking at these paintings again and again. And then I worked out a design. Finally, however, they decided that Berlage should do the building.

This short stay in Holland – and especially the opportunity to see Berlage's buildings – was, however, of great value to Mies.

The Stock Exchange really made a great impression on me. Behrens was of the opinion that all of Berlage's work was passé, but I said to him, 'You may well be mistaken.' He looked at me furiously; no doubt, he would have liked to slap me in the face.

Well, what did you see that was so important for the future in Berlage's way of building?

Mainly, it was the careful construction. To be absolutely honest, this was what interested me most, and also the totally different spirit that had nothing to do with Classicism – there was nothing historical in it. It was really a modern building. After I returned from Holland, I fought with myself to get away from Schinkel's Classicism.

After the war, I believe it was in 1919, I tried making buildings in glass, and to avoid large dead or highly mirroring surfaces, I broke the glass into long strips and put them at slight angles to each other so that the light would reflect in different planes like a crystal, a polished crystal. Actually, this was a project for a competition in Berlin. At the exhibition of all the projects my drawings were hung in the darkest corner because they thought it was a joke.

After that, I tried to work with small areas of glass because I was not satisfied with the first results. This time, I stuck narrow glass strips in plasticine, following the light reflections that they gave. This method determined the final curve of the plane. People say I got this idea from Arp, but that is not true, of course. My intention was not expressionistic. It was to show the skeleton of the building, and I thought the best thing would be to simply wrap it in a glass skin.

This study model on Mies' balcony in Berlin is the source of the great building idea to which Mies has devoted his whole life. Structure reduced to a load-bearing skeleton and enclosed within a clearly recognisable skin: these were the means by which the plan became free and new spaces became possible. Interior and exterior spaces could float together.

The year 1923 brought the important design for the house in brick. [...] Three years later, Mies van der Rohe was able to realise some of these new ideas in his houses in Guben and Krefeld [Wolf House, Guben/Gubin, Germany/Poland, 1926; Lange and Esters Houses, Krefeld, Germany, 1930].

In 1919 Gropius returned to Mies his drawings for the Kröller house of 1912.

He said, 'No, we don't want to exhibit that. We are looking for something quite different.'

1927 found Mies already directing the construction of the Weissenhofsiedlung in Stuttgart. Many architects who are now well known were building there, including Le Corbusier, [Walter] Gropius, Bruno Taut, Richard Döcker, Hans Poelzig, Peter Behrens, and Hans Scharoun. Mies van der Rohe, primus inter pares, was the head of the whole project.

In 1928 Mies received the commission for the Barcelona Pavilion and in 1930 was asked by

Gropius to accept the post of director of the Bauhaus in Dessau. On 5 August 1930 the city of Dessau officially appointed Mies van der Rohe director of the Bauhaus with a free hand in both administrative and artistic matters. Two years later, in August 1932, the city's parliament decided under pressure from the National Socialist majority that the Bauhaus should be closed.

This came about because Anhalt was the first National Socialist state in Germany and the Bauhaus was controlled by the state but at the same time financially supported by the democratic city government, which was likewise National Socialist. They wanted to come to us with an examining commission, and the mayor asked me whether I wanted to go on vacation during the visit. I said, 'No, I would like to see these people' – and we prepared a fine exhibition, probably the best exhibition the Bauhaus ever held. But, of course, the decision was simply a matter of formality. They wrote a scathing report, and that was the end of it.

On 5 October 1932 the Bauhaus was dissolved. Together with almost the entire faculty and a large part of the student body, Mies moved to Berlin to continue the Bauhaus there, as his private institute largely financed by himself.

Since I knew that we could not stay in Anhalt, I rented a factory somewhere between Steglitz and Lichterfelde, near a canal. We painted the interior of the factory white. That looked very nice, and we all liked it much better there than at the Bauhaus – it was not so pretentious since the building was located behind a dirty, run-down fence. Whoever came to see us there really wanted to come to us. We did not need much; all we needed were drawing boards.

How long did you stay in Berlin?

I believe we worked there for a year and a half. We had one costume-party, not two. One morning, as I was approaching the building, I saw that everything was cordoned off. As I came closer, they said, 'Stop,' and I said to them, 'What do you mean? That's my school, it belongs to me.' These people were from the Gestapo. They had been ordered to search the building because they were looking for the founding documents of the Bauhaus to get material against the mayor of Dessau. That had really nothing to do with us; they thought we were quite harmless – which we were, of course.

For hours they interrogated me. They had searched the building the night before, without our knowing it, but they had waited for us there in order to interrogate me and the faculty. And then there were these soldiers outside with their rifles. They became hungry and telephoned their headquarters on Alexanderplatz. 'Well,' they said, 'what shall we do? We have to eat something.' And their superiors at Alexanderplatz said, 'Why don't you lock the place up and come back.' Well, then we were outside, and we could not get back in.

Mies van der Rohe went to see Alfred Rosenberg, from whom he expected support. Rosenberg answered, 'Listen, the Bauhaus is backed by forces which are our enemies, and this is impossible.' And then he said, 'Why didn't you rename it when you came to Berlin?' And I said that I thought one of the best things Gropius ever did was to invent the name 'Bauhaus'. I thought it so good, it should not be changed; and he said he would see what he could do. *But nothing happened. The Bauhaus remained closed. Mies continued for weeks to go to Alexanderplatz to see Rosenberg. He tells the story without any sign of resentment.*

One had to sit outside in the lobby on one of those very narrow benches like the ones in Sanssouci *[Potsdam]* that Frederick the Great built for his pages to prevent them falling asleep. So, there were these very narrow benches on which it was impossible to sit for any length of time. All one could do was go home again. But finally, one day, I reached him, and he said: 'I know exactly what the Bauhaus is doing, and I am very interested in it and will try to persuade *[Hermann]* Göring that it should be reopened.' And then they wrote us that we could open it again.

But before that, I was asked to go to the Culture Ministry to discuss certain questions with them. And then I called the faculty together and told them we can continue the Bauhaus. But I proposed we voluntarily close and I would write a polite letter saying that the faculty had decided to close the Bauhaus. And that's what I did.

Mies does not mention – and this is also part of his character – the conditions set out in the letter from the secret police. Ludwig Hilberseimer and Wassily Kandinsky were to stop teaching, to be replaced by adherents of the National Socialist philosophy. Furthermore, a new curriculum was stipulated, and the old instructors had to fill out questionnaires in accordance with the new National Socialist laws.

Mies van der Rohe's answer to the Gestapo read:

I beg to inform you that the faculty of the Bauhaus has been forced to dissolve the Bauhaus because of the economic difficulties resulting from the shutting down of the building. Respectfully yours.

In 1938 Mies van der Rohe emigrated to the United States, where he continued teaching. America and the whole world learned from his teaching and work. This period saw him design important buildings such as Farnsworth House, the Illinois Institute of Technology, Crown Hall, the Seagram Building, and numerous apartment buildings. His work became a symbol of the epoch.

Thirty-four years passed between the commission for the German Pavilion in Barcelona and the new Nationalgalerie in Berlin. Between Mies' first and last public commissions in Germany lies the span of an entire generation.

In 1905 Mies came to Berlin for the first time. Sixty years later, now almost 80 years old, he has attended the ground-breaking ceremony for a building which once more carries his name, his philosophy, his learning, and his mastery.

This building comes with my sincere wishes that it will become a dignified framework for a great collection – for the enjoyment of all, and to serve art and the spirit.

After 26 years, Mies van der Rohe is back in Berlin. As he remembers, pictures come back to his mind, and his very straightforward thinking puts the tremendous content of his life in front of us – with absolute modesty, somewhat wistfully, and with a tiredness induced by the reminiscing. Smiling to himself, he suddenly listens closely again. Outside in the light of the late morning broils the city – his city, despite Chicago. Berlin, the city for which he is building once more.

Naturally, I was glad to build here again, especially since there was a possibility of doing something – you know, we like very much to have a free hand. I would not have been interested in building an ordinary structure. That would have not been necessary since you have many capable architects in Berlin who could do this.

When we started working on the museum, we studied the programme and looked for a solution. Since the site slopes from the new Potsdamer Street (from the new bridge), the idea of making a building with two levels – the lower level for the permanent museum and the main level for the exhibitions – came almost by itself.

111 Against Arbitrary and Childish Play

Published newspaper interview (given on 9 October 1964).
Source: Anna Teut, 'Gegen Willkür und Spielerei', *Die Welt*, 10 October 1964, p. 7.
Mies was interviewed in his hotel room in Berlin.
Translated from German by John Nicolson.
Republished in Pizzigoni 2010, pp. 287–288; Walter 2022, pp. 309–312.

[...] *We visited Mies in his hotel apartment, high above the city centre. He sat opposite the window smoking a cigar – as he's been doing since he was 15 – and grumbled about the architect of the building – for placing the high parapet blocking (for reasons to do with the façade) his view of the autumnal Tiergarten and the bizarre play of the roofs. That is not something for which you could fault his '860s', the glass residential towers on Lake Michigan in Chicago [860–880 Lake Shore Drive Building, Chicago, 1951]. There people live high up and free and yet are protected. Mies is committed to works of urban civilisation and trusts in their permanence.*

His grumbling about his colleague gave us the opportunity to ask what, in view of the large number of his students and imitators and, above all, of a world without beauty and spirit, he thought of the misunderstood declaration of 1923: There is no problem of form; there are just problems of structural design. *Mies vigorously refused to take responsibility for the can't-dos and can't-thinks. He said it was not his style to go scattering abstract realities about the room; every statement is rooted in the situation. The quote from 1923 was the result of a long piece of research; its intended meaning was that* no innovation of architecture can be expected from form.

This is also Mies' opinion today: What is truly important is only the very slow development of a form which is an objective expression of a civilisation; everything else is caprice or loose playing around.

When we followed this up with a question about how 'Neues Bauen' [New Construction] fits into tradition, Mies answered in Solomonic fashion: If you live and work seriously, then you are part of tradition. The relation to tradition will only be felt as a break for as long as the tasks of the present have not been mastered. *Mies rejected, however, the assumption that there has been no 'revolution' at all in construction:* We are in the midst of one.

On the question of how highly he rated the part played by social ideas in the 'revolution', his opinion was: Social circumstances have certainly played a role in this, *but here too it's a matter of a process of emergence and a complex phenomenon. There have been many interdependences and actions, and not all of them can be grasped conceptually.* Building art is a crystal formed from the essence of the age or it does not exist.

Contact with civilisation *has also been decisive for his own development, and* transplantation *to Chicago in 1937 was difficult.* In America architecture is business. There are no debates and discussions like there were in Berlin in the twenties. *He regards it as important to teach and build since only* construction founded on clear rationality *can provide proof of the rightness of an architect's concepts and teaching. Mies places a high value on his activities as a teacher. IIT (Illinois Institute of Technology), which was for a long time under the influence of the École des Beaux Arts, has under his gentle direction developed into 'a school of seeing'. For Mies* learning to see a building correctly *is still the point of teaching today, and he places great trust in the power of thinking:* Once you have learnt to think correctly, you can never think differently.

[...] *When we asked him whether he believed in the further development of modern architecture, Mies said:* Of course! New concepts will have to be developed from new briefs, new materials. *We asked whether he saw such a development right now, for instance in Le Corbusier's experiments with sculptural form; Mies said,* No [...]

Bindingness, order, rationality: these are the words around which Mies' thoughts constantly circle. We asked him whether he had never thought about testing them out in urban planning. I have often been tempted by urban planning *was his answer*; it's always interested me, it's just that I've never received a specific brief.
We came to the subject of the architectural client. Mies sees no problems here. I have never chased commissions, *he said*, I've let clients come to me. Whoever comes to me knows what he is getting. A real Mies. It's simplest and best that way – not least for the client. *Mies does not suffer from a lack of self-confidence. But he is right. His enormous authority rests not least on the fact that he is aware of being an architect of a highly industrialised age and an urban society and he has never wanted to be anything different. 'Compromise' is a word that does not exist in his vocabulary [...]*
When will he return to Berlin? Two years from now, for the opening of the 'Galerie des 20. Jahrhunderts', definitely. And probably once more before then. But incognito – definitely.

112 Modern Classicist

Published magazine interview (interview recorded in January 1965).
Source: Katherine Kuh, 'Mies van der Rohe: Modern Classicist',
Saturday Review of Literature, vol. 48, no. 4, 1965, pp. 22–23, 61; also
Der Architekt, vol. XV, no. 10, 1966, p. 324.
Republished in Pizzigoni 2010, pp. 292–295; Walter 2022, pp. 313–320.

Which buildings do you consider your most important?
My whole life has been a search for good architecture. Everything I've read (and I've read a lot in my life) has been directed toward finding an answer to the question of truth. What is this thing called 'truth'? Everyone uses the word, but who can really explain it? To learn that truth is relative requires a long search. It took me years to find out, to find out how to make a clear, honest construction. My entire life has been one trip in that direction – so no single building stands out.
In the beginning I worked with small units. At the time I started, I still had to grow up. When I was young, mostly small houses came my way. Of my European work, the Tugendhat House is considered outstanding, but I think only because it was the first modern house to use rich materials, to have great elegance. At that time modern buildings were still austerely functional. I personally don't consider the Tugendhat House more important than other works that I designed considerably earlier.
Another example is the German Pavilion at the Barcelona Exposition, built half a year earlier. You know there were already 17 enormous general buildings – really palaces – planned for the exhibition when representatives of the German government heard that France and England were each putting up separate national pavilions. So, they decided to have one too. I asked, 'For what purpose?' They said, 'We don't know – just build a pavilion, but not too much glass!' If I'd used brick, the pavilion would have been equally good architecture (I like brick), but I doubt if it would

have become as celebrated, for this was really the first modern building to use rich materials, even before the Tugendhat House.

Which projects have you designed that you most regret were never built?

I never regret. I knew, for instance, that the glass skyscraper I designed in Germany around 1920 would never be built. I designed it for a competition. As a matter of fact, nothing was built; the whole project was dropped. I realised that at the time Germany was not ready for my design, but I was interested in the idea. I did it for that reason, not to win a competition. Much later – in Chicago in 1954 – I designed a square building with no interior columns, 720 feet by 720 feet, planned as a convention hall. I'll tell you why I particularly wanted to design that building. When I was young, I started with simple brick structures, then went on to larger buildings like the Barcelona Pavilion and then to office buildings. I had already tried to solve these various types of construction, but during my life one type was still missing – an enormous open building. Of course, by this time I'd put up Crown Hall at Illinois Institute of Technology, yet I had never designed a structure of really monumental quality until the convention hall.

Would it be possible for this design to be used elsewhere?

Of course. I don't feel site is 'that' important. I am first interested in a good building, then I place it in the best possible spot.

What is a good building?

That's the question I'm pursuing: the question of truth. Long ago, I knew that architecture had to be related to our time, but now I feel it can 'only' be the expression of our civilisation.

Are you saying that your architecture is a reaction against the chaos around us?

Yes, in a sense, but it is more than that. It is very difficult to define our civilisation. And it is far different to put this thought into words than to build it.

Do you design for yourself or for your client?

I build not for myself, not for my client. I build for the sake of architecture.

Do you consider design in general more important than the needs of people using your buildings?

I think personal needs are taken care of in all my buildings, but not personal whims. There is an aphorism by Goethe: 'It is neither core nor shell, it is all one.' The interiors and exteriors of my buildings are one – you can't divorce them. The outside takes care of the inside.

Modern buildings of our time are so huge that they have to be grouped. Often the space between these buildings is as important as the buildings themselves. I'm working now on a project for San Francisco, a group of three structures – two apartment buildings and one for recreation. What's important to me is how these buildings relate to each other. You can see an example of this here in Chicago. In the group of apartments between 860 and 900 Lake Shore Drive we purposely opened up the surrounding and intervening spaces; now this space is being filled up with additional buildings. *[This might refer to the one-storey building that has been added between 900 and 910 Lake Shore Drive.]* How ridiculous!

From your experience as director of the Bauhaus and later of the School of Architecture at Illinois Institute of Technology, do you feel that architecture can be taught?

You can teach students how to work; you can teach them technique – how to use reason. You can even give them a sense of proportions – of order. You can teach general principles. If someone knows these principles, they are at least able to reach their native potential; this differs, of course, for each student. But the different potentials are not the teacher's problem. As far as I was concerned, every student working under me was given the same problem – if only to make the general principles clearer.

Some students you simply cannot teach. What's important is not to act as if everyone is a genius. As I have often said, architecture starts when you carefully put two bricks together. That's where it begins. When I came to the Illinois Institute of Technology, I figured we'd have about 20 students a year and if there were two good ones each year, that meant ten in five years. I thought we really only needed two good ones to change Chicago.

Have you been consistently following a specific direction since the beginning?

Yes – I've simply tried to make my direction clearer and clearer. I feel my work has become clearer. I don't think every building I put up needs to be different, since I always apply the same principles. For me novelty has no interest, none whatsoever.

What have been the most important influences on your work?

I thought a lot and I controlled my thoughts in my work – and I controlled my work through my thoughts. I read voraciously when I was young – philosophy, natural science, sociology. I wasted a lot of time on sociology; I don't believe it has much to do with building – it's another problem. My father was a stonemason, so it was natural that I would either continue his work or turn to building. I had no conventional architectural education. I worked under a few good architects, I read a few good books, and that's about it.

What architecture from the past has impressed you the most?

I was impressed by Romanesque and Gothic cathedrals, by Roman aqueducts, by the Pitti Palace in Florence, and by modern suspension bridges. They're still the best buildings in New York.

Has living in Chicago all these years affected your work? Has the proximity of the so-called 'Chicago school' changed your thinking in any way?

I really don't know the Chicago school. You see, I never walk. I always take taxis to and from work. I rarely see the city. In 1912, when I was working in The Hague, I first saw a drawing by Louis Sullivan of one of his buildings. It interested me. Before I came to Chicago, I also knew about Frank Lloyd Wright and particularly the Robie House. If you remember, I wrote about Wright in the Museum of Modern Art catalogue for my 1947 exhibition *[see Johnson (New York, 1947)]*.

(*In a discussion of Sullivan and Wright a few years ago, Mies was quoted in the British magazine* Architectural Design *as saying that their work was very interesting and very important ... Yet we would not do what Sullivan did. We see things with different eyes because now is a different time. Sullivan still believed in the façade; this was still the old architecture. He did not think that just the structure could be enough. Now we would go on for our own time – and we would make architecture with the structure only. Likewise with Wright. He was different from Sullivan, and we for equal reasons are different from Wright.*) *[Reference not found.]*

[...] As to your question, no: living in Chicago has had no effect on me. When I first arrived, I immediately went to the campus of the then Armour Institute (now the Illinois Institute of Technology). I felt I ought to turn around and go home.

Speaking of campuses, how important is continuity of design?

I firmly believe a campus must have unity. Allowing every building or group of buildings to be designed by a different architect is sometimes considered democratic, but from my point of view this is just an excuse to avoid the responsibility of accepting one clear idea. The only American campus worth the name was built by Thomas Jefferson at the University of Virginia.

What should be the relationship of architecture to sculpture and architecture to painting?

What I like most is to come upon a fine work of art and then find a place for it. But first, the architecture must be good. I do not believe that sculpture or painting can be included in the original design of a building. To start with, the architect must work alone, because I believe above all in clear structure itself. Here I differ from Corbusier. Since he is also a painter, he tends to incorporate colour in his buildings. I prefer natural materials.

In the initial design of my buildings I do not believe there can be cooperation between the artist and the architect. The reason is simple: my structural objectives always have an objective character, never subjective. I get along well with artists, but their work has nothing to do with my work.

113 [Peterhans' Seminar for Visual Training]

Unpublished typewritten introduction (5 February 1965).
Source: LoC, Mies, Box 49, Peterhans.
Introduction to a planned publication on Peterhans' IIT Visual Training course. Republished in Blaser 1977, pp. 34–35; Neumeyer (1986) 1991, p. 334; Pizzigoni 2010, pp. 289–290; Walter 2022, pp. 362–363.

When friends and students of Walter Peterhans decided to publish a selection of plates from the Visual Training course he developed at Illinois Institute of Technology, I was asked to write an introduction to the publication because of the part I had played at the inception of the course. In 1930, when I took over the Bauhaus in Dessau, Walter Peterhans was head of the Department of Photography. There I became acquainted with his painstaking work with students and with the great discipline he taught and demanded of them. Not only was he a photographer second to none, but he was a strong personality with a broad education in many fields, notably in mathematics, history, and philosophy.

When I later came to Chicago to head the Department of Architecture at Illinois Institute of Technology, I asked Ludwig Hilberseimer, a leading theoretician in city planning, and Walter Peterhans to become members of the faculty and to work closely with me in initiating our own curriculum for training and educating young architects.

Confronted with the problem of changing a school containing students at different levels, from freshmen to graduates, it was obvious that the only possible starting point was at the freshman level. As properly trained freshmen progressed from level to level, a curriculum conforming to our ideas and consonant with our aims could gradually be evolved.

It was my conviction that any freshman, given the right exercises and guidance, could become a good draughtsman in one year. I asked Peterhans to set up a course to this end, so that at the upper level we would have students to our liking. He succeeded admirably, and in the course he organised a foundation was laid for clean, clear, exact work – the basic prerequisite for what was to follow.

Somewhat later, I made the startling discovery that although the students appeared to understand what I said about the importance of proportion, they did not demonstrate the slightest sense for it in their exercises. I realised that their eyes simply could not see proportion. This problem was discussed with Peterhans, and we decided to introduce a new course, especially designed for training the eyes and forming and maturing a sensitivity for proportion. It was to be a continuation of the basic freshman course but starting at the sophomore level. To achieve this end, Peterhans developed the course he called 'Visual Training'.

The effect of the Visual Training course was a radical change in the whole mental attitude of the students. All fuzziness and sloppiness disappeared from their work; they learned to discard any line that did not fulfil a purpose, and a real understanding of proportion emerged. Although specially gifted students sometimes produced plates that would have enriched the collection of a museum, the purpose of the course was never to produce works of art but to train the eyes.

114 [Eulogy for Le Corbusier]

Published eulogy (7 September 1965; Le Corbusier died on 27 August 1965). Source: LoC, Mies, Box62, ReLeCorbusier; LMvdR, untitled, *Arts and Architecture*, vol. 82, no. 10, 1965, p. 10; also published in *Progressive Architecture* and *L'architecture d'aujourd'hui*.
Republished in Neumeyer (1986) 1991, p. 334; Pizzigoni 2010, p. 291; Walter 2022, p. 321.

Everyone recognises by now that Le Corbusier was a great architect and artist and a real innovator. Ever since 1910, when I first knew him, he reminded me of the great Renaissance artists who built, painted, and sculpted all at the same time. To me his deepest significance lies in the fact that he was a true liberator in the fields of architecture and city planning. Only the future can reveal how those who have been liberated will use the freedom opened up to them by his courage and imagination. Any liberation can result in a new confusion, a new Baroque, or in what we can hope for from those who will follow Le Corbusier: an essential expression of our civilisation.

115 [My Professional Career]

Published foreword (1965).
Source: LMvdR, untitled, Werner Blaser, *Mies van der Rohe. The Art of Structure,* Praeger, New York, 1965, pp. 5–6.
Republished in Neumeyer (1986) 1991, p. 335; Walter 2022, pp. 322–324.

It was about 1910 that I first realised I was embarking on my professional career. At that time the Jugendstil and Art Nouveau movements had run their course. Buildings designed to be worthy representatives of their owners were influenced to a greater or lesser extent by Palladio and Schinkel. But it was the industrial and other purely technical buildings that were the greatest achievements of the period. Those were confused days, and nobody would venture an answer to questions about the nature of architecture. Perhaps it was still too early for an answer. All the same, I posed the question and was determined to find an answer to it.

It was only after the war, in the twenties, that the influence technical developments were beginning to exert on many aspects of life became increasingly apparent. We recognised technology to be a civilising force and one to be reckoned with.

Advancing technology provided the builder with new materials and more efficient methods which were often in glaring contrast to our traditional conception of architecture. I believed, nevertheless, that it would be possible to evolve an architecture with these means. I felt that it must be possible to harmonise the old and the new in our civilisation. Each of my buildings was a statement of this idea and a further step in my search for clarity.

It was my growing conviction that there could be no architecture of our time without the prior acceptance of these new scientific and technical developments. I have never lost this conviction. Today, as for a long time past, I believe that architecture has little or nothing to do with the invention of interesting forms or with personal inclinations.

True architecture is always objective and is the expression of the inner structure of our time, from which it stems.

116 Mies van der Rohe, an Architect of Our Time

Broadcast interview (1965–1966).
Source: Bayerischer Rundfunk Archives. Partially published in 'BDA ehrt Mies van der Rohe in Berlin [BDA Honours Mies van der Rohe in Berlin]', *Der Architekt*, vol. XV, no. 10, 1966, pp. 322–324.
Here Mies appears in Chicago, at IIT, and at his own office.
Republished in Walter 2022, pp. 325–327

To mark Mies van der Rohe's 80th birthday, a television film was produced for the study programme of the Bavarian Radio (authors: the architects Detlef Schreiber and Peter C von Seidlein; director and cameraman: Pitt Koch). For this Mies van der Rohe was interviewed several times. From his recorded remarks the following edited selection was compiled.

You won't be angry, my ladies and gentlemen, if we present to you the life's work and the personality of Mies van der Rohe not in a speech but in a film which the Bavarian Radio has produced under the title 'Mies van der Rohe, an Architect of our Time'. [...]
In addition to scientific education, students first have to learn signs so as to master technical means of expression and how to train their eyes and hands.
[...]
I have often compared architecture with language because in order to truly master a language, you have, of course, to master the grammar. Then you can express yourself clearly. You can say very standard things in a language, you can express very logical things, and if you are a poet, you can even use it to express artistic things. And I think it is just the same in architecture.
[...]
The problem of architecture has always been the same. Quality comes through buildings' proportions, and proportions don't cost anything. For the most part, proportions are between things; they are never the things themselves. That, of course, creates a lot of work for the architect in forming the intermediate spaces. The artistic is almost always a question of proportions.
When Sullivan said that form should follow function, that was more a reaction to what he saw. Today I can no longer believe that this dictum is binding. We have learnt that our buildings last for much longer and functions become obsolete. Today functions change so rapidly that really the only thing that has value in a building is great flexibility. I believe flexibility is, when it comes down to it, the most important and distinctive thing in our buildings – and no longer expression of function.
Structural design follows clear laws, and there is nothing more that it can achieve. But if structural design is elevated to the level of expression – giving it a meaning – then we are in fact already talking of structure. The structural design in fact fulfils a purpose, and the structure gives this state of affairs a meaning.
[...]
If you observe our time, then you get the impression of a great confusion created by the abundance of the things which we see and experience. And what we see in this way, this multiplicity, is essentially chaos. This is not what the Middle Ages called 'multiplicity' but something completely different. Neither is it 'richness'. The Middle Ages had richness even though they were under the high law of theology. That is why medieval cities also look so wonderful even though they were so schematic. All building types were essentially the same.
The confusion that is now spreading everywhere is essentially the result of a failure to understand the problem and of a lack of clarity with regard to the fundamental interconnectedness of architecture with an epoch or civilisation …
[...]
I am convinced that architecture can in fact only be the expression of a civilisation. The essential expression of a civilisation.
Technology has, of course, placed at our disposal entirely unexpected capabilities, but I am not of the

opinion that we should use them arbitrarily. I do not believe that you can attain a clear expression of our time without employing a clear architectural discipline. Someone said I have looked for a special path just for me. In fact I have only been trying to find a path for everyone. Not a personal one.

117 Light 80 Candles on the Library

Excerpts of a conversation published in a newspaper (20 February 1966). Source: Wolf Von Eckardt, 'Light 80 Candles on the Library', in *The Washington Post*, Sunday 20 February 1966, G7.

Ludwig Mies was born in Aachen, Germany, 80 years ago. New York's Museum of Modern Art is celebrating that event with an exhibition of the master's drawings. Washington's officials have done even better. They have commissioned Mies to design the new public library in the nation's capital.
[...] What Mies set out to do was and is nothing less than to find a valid and, if you will, universal architectural expression of our time. Ours, he feels, is a totally new epoch, and history holds no answers for him. We must start to think for ourselves, *he has said,* and try to follow reason, not grand ideas. We must build again in a reasonable way.
The reasonable way for him was to free the practice of building from the control of the aesthetic speculators and restore it to what it should exclusively be: building.
[...] What matters to Mies is the integrity of structure. He presents his buildings, in Louis Sullivan's wonderful phrase 'well-formed and comely in the nude'. He likes to quote Thomas Aquinas and his definition of truth as 'the equation of thought and thing'.
[...] If the Washington Library looks much like a great many other of Mies' buildings, that is very much part of Mies' consistent philosophy too. You don't have to invent a new architecture every Monday morning, *he says.* I'd rather be good than original.
And if that library reminds you too much of all the many, often insipid glass boxes the mini-Mieses have perpetrated all over the place, that is no more his fault than the fact that Rubens or Roman temples have far too often been poorly imitated. As a library, says Harry N Peterson, Washington's director of public libraries with several decades of experience in the field,

Mies' design will function superbly. To some, however, the structure may seem cold and impersonal. An almost shy man who believes in the logic of his cause rather than his ego, Mies laughed in a friendly and genuinely amused way when I asked him about that in a recent interview. What does 'cold' mean? *he said.* You can have cold milk or warm milk. But you can't have cold or warm architecture! Nor can you have a personal architecture. Architecture is impersonal. If it isn't, it is arbitrary, as nowadays it so often is.

[…] Mies, who had been imitated most, now stands practically alone. If others have idealistically wanted to change the concept of what a total, environmental architecture is, Mies keeps showing us what precise, craftsman-like building is. We cannot expect too much, we should not talk so big, *he told me.* If anyone will tell us architects what people need, we'll tell them how to build it. We can only reflect what civilisation and what culture we have.

118 The Life and Times of an Old Master

Published newspaper interview (27 April 1968).
Source: M. W. Newman, 'Mies the Man: the Life and Times of an Old Master', *Chicago Daily News* ('Panorama' supplement), 27 April 1968, pp. 3–4.
Republished in Pizzigoni 2010, p. 296; Walter 2022, pp. 341–342.

It was another time, another day, when Ludwig Mies van der Rohe first came to Chicago and wondered if it was worth it.

The year was 1938, and he was already 52, with an international renown as an architect, although he had built relatively little. Armour Institute (now the Illinois Institute of Technology) wanted him to head its department of architecture. A great sea of slums lapped at the edge of the old South Side campus. Was there a worse slum anywhere? Chicago was drab, dim, depressed.

'What are your terms?' the Chicago architect John Holabird asked the quiet master of Germany's Bauhaus, the 'Haus of Building'. Mies was only a few months out of the nightmare of Naziland.

So Mies' answer to Holabird was most fitting. I would like a completely free hand, *he said.* And $10,000 a year.

Henry Heald, Armour's president, was happy to give him the free hand – but the salary apparently was closer to $8000 than $10,000. Fortunately for Chicago, Mies said 'yes'.

In the 30 years since then, Chicago has become a Miesian city, thanks to the free hand it gave a German exile. He began by designing the Illinois Tech campus (a task he was unfortunately never given the chance to finish; the campus has now been mutilated by other hands).

Symbolically, however, its noblest building, the glass-and-steel Crown Hall at 34th and State St, stands on the site of the squalid old Mecca Flats. That notorious slum, peopled with 1500 squatters, was hymned by blues singers –'*Mecca Flat Woman, must been a jazzin' hound.*'

In 1955, when Crown Hall opened, the students held a prom in its majestic open space. Duke Ellington's orchestra played, and the Duke was blown over by the brilliant acoustics in Miesian crystal. And no one sang then about the Mecca Flats.

Mies (pronounced 'Meece') has tried to create a sort of anonymous architecture for our time, so flexible it can be used for almost any purpose. It is controlled, orderly, logical, and not everyone can live as easily with it as a Duke Ellington happily playing jazz in a hall designed for work and study.

Frank Lloyd Wright's granddaughter [Elizabeth Wright Ingraham], so the story goes, once worked for Mies, and walked up to his desk one day, worried.

'But Mies, what about self-expression in architecture?' she asked him point-blank.

Mies, grandly massive and a slow starter, told her: Wait, first let me get a cup of coffee. Come back in two hours. *She did, and the elderly master politely asked her to write her name on a slip of paper.*

There, *he said,* so much for self-expression. Now let's design a good building. [...]

This rugged man also must have learned self-discipline quite early, because it is the root of his character.

'The only time I ever saw Mies lose his temper was after he stayed up all night on a student design project at IIT,' a Chicago architectural recalled. 'He ran out of cigars around 2 a.m.' There weren't any available in the neighbourhood, and about an hour later, Mies became irritable and blew up at a student. 'But at 6 a.m., a store opened and Mies finally got some cigars and relaxed.'

Cigars and brandy must be considered Miesian. The story is told about him that late at night he has sometimes felt an overwhelming desire to work at something he liked.

I shake it off by smoking a cigar and drinking a glass of brandy and going to bed, *this iron-willed elder confided.*

I don't want to do what I like. I want to do what is right. [...] For it is Mies' controversial thesis that form no longer follows function *in architectural design. Rather, he says, we need* 'universal spaces' *that can be put to varying uses in a time of expanding population and vast demand for buildings. Structures designed for one purpose are often used for another, he points out.*

As if to underline his point, there are the three famous houses that dominated home architecture in our century until World War II. Frank Lloyd Wright's Robie House at 5757 S Woodlawn is now the home of the Adlai Stevenson Institute of International Affairs. Le Corbusier's light, clean-lined Villa Savoye in France, a masterpiece, was used for a time as a hayloft! And Mies' Tugendhat house in Brno, Czechoslovakia – in some ways the first modern glass house – was brutally turned into a Gestapo headquarters by Nazis in World War II. Still later, Czech authorities converted it to a children's gymnasium. Someone took a snapshot of it and showed it to Mies, who said with a grin: And you know, it didn't look bad at all!

119   I Really Always Wanted to Know About Truth

Published newspaper interview (27 April 1968).
Source: Franz Schulze, 'I Really Always Wanted to Know About Truth', *Chicago Daily* (**'Panorama'** supplement), April 27, 1968, p. 4.
Republished in Pizzigoni 2010, pp. 297–298; Walter 2022, pp. 343–346.

Relaxing in his living room, cigar in hand, his keen, clear, 82-year-old eyes measuring the visitor and his secure mind weighing his own remarks, Mies van der Rohe is a study in credibility. Between the man and his works there appears no discrepancy; he seems to form his thoughts the way he forms his buildings. The thoughts take shape in reflective, even grave, deliberation, but when they are uttered, they are brief and compact, light and buoyant, with no loose ends, no rhetorical embroidery.

He was talking about Peter Behrens, the great German architect in whose atelier he served as a draughtsman between 1908 and 1911 (Mies had no formal architectural training). Behrens, *he recalled,* was working in steel-and-glass skeletal construction as early as 1909, in his Berlin turbine factory. But he did not seriously apply the method to other buildings, *Mies reminisced.* Funny. It takes quite a while before people realise what they are doing.

Mies himself had realised the possibilities of what he calls 'skin and bones' architecture by 1919, when he designed a 20-storey steel-core building for Berlin which was covered from street level to roofline with an uninterrupted sheath of glass. This was the radical concept (the building was never actually erected) that thrust him into the forefront of modern architecture. But how, one wonders, did he come upon this notion with virtually no European work around him to serve as a precedent?

America, *he replied.* I liked the clarity of American skeleton buildings. *Did he mean, perhaps, the buildings of the Chicago school of the '80s and '90s?* I was interested in anything in America that was steel construction and rational. But you see, I liked these buildings best when they were half-finished, for that is when they were clearest: when the skeleton was already built, but before all the 'style' was applied to the surface to hide what was true, what was at the foundation. I have not much sense for the stylistic. But I care about the truth.

Mies is quiet and slow to speak, as his biographers love to say, but he is capable of ardour and volubility, and when he mentioned truth, these qualities became apparent. I really always wanted to know about 'truth'. He leaned his great bulk forward and spoke with intensity, enunciating each word carefully. Truth and reason are what matter most, and reason is the first principle of all human work. My pencil would bend if I did not follow this.

But is reason all that important for an artist? Is it enough in architecture?

In architecture, *he said firmly,* one faces problems and finds solutions. The best architecture is the clearest and most direct solution in a problem.

Is the architect bound only by problem and solutions? Can he not express himself?

Na, if he is so dumb, *Mies responded with a magnanimous grin,* let him do it. But you see, architecture has nothing to do with self-expression. It must express something other than 'self' if it is going to express anything. That something is the essence, the spirit, of the civilisation the architecture represents. That is what all great buildings have done. They have said something about an age, not a man. If a man has to express himself, let him be a painter.

Look at the medieval cathedral. How clear it is, and what it tells us of the time; how truly enlightened that time was. *Mies loves the Middle Ages and claims to have found many of the answers in his search for truth in the writings of the Scholastics. It is a little startling – and refreshing – to hear this most modern of architects quoting St Thomas Aquinas.*

That Mies knows painting well enough to contrast its nature with that of architecture is attested by the soundness of his own collecting, most notably of Paul Klee and Edvard Munch. One would think, perhaps, that he would favour [Piet] Mondrian. His work might seem to be influenced by the clean lines of the great Dutch abstractionist. Is this true, Mies?
With emphasis: The Museum of Modern Art thinks so. I don't. Really, my ideas were arrived at independently of Mondrian. I like him, don't misunderstand. But I bought Klee.
Why didn't you also buy Mondrian?
You don't have to have everything.
One more question: remembering that so many of your finest designs were never built, for one reason or another (World War I, inflation in the 1920s, the Nazis in the 1930s, etc.), do you have any regrets about this?
A pause, a shrug, a little smile, and an answer appropriate to a man full of years and past honours, who nonetheless lives wholeheartedly in the present: I don't care much. I hope for the next possibility.

120 The Will of the Epoch Shown in Construction

Published newspaper interview (circa 1968).
Source: Lisa Dechêne, 'Im Bauen den Zeitwillen darstellen. Ein 1968 mit Mies van der Rohe geführtes Gespräch [Representing the Will of the Epoch in Construction. A Conversation With Mies van der Rohe in 1968]', *Deutsche Volkszeitung. Wochenzeitung für demokratischen Fortschritt*, no. 36, 5 September 1969, p. 14.
Transcript of an interview originally recorded for radio, given in Berlin in 1968.
Translated from German by John Nicolson.
Republished in Pizzigoni 2010, pp. 299–302; Walter 2022, pp. 349–353.

With the death of Ludwig Mies van der Rohe this summer died one of the last major German architects who defined functional building from the 1920s forwards. The previous year, Mies, born the son of a stonemason in 1886 in Aachen, visited his native city for the last time. Lisa Dechêne spoke with the 'grand old man' of architects on that occasion. Below we publish a transcript of this conversation, which was originally recorded for radio.
They say you have never lived in a building you have designed yourself. Is this an anecdote, a reflection of biographical destiny – or just chance?
[Laughing.] All at the same time, you could say. It is the truth and it's an anecdote and it's fate and chance, and you probably can't do anything to change it. It was in the twenties that our Neues Bauen *[New Building]* came of age. At that time I belonged to the 'November Group' …
The November Group to the bitter end and beyond. You also designed the gravestone for Karl Liebknecht and Rosa Luxemburg?
Yes, in the form of a cuboid. Clarity and reality had to come together – against the haze which had risen and killed hope. The hope, as we then very correctly saw, of a lasting German republic. That was supposed to be a consistent democracy. Everything else led back to the black-white-red reactionism which in any case no longer held any attraction for us Aacheners. We were Rhenish revolutionaries.

What was it like to take that leap to America – was it a matter of compulsion? Had everything here become too stifling, even before the Nazis?

To be sure, this dullness, this impending doom, was no climate for an architect. You always want to move forward into space and time, into spatial time, into new realities.

It's often been said and written that Ludwig Mies van der Rohe is building the Tower of Babel of our century. Does that amuse you, or do you feel annoyingly misunderstood, or is there something to it?

At some point the Tower of Babel comes to the mind of every architect who travels to America from Europe, or at least that was still the case at the end of the twe nties and in the thirties. To make the tower from glass, concrete, and light – that could also be a liberation. We have to solve the problem of skyscrapers functionally, in the sense of purposefulness and proportionality and, not least, permeability to the atmosphere.

The Tower of Babel demythologised, so to speak. Nothing at all about a ritual of civilisation, or am I wrong?

Yes, you probably know of the court cases I went through with Mrs Farnsworth. Because all that played a role in the argumentation. Farnsworth House, which I designed for the eminent doctor, was an almost completely hollow space. It stood on stilts so as to emphasise its floating, fantastical equilibrium. It was like a crystal. And I thought I had translated, so to speak – not irrationally but with the help of proportion – the emancipation of mankind from the power of gravity into the form of a building. But Mrs Farnsworth accused me of having realised an ice-cold and very male, typically masculine obsession in which people could not live, and certainly not as a woman. And she sued me for damages, in all seriousness. And I had to prove – and here the word probably occurred for the first time – that I had not built a Tower of Babel for Mrs Farnsworth. Well, there was a settlement eventually. And Mrs Farnsworth sold the house, quite advantageously, to a designer of machines. And he was comfortable in it.

An American tragicomedy. But then came your famous high-rise buildings, which, like your buildings on Lake Michigan, were for the most part specifically residential buildings. And the Seagram Building on Manhattan remains to this day a symbol of New York, containing both passable offices and practical apartments. It was also thought that during the thirties your emphasis was more and more on use and that – after your revolutionary sketches and visions – this was, so to speak, practical work on democratising housing.

You should not overlook the fact that I was always, regardless of official honours, fundamentally at odds with the Americans. But this was not just my experience – it was also that of other architects who were very famous there, such as Le Corbusier and Gropius. The skyscrapers that I came upon there, mostly dressed up in the Neogothic or Tudor styles, were for a nation of engineers an annoyingly sentimental style, and they were also ill fitted to purpose. And I said so straightaway. And then they wanted to know how things could be done differently. Then followed the dispute over the institutional buildings for Illinois Institute of Technology. Because this was the first realisation of the principle of flowing space – with open, almost never enclosing but merely touching alignments and free-standing walls. And then things really got going when I applied the idea of hollow space – space that is a box, people said, and which in its turn contains an empty box. But the use of space and the functional purposefulness and the avoidance of the bourgeois-decorative – all this only became clear to many Americans when the buildings were subsequently used and lived in.

Now, however, people have attributed to you a secret Classicism. Here in Aachen, where you spent your childhood, you saw buildings by Schinkel and his school, the Elisenbrunnen, the theatre. And is not this ordering carefulness, this symmetry of Schinkel, ultimately to be found in all your buildings – even where they stretch gigantically into the heavens or where they encompass every hollow space?

Schinkel as a measure that we should apply to a changed world, to the new mobility processes in this world – why not? That alone doesn't have to be Classicism. After all, you couldn't call me one of the stylists of the restoration, and for this reason I was also so cautious with commissions from the German republic.

The tower buildings – do you now see in them the structure that frees the skyscraper from its formlessness forever?

No, I have built for eternity. And who builds in the USA for centuries? However, I wanted to think through certain constructional principles functionally in order to introduce them into the actual development process as forcefully as possible.

Have you always – from when you were young in the November Group, a time that is associated with Karl Liebknecht and Rosa Luxemburg, until today – seen architecture as linked to the will of the epoch?

That architecture should represent the will of the time remains my conviction. Incidentally, that is not necessarily new. The Roman aqueducts and the cathedrals of the Middle Ages also expressed the will of their time. Admittedly, this is hardly congruent with the will of my epoch. It has still to fundamentally assert itself against the dominant constraints of the nineteenth century. That is the problem that today's young students, in America as in Europe, are struggling with. And students from Berkeley and Berlin …

And from the SDS at Aachen University of Technology?

Yes, that here in Aachen the SDS is the majority in the General Students' Committee of Universities of Technology was a surprise for me; it's shown me that the student movement in the Republic of Germany is not limited to specific centres. So, I would also like to say that we cannot compromise when dealing with the social problems of this century. This is a lesson the student movement has learnt very well. We wanted to give young people like this a couple of signs of the new direction through uncompromising building design. And possibly we achieved this, in the old and in the new world.

121 [Dirk Lohan Interview]

Unpublished interview by Mies' nephew Dirk Lohan (summer 1969). Published in F. Neumeyer, *The Lost, Last Words of Mies van der Rohe. The Lohan Tapes from 1969* (Berlin, 2021).

When you first arrived in New York, in those early days before the Seagram Building ... You must have met a lot of people, other than the gallery types. I know you met Nierendorf and Peterhans there for example. Did you meet anyone else?
Well, other than museum people ... I suppose I met d'Harnoncourt, who was run over in an accident ... And I already knew Sweeney from earlier. He and I would get into some very lively discussions.
When did you meet Sweeney for the first time? Was it back in 1938? Or 1939?
It must have been around then. I don't remember the exact dates anymore. I met Sweeney in Berlin, but I'm fuzzy on the details beyond that. Philip and Neumann introduced me to a lot of people. They were the first ones I met. I believe it was Philip and ....
In Berlin you mean?
Yes.
So Philip Johnson came to you.
Yes. He visited me in Berlin every few years. And he began to take an interest in architecture, collecting photographs and so on.
Was he actually an art historian or an architect?
Neither. He'd studied at Harvard before making some contacts at the Museum of Modern Art. He calls himself a historian every now and then if he wants to make a point about something. Later, when he came to us, he took a serious interest in architecture. He did an exhibition on modern architecture later, with ... with that one with the beard ...
From England?
No, no, from here.
Oh, you mean Hitchcock.
Hitchcock, yes. He did an exhibition with Hitchcock about modern architecture. That was quite a while ago.
I read that they recently published a revised edition of the book.
Is that true? I haven't heard anything about it.
But Hitchcock is actually a historian.
Yes.
Didn't he attack you once, some time ago?
No, it was actually only Mumford who went after me.
Yes, he's the one I meant, I was getting mixed up. Why did he attack you?
He didn't like my buildings for his cities. And frankly, I didn't like his cities for my buildings. Not that any of that really mattered. People take themselves so seriously. But I suppose everybody's like that. Once Philip discovered his interest in architecture, he went back to Harvard to study with Gropius.
With Gropius? But weren't you already here in Chicago at that point?
Yes. Then later, he built a court house from wood, though it was poorly done.
Before he did the Glass House?
Yes.
I've never seen it.
I don't think he ever published it.
Why did he go to Gropius instead of coming here?
Well, you know, Harvard is a special school, where only the most refined people go. Though they've gone on strike now, the refined people ... I suppose in the end, he'd already been at Harvard earlier, as a poor student, and it wasn't like Gropius was so bad that he would abandon his alma mater because of him.
I only meant because he'd spent so much time with you in Berlin.
He also came here to Chicago very often. He would snoop around my work and copy my details. But he would make mistakes in his details, because he did not work through them himself. He only lifted them. ... stole them.

Yes, when in fact you should always work them out yourself.

Could you say something about your childhood home? Where your parents came from. What your father was like. The whole story.

But that is all rather tedious.

I'd like to hear about your home, back when your father had his stone-carving shop.

He'd taken over the business from his father. It used to be a big operation, and my father's brother was still involved at the time. In fact, his brother took care of the business side of things. He'd often travel to Belgium, Paris, Africa, and so on.

To Africa?

Yes, to procure the marble. It was rather excessive, but to be fair, a large share of the business came from fireplace mantels, which did not require a lot of material. So of course, you would use expensive materials to charge higher prices. Having said that, price did not play such an important role at the time. People were not so profit-oriented when my father was young or when my grandfather was running the shop. They had clients asking for mantlepieces from all over, from the Rhine to Brussels. I think it was quite common at the time for a business to serve such a vast area. There was a company, Kufen, run by a father and son, which also had clients everywhere, from the Rhine to Brussels. They built a large number of Baroque-style buildings in Aachen, which was an important, lively city at the time. Full of industries – tube manufacturers, nail factories, and so on. Big fires would often break out in Aachen, and the last of them destroyed the residences of many factory owners. I always wondered how the Kufens received so many commissions until the connection with the fire dawned on me. They were the best people for the job, and there weren't that many others.

Your father also did a lot of headstones when people began to build less.

Yes, people stopped commissioning fireplaces. They began to use ovens instead and would mostly burn coal or slurry from washed coal.

That brown stuff?

No, that's lignite, which is yet another kind of burning material. This was really very valuable coal which had been washed to remove the impurities.

This slurry that you're talking about ... is it made of small grains, like soot?

Yes, it had the consistency of porridge.

How did people buy it? In sacks?

No, it would have all leaked out. You could have a batch delivered in a large handcart, in the form of a half cylinder, about this wide. The same kind of cart that was used to transport white lime.

Like a tub?

Yes, and that was simply passed through a window into the cellar. People would also buy clay so the coal wouldn't burn so fast. It was an excellent burning material. Of course, not the best coal, only the dust from the best coal.

Going back to your father ... You were saying he made a lot of headstones.

Yes, increasingly so.

I saw Ewald [Mies' older brother] when I was in Aachen some time ago. He showed me a lot of other things you can make with stone. Wells, for example, or decorative cornices for old buildings.

Yes, and above all for old churches. Clients trusted him to work very carefully, and he knew his craft rather well. He was more practical than theoretical.

When you were young, did you mostly stay at home for your school work? Or did you also have to help out with the business?

I helped out for fun, and always during the holidays. I still remember how everyone wanted a new gravestone monument when All Saints' Day came round and how the whole family would get involved. I did the lettering, my brother did the carving, and my sisters did the gilding. The whole place came alive. I doubt this helped the business too much – perhaps just a little bit. But after a certain point, we began to feel the pressure from new, richer competitors entering the business explicitly to make a profit. My father didn't have a business mind at all. He would simply assess how long each job would take and name the price. No shrewdness, not a single thought about profit or making a little extra to get through a rainy day. He and my brother would get into such heated arguments. My brother would say, 'For heaven's sake, we could do it much faster! No one will see that section all the way up there anyway. It's not like it's a door frame that everyone can see!' But my father would have none of it. He would say, 'I see I'm the last stonemason left in this house! No one has climbed up Cologne Cathedral to look at the finial either. But it was conceived and created for God!' And so on. But of course, it became harder and harder to go on that way. Eventually, my brother took over the business side of things.

This was when you were still in Aachen? Or were you already in Berlin by then?

Yes, I was already in Berlin.

Was it always assumed that Ewald would take over the business and that you, as the second son, so to speak, would go your own way and do something else?

Yes, though we did also know of other businesses – not stonemasons but carpenters, for example – that were run by several sons. But such enterprises would quickly descend into chaos. There were too many cooks minding the broth. So after I left school, I went to do practical work as a building apprentice.

What made you decide to go into building?

We had a teacher at school who was an architect, and he looked very sharp. I liked that, so I became one too. But it also had something to do with our family business. I spent so much time as a child running around buildings, helping out at the workshop, and I always found that fun.

The school, where you had an architect as a teacher. Was that a crafts school [Werkschule]?

Not in the strictest sense. It was a trade school [Gewerbeschule] with a two-year curriculum, designed to prepare students for a job at an office or workshop. It included some maths and geometry and also German and a bit of French for one or two years, one or two hours per week. But the school emphasised drawing above all because that was a skill everyone could use. It wasn't an airy, theoretically concocted programme. It was grounded in practical experience. Students were taught what they really needed. Of course, there were also other schools. The Baugewerbeschule for example, which was yet another level higher and very specialised. But such schools also took longer – they offered a four-year curriculum.

I think it's called a 'Baufachschule' nowadays. It offers a technical, higher-level degree. The graduates are very practically minded.

Their work was always flawless. I always preferred working with them over those from the [more theoretically oriented] Technische Hochschule. They could draw a roof truss impeccably. They knew how to do such a thing because they had learned it.

Then afterwards, you did a year of practical work on the building site.

Yes.

What kind of building were you constructing? Was it a house?

Yes, a house with multiple storeys – two, four, three – I can't remember anymore.

Could you describe the building process?

We first dug a pit for the foundation. Then we dug a second pit for the slaked lime. Bricks were delivered to us in enormous piles. They covered the whole pavement. We didn't have concrete back then, not for these purposes; foundations were made of bricks. So we laid a dry layer of bricks and began to apply the mortar, which we had to mix ourselves using sand delivered to the site. We carried the mortar, with the bricks, on our shoulders, on a flat board cut in the shape of a semi-circle, using one hand to keep the pile steady and the other to climb down the ladder. We'd compete to see who could carry the biggest pile of bricks. There were other tasks once the foundation was completed. Some of us worked with the bricklayers, for example. You learned to work slowly – not like a savage that grows weary within minutes but steadily, so you could keep at it for several hours. If you were good, the foreman allowed you to do a corner, which was very complex. We mostly used the English cross bond, and of course, sometimes we'd make mistakes. But if we did, the foreman would let us continue until we were finished with the whole section before telling us to tear it down and try again. Then we'd have to scrape off the mortar and start over. Later, the carpenters arrived on the site, and we would help them out as well. But one of our most important tasks at the beginning – in fact throughout the whole year – was to fetch hot water for the coffee. You could get a small jug filled with boiling water for two pfennigs. We would pour coffee powder into the jug and fill it up with hot water. For five pfennigs you could buy a sausage, black pudding, or cheese. That was our main meal. The bread we brought from home.

Did people not drink as much beer on the building site as they do today? I'm always surprised by how much beer people drink in Germany.

They did, actually. After all, in my hometown, there was a brewery at every corner. But most people would only go there at the end of the week, once they'd been paid their wages, and drink schnapps.

So perhaps beer is more popular in the north ... I assume you made the ceilings out of wood back then?

Yes. We used thin beams – positioning the longer face vertically – and fixed them together so they wouldn't move. We wove a thin iron band, around one centimetre wide, over and under the beams and nailed them in place at the two ends. But what's interesting is that back then we still tried to make the true half-barrel vaulting in the basement. This was before people began to use iron girders instead of wood. We carved a groove down the sides of the beams and inserted sapwood boards between them. Then we layered clay on top of the boards, and ash on top of that, to exclude moisture and noise.

That is very interesting, I've only heard about these building methods during my studies. It's remarkable that people really used them back then.

And of course, once iron girders arrived on the scene, people began to make Prussian cap vaults instead.

Over the girders?

No, in the flanges.

Yes, yes, that's what I meant.

And then you filled in the rest from above.

When people were making wood ceilings, you could still get proper Plister boards, which were thin and rough sawn so the mortar would stick to them.

I've only seen them in old run-down buildings. There are still some here in Chicago.

Yes, they must have been built around the same time ... The wooden boards were attached below the beams, and the bricks were simply layered above horizontally. Every third layer had either a round rod or a very thin steel band in the joint, which was of course filled with mortar. And I've just remembered something else. The concrete. We called it 'Monier concrete'. Monier was probably the name of the inventor – a Frenchman.

Were such buildings, and the one you were working on, rendered on the outside? So many buildings in Aachen have exposed brickwork.

Exposed brickwork was out of fashion by the time we were building. Instead, people would apply a cement render with ornaments, profiles, and window frames. Of course, you still came across proper old brick buildings. The Kufens did a lot of them, making the window and door frames out of blue stone. It was actually very nice work, on the inside. They often erected a building entirely out of brick and stone.

How old were you when you were on the building site?

Not yet 15, I would say.

And that was only for a year?

Yes. Once the construction was complete, I had to do the lettering for the signs saying 'ROOMS TO LET' in capital letters. It wasn't hard since I'd already learnt how to draw and was already very familiar with the typefaces. I did it quite quickly, though I had to make the ink myself. It was a Chinese ink, very oily, and I had to produce it by grinding an inkstick. Afterwards, my father said it was time I earn something now, having already worked without pay for so long. So I went to my boss and asked for a wage, saying it didn't have to be much ... There's that flash of stupidity again. No business sense whatsoever. But he remained stubborn and refused. Then an old school friend of mine told me about a stucco company that was looking for a draughtsman, so I went to work for them. But they placed me in the administrative office at first, where I was stuck doing the book-keeping, filing, licking stamps, and dealing with employee medical forms. I also had to answer the phone and deliver the workers' wages to the building sites on a bicycle. But I got lucky after a short while, maybe half a year later. The head draughtsman was called up for military service. So I rose up the ranks overnight and ended up in the drawing room. That's where I really learned how to draw. At that point, I was rather good at geometric forms, but otherwise my drawing skills were unrefined. So I learned. We worked on a large, upright, wooden board, as tall as this wall, from floor to ceiling, where we drew the designs full size. You weren't allowed to lean against it. You had to stand with your feet planted firmly in the ground, and the motion had to come from your whole arm rather than your wrist. The drawings were enormous – large enough to cover a quarter of a ceiling. Once we were finished with them, the drawings were taken to the modelling room. I truly learned how to draw. I can still draw cartouches today, virtually from memory.

The drawings were in all kinds of styles?
Yes. We also drew modern patterns, based on chesnut leaves or fruits in full bloom, for example. The modellers were more at home with the old forms since they'd done them hundreds of times. We copied the new ornaments from photographs in books.

Were you allowed to design your own ornaments?
Yes, of course, if you had the skills. It is a difficult task of course. Not at all easy.

This must have been the first time you could try your hand at creating something of your own.
I'm not sure. We certainly could have done. Of course, we always avoided making exact copies. And variations are easy to add.

Then you went to an architectural practice?
Yes.

How did you make this transition?
The head of the stucco company had some kind of lung disease. He would go to Davos every winter and stay for several months. One day, we got into a terrible row. He must have been unhappy with my work. He made as if to box my ears, and I said to him, 'Just you go ahead and try it!' Then I took my hat and stormed off. He sent the police after me, to my home, as if I were an apprentice. But I was no apprentice – I was just a beginner as a draughtsman. My brother was at home at the time, and he told the officer, 'Good sir, listen to me. That man is speaking nonsense. My brother was never an apprentice there.' Then the officer left, and things quietened down after that.

How long were you at the stucco company? A year? Or longer?
Two years.

So you were 17. You could already draw, and you knew a thing or two about construction. You could essentially build an entire building. No 17-year-old can do that today. What happened after you left the stucco company?
I ended up working for an architect who was designing a building for a new branch of [Leonard] Tietz, a department store chain. His practice had come up with a richly decorated façade. But their reach had exceeded their grasp. Nobody knew how to draw it. A friend put me in touch with the practice, and I agreed to work for them, just to draw the façade. I wasn't thinking of staying there for longer. The architect asked me how much time I needed, and

I replied, 'It depends on when you need it. Do you need it by this evening? Or can you spare a day or two?' He looked at me quizzically, as if I were the wrong person for the job for thinking I could do all those ornaments so quickly. But for me drawing ornaments was a breeze. I was finished with them by the next day, and he was very pleased, so he asked me to stay on.

He was an architect? Based in Aachen?

Yes. But in the end, the Tietz people, based in Cologne, decided that they couldn't trust him with the job because he lacked the experience. They signed a new contract with Boswau & Knauer, a big architectural firm in Berlin, and rented a building for them to work in. A horde of architects, engineers, and typists arrived the next month. That's how it began. No one could do anything about it even if they wanted to.

We left off last time when you were about to move from Aachen to Berlin.

The first time.

I heard that someone at the architectural firm gave you the idea of going to Berlin.

Yes, it was an architect, [Rudolf] Dullo, from Königsberg. He was a great admirer of Schopenhauer. He invited me to a dinner once, to celebrate Schopenhauer's birthday. I wasn't particularly well versed in such intellectual matters.

But you must have already had an interest at the time.

Yes of course.

So he suggested you move to Berlin?

Yes. He took me aside one day and said, 'Listen. What are you doing in this sleepy town? Go to Berlin, where there are actually things going on!' I replied, 'That's easier said than done. I can't just buy a ticket and go to Berlin, where I'll end up standing around at Potsdamer Bahnhof without a clue where to go.' Then he glanced around before opening his desk drawer to show me a building magazine – I'm not sure which, the *Bauwelt* perhaps – where two vacancies were being advertised in the jobs section: one for the new town hall in Rixdorf, and another for a position at [Heinrich] Reinhardt und [Georg] Süßengut, which was quite a big company, not unlike Boswau & Knauer. It wasn't an architecture firm exactly. The boundaries weren't as clearly defined back then. Anyone could build as long as the authorities would allow it. You didn't need to have passed any exams. The work itself was the test. Both companies asked for a few sketches, just to see if you could draw, and advertised that they would do the rest of the tasks themselves. So I sent off two piles of mostly free-hand drawings, and I received an offer for both positions. I was unsure about the job in Rixdorf, because they would only pay 200 marks per month, which was 50 less than what Reinhardt and Süssenguth were offering. But Dullo told me to go to Rixdorf, saying a good friend of his was heading the office. Martens was his name. A very fine man. From the Baltics. A meticulous architect and an artist, above all. I followed Dullo's advice and went to Rixdorf. It was a long journey.

That was your first trip then? The first time you moved away from Aachen.

Yes, and for the better I would say. I had to journey to Cologne first, where I had to transfer to another train to Berlin. The train departed from Cologne at 8:15 a.m., and by 8:16 a.m. I was already heaving out the window. It was a huge relief when I arrived in Berlin, with solid ground beneath my feet once more. Then I took a taxi, but I began to feel unwell again after a few blocks, so I took a tram for the rest of the journey to Rixdorf. The firm in Rixdorf gave me the task of designing the large councillors' chamber with wood. Now, at the time, I was familiar with all kinds of materials – stone, brick, stucco – but I had never properly worked with wood before. I'd only picked up a few things from the carpenters during my year as a building apprentice. I stayed at the firm until I was called up for military service.

Do you know which year you went from Aachen to Berlin?

I don't know exactly anymore.

But you weren't yet 20.

No, you didn't need to be 20 to be a soldier.

No, I can believe that, I just wanted to figure out the year.

One time, when I was in the military, our unit was doing a drill in the pouring rain. We were wearing those funny old helmets with a pickaxe on top, and water was splashing all over the place. During this drill, we were given the command 'Attention!', and one of the recruits in the first row wiped away the rain from his face. The inspecting officer was furious and stormed off. And our captain was livid that we'd embarrassed him. So he had us practising drills for hours in the rain until eight in the evening. It was absolutely senseless – pure soldierly nonsense. As a result, I couldn't get out of bed the next morning. I was feeling so strange, as were six others in my unit. We were all taken to hospital, where I was diagnosed with a lung infection. And since they had so many healthy young bodies, they didn't want cripples like us. So I was discharged as 'unfit for service'. I don't know what happened to the others. That's when I went to work for Bruno Paul. I didn't go back to Rixdorf.

How long were you in the army? Around a year? Half a year?

It must have been half a year. I'm not sure anymore. It's been a long while. I wanted to learn more about working with wood, so I went to Bruno Paul's practice to study how to do details – furniture details, claddings, and so on. Bruno Paul was working with Deutsche Werkstätten Hellerau *[a furniture manufacturer]* at the time.

Did he have a furniture company of his own?

Yes. And he also received his first commission to design a house while I was there. It was a very nice house, a small tennis club, in Grunewald. It is still standing today, as far as I know. He wanted me to work on this project because he knew I could do it and he otherwise only had furniture people working for him. But I wasn't interested. I didn't want to give up my furniture. So I recommended a friend who was working for Olbrich in Düsseldorf at the time. Bruno Paul asked to see some of his drawings, to make sure he could really draw, but my friend didn't have any at hand. At this point, I really wanted to see this process through, so I gathered some of my own drawings and showed them to Paul, passing them off as my friend's. He never caught on.

My friend arrived in Berlin on a Saturday, and he had to show up at the office the following Monday. So we spent the whole weekend together, drawing and practising, to make sure his sketches would look more or less like mine. We got into a heated argument later because I didn't consider Bruno Paul such a great architect. In my eyes he was more an interior designer. But my friend was precisely the opposite. He was a great admirer of Bruno Paul. Our argument became rather hostile. I would tell him, 'For heaven's sake, this has nothing to do with architecture at all!'

What kind of furniture did Bruno Paul make?

He always drew inspiration from older works. But his furniture pieces were very beautiful. Not simply replicas. They were inscribed with his handwriting. The way a storyteller's personality shines through while he is retelling an old fairy tale. He could do that very well.

This was just after he'd done all the caricatures?

No, that was way back, when he was in Munich.

Why did he give those up? He went from drawing caricatures to designing furniture. Then from furniture to architecture. An interesting trajectory…

Well, Behrens was a painter, Van de Velde was a painter, that was the trend. Riemerschmid, I think, was also a painter. In the end, it was often the outsiders who introduced the most radical changes. Though it was the English – Morris and the like – who actually led the way.

Did you meet other architects while you were with Bruno Paul? Or while you were in Rixdorf? Peter Behrens for example …

No, no.

Did you engage with the works of Schinkel during that time? Did you go and see his buildings?

I was more interested in Messel at the time. The great Wertheim department store, in the city centre, had such a wonderful front side. All of Messel's works were wonderful. He was rather like Palladio. He could perfectly imitate the Gothic style. Of course, there were plenty of works by Schinkel in Berlin as well. The Altes Museum, for example. I often went for a walk on Sundays to look at them. But that was mostly later, after I'd gone to Neubabelsberg to work for Behrens.

So Behrens was your next destination, so to speak, after Paul.

Well, I stayed with Bruno Paul for a while and continued to design furniture. At the same time, I was taking classes at two schools where Paul was teaching: at the Kunstgewerbemuseum and at the Akademie. The Kunstgewerbemuseum was on Prinz Albrecht Strasse, inside a damaged corner building. I think Gropius renovated or rebuilt it, because his uncle had originally designed it. It was a very fine building, very beautiful, and we had our classes inside. We'd go inside, all together, or one after the other, and do free-hand sketches of furniture. The other rooms were used for life-drawing classes and the like. I could only spare a few hours to practise what I was learning, since I was working at the same time. But I was certainly learning. Orlik was one of the teachers. He was a painter, but he did a lot of woodcuts which were very fine, with a touch of the Japanese manner. Nothing like Munch. He had his own style. I became friends with his assistant – Potz or Popp *[Propp]*, I think, was his name. I would have liked to have learned woodcutting with him.

One day, when I was in Propp's studio, Frau Riehl, the wife of my future client, walked in, looking for a young man who could help her design a bird bath. It was one of those flat bowls. Propp helped her by drawing the sketches. Later on, the Riehls decided to build a house. But they were so idealistic. They wanted a young architect rather than an old hand. They came to Propp, asking if he knew anyone who was up for the job. He said, 'Yes, of course I know someone.' So I was asked to visit their home for an interview with Frau Riehl, the professor's wife. She asked me: 'So, what have you built alone?' I answered, 'Nothing.' To which she replied, 'That won't do. We don't want to be guinea pigs.' Then I said, 'But I can build a house. I've just never done it alone – but I have certainly done it. Please imagine what would happen if everyone were to ask me the same question before trusting me to do a task. I'd end up on my deathbed having accomplished absolutely nothing.' This made her laugh, and she decided to introduce me to her husband.

She was hosting a dinner party that very evening, and she invited me to attend. I'll never forget how Propp told me, no earlier than noon, that I'd have to wear a frock coat. I didn't have the faintest idea what a frock coat even was. He said, 'Just make sure you get your hands on one. You can buy one anywhere, or perhaps even rent one.' I ended up going round the whole office to borrow enough money to buy a frock coat. Of course, I didn't know which tie to wear. I ended up going with one that was a garish yellow. Completely out of place. I arrived at the Riehl residence later that evening. Several people were with me in the lift, all of them dressed to the nines, in tail coats and donning medals. I thought to myself, 'Surely they're going where I am!' I let them out first, and it turned out I was right. The doors opened, and I almost became dizzy at the sight before me. The man and his wife were zooming across the parquet floor like ice skaters – I was afraid I would break my neck. The professor dashed from one guest to the next to greet them. It was a peculiar scene.

After the dinner, the professor invited me into his library, where he proceeded to ask me a barrage of questions. After that, he suddenly announced, 'We shouldn't keep the other guests waiting,' and as we were returning to the salon, he turned to his wife and said, 'This is the man who will build our house!' Here I must correct what I said earlier. Frau Riehl was in such a shock – she didn't quite trust her husband's judgement – so she asked me to come and see her the next day. The meeting with her took place after the party, not before. Towards the end of my interview with Frau Riehl, I told her I was working for Bruno Paul and that he'd wanted me to design a tennis club for him. I suggested she ask him what he thought of me. Bruno Paul later told me what she said to him, 'You know, that Mies is a genius, but he is simply too young. He doesn't have the experience.' Bruno Paul proposed I design the house together with his practice, but I refused. He asked where I get the nerve to say no. He couldn't understand. Probably I just wanted to do it all alone. And I was given the project in the end. When the house was finished, Bruno Paul asked me if I would give him photos of the Riehl House. He wanted them for an exhibition he was showing of his current and former students' works. Apparently, later, during a tour of the exhibition, he said to one of the visitors, 'Do you see that house? There is only one thing wrong with it, and that's the fact that I wasn't the one who designed it.' He was very kind to me in the end. Not at all petty.

So the Riehls were very pleased with your work?
Oh yes, of course. They were a bit shocked that it turned out to be more expensive than we'd planned. But that was to be expected. It almost always becomes more expensive. Soon after I'd completed the house, I was approached by Thiersch. He'd worked with Behrens before becoming Bruno Paul's office manager. Behrens had asked him to keep an eye out for any young talents and to send them his way if he ever found any. Thiersch told me, 'You should go to Behrens. He's a first-class man.' And so I came to work for Behrens. There are a lot of stories floating around that the three of us [*Mies van der Rohe, Walter Gropius, and Le Corbusier*] were working there together. But Corbusier was already on his way out by the time I arrived. Of course, Gropius headed the office. And what a gentleman chief he was – simply there to learn. I don't think he ever received a salary.

Is Gropius a trained, academic architect?
I would say so, yes.
But you came to know Corbusier later. When was that? It must have been during the Weissenhof Housing Estate project at the latest.
Yes, not much earlier ... Of course, I'd already met Corbusier while I was working for Behrens. But there wasn't enough time to really get to know him.
There was an exhibition of decorative and industrial arts in Paris in 1925. And Le Corbusier built a house for it, using pressed wood-wool panels and sprayed cement. I sent him a note to congratulate him afterwards, because I liked the house. It was a completely new idea. Hardly anyone had used limewash for smaller buildings before then.
You must have spent a lot of time with the Riehls while you were building their house. Did you meet a lot of people during this time?
Oh yes, I met some very nice people. And Frau Riehl also gave me and Propp some money to travel to Italy for six weeks. That was my first trip to Italy.
Was that the trip to Naples that made you feel homesick for a grey sky above you?
Yes, yes.
Did anything especially leave a mark on you during this trip?
We were to go to Munich first. There was an exhibition there, I can't remember which anymore, where Riemerschmid had designed a building and its interiors. It was to Frau Riehl's taste, so she wanted us to see it, but she also sent us on that trip so we could refine our sensibilities as designers. It was a very interesting trip, though Propp spent too much time in the museums for my taste, looking at paintings. Of course, I understand why, but I often stayed outside to look at the city. It was wonderful. Afterwards, we travelled onwards to Italy, through Brenner and Bolzano and from there onwards to Vicenza, where Palladio did many of his buildings. Some of his most important works are there. Wonderful country houses – not only the Villa Rotonda, which is very formal, but also

others that are freer. Messel did a beautiful country house by the Wannsee Lake in Berlin – very flat and elongated – that always reminded me of Palladio's villa outside Vicenza. Messel and Palladio did very fine details, though Messel's details were even finer. He had a kind of sensitivity that some people are just born with. When we were still in Rixdorf, we would go to the centre of Berlin on Sundays to look at one of Messel's buildings. It had large stone snails – wonderful and perfectly detailed. We should see if we can find a book on Messel so I can show you. The building is no longer there. It used to be where the Philharmonie now stands. Those were our visits. There was always something going on in Berlin. Especially at Unter den Linden, in the area in front of the Brandenburg Gate. At the other end of the avenue was Tessenow's Neue Wache, the memorial to dead soldiers. And behind it was a beautiful grove of chestnut trees. You could see how they used to work back in the past. How slowly life would saunter on. They still had time back then, to do it all nicely, and not everything helter skelter.

All of that was before the First World War? So the Riehls introduced you to the intellectual world. Did you also meet any politicians?
Not while I was with the Riehls. I did meet the young Rathenau, but he hadn't yet become a politician. He didn't come to power until after the First World War. I also met Werner Jäger, a classicist, who had a Jewish wife. I don't know if he was married to her from the start, or if he got divorced to marry her some time after the Nazis rose to power. Of course, it wasn't a good situation for him. But then he was offered a teaching position here in Chicago.

He was also a politician?
No, just a classicist. *Paideia*, in two volumes, is one of the most important books. He spoke many different Greek dialects and became a professor, in Kiel I believe, when he was 22 years old. Later, [Ulrich von] Wilamowitz-Moellendorff gave him a professorship in Berlin. And later he became Wilamowitz's successor.

Today is the 24th. I'll read out loud Howard Dearstyne's article, titled 'Mies van der Rohe at the Bauhaus', just so you know what it says. Dearstyne writes here for example that the mayor of Dessau closed the school for a couple of weeks.
That is probably not incorrect because no one else had the authority to close it. He was in charge.

But you were the one who called him in.
That was some time after we'd thrown out the students, when they weren't working anymore. They were just standing around in the corridors, having rowdy discussions and holding rallies. So I gathered all the Bauhaus masters for a meeting and asked them, 'Do you think this is a normal state of affairs for a school? Are you pleased with your people? I want to hear a yes or a no.' They were hesitant to say anything, so I insisted: 'Yes or no, I'm not interested in any other answers.' Then I went from person to person individually, repeating the question. In the end, the consensus was, no, they were not pleased. They said, 'Of course, this is no longer a school. It is all nonsense. We cannot teach if we are inside and they are standing around outside in the corridors,' and so on. Then I said, 'This is all happening because no one has a clear idea of what the rights and duties of the students are, of what the rights and duties of the teachers are. We need to make that clear.'

I can't remember if I asked for the faculty's blessing in advance, but I called up the mayor and told him we were closing the Bauhaus for a couple of weeks to give the school a clear constitution. Then I did just that. Gropius and the mayor had asked me to take over the school, saying that the Dessau city administration trusted me and no one else. I don't know whether or not that was true. But I went there to restore order, to clean up the school.

How had it become so chaotic in the first place?
Hannes Meyer had wanted to turn the Bauhaus into a political, communist school. I had no interest in that at all. I am no world-improver. I have never claimed to be nor wanted to be such a person. I am an architect.

My interest is in building and in design in general. After all, building can be understood in broad terms. Making a good poster is ultimately no different from doing architecture. When I closed the Bauhaus, even Heinrich Simon, a good acquaintance of mine through Lilly Reich, from the *Frankfurter Zeitung*, described it as a 'cultural revolution at the Bauhaus'.
What did he mean by that?
He meant it literally.
Against the old Bauhaus? Against Hannes Meyer's Bauhaus?
Yes. Though I'd call it more a cultural reaction than a revolution.
And then you gave the Bauhaus a constitution?
The teachers and I drafted a constitution together, and the government approved it. The government had the final say, even though it was the city that funded the Bauhaus.
Who were the masters, the main teachers, when you arrived there?
I am sure Albers and Kandinsky were still there. Klee was on holiday.
Was Itten there?
He had been gone for a while. He left during the early years of the school.
Was Hilberseimer there?
Hilbs was there, yes.
Was he new?
He'd been appointed by Hannes Meyer, I think. In fact I'm almost certain.
And Peterhans?
Peterhans was also there.
So they were there before you.
Yes. And Klee was on holiday. And I believe Feininger had simply resigned. There was still *[Joost]* Schmidt, *[Josef]* Albers, and *[Hinnerk]* Scheper, who later gave classes in colour theory.
I know his son. He's in Berlin now. In the early years of the Bauhaus, when you were still in Berlin, you had a somewhat hostile stance towards the school. That's how it comes across in the magazine G.

Yes.
Hilbs was too, was he not? So why did he choose to join the school?
Well, he wanted to build cities, and if you are offered a position as city planner, you take it. Regarding our position towards the Bauhaus ... We were against a particular direction that Gropius was taking. The Bauhaus celebrated its fourth anniversary in 1923, when the school was still located in Weimar. The main celebration was moved to Jena, where Gropius had either built or rebuilt – I think rebuilt – a theatre, in collaboration with Adolf Meyer. We were quite disappointed when we saw the building. We all thought, 'That's a bit strange. It's all so decorative, like the Viennese workshops.' In particular, it reminded us of Gropius' desk, which had a meandering ribbon at each end – not inlaid but built out of solid wood. It wasn't a decoration – the whole thing was a decoration. Then he added some lighting elements with a couple of wires, light tubes, and so on. Looking at the theatre building, we realised that everything could go in the wrong direction again if we didn't pay attention. So we launched the magazine G. The 'G' stands for 'Gestaltung'. We wanted to emphasise that word. Our architectural culture allows you to do everything, but 'Gestaltung' is in fact something very particular. It is not frippery, nor decorative design. You can see the same difference when you compare the Pan Am Building in New York with our own works, which are carefully constructed into coherent structures. Though, funnily enough, I have never seen the Pan Am Building with my own eyes. It's been that long since I've been in New York.
Around 10 years ...
The *Frankfurter Zeitung* was against the Bauhaus. In fact many people were against it. After I became the director of the school, we thought that as soon as we had a clear constitution set in stone, the communists would stay away. What happened in reality though, is that all the champagne communists kept

their distance, but the true communists remained. They came and signed the agreement.

You had every student sign an agreement, so you would have some kind of leverage to keep order.

Yes, so that I could tell them: you agreed to the constitution yourself. It wasn't as if I was behaving like a dictator. I just wanted to keep the place in order, which wasn't possible without having rules laid down. I'll continue to read from the article.

'During the lull a number of the ringleaders of the revolt were expelled, and when the school reopened, things had quietened down.'

That is also not true, really. They were not expelled – they just didn't sign up, as you say, so they left, of their own volition. I didn't consider anyone in particular a ringleader. But he would know better. He'd known them for two years.

'Mies deemed it advisable, nevertheless, as a precautionary measure, to interview each and every student, individually, in his private office.'

I don't know about that. Maybe I wanted to speak to the students, but not to grill them or anything like that. No, I calmly assumed, as a matter of fact, that if they signed the agreement, they would respect the constitution and otherwise stay away. But they did not want to give up the school.

Dearstyne writes here:

'When my turn came I was at a loss for something to say to the director for he himself failed to open the conversation. So I ventured to raise a question which was close to my heart, asking, "Is it no longer right to seek beauty in architecture?" He quickly assured me that it was right. The very fact that I asked the questions shows how completely ignorant I was at the time of Mies' nature and aims. I was to find, indeed, that the attainment of beauty in architecture had been his own lifelong goal and that he would soon launch his students in quest of it.

By the time Mies arrived in Dessau, I had completed the studies which were prerequisite to entry into the architecture department, so I became one of his students. This was the first architecture class which Mies taught at the Bauhaus and, in fact, the first teaching he had done anywhere. There were only a half dozen people in the group, and some of these, Eduard Ludwig, Hermann Blomeier, and Willi Heyerhoff, became my particular friends. Mies started us off with a simple problem, the design of a single-bedroom 'court house', a house. That is, facing a walled garden. The plans we did for this house were all pretty much alike, varying only in details. Mr [Hans] Wingler has published Ludwig's version in his book on the Bauhaus and Philip Johnson based the design of his house in Cambridge, Massachusetts on a solution of this project made at the school. Mies was so concerned with the uprooting of misconceptions and setting us on the right track that he sometimes, unintentionally, injured the sensitivities of his students. Those inseparable friends, Blomeier and Heyerhoff, for example, had been prize students at Paul Klopfer's architecture school in Holzminden. On one occasion, early in the term, they showed Mies prints of building plans made by them there, confident that he would praise them. I was standing by and winced when Mies rode roughshod over them, marking them up with a black pencil to indicate how they should have been done. Hermann and Willi were so hurt by Mies' ruthlessness that they remained away from class for a month. Nursing their wounds ... But we all had to get used to having our fondest schemes rejected. Time after time when I had made sketch plans which seemed good to me, Mies would examine them and say laconically, "try it again," and I had the good sense not to argue with him. Little by little we began to understand.

Mies himself was mostly doing houses at that time, and he kept up planning houses, one after another. He used to remark that if you could design a house well, you could design anything. I have become so firmly convinced of the truth of this that I repeat it to my students today to impress upon their minds the importance of mastering the simpler problems.

After making many sketches (Mies said that one should do at least 100), I finally came up with a house plan which he liked. The house was a one-storey court house with an elongated living-dining room and a single bedroom which communicated with it. Two external sides of the house were continuous with the walls of the court, while the living room and bedroom had floor-to-ceiling glass facing the garden. A porch roof supported by free-standing columns connected the house with the court wall opposite. I shall never forget the trouble we had smoothing out the rough spots. At one point we were about to abandon the scheme because we could find no place in the kitchen for the garbage pail! The entrance also posed a difficult problem. In my original plan the connection of the foyer with the living room was too abrupt. After sketching over my layout for hours, Mies finally hit upon a solution which provided an indirect transition from the foyer to the living room and, at the same time, an indirect route from the kitchen to the dining area. This kind of circuitous passage from one space to another is a continuing characteristic of Mies' work.

I kept my folks in the United States informed about my studies at the Bauhaus, and, fortunately, my mother saved every scrap of mail I sent her. In a letter written on 20 December 1931, I spoke as follows of the work with Mies: "I'm using the few days until Christmas to put the finishing touches on the house design I've been working on since I arrived [from a trip to the United States]. The house is a small one with a living room, one bedroom, and the necessary utility rooms such as bathroom, kitchen, etc. The house is of the same character as the two I had with me in America. Mies van der Rohe continues to hold us to the small problems. But that he is right in doing this is indicated by the fact that it takes weeks or months to do a small house of this nature in a decent way. The very simplicity of these houses is their chief difficulty. It's much easier to do a complicated affair than something clear and simple.

We're learning a tremendous lot from Mies van der Rohe. If he doesn't make good architects of us, he'll at least teach us to judge what good architecture is. One of the uncomfortable sides of associating with an architect of the first rank is that he ruins your taste for about all but one-half of one percent of all the architecture that's being done the world over. Mies van der Rohe not only comes down hard on the American architects (for which he has, without the shadow of a doubt, the most perfect justification) but holds that one doesn't need the fingers of one hand to count the German architects who are doing good work. He sets a very high standard, which is a fact that should only cause us to rejoice. It's much easier to work under less critical men and content yourself with middle-rate work. That's what I was doing at Columbia and what most of the students in America (and here) are doing. But I thank my stars that I landed where I did."

Mies had taken one of the master houses and he spent three days each week in Dessau. He and Ludwig Hilberseimer, who taught city planning at the Bauhaus, had worked out an arrangement whereby they commuted between Berlin and Dessau alternately, so that one of them was in the capital while the other was at the Bauhaus. We saw much of Mies during his weekly sojourn in Dessau and I often think how privileged we were to have this close association with him. Our students in the department of architecture of the Illinois Institute of Technology, who revere him as their great master, are lucky today if they lay eyes on him once during their entire five-year course.

When the final semester arrived, our class was reduced to four people. I know that Eduard Ludwig and Edgar Hecht were two of these, and I am fairly certain that Hubert Dollner was the fourth man who, with me, completed the quartet. We moved to a private ground-floor studio, which was kept locked and to which we each had a key. Here we worked on our "diploma problems" (Diplomarbeiten). I chose to do a bathing pavilion for the Kühnauer Lake on the outskirts of Dessau, and Mies walked out with me to see the site. In this last semester we had enviable opportunities to talk with Mies, isolated from the rest of the school in our private room. We had him to ourselves for hours at a time. I wrote to my folks at home about this on 12 June 1932: "We saw a lot of Mies van der Rohe last week. He came on three different days to our atelier. Wednesday, he spent over three hours with us and ordered coffee for us from the canteen. Thursday, he came for about an hour. Friday, he came twice and spent about five hours with us, all told. We had coffee again. We (our semester, four people) have gotten well acquainted with him, and he seems to enjoy talking with us more than with the lower semesters. We discuss everything, architecture, art, philosophy, politics, etc. These discussions don't, therefore, always have a direct bearing upon our work but are tremendously interesting and valuable because Mies van der Rohe is a man of profundity and richness of experience. It would be worth my while being here just for these discussions if I did no designing whatever. My hope is that the Bauhaus doesn't break up and that I can return (from a planned trip to America)."

All four of us, as I recall, received our Bauhaus diplomas in July 1932, although Hecht almost failed to make it, chiefly because he put such atrocious-looking trees in a rendering of his project. We got in just under the wire, for political coercion, which for years had hung over our heads like a Damocles sword, was finally brought to bear upon the Bauhaus. The Nazis, who had persistently sworn to close the school and, for that matter, to raze the building, at last gained control of the Dessau legislature. Fully intending to do away with the hated Bauhaus, they nevertheless saw fit to give their contemplated action the appearance of legality by arranging a trial bearing the semblance of justice. They required the director to make an exhibition of Bauhaus work and appointed as judge Paul Schultze-Naumburg, an ultra-conservative architect, who despised the Bauhaus and who, in turn, was despised by it. So Mies assembled the best of the student work for the fruitless exhibit. We were all intent upon putting our best foot forward, so I asked Hinnerk Scheper, our colour teacher at the Bauhaus, to make a rendering of my bathing pavilion for the exhibition. He cheerfully complied, and I am happy today still to possess this memento of that talented and modest man. Before the inevitable blow fell, I left for a vacation in the United States. When I returned to Dessau in October 1932, the Bauhaus was closed and Mies and most of the instructors and students had departed for Berlin, where Mies established a new Bauhaus on a private basis. I gave up my apartment in Dessau and followed them.'

Did Kandinsky also go to Berlin?
Yes.
And Albers also?
I'm not sure. Albers was the first to leave for America. He had received an offer from Black Mountain College through Philip Johnson.
Was Philip Johnson also a Bauhaus student?
No, he was just a visitor.
Was he there for a while? Like a couple of months or so?
No. But he came often.
What else did he do? Was he just travelling around?
He was the director of the architecture department at the Museum of Modern Art. After he learned about the New Architecture, he wanted to become an architect himself and went to Harvard, where Gropius had been teaching since 1937. He studied with Gropius and soon built his own house – a court house – from wood, though it wasn't very good. It's not something you can simply do if you don't understand anything about it.
How many Bauhaus students were there in Berlin? Were the other classes also being offered?
Yes, of course, all of it.
Then there must have been around 200 students ...
Oh no, even in Dessau there were only 100.

I find that astonishing. So it was never a large school. And you financed it privately? Who paid the instructors?
The city.
You mean Berlin?
Yes, we still received a salary from the city.
Did they continue to pay when the school moved to Berlin?
Yes. Not to the school, but to each instructor individually. We had contracts with the city. But the Nazis had that vague paragraph stating that anyone who was politically untrustworthy would lose their contractual rights. Then the payments stopped coming.
We know the story about how the Bauhaus was closed. You've told the story yourself before. But you still had files from the Bauhaus, which were in that box with Ludwig. What kinds of files were they?
From the Bauhaus in Berlin.
Including information about who was there, and the correspondence? ...
But surely also the official papers, the founding documents and ...
Those disappeared before the Nazis came.
What do you mean?
They simply weren't there. I never saw them. I'm sure they must have been taken somewhere safe.
By whom?
By the mayor perhaps. I don't know anymore.
Were any of the students Nazis?
As the communists grew in numbers, Nazis came as well. But not from outside. Only from amongst the students. There weren't many.
Did they also, in a sense, play the role of Nazi collaborators?
I believe there was little of that, if any.
I mean, did they spy on anyone, or pass on information to the party?
I couldn't tell you. I never had any suspicions.
I met with [Richard] Neutra some time ago in Los Angeles. He was acting very strange. He was telling me that he was the one who'd convinced Edith Farnsworth to build the house. Does he even know her?
I don't believe so.
He spoke as if he'd had a hand in designing the house. As if everything you achieved could ultimately be traced back to him. That's the impression he gave.
Is he ill?
I believe so, yes. People were also talking about it – Craig Ellwood and the others – that he was under some kind of delusion. But he established a foundation. He told me he was the last person to ever speak to Gropius. They didn't want to let him in, but he fought his way through and spoke to Gropius before he died. And then he wrote a letter to the Architectural Forum, saying he was the one who had brought Gropius to America and that if they wanted to do an obituary on Gropius, he should be the one to write it. I found it strange.

122 [Eulogy for Walter Gropius]

Published eulogy (16 July 1969; Gropius died on 5 July 1969).
Source: LoC, Box 62, reGropius; LMvdR, 'Walter Gropius', *Deutsche Bauzeitung*, vol. CIII, no. 12, August 1969, p. 597.
Republished in Neumeyer 1991, p. 337; Pizzigoni 2010, p. 303; Walter 2022, pp. 347–348.

It was a kindness of fortune that allowed Walter Gropius, so near the end of his life, to be present in Stuttgart at the opening of the 50th-anniversary exhibition of the Bauhaus – the school he founded and which embodied one of the most vital ideas for education in our epoch.

As I look back over the 60 years I have known him as one of the leading architects of our time and the greatest educator in his field, I am struck by his generosity of spirit.

The divisive forces in this century have been powerful: disorder, competitiveness, specialisation, materialism. This condition never discouraged Gropius from seeking unity in diversity. It never undermined his conviction that people could work more fruitfully in collaboration than in competition. It never shook his courage in pursuing a course of coordinating and integrating the efforts of many. He had the rare talent for bringing people together.

As I said of him years ago, he was always a gallant fighter in the never-ending battle for new ideas. His participation in this battle endured to the end of a long and productive life.

These are, in my opinion, Gropius' noblest legacies to all of us.

INDEX

Note: A page number in italics indicates a figure.

Aachen Industrial School speech, 237
Academy of Weimar, 136
Achilles, Rolf, 11
acoustics, 81
Adam Department Store, 25, 84, 209
AEG Turbine Factory (Berlin), 204, 228, 260, 275
Albers, Josef, 135, 136, 289, 292
Alegria, Ricardo, 175
Alexanderplatz project, 209
Alfonso XIII (king of Spain), 173
Altes Museum (Berlin), 150, 197, 286
American Institute of Architecture (AIA), 201
aqueducts, 20, 80, 203, 267, 278
Arbeitsrat für Kunst, 207
architects
- European, 101–103
- training of, 125, 127–130
- see also individual architects by name
Architectural Association, 187
architectural competitions, 23, 25, 85, 100, 101, 102, 115, 170, 207, 213, 218, 229, 261, 266, 294
Architectural Forum, 192
Architectural League (New York), 164–172
architecture
- anti-Classical, 223
- Art Nouveau (Jugendstil), 150, 164, 181, 188, 197, 242, 243, 270
- Arts and Crafts, 223, 260
- Baroque, 126, 162, 167, 175, 178, 202, 245, 247, 251, 269, 280
- Beaux Arts, 102, 213, 238, 253, 264
- Chicago school, 21, 206, 267, 275
- Classical, 19–20, 111, 188, 223, 260
- Constructivist, 232
- future of, 139–142, 245–251
- Gothic, 20, 62, 69, 109, 110, 122, 126, 128, 133, 146, 147, 161, 168, 194, 202–203, 204, 228, 247, 260, 267, 286
- International Style, 189
- Japanese, 192
- Neoclassical, 150, 197, 260
- Neogothic, 277
- Renaissance, 22, 101, 164, 168, 175, 176, 202, 222, 228, 259, 269
- Romanesque, 62, 64, 110, 122, 127, 128, 203, 247, 267
- Romantic, 57, 61, 109, 223
- 'skin and bones,' 54, 256, 275
- and technology, 124
- Tudor, 277, 286
Armour Institute of Technology, 9, 17, 109, 212–213, 240, 241, 267, 273
- curriculum, 106–108
- inaugural address, 104–105
- see also Illinois Institute of Technology (IIT)
Arp, Hans, 261
Art Institute of Chicago, *47*
Art Nouveau (Jugendstil), 150, 164, 181, 188, 197, 242, 243, 270
Arts and Crafts, 223, 260
Association of German Architects, 100
Association of German Architects and Engineers, 100
Augustine (saint), 18, 114, 146, 151, 194, 199
Ausstellung für unbekannte Architekten (Exhibition for Unknown Architects), 15
Athens, 20; *see also* Greek culture

Bacardi Building (Cuba), 149, 196, 219–220, 251
Bacardi Building (Mexico City), 220, 251
Bacon, Francis, 79
Baeza, Arturo, 174, 176–180
Barcelona Pavilion. *See* German Pavilion (Barcelona)
Baroque style, 126, 162, 167, 175, 178, 202, 245, 247, 251, 269, 280
Bartning, Otto, 77
Battery Park City Apartment Buildings (New York), 178, 220
Bau und Wohnung, 74
Baudelaire, Charles, 18
Bauhaus, 15, 17, 21, 91, 102, 171, 213, 232–233, 236, 240, 246–247, 268, 286, 288
- 50th anniversary exhibition, 294
- beginning of, 137
- Dearstyne's account of studying at, 290–292
- dissolution of, 99, 133–136, 233–234, 262–263, 288, 293
- future of, 97–98
- syllabus and curriculum, 94–97
Weimar exhibition, 229
Baukunst, 158, 165, 171, 238, 247–248, 253
BDA ehrt Mies van der Rohe in Berlin (1966 film), 10, 26, *43*
beauty, 86–87, 90, 105
Beaux Arts, 102, 213, 238, 253, 264
Behrendt, Walter Curt, 55, 77
Behrens, Peter, 15, 20, 77, 101, 111, 136, 139, 152, 164, 170, 182, 201, 204, 205, 206, 224, 228, 230, 231, 236, 245, 260, 261, 275, 285, 186, 187
Beton, Stahl und Glas (film), 11
Berlage, Hendrik Petrus, 21, 111, 139, 164, 182, 201, 205, 223, 228, 239
Berlin Building Exposition, 102
- Hall II, 89
Berlin Stadium, 80

Bismarck Memorial Competition, 25, 101
Blake, Peter, 221–236
Blessing, Hedrich, 10, *36–39*
Blomeier, Hermann, 290
Boswau & Knauer, 284
Brandenburger Tor, 260, 288
Braque, Georges, 232
Brick Country House, 21, 188, 208
bridges, 57, 61
- George Washington, 139, 152, 242, 256
- Hudson, 80
- Maillart, 249
- suspension, 20, 267
Bronfman, Samuel, 23, 171, 219
Bruhn, Ada, 15
building materials, 55–56, 58, 64, 75
- aluminum, 170, 178, 218, 219, 248
- brick, 104, 107, 136, 156, 167, 189, 190, 231, 266, 282, 284
- bronze, 159, 169, 170, 171, 176, 219, 248, 250
- cement (sprayed), 287
- concrete (ferroconcrete), 59–60, 80, 98, 104–107, 136, 166, 170, 174, 179, 192, 220, 248, 249
- glass, 98, 101, 112, 118–119, 126, 132, 136, 144, 145, 154, 159, 162, 167, 169, 170, 171, 173, 176, 178, 185, 207, 210–211, 221, 224, 229, 241, 248, 257, 258, 261, 266
- marble, 141, 159, 176, 179, 187, 277
- onyx, 22, 141, 210, 256, 258
- plaster, 189
- plastic, 174
- Rudeglass, 59
- steel, 98, 105, 106, 126, 136, 141, 144, 145, 169, 170–171, 185, 189, 190, 216, 220, 241, 249, 257, 258
- stone, 104, 106, 107, 159
- stucco, 22, 176, 228, 239, 259, 260, 283, 284
- teak, 141
- travertine, 112, 148, 159, 190
- wood, 106, 107, 260, 284, 285, 286, 287, 289, 292
building-art movement, 61–62, 73, 78–82, 83
buildings
- apartment, 53–54, 55, 75, 126, 130–131, 184, 185, 208, 217–218, 220, 224, 239, 241, 248
- concrete (ferroconcrete), 66
- nature of, 62–67
- office buildings, 51–52, 59–60, 153, 209, 219–220
- residential, 52–53, 59, 60, 66, 76, 102, 116, 126, 147, 188
- *see also* skyscrapers
Bund Deutscher Architekten, 10
Burleigh, Thomas, *47*
Burzi, E, *46*

296

Cadbury-Brown, HT, 187–193
Cantor drive-in restaurant, 218
cathedrals, 16, 57, 61–62, 65, 110, 127, 146, 147, 161, 169, 226, 238, 248, 256, 267, 275
- Aachen, 245
- Amiens, 204
- Cologne, 203, 204, 281
- St Peter's, 80, 203
- *see also* churches
Chang, Pao-Chi, 11
Chicago, 199
- convention hall, 149, 218–219, 249, 252, 266
- federal court building, 149, 196, 250
- Chicago school, 21, 206, 267, 275
churches, 65, 123, 146, 153, 194, 203, 214, 226–227
- *see also* cathedrals

City Hall (Rixdorf/Neukölln), 260
city planning, 114, 116, 149, 160, 196–197, 249–250, 268, 269, 291
civilisation, 155–157, 200, 220–221, 224, 234, 251, 252–253, 264
Classical style, 19–20, 111, 188, 223, 260
clear construction, 160–161, 167, 169, 194–197, 244, 258
Cobo, Albert, 151
Cocteau, Jean, 129
Cologne Cathedral, 204
colour
- in architecture, 141, 159, 160, 162, 171, 176, 189, 190, 193, 195, 267
- of glass, 84, 112, 138, 154, 159, 208, 210
- of marble, 86
- theory of, 96, 289
Columbus Haus (Berlin), 101
Concrete House, 24
Constructivists, 232
Continental-Caoutchouc und Gutta-Percha Compagnie offices (Hannover), 224
Crown, SR, 143
- see also SR Crown Hall
Cullinan, Nina, 163
Cullinan Hall (Houston), 192
curtain wall, 121, 170, 175, 176

Danforth, George, 10, 26, 202–220, 237–238
De Stijl movement, 15, 20–21, 232
Dearstyne, Howard, *46*, 288, 290–292
Dechêne, Lisa, 276–278
Deutscher Werkbund, 70, 76, 102, 231, 247
- see also *Werkbund* exhibition
Deutsche Werkstätten Hellerau, 285
Die Form, 16, 68, 70–72
Die neue Wohnung (film), 26
Die Wohnung exhibition, 74
Die Zukunft, 18, 245
Döcker, Richard, 77, 261

Dollner, Hubert, 291
Dominion Center (Toronto), 250
Duns Scotus, 79
Duquesne University, Mellon Hall of Science, 250

Eckhart von Hochheim (Meister Eckhart), 160
École des Beaux Arts. *See* Beaux Arts
Elisenbrunnen, 277
Ellwood, Craig, 293
Empire style, 239
Esters House (Krefeld), 261
exhibitions, 82–83, 88–89
- *Ausstellung für unbekannte Architekten* (Exhibition for Unknown Architects), 15
- Bauhaus (Weimar), 229
- Bauhaus 50th anniversary, 294
- *Die Wohnung*, 74
- of Frank Lloyd Wright, 112, 206
- *Grosse Berliner Kunstaustellung*, 15, 188, 189
- *Internationale Architektur*, 15
- *Les architects du groupe De Stijl*, 15
- *Mies van der Rohe: Architect as Educator*, 11
- MoMA (1947), 30, 267
- in Munich, 285
- *Neue Amerikanische Architektur*, 21, 68
- for the Novembergruppe, 207–208, 230
- in Stuttgart, 188
- *Werkbund* exhibition, 68, 76, 93–94, 136, 208, 231, 247
- *Exposition Universelle* (Paris), 260

Fagus Factory, 136
Fallingwater, 24
Farnsworth, Edith, 277, 293
Farnsworth House, 23, 141, 148, 162, 169, 190, 195, 218, 263, 277, 293
Feininger, Lyonel, 137, 289
flat roofs, 73, 77–78, 174, 233
form-giving, 57–60
Frankfurter Zeitung, 289
Friedrichstrasse railway station (Berlin), 25, 118
Friedrichstrasse skyscraper, 207
Fuchs, Eduard, 21, 230–231
Fujikawa, Joseph, 199
furniture design, 102, 130, 179, 188, 204, 209, 248, 282–283

G (magazine), 229, 287
Garretón, Jaime, 175–176, 179
Geininger, Lyonel, 137
German Building Exhibition. See *Grosse Berliner Kunstaustellung*
German Embassy (St Petersburg), 228, 260
German Pavilion (Barcelona), 21, 86, 102, 129, 141, 145, 166, 173, 179, 187, 209–210, 223, 224, 231, 258–259, 262, 263, 265–266

Germanic villages, 64–65
Glass House, 277
Glass Room (Stuttgart), 208
Godoy, Ivan, 179–180
Goethe, Johann Wolfgang von, 266
Goldsmith, Myron, *40–41*
Goodhue, Bertram, 101
Göring, Hermann, 135, 234, 263
Gothic style, 20, 62, 69, 109, 110, 122, 126, 128, 133, 146, 147, 161, 168, 194, 202–203, 204, 228, 247, 260, 267, 286
Graham, Bruce, 175, 179
Gravensteen Castle (Ghent), 20, 54
Greek culture, 20, 140, 238
Acropolis, 256
Parthenon, 20
Temple of Poseidon, 20
Greenwald, Herbert, 23, 178, 199, 217, 229
- eulogy for, 172–173
Greenwald, Lilian, 172
Gropius, Walter, 15, 21, 23, 77, 102, 133, 136–137, 189, 208, 213, 227, 229, 231, 232, 233, 240, 242, 246–247, 260, 261, 277, 279, 286, 287, 288, 289, 292, 293
- eulogy for, 294
Grosse Berliner Kunstaustellung (exhibition), 15, 188, 189
Guggenheim Museum, 167, 224

H House (Magdeburg), 103
Haesler, Otto, 77
Haid, David, 163
Häring, Hugo, 19, 59, 77, 258
Harkness, John C., 117
Harrington, Kevin, 11
Harris, Cynthia, 153
Harvard University, 137, 276, 279, 292
Haus Behrens, 204
Haus der Deutschen Kunst, 135
Haussmann, Georges Eugène, 67
Headquarters Administration Building (Friedrich Krupp; Essen), 241
Heald, Henry, 120, 190, 212, 215, 223, 241, 273
Hecht, Edgar, 291
Hegemann, Werner, 21
Hesse, Fritz, 133, 232
Heyerhoff, Willi, 290
Hilberseimer, Ludwig Karl, *40–41*, 77, 20, 21, 80, 114, 134, 135, 208, 212, 219, 238, 263, 268, 289, 291
historical architecture and engineering
- aqueducts, 20, 80, 203, 267, 278
- Acropolis, 256
- basilicas, 20, 62, 203, 238
- Ghent (Gravensteen Castle), 20, 54
- Greek, 20, 140, 238
- Palatine Chapel, 202
- Parthenon, 20

297

- Pitti Palace, 20, 139, 203, 207, 267
- Pont du Gard, 203
- Roman, 80, 203
- St Peters Cathedral, 80, 203
- see also bridges; cathedrals; churches

Hitchcock, Henry-Russell, 189, 276–277
Hitler, Adolf, 135, 240
Holabird, John, 211, 212, 273
Holsman, Holsman, Klekamp & Taylor, 130
hospital design, 115–117
Hudson Bridge, 80

Illinois Institute of Technology (IIT), 9, 11, 21, 24, 141, 235, 237–238, 253, 264, 267, 268, 273, 277, 291
- Alumni Memorial Hall, 10, 216
- Bailey Hall, 192
- campus design, 119–122, 131, 186, 190–192, 215, 216–217, 223, 250, 263, 273
- Carman Hall, 192
- chapel, 20, 133, 191
- Commons Building, 24, 132
- Cullinan Hall, 163
- Cunningham Hall, 192
- Department of Architecture, 143, 161
- dormitories, 192
- Institute of Design, 143, 161
- Library and Administration Building, 118, 216
- Mineral and Metals Research Building, 21, 232, 250
- School of Architecture, 26, 191
- SR Crown Hall, 9, *35*, 143–145, 161, 191, 194, 216, 218, 220, 259, 263, 266, 273–274
- symmetry, 161
- television series about Mies, 157–159
- Visual Training course, 268–269
- see also Armour Institute of Technology

Ingraham, Elizabeth Wright, 274
International Congress of Modern Architecture (CIAM), 137
International Style, 189
Internationale Architektur, 15
interviews, 25
- on the Barcelona Pavilion, 86
- in *Baukunst und Werkform*, 160–162
- Bayerischer Rundfunk, 271–272
- with the BBC, 145–150, 186
- with Peter Blake, 221–236
- with Mervin Block, 198–200
- on campus design, 120–122
- *Chicago Daily News*, 273–274, 275–276
- in *Christian Science Monitor*, 255–256
- in *Construction Record*, 160
- with George Danforth, 202–220
- in *Deutsche Volkszeitung*, 276–278
- in *Die Welt*, 264–265
- on the end of the Bauhaus, 133–136
- excerpts and paraphrasing, 252–255
- on the future of architecture (part I), 139–142

- on the future of architecture (part II), 245–251
- on hospital design, 115–117
- in *Interbuild*, 183–187
- with Philip Johnson, 30
- on Lake Shore Drive Buildings, 130–131
- with Le Corbusier and Stam, 68–70
- in *The Listener*, 194–197
- with Dirk Lohan, 10–11, 279–293
- at the New York Architectural League, 164–172
- for *Pencil Points*, 20, 101–103
- with John Peter, 10
- for *Rundfunk im amerikanischen Sektor* (RIAS), 257–263
- in *Saturday Review of Literature*, 265–268
- in *Show: The Magazine of the Arts*, 237–241
- with students, 127–130, 157–159, 174–180
- with Georgia van der Rohe, 11
- 'What Should a Church Look Like?', 123

Jäger, Werner, 288
Jahrhunderthalle (Breslau), 80
Jarzombek, Mark, 30
Jefferson, Thomas, 267
Jenney, William Le Baron, 206
Johnson, Philip, 25, 30, 118–119, 129, 164, 170, 224, 256, 276, 290, 292
Jugendstil movement, 150, 242, 243, 270
- see also Art Nouveau (Jugendstil)

Kahn, Louis, 226
Kandinsky, Wassily, 133, 135, 137, 234, 240, 263, 292
Kant-Laplace-Theorie, 155–156, 214, 245
Kauffmann family, 24
Klee, Paul, 91, 137, 162, 198, 232, 239, 276, 289
Klopfer, Paul, 290
Knobelsdorff, Hans Georg Wenzeslaus von, 236
Koch, Pitt, 271
Kolbe, Georg, 190, 210, 231–232
Korn, Arthur, 77
Krayl, Carl, 77
Kröller-Müller house-museum, 15, 17, 25, 164, 188, 205–206, 223, 228, 260–261
Krupp, Friedrich, 241, 250
Krupp office building (Essen), 250
Kunstgewerbemuseum, 286

Lafayette Park (Detroit), 151, 219
Lafayette Plaisance project, 184
Lake Shore Drive apartment buildings, 24, 130–131, 147, 179, 184, 192–193, 195, 217–218, 221–222, 224, 239, 241, 248, 264, 266
Lambert, Phyllis, 154, 219

landscaping, 92, 143, 169
Lange, Hermann, 189
Lange House (Krefeld), 189, 261
Langhans, Carl Gotthard, 260
Laplace, Pierre-Simon, 18, 245
Laplace Theory. *See* Kant-Laplace-Theorie
Larkin Administration Building (Buffalo, NY), 224
Le Corbusier, 9, 66, 67, 68–70, 80, 101, 137, 167, 189, 198, 208, 222, 225, 226, 227, 231, 260, 261, 264, 267, 274, 277, 287
- eulogy for, 269
- lectures, 57–60, 62–67, 73, 78–82, 106, 107, 109–111
Lehmbruck, Wilhelm, 189, 206, 231, 232
Les architects du groupe De Stijl (exhibition), 15
letters
- describing the Adam Department Store, 84
- on the end of the Bauhaus, 99
- on the roof question, 77–78
Lever House, 168, 176, 250
Liebermann, Max, 230–231
Liebknecht, Karl, 22–23, 230, 276, 278
Lindner, Werner, 21
Lohan, Dirk, 9, *33, 34, 45*, 279–293
Loos, Adolf, 201
Louis V style, 239
Louis XIV style, 176, 228, 239, 259
Luckhardt, Hans, 77
Luckhardt, Wassily, 77
Ludwig, Eduard, 290, 291
Luther, Martin, 200, 254
Lutyens, Edwin, 182
Luxemburg, Rosa, 22–23, 230, 231, 276, 278

Mackintosh, Charles Rennie, 182
Maillart, Robert, 249
Maillart bridges, 249
Mannheim theatre, 24, 161–162
Márquez, Jaime, 175, 178–179
May, Ernst, 77
McConoughey, Connie, 199
McCormick, Robert, 195
McCormick House, 195
McKin, Mead, and White, 250
Meier Gräfe, Julius, 206
Mendelsohn, Erich, 77, 101, 102
Mendelssohn & Co., 230
Messel, Alfred, 182, 245, 286, 288
metropolis, 66, 149, 196–197
Meyer, Adolf, 77, 289
Meyer, Hans Emil 'Hannes', 81, 102, 213, 232, 246, 288–289
Michelangelo, 203
Mies van der Rohe
- in Chicago, 18, 21
- education of, 12, 17, 18, 227, 237, 239, 280
- as educator, 10, 11, 21, 127–130, 177, 232–233, 253–254, 264–267, 291–292

298

- in Germany, 15–18
- letters, 68, 70–72
- library of, 18, 156, 168–169, 214, 245, 246
- in the military, 284–285
- photos of, 9–10, 12, *33–47*
- see also Bauhaus
- *Mies van der Rohe* (1986 film), 11
- 'Mies van der Rohe: A Special Kind of Order' (television series), 157–159
- 'Mies van der Rohe: An Architect of our Time' (Bavarian Radio), 271–272
- *Mies van der Rohe: Architect as Educator* (exhibition and catalogue), 11
- Mies van der Rohe Centennial Project, 11
- 'Mies van der Rohe' (WTTW Heritage Program), 10, 26, *42, 43*
Milton, Henry, 18
mixed development concept, 184
Mondrian, Piet, 21, 232, 276
Moraleda, Lautaro, 175
Morris, William, 111, 223
Moses, Robert, 165
Mumford, Lewis, 68, 277
Munch, Edvard, 276
Munich Cultural Award, 243–244
museum for a small city, 113
Museum of Modern Art, 30, 147, 195, 212, 219, 267, 276, 292
Myhrum, Charlotte, 11

Naeff, Paul, *46*
National Institute of Arts and Letters, Gold Medal in Architecture, 242–243
National Theatre building (Mannheim), 138, 218
Nazi movement, 133, 233
Neoclassical style, 150, 197, 260
Neogothic style, 277
Nervi, Pier Luigi, 174, 186
Neue Amerikanische Architektur (exhibition), 21, 68
Neue Nationalgalerie (Berlin), 20, 257
Neue Wache, 288
Neuhaus, Hugo, 163
Neumann, Dietrich, 11, 276
Neumeyer, Fritz, 11, 29–30
Neutra, Richard, 293
New York Architectural League, 164–172
Nierendorf, Karl, 276
Norberg-Schulz, Christian, 12
Novembergruppe, 15, 207–208, 230, 276, 278

office organisation, 153
Olbrich, Joseph Maria, 182, 201, 285
Order of Merit, 181
Orlik, Emil, 260
Oud, Jacobus JP, 189, 208, 231

Palace of the League of Nations, 81
Palatine Chapel, 202
Palazzo Pitti, 20, 139, 203, 207, 267
Palladio, Andrea, 141, 243, 245, 260, 270, 286–287
Pan Am Building, 289
Pankok, Bernhard, 77
Paris, France, 67
Paul, Bruno, 101, 204, 228, 236, 260, 285–286, 287
Pechstein, Max, 230
Perls, Hugo, 230
Perls, Klaus, 230
Perls House (Berlin), 230
Peter, John, 10
Peterhans, Walter, 135, 212, 268–269, 279, 289
Peterson, Harry N, 272
photomontage, 25
Picasso, Pablo, 232
Planetarium (Jena), 80
Plato, 79
Poelzig, Hans, 77, 208, 261
prefabrication, 137, 148, 175, 183–184, 196, 217
Promontory Apartment Building, 185, 217
proportion, 178–179, 238, 269
Propp, Adolf, 286, 287
Puente, Moisés, 30

Racquet and Tennis Club (New York), 250
Rading, Adolf, 77
Rathenau, Walther, 288
Reich, Lilly, 102, 135, 208–209, 240, 289
Reinhardt and Süßenguth, 284
Renaissance art/style, 175, 176, 202, 222, 228
Resor, Mrs Stanley, 211, 240
Resor House (Jackson Hole, WY), 141, 211–212, 240–241
Rettaliata, John T, 155
Richardson, Henry Hobson, 223
Richter, Hans, 26
Riehl, Alois, 15, 18, 156, 204, 214, 245, 260, 286, 287, 288
Riehl, Sophia, 21, 228, 260, 286, 287, 288
Riehl House (Potsdam), 21, 156, 160, 188, 204, 211, 214, 228, 229, 245, 260, 286, 287
Riemerschmid, Richard, 285, 287
Riezler, Walter, 70–72
Robie House, 224, 267, 274
Rockefeller Center, 142
Rodgers, John Barney (Jack), *46*, 212
Roman culture, 80, 203
- basilicas, 20, 61, 203, 238
- Palatine Chapel, 202
- Palazzo Pitti, 20, 139, 203, 207, 267
- St Peter's Cathedral, 80, 203

Romanesque style, 62, 64, 110, 122, 127, 128, 203, 247, 267
Romantic style, 57, 61, 109, 223
Ronchamp chapel, 167
Rosenberg, Alfred, 134–135, 233–234, 240
Royal Institute of British Architects, 20, 182–183
Rudolph, Paul, 226
Ruegenberg, Sergius, 17
Ruhr Settlement Association, 67
Ruskin, John, 19, 150, 197
Russian Constructivists, 232

Santiago de Cuba, 178
Scharoun, Hans, 77, 261
Scheler, Max, 18, 149, 182
Scheper, Hinnerk, 289, 292
Scherschel, Frank, 10, 12, *35, 44*
Schilbach, Walter, 77
Schinkel, Karl Friedrich, 20, 150, 188, 197, 205, 222–223, 230, 236, 243, 261, 270, 277–278, 286
Schlüter, Andreas, 236
Schmidt, Joost, 289
Schneider, Karl, 77
Schlotfeldt, Francisco, 177
Schopenhauer, Arthur, 284
Schreiber, Detlef, 271
Schreiber, Fritz, *46*
Schrödinger, Erwin Rudolf Josef Alexander, 140, 244, 253
Schultze-Naumburg, Paul, 22, 133, 233, 292
Schwarz, Rudolf, 150, 153, 182
- eulogy for, 242
Schwitters, Kurt, 198
Scott, Mackay Hugh Baily, 182
sculpture, 166, 189–190
Seagram Building, 23, 24, 142, 149, 154, 165, 166, 168, 169, 170, 171, 175, 176, 178, 180, 199, 219, 222, 248, 250, 256, 263, 277
Simon, Heinrich, 289
skyscrapers, 59, 66
- Friedrichstrasse, 207
- glass, 15, 25, 50, 101, 118–119, 185, 207, 229, 239, 248, 266
- 'Mile High,' 160
- Neogothic and Tudor style, 277
- steel, 25, 58
Soeder, Hans, 77
Sommerfeld, 56
space age, 186
'Special Kind of Order, A' (documentary), 26
Spinoza, Baruch, 201
Springs, Bernard, 174, 176
SR Crown Hall, 9, *35*, 143–145, 161, 191, 194, 216, 218, 220, 259, 263, 266, 273–274
Stam, Mart, 68–69, 189, 208, 231
Stevens Chicago note, 109

Stock Exchange building (Amsterdam), 165, 205, 261
Stone, Edward D., 198
Stotz, Gustav, 231
Strauss, Richard, 189
structure, 164–165, 168, 171, 179–180, 197, 202–203, 222, 226, 238
Stuttgart Bank competition, 85
suburbs, 184
Sullivan, Louis, 19, 130, 147, 174–175, 177, 238, 249, 267, 271, 272
Summers, Gene, 199
Sweeney, James Johnson, 167, 276
Swenson, Alfred, 11
symmetry, 161, 250, 277

Taut, Bruno, 59, 77, 102, 208, 261
Taut, Max, 77, 102, 189
Taut House (Stuttgart), 189
Technical Administration Building (Frankfurt), 231
technology, 124, 220–221, 243–244, 270
Tessenow, Heinrich, 77, 288
Thiersch, Paul, 287
Thomas Aquinas, 18, 105, 128, 152, 180, 181, 182, 199, 201, 239, 246, 253, 275
Tood, Anderson, 163
Toole, Edward J, 117
Tower of Babel, 277
traffic, 59, 64, 65, 66, 67, 80, 83, 91–92, 115, 151, 215, 219, 250
Tropp, Paul, 55
Tudor style, 277, 286
Tugendhat, Fritz, 229
Tugendhat House (Brno), 23, 166, 187–188, 211, 229, 239–240, 265, 274

underwear ad, 24
University of Virginia, 267
urban planning. See city planning
Urbig house (Potsdam), 229

van de Velde, Henry, 111, 136–137, 178, 182, 201, 205, 247, 285
van der Rohe, Ewald, 25, 278
van der Rohe, Georgia, 11
van der Rohe, Ludwig Mies. See Mies van der Rohe
van Doesburg, Theo, 188, 232
van Eesteren, Cornelis, 232
Van Gogh, Vincent, 205–206, 232, 261
Velvet and Silk Café, 102, 179, 208, 209
Vendôme Shop (Pittsburgh), 24, 112
Ventura, Sam, 11
Vico, Giambattista, 18, 181, 201
Villa Rotonda, 288
Villa Savoye, 274
Viollet-le-Duc, Eugène, 150, 161
Visual Training course, 268–269

Voice of America speech, 236
von Hutten, Ulrich, 181, 182
von Seidlein, Peter C., 271
Voysey, Charles Francis Annesley, 182

Wagner, Martin, 77
Walter Thompson (advertising), 211
Washington Bridge (New York), 139, 152, 247, 256
Webb, Aston, 182
Weber, Hugo, *34*
Weissenhof Housing Estate project, 74, 76, 137, 149, 196, 208, 247, 261, 287
Werkbund exhibition, 68, 76, 93–94, 136, 208, 231, 247
Westmount Square (Montreal), 250
Whitehead, Alfred North, 18, 110, 150, 181, 182
Whitman, Walt, 18
Wiegand, Theodor, 230
Wilamowitz-Moellendorff, Ulrich von, 288
Wiley, Charles D., 117
William of Occam, 79
William the Silent, 156, 172
Wolf House (Guben/Gubin), 261
Wright, Frank Lloyd, 9, 19, 21, 23, 24, 101, 139, 141, 147, 152, 160, 167, 177, 195, 198, 201, 206, 223, 224, 225, 227, 241, 267, 274
tribute to, 111–112

Zevi, Bruno, 148, 195

ACKNOWLEDGEMENTS

The co-editors wish to thank our dedicated team at DOM publishers in Berlin. Publisher Philipp Meuser believed in *Mies in His Own Words* early on and exercised great patience during the extended gestation period that the project required to be completed. Working with publishing director Björn Rosen and graphic designer Nicole Wolf was enjoyable, as was collaborating with our proofreader/translator John Nicolson. Financial support for this book was provided by IIT's College of Architecture through the John Vinci Distinguished Research Fellowship/PhD Program in Architecture, as well as by the dean, Reed Kroloff. Thanks also to Dr Cynthia Vranas, executive director of IIT's Mies van der Rohe Society, for promoting this book as part of a broader mission dedicated to the preservation of the IIT campus and its history.

All works of new scholarship inevitably draw on previous efforts and our *Mies in His Own Words* is no different. We owe a particular debt of gratitude to Fritz Neumeyer's pioneering *The Artless Word. Mies van der Rohe on the Building Art* (originally published in German in 1986 and first translated into English by Mark M Jarzombek in 1991). For texts published before 1935 we almost always used translations by Jarzombek. On a more personal note Mark deserves a special thank you for his support throughout the process. Various other scholars have published Mies' writings, speeches, and interviews. To all of them spread throughout the world we owe a collective thank you. Most recently Tom Lamberty of Merve Publishing House assisted us with a handful of additional Mies texts. Special thanks to Dietrich Neumann for his ongoing support.

Michelangelo Sabatino wishes to personally thank Dirk Lohan for generously sharing over the years his expertise and insights about Mies. I first met Dirk shortly after arriving in Chicago to serve as professor and director of the PhD programme at IIT's College of Architecture. Dirk's support and collaboration continued during my recent tenure as interim dean of the College of Architecture when I started co-editing *Mies in His Own Words*. Additionally, the co-authors wish to thank Dirk for authorising the reprint of his *Lohan Tapes*, recently published with an introduction and notes by Fritz Neumeyer as *The Lost, Last Words of Mies van der Rohe. The Lohan Tapes from 1969* (Berlin, 2021).

Photo of Mies and Dirk Lohan entering a meeting at the Graham Foundation, Chicago, c. 1965, photography unknown, courtesy Dirk Lohan.

Vittorio Pizzigoni wishes to thank IIT's College of Architecture for inviting him as a visiting researcher in autumn 2018. During this time, while Michelangelo served as interim dean, we also developed the idea of an expanded anthology of Mies' complete writings based on my previous Italian edition of 2010. While in Chicago, I also had the pleasure of meeting Dirk Lohan, who was extremely supportive and helpful. Finally, I wish to thank the Università degli Studi di Genova, my home institution, for their ongoing support.

The co-editors first met during our architectural education at the Università Iuav di Venezia. Our time in Venice was greatly enhanced by the presence of an extraordinary group of architects and historians, many of whom are sadly no longer alive. In particular, our shared admiration for Manfredo Tafuri continues to inspire our work as educators and researchers. Finally, this anthology of *Mies in His Own Words* is dedicated to all those who continue to believe in the power of the written and spoken word to communicate the value of architecture in enriching contemporary culture and society.

The *Deutsche Nationalbibliothek* lists this publication in the *Deutsche Nationalbibliografie*; detailed bibliographic data are available at http://dnb.d-nb.de

ISBN 978-3-86922-307-0

© 2024 by DOM publishers, Berlin
www.dom-publishers.com

This work is subject to copyright. All rights are reserved, whether the whole or part of the material is concerned, specifically the rights of translation, reprinting, recitation, broadcasting, reproduction on microfilms or in other ways, and storage or processing on databases. Sources and owners of rights are stated to the best of our knowledge; please point out any we might have omitted.

The original texts are here reprinted with the kind permission of the heirs of Ludwig Mies van der Rohe.

Design
Nicole Wolf

Fonts
Akzidenz-Grotesk Pro, Sabon LT Std

Proofreading
John Nicolson

Indexing
Meridith L. Murray
MLM Indexing Service

Printing
Tiger Printing (Hong Kong) Co., Ltd.
www.tigerprinting.hk

Front and back cover flaps: Mies in his IIT office in Alumni Memorial Hall, photos by Hedrich Blessing, Courtesy Chicago History Museum [hb35283y; hb35283s].

ILLINOIS INSTITUTE OF TECHNOLOGY
College of Architecture